DOES
GOD
EXIST

DOES GOD EXIST

The Debate between Theists & Atheists

J. P. MORELAND AND
KAI NIELSEN

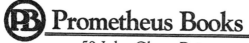

Prometheus Books

59 John Glenn Drive
Amherst, NewYork 14228-2197

Published 1993 by Prometheus Books.

Unless otherwise noted, Scripture quotations are from the New King James Version of the Bible. Copyright © 1979, 1980, 1982, Thomas Nelson, Inc., Publishers.

99 98 97   5 4 3

Library of Congress Cataloging-in-Publication Data

Moreland, James Porter, 1948–
    Does God exist? : the debate between theists and atheists / J. P. Moreland and Kai Nielsen.
        p.   cm.
    Originally published: Nashville : T. Nelson, © 1990.
    Record of a debate held at the University of Mississippi, March 24, 1988.
    Includes bibliographical references.
    ISBN 0–87975–823–6 (pbk.)
    1. God—Proof. 2. Theism. 3. Theism—Controversial literature.
I. Nielsen, Kai, 1926–   . I. Title.
[BT102.M642   1993]
212′.1—dc20   92–41375
                                                        CIP

Printed in the United States of America on acid-free paper.

To the staff of
Campus Crusade for Christ
J. P. Moreland

To Merlette Schnell
Kai Nielsen

CONTENTS

PART III
What Do Others Think?
Responses to the Debate

PART IV
What Would the Debaters Say?
Some Closing Arguments

PART V
How Can I Decide for Myself?
The Debate Made Personal

PREFACE

Professors J. P. Moreland (theist) and Kai Nielsen (atheist) went head-to-head over the question "Does God exist?" at the University of Mississippi on the evening of March 24, 1988. At the end of their formal presentations, rebuttals, and counter-rebuttals, they answered questions from the almost eight-hundred member audience. That evening's interchange comprises Part I of this book.

On that same day, before they met to debate God's existence, Moreland and Nielsen lectured and answered questions on whether or not ethics depend on God—on either His will or His nature or both. In other words, what role, if any, should the existence of God play in our day-to-day decisions of what's right and what's wrong? Can we be moral without God? Must ethical standards be grounded in God for them to be truly ethical or truly standards? Our debaters' presentations of their positions on this issue make up Part II.

After their debate on God's existence and presentations on ethics were transcribed, they were given to two theists and two atheists for their responses (Part III). With the respondents' essays in hand, Moreland and Nielsen wrote their closing arguments, making their final responses to each other and to the respondents (Part IV).

Opening and concluding the book are contributions by philosopher and author Peter Kreeft. And for those who wish to dig deeper into the issues raised by the debaters, Professor Kreeft has provided an appendix, "Facing the Specific Questions."

Finally, a bibliography on atheism (compiled by Nielsen) and Christian theism (compiled by Moreland) wraps up this volume.

The desire behind this book's undertaking was to bring to your attention many of the critical and life-changing issues that surround the question of the existence of God. We hope you will weigh the "pros" and "cons" carefully and rationally. Then make a decision—to choose a position or engage in more reflection and study. But whatever you do, we hope you don't put the matter aside and press on with your life. This question is too great, too fundamental, too all-impacting to set aside. Indeed, to ignore it *is* to decide—to decide how you will think and live. So read on, consider, decide.

William D. Watkins
Editor

INTRODUCTION

Peter Kreeft

Why Debate the Existence of God?

The Primacy of the Question

The idea of God is either a fact, like sand, or a fantasy, like Santa.

If it is a fantasy, a human invention, it is the greatest invention in all of human history. Measure it against all the other inventions, mental or physical. Put on one side of the scale the control of fire, the domestication of animals, and the cultivation of wheat; the wheel, the ship, and the rocket ship; baseball, the symphony orchestra, and anesthetics—and a million other similarly great and wonderful things. Then put on the other side of the scale a single idea: the idea of a being that is actual, absolute, perfect, eternal, one, and personal; all-knowing, all-loving, all-just, all-merciful, and all-powerful; undying, impervious, unbribeable, uncompromising, and unchangeable; a cosmic creator, designer, redeemer, and provider; cosmic artist, musician, scientist, and sage; the infinite abyss of pure Being who is yet a person, a self, an "I." It is disputable whether such a being is a fact or a fantasy, but it is indisputable that if it is a fantasy, it is by far the greatest fantasy in history. If it is humanity's invention, it is humanity's masterpiece.

The idea of God has guided or deluded more lives, changed more history, inspired more music and poetry and philosophy than anything else, real or imagined. It has made more of a difference to human life on this planet, both individually and collectively, than anything else ever has. To see this clearly for yourself, just try this thought experiment: suppose no one in history had ever conceived the idea of God. Now, rewrite history following that premise. The task daunts and staggers the imagination. From the earliest human remains—religious funeral artifacts—to the most recent wars in the Mideast, religion—belief in a God or gods—has been the mainspring of the whole watch that is human history.

The debate recorded in this book was designed to aid anyone who wishes to investigate the question whether God is the greatest of fantasies or the greatest of facts. Those are the only two possibilities. "To be or not to be, that is the question." There are endless variations and refinements within the concept of the *nature* of God, but the Law of Excluded Middle prevents any compromise on the question of God's *existence*.

Why are we reluctant to admit this eminently logical truism with respect to God, though not with respect to anything else? Because it means that one of the two sides, either the believers or the unbelievers, have been basing their entire lives on the most fundamental illusion that has ever bedeviled humanity. Sigmund Freud's argument, though often shocking to believers, is consistently logical: If religion is an illusion, it is the greatest of all illusions, in fact, a species of collective insanity, like the imaginary friend of a child who never grew up. The same is true, of course, about atheism if theism is true: It is the child's denial of the parent's existence.

How could anyone be indifferent to this question? If God equals only Santa Claus for adults, who in his right mind would want to believe in such a myth all his life? If God equals the heavenly Father, who in his right mind would want to disbelieve in his own father? Of all the questions of philosophy, this is the one that ordinary people naturally find the most interesting and important. And ordinary people are usually right. (They are not always and infallibly right, or else the fact that believers vastly outnumber unbelievers would settle the God question immediately.)

The Nature of the Question

The question of God is what Gabriel Marcel calls a "mystery" rather than a "problem." Marcel means by a "mystery" not an unexplorable and unintelligible question, but one in which the questioner is so personally and inextricably *involved* that he cannot detach himself from it and surround and confront the question as an object. Mysteries transcend the subject-object dualism. Death, evil, suffering, and love are mysteries. The number of atoms in the sun, how to cure cancer, and whether Shakespeare wrote Shakespeare are problems. How to make people good is a mystery; how to kill them is a problem.

A second characteristic of a "mystery" is the more popularly known one: a mystery is "deep," profound, inexhaustible, impossible to completely illuminate, understand, or solve with certainty. This second characteristic of a mystery obviously follows from the first: mysteries are dark *to* us because they are *in* us.

The question of God is a mystery in the first sense to the believer but not to the unbeliever. It is a mystery to the believer because he finds his identity, the meaning and purpose and hope of his life, and the ultimate foundation for his morality in God. The question of God is not a mystery for the unbeliever because he believes that he has freed and detached himself from the idea of God, as from an illusion, like a man waking up from a dream, no longer under its spell.

But for both believer and unbeliever, the question of God is a mystery in the second sense. For no one, not even Spinoza or Hegel, ever claimed to know *everything* knowable about God, or to fully and adequately comprehend the nature or essence referred to by that concept. The theist thinks this is because there is too much reality there for the human mind to contain; the atheist thinks it is because there is too little.

But we can often prove or disprove the existence of something whose essence we cannot fully understand (e.g., quarks or love). But on the God question, neither side has been able to eliminate the other's belief by logically convincing and converting them, though both sides have occasionally tried to eliminate its opponents by less rational means, such as intimidation, torture, and murder.

But this does not mean that the question of God's existence cannot be intelligently and logically argued, or even that it cannot be rationally decided. An argument need not be accepted by everyone for it to be conclusive; one stubborn mind does not hold logic hostage. Though the question is a mystery, a mystery is not simply an unintelligible darkness; it is a little circle of light surrounded by a large darkness, and we can hope to increase the light and decrease the darkness a little, or even a lot. A mystery invites exploration. Maps can be made.

The Definition of the Question

In exploring the general question of "proofs for or against the existence of God," we must distinguish five different questions which are often confused, five different questions we can ask about God or anything else, any *X:* the questions of *existence, knowledge, proof,* and *method.*

(1) Does *X* really *exist?*
(2) If it does, can I *know* that it exists? (A thing can obviously exist without my knowing it exists: for example, a pink rock on the other side of the moon.)
(3) If I know *X* exists, is that knowledge *certain?* (Much or most of our knowledge is only probable, not certain: for example, that I do not have cancer, or that all dinosaurs died before mankind evolved.)

(4) If I can be certain *X* exists, is there a *proof*, a demonstration of my right to certainty? (I can be certain of some things without being able to give a proof of them to others so that others can share my certainty: for example, that I exist and am conscious and sane, or that my wife's soul is beautiful, like her face.)

(5) If there is such a proof, is it a *scientific* proof in the modern sense of *scientific*—that is, according to the rules of the "scientific method"? Are the premises reducible to evidence that is either empirical or logical and mathematical (something like Positivism's softened version of the Verification Principle)? (Not only the arguments both for and against the existence of God, but *most* arguments in philosophy that claim to be proofs are not "scientific" in this sense: for instance, Plato's demonstration in the *Republic* that "justice is more profitable than injustice.")

Atheists answer all five of these questions about God in the negative. Logically, this is because answering question (1) negatively entails answering (2) negatively; a negative answer to (2) entails a negative answer to (3); etc. Some rationalist atheists reason the other way round: from a negative answer to question (5) to a negative answer to question (4), from (4) to (3), etc. That implies that all proofs should be scientific; that all certainty requires proof; that all real knowledge requires certainty; and also (if they go that far) that all reality must be humanly knowable.

Agnostics claim not to know the answer to Question (1), and therefore not to know the answers to all the subsequent questions either.

Theists answer the first two questions yes, but differ on the other three. Most traditional theists, like Dr. J. P. Moreland in this debate, answer questions (1) to (4) yes and (5) no.

(By the way, the claim to *certainty* does not mean the claim to *infallibility*. One may claim to have a more-than-probable proof that God exists without claiming to be a divinely guaranteed authority.)

The Parameters of the Question

There are gods and goddesses aplenty, and religions aplenty. How shall we narrow the focus of this debate, and by how much?

Religions, and ideas of God, can be divided into seven basic kinds by the following seven divisions, which are also laid out in chart form in Figure One.

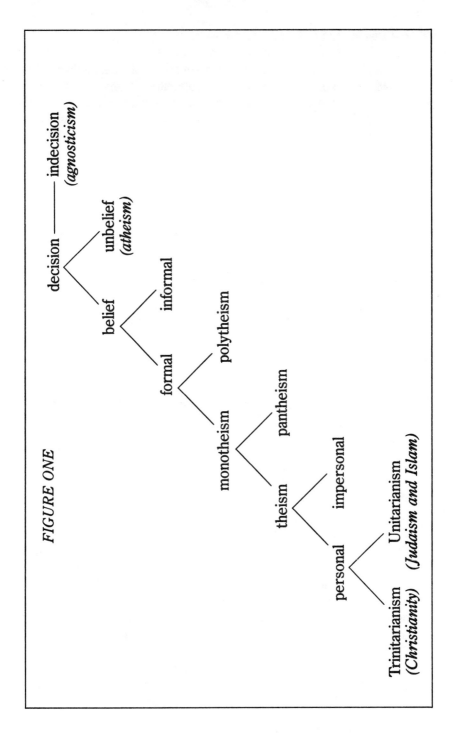

FIGURE ONE

1. Indecision (agnosticism) vs. decision.
2. Among decisions, unbelief (atheism) vs. belief.
3. Among beliefs, those that are only instinctive, informal, individualistic, or idiosyncratic vs. formal, institutional religions.
4. Among formal religions, polytheism vs. monotheism. (By the way, I wonder why of all these religious options, polytheism is the only one that almost no one in the modern West believes? It is at least a simple and obvious answer to the problem of evil.)
5. Among monotheism, pantheism or monism (Eastern religions) vs. theism or Creator-creature dualism (Western religions).
6. Within theism, impersonal theism ("Nature and Nature's God") vs. personal theism (God as "I AM").
7. Within personal theism, Trinitarianism (Christianity) vs. Unitarianism (Judaism and Islam).

The parameters of this debate restrict the God-idea to theism, but not much farther. Sometimes, the debaters address themselves to specifically Christian claims, especially the divinity and resurrection of Jesus; but most of the debate is in the medieval mold, in which Jews, Christians, and Muslims argued in common about the common God of the Hebrew scriptures in the common terms of classical philosophy.

The Motives Behind the Question

Why would someone want to prove that God exists? Why would someone want to prove that God does *not* exist? What is the point behind the arguments? Why this book?

There seem to be at least five possible motives behind each attempt. An individual may want to prove God exists (1) to convince and convert others; (2) to leave atheism or agnosticism and become a believer; (3) to strengthen his faith if he is a believer but has doubts (faith is compatible with doubt); (4) to glorify God; or (5) simply for the sake of truth.

Someone else may want to prove God does not exist for similar reasons: (1) to liberate others from illusion; (2) to leave belief and become an atheist; (3) to strengthen his unbelief (which is also compatible with doubt); (4) to glorify man; or (5) simply for the sake of truth.

Regarding the first purpose, which I think is the most usual one, we must carefully distinguish between an argument that is *objectively* strong by the rules of logic and evidence, and an argument that is *subjectively* strong (effective in changing others' minds). The two categories overlap but do not coincide. Thus there are four possibilities for any argument. One could give:

1. an objectively logical argument that is also subjectively convincing;
2. an objectively logical argument that is nevertheless unconvincing to someone because of his ignorance, prejudice, or passion;
3. an objectively weak argument that is nevertheless subjectively convincing to someone for the same reasons;
4. an objectively weak argument that is also subjectively weak.

Even the fourth category may contain some important and valuable arguments—for instance, the most famous argument in the history of philosophy, Anselm's ontological argument, seems to fit here.

William James distinguished two types of minds: those who are swayed primarily by subjective and personal factors he called "tender-minded," and those who are swayed primarily by objective facts and factors he called "tough-minded." These two attitudes can be found among both believers and unbelievers. The "tender-minded" on both sides would argue their case for a motive not listed here as one of the five—namely, for happiness or goodness or utility or comfort or peace or "needs" (usually a code word for *wants*) or something of that kind. The "tough-minded" put truth above even happiness. They want to know the truth whether or not they think it will help them to be happy. Thus we could have:

1. A tough-minded believer who believes God exists because the reasons seem to point that way, even though he may find the existence of God inconvenient or uncomfortable, as C. S. Lewis says he did in his autobiography *Surprised by Joy*.
2. A tough-minded unbeliever who does not believe God exists because the reasons and evidence seem to point that way, even though he may find the nonexistence of God inconvenient or uncomfortable, as Sartre says he does in *Existentialism and Humanism*.
3. A tender-minded believer who believes in God not because of objective evidence but because it makes him feel good, or, much more seriously, because it is his only hope for real happiness (Pascal's Wager) or his only adequate foundation for his moral ideal (Kant).
4. A tender-minded unbeliever who does not believe in God not because the objective evidence points that way but because he needs or wants there to be no God—like Nietzsche, who wrote, "If there were gods, how could I bear not to be a god? *Consequently,* there are no gods"—or, less candidly, because admitting God would mean

admitting the claims of His moral law in some area of life (usually sexual) where selfish desires would be thwarted.

I think two tough-minded people could understand and respect each other better, even if one were an atheist and the other a theist, than either one could understand and respect and fruitfully argue with a tender-minded person, even if the tender-minded person shared the same belief about God. Thomas Aquinas could debate on common ground with Bertrand Russell (or Kai Nielsen) more than with Kant or Kierkegaard; and Russell would find more common ground to argue with Aquinas (or J. P. Moreland) than with Nietzsche.

Both debaters in this book are tough-minded, and I think that when push comes to shove, most honest people are too. Although the Freudian can find much evidence that people choose their beliefs on the basis of their desires rather than on the basis of objective evidence, there is also strong and simple evidence that they do not. For instance, why do we not all believe in Santa Claus right now? That belief made us very happy once. Why did we abandon it and why don't we simply re-capture it? Obviously, because reason has told us Santa is a myth. But why do we follow reason instead of desire and wish? Because we are honest—tough-minded. If we only believed that we were in heaven right now in infinite joy—if we really believed that—we would be much hap-pier than we are. Why don't we then? Simply because we embrace our beliefs with the cold arms of truth-seeking more than with the warm arms of happiness-seeking.

This does not mean there must always be a conflict between truth and happiness. Both participants in this debate may be quite happy with their beliefs. But that was not their motive for adopting it.

The Existential Import of the Questions

William James says that a philosophical question is meaningless if it makes no *difference* to anything in our experience, either past or future. It is a useful practice to ask this question of every idea before spending time with it: Does it make a difference? How big a difference? There are at least three possible answers to that question when we apply it to the existence of God.

First, there seems to be a relationship between the question of God and the question of our own *identity*. For either God created us in His image, or we created Him in ours. (It could be both options, of course; as one wag put it, "God created us in His image and we've been returning the compliment ever since.") Either way, God and human identity are intimately related. For the atheist, we are emancipated to become our true selves (that is, autonomous individuals) only when we are freed from intellectual and moral slavery to the myth of subservience to God. For the theist, God's nature as Person or Self ("I AM") is the model or archetype for our own nature as persons. (This connection between the divine "I AM" and the human "I am" may account for the teasing similarity between the two most famous arguments in the whole history of human thought: Anselm's ontological argument for the divine being and Descartes's *cogito ergo sum* argument for his own being.)

Second, as Pascal perceives with the Wager, the God-question concerns us *eschatologically,* or *thanatologically.* At the end of our lives, at death, we shall all face either God or nothingness. It obviously concerns us to know ahead of time which is the case, just as it concerns one who is falling to know whether there is a fireman's net below or just a concrete street. Nearly everyone sees God and immortality as a single package deal.

Third, God may (or may not) make a difference to *morality.* That is the second of the two questions our debaters debate here, in Part II.

The relationship between God and morality can move in different ways (see Figure Two):

(1) The moral argument for the existence of God argues that if there is a real, objective morality, there must be a real, objective God. C. S. Lewis, following Cardinal Newman, uses this argument at the beginning of *Mere Christianity.*

(2) The atheist sometimes perceives the same tie between God and morality but argues in the opposite direction: there is no God, therefore there is no objective morality. As Ivan Karamazov and Jean-Paul Sartre contend, "If God does not exist, everything is permissible."

(3) Many atheists, especially anthropologists like Ruth Benedict and Margaret Mead, argue that there is no objective and universal morality, therefore there is no single, objective, and universal God.

(4) Many theists try to persuade people to obey moral laws on the basis that these laws stem from God, but I know of no one who tries to *deduce* the existence of morality from the existence of God—and this for a good reason: We do not argue from the lesser-known to the better-known. No one can deduce from the nature of God (how well does anyone know *that*, anyway?) how He will act, what He will will, and so forth.

FIGURE TWO

GOD	NO GOD	NO GOD	GOD	GOD	NO GOD
MORALITY (1)	NO MORALITY (2)	NO MORALITY (3)	MORALITY (4)	NO MORALITY (5)	MORALITY (6)
Newman; Lewis	Karamazov; Sartre	Mead; Benedict	(No One)	Pagan Religions	Camus
(Moral Argument)	*(Existentialist Atheism)*	*(Sociological Atheism)*			*(Humanism)*

(5) All four positions above see a "package deal" relationship between God and morality. One denial of such a relationship comes from ancient pagan Gentile religions, which, unlike Judaism, often did not believe that their gods instituted a moral law at all. Gentiles got their morality from one source (such as social legislators) and their religion from another (such as shamans). Jews united the two.

(6) The other denial of the "package deal" is the position of the humanist like Camus's Dr. Rieux in *The Plague,* who agonizes over the question, "How can one be a saint without God?" He knows one must be a saint (practice a high and binding moral ideal), yet he does not believe there is a God; and he wonders whether this is possible in logic or in life. This is one of the issues Drs. Nielsen and Moreland debate here.

Because the moral question of how to live has existential import for everyone, believer and unbeliever alike, the question of the connection between morality and God also has existential import. Other arguments for the existence of God (such as the First Cause argument) and arguments against God as well (such as the supposed logical contradictions in the idea of God) have existential import at least indirectly, in that the God they seek to prove or disprove may make a very intimate difference to our lives, especially in the area of morality. So the other arguments borrow at least part of their existential import from the moral argument. The debaters were wise to single out this aspect of the God-question for special emphasis, for that is just what ordinary people would do.

The Validity of the Question

By the "validity of the question," I mean the validity of putting the question of God's existence to the test of two philosophers, the validity of using philosophical reasoning to try to settle this existential question. Is impersonal logical argument the proper approach to such a personal question?

Yes, it is. The God-question is *not* "personal" in the sense that a preference for olives, rock music, or large houses is personal—that is, not subjective and individual and dependent on feelings. But it *is* "personal" in the sense that death is personal—that is, it touches and concerns each person deeply. The fact that I and all of us will die some day is not a subjective personal preference but an objective truth; yet it is one that touches me (and you) personally.

Partly because of the confusion between these two meanings of "personal," many people think that logical reasoning is an inappropriate method to use to address the question of God. Both our debaters disagree with this popular prejudice. They do not think that rational clarity and existential profundity need exclude each other. They do not think it is silly or hopeless to use reason to explore the deepest issues (though I suspect they mean somewhat different things by "reason," Dr. Nielsen being a kind of Positivist and Dr. Moreland a kind of Aristotelian). They agree, in fact, that we *must* use reason, *especially* here. For the alternatives are to follow fashion, force, passion, or propaganda to decide this consumingly important issue of which view is the dream and which the reality. (For if atheism is true, theists are living in a dream, and if theism is true, atheists are not living in reality.)

Nielsen and Moreland also agree that it is right and fair to explore and test faith by reason. They are not fideists, believing that faith independent of reason is the only valid test for truth. (Atheism too can be a fideism.) Sometimes fideism is due to fear; but usually, I think, it is due to a misunderstanding of the nature and power of reason, or to ignorance of the arguments and the evidences on both sides.

Both sides of this debate would disagree, I believe, with Kant's compromise solution, which his disciple Vahinger called "the philosophy of the 'as if'"—living "as if" God existed, so that you can have an ultimate basis for a moral code, even though (Kant thought) no one can know or prove whether God exists or not.

Both debaters also seem to disagree with the currently fashionable attack by some Christian philosophers on "epistemological foundationalism," which is a kind of moderate rationalism. These Christians contend that "belief in God is 'properly basic'"—which means, as far as I can see, that they have invented a new and technical way of saying that they need give no reason for this particular belief, that no onus of proof is on the believer. Dr. Moreland prefers to obey the apostle's command to "be ready to give a reason for the hope that is in you" (1 Pet. 3:15), and even Dr. Nielsen's atheism comes from his attempt to follow the (biblical) command "test all things; hold fast what is good" (1 Thess. 5:21).

I think both debaters would agree with Thomas Aquinas's deduction of a remarkable but logical conclusion from five premises, in his *Summa Contra Gentiles* I, 7. Although Dr. Nielsen would disagree with the premises, and Dr. Moreland would agree with them, both would agree that the premises logically entail their conclusion. Here is Aquinas's argument:

1. God is the author and designer of the human mind and its power to reason.
2. God is also the author and designer of nature and the evidence in nature that human reason can know.
3. God is also the author and teacher of the Christian faith as a "divine revelation" in the Bible, as summarized by the Church's Creeds.
4. God does not contradict Himself or teach error.
5. Truth cannot be opposed to (contradict) truth, but only untruth.

From these premises, it necessarily follows that there can never be any real contradiction between any article of the Christian faith and any valid argument or true discovery of natural reason in the sciences or in philosophy. Further, the surprising (to many) corollary also follows that every objection and argument that anyone ever brings against any article of faith can be answered by reason alone without appeal to faith. For every such objection must contain some rational mistake. For truth (revealed by God to faith) cannot contradict truth (revealed by God to reason).

Both debaters, I think, agree with that logic, and therefore welcome the opportunity to test faith by reason. Thus this debate really investigates, not only (1) whether God exists and (2) whether it can be proved that God does or does not exist, but also (3) whether all the other side's objections can be answered, whether the case can be closed, whether one side can win this war of words and wisdoms.

The History of the Question

The Origin of the Idea of God

No one knows the exact origin of the idea of God in the human mind. If the idea is true, it originated either from human reasoning, or from divine revelation, or from the experience and memory of a supernatural intimacy in Eden, or from the experiences of the mystics, or from ordinary, present-type religious experiences. If the idea is false, then it originated in either fantasy, fallacy, folly, or fear (or all four or any combination thereof).

One of the atheist's strongest arguments has been his ability to explain the origin of the idea of God without a God. Freud, for example, makes a reasonable case for fear and wishful thinking as its origin. Voltaire puts it simply and elegantly: "If God does not exist, it would be necessary to invent Him."

But *when* is it reasonable for us to look for such psychological explanations for the origin of an idea? Only *after* we know, or think we know, that the idea is false. We don't give psychological explanations for the origin of the idea that $2+3=5$ or that the sun is round. Thus the Freudian argument begs the question. The God-question cannot be settled that way, psychologically. The theist could fairly turn the argument around and psychoanalyze the atheist's motives as the atheist has analyzed his. He could argue, for example, that Freud had a bad relationship with his father, and explain that that was why he became an atheist: it was the Oedipus complex. Instead of killing his earthly father, Freud took vengeance on his heavenly Father. Such an "argument" has no more (*and* no less) validity than Freud's own explanation of the heavenly Father as a substitute for the lost earthly father.

In other words, both sides must avoid the "genetic fallacy": deciding whether an idea is objectively true by looking at its subjective origin. If Hitler had discovered Einsteinian relativity theory and done so, not out of any love of truth, but only out of a mad desire to conquer the world through nuclear weapons, that would not have made E *not* equal MC^2.

The Historical Development of the Idea of God

The question of how the idea of God developed through human history is also unprofitable here not because there is a paucity of data, but because there is such a surplus. The whole history of philosophical theology cannot be summed up in a few pages. So we must turn to the more manageable question:

The Present Status of the Idea of God

The history of human thinking about the question of this debate has deposited into our hands so far two cases, which can be summarized in a number of distinct arguments. The "con" case seems to consist basically of five arguments against God's existence, and the "pro" case has at least twenty-five arguments for it. (Of course, that count is not itself a "pro" argument, for quality of truth has no necessary relation to quantity of arguments, though it *may* be a probable consideration or a clue.)

"Con"

There are many arguments against *religion*—that it is "the opiate of the people" and distracts us from the good life here and now; that it is a power play by hypocritical clerics; that it is a failure to grow out of infantile dependency; that it comforts us too much or too little; that it challenges us too little or too much; that it oppresses or suppresses the poor or the rich or women or manliness. The list of charges is almost endless, and sometimes self-contradictory. But the arguments against *the existence of God* are far fewer and more manageable. They can all be grouped into five classes.

1. The strongest argument for atheism has always been the problem of evil. This is the only one of the five "con" arguments that tries to conclusively prove that *God does not exist.* The others only try to prove that belief in God's existence is not *necessary* (argument 2), or is logically confused or meaningless (argument 3), or is not *proved* (argument 4), or produces bad consequences in practice (argument 5).

The argument for atheism from evil is also strong because it is based on a strong premise, on universally acknowledged data which is open to immediate daily experience—namely, the fact that there is evil. The reality of evil seems logically incompatible with the reality of an all-good, all-powerful God.

Dr. Nielsen, however, does not use this argument, because he contends that the very *concept* of God is logically confused or meaningless (argument 3). If he is right, then *both* sides in the traditional argument about evil are confused: the theist side, which thinks (1) that 'God' is a meaningful term and (2) that belief in the existence of God is logically compatible with belief in the existence of evil, *and* the atheist side, which thinks (1) that 'God' is a meaningful term and (2) that belief in the existence of God is logically incompatible with belief in the existence of evil. Since Nielsen denies the assumption (premise 1) common to both the traditional theist and the traditional atheist, he cannot use the traditionally strongest objection against God—the problem of evil.

(If you are interested in pursuing the problem of evil further, you would do well to turn to Ivan Karamazov's stirring arguments in Dostoyevski's *The Brothers Karamazov*. It is the most powerful argument for atheism I know. For the theist's reply, you could read the rest of that novel, or C. S. Lewis's *The Problem of Pain*. On a more advanced and technical level, see John Hick's *Evil and the God of Love*, and on a more elementary and popular level, my *Making Sense Out of Suffering*.)

2. A second major argument for atheism is the apparent ability of science to explain all the data in human experience without God. God then becomes something like an extraterrestrial or leprechaun or witch. You can appeal to ancient extraterrestrial astronauts to explain

strange markings atop Peruvian mesas, or to leprechauns to explain disappearing Irish money, or to witchcraft to explain a woman's power or fascination. But there is no proof for any of these "accounts," and it is much simpler and more reasonable to use other, more natural explanations. Everything in nature, it seems, can be explained by physical laws, and everything in human life and history by psychological laws. Thus nature and human wills are the only two kinds of causes needed to explain anything. And God, a supernatural and superhuman cause, becomes a useless hypothesis, a superfluity.

(In his *Summa Theologica* [I,2,3], the above arguments [1] and [2] were the only two Thomas Aquinas could find against the thesis that God exists, even though he usually listed at least three objections to each of the hundreds of theses he tried to prove, and even though he always bent over backwards to present his opponent's case as thoroughly and fairly as possible.)

3. The argument used by most English-speaking philosophers for atheism today is *epistemological* and *linguistic* rather than *ontological*. In other words, rather than trying to prove that "being," or reality, does not include a God, this argument challenges our claim to know or understand the concept "God" and our ability to use the term "God" in obedience to the rules of ordinary linguistic usage.

Philosophers in previous centuries sometimes argued that there were logical self-contradictions within the idea of God—for example, within the claim that God is both just and merciful, or the claim that He is both changeless and a person. In this century, Sartre has developed a complex and technical version of this last argument, contending that "the idea of God is the impossible synthesis of being-in-itself [which is a changeless, perfect, and positive *object*] and being-for-itself [which is a changing, imperfect, nay-saying *subject*]." Dr. Nielsen uses an argument similar to this one but emphasizes the linguistic angle of the problem.

4. There are objections against *each* of the arguments *for* the existence of God, no matter how many there are. (However, even if all these objections were valid, that would leave us only in agnosticism, not atheism. To find a fallacy in an argument is not to prove the opposite conclusion.)

5. Finally, atheists often point to negative consequences of belief that can be seen in individual lives (Jim Jones, Jim Bakker, and Jimmy Swaggart) and in history (the Spanish Inquisition): moral weakness, dishonesty, or cruelty. G. K. Chesterton said there was only one really convincing argument against Christianity—Christians. (Someone also

said there was only one really convincing argument *for* Christianity—saints.)

"Pro"

The arguments for the existence of God are a mixed bag. Almost no one holds all twenty-five, and some of them are probably not demonstrative (the first seven here, at least). Here is a quick rundown:

1. The argument from "common consent," or human authority, either quantitative (most people believe) or qualitative (most sages believe).
2. The argument from the reliability of the Bible.
3. The argument from (ordinary) religious experience.
4. The argument from mystical experiences.
5. The argument from miracles, especially the resurrection of Jesus.
6. The argument from history: martyrs, saints, the survival of the Church.
7. The argument from Jesus: like Son, like Father (compare John 14: 8–9).
8. Anselm's "ontological argument" from the idea of God as including all perfections to including the perfection of actual existence.
9. Descartes's psychological version of Anselm's argument: from the perfection of the idea of God to the equal perfection of its cause.
10. The moral argument from conscience: from an absolute moral law to an absolute moral Lawgiver (Newman, C. S. Lewis).
11. The moral argument from the need for the moral ideal of perfection to be actual or instantiated (Kant).
12. The moral argument from the consequences of atheism ("If God did not exist, everything would be permissible"—Dostoyevski).
13. The epistemological argument from the eternity of truth to the existence of an eternal Mind (Augustine).
14. The aesthetic argument: "There is the music of Bach, therefore there must be a God." (I personally know three ex-atheists who were swayed by this argument; two are philosophy professors and one is a monk.)
15. The existential argument from the need for an ultimate meaning to life (Søren Kierkegaard).
16. Pascal's Wager: Your only chance of winning eternal happiness is believing, and your only chance of losing it is not believing.
17. C. S. Lewis's Argument from Desire: Every innate desire corresponds to a real object, and there is an innate desire for God.

18. The design argument from nature: The watch proves the watch-maker (Paley).
19. The design argument from the human brain: If that computer was programmed by chance, not by God, why trust it? (J.B.S. Haldane).
20. The cosmological argument from motion to a First, Unmoved Mover.
21. The cosmological "First Cause" argument from second (caused) causes to a first (uncaused) cause of existence (a self-existing being).
22. The cosmological argument from contingent and mortal beings to a necessary and immortal being (otherwise all things would eventually perish).
23. The cosmological argument from degrees of perfection to a Most Perfect Being (arguments 20–23 and 18 are Aquinas's "five ways").
24. The cosmological "kalam" (time) argument from the impossibility of arriving at the present moment if time past is infinite and beginningless (uncreated) (medieval Muslim philosophers).
25. The metaphysical argument from the existence of beings whose essence does not contain existence, and which therefore need a cause for their existence, to the existence of a being whose essence is existence, and which therefore has no cause (Aquinas in *De Ente et Essentia*).

This debate focuses especially on "con" argument 3 and "pro" arguments 5, 7, 12, 15, 18, and 24.

The Debaters and Respondents

Philosophy developed out of debate. Specifically, it developed in ancient Athens from the jury system of court trials, with its method of finding the truth by each side cross-examining the other. Socrates began to cross-examine not only people but ideas, and this began the great philosophical tradition of dialectic and debate—for example, the Scholastic Disputations in the medieval schools. (Our present-day presidential "debates" share the same name only in the same sense that a virus shares the name "animate" with an elephant.)

You are invited to look at this book as a law court. To find the truth in court, you need strong, well-qualified advocates to argue both sides. So we have here two good philosophical lawyers to plead the case for

God and the case against God: *Professors Kai Nielsen and J. P. Moreland.*

Dr. Nielsen is the prosecutor. Professor and head of the Department of Philosophy at the University of Calgary in Canada, Dr. Nielsen has presented and defended the atheistic perspective in more than sixteen books—including *Philosophy and Atheism, Ethics Without God,* and *God, Scepticism and Modernity*—and through almost 400 articles. His writings on the subject span three decades, and there are no signs of his letting up. Next to Antony Flew, he is probably the most well-known atheist in contemporary philosophy.

Dr. Moreland, though a newer arrival in the philosophical courtroom, has already offered several well-received defenses of various aspects of Christian theism. *Scaling the Secular City* and *Christianity and the Nature of Science* are two of his longer briefs. Dr. Moreland is Professor of Philosophy of Religion at Talbot School of Theology, Biola University, in La Mirada, California. He is quickly becoming recognized as one of Christianity's bright philosophical minds in the twentieth century.

Joining ranks with Professor Nielsen are two atheistic respondents, Professors Antony Flew and Keith Parsons. They were assigned the task of further supporting the case against God. Aside from Dr. Flew's numerous teaching assignments at universities such as Oxford, Aberdeen, and Keele, his many published works have had a tremendous impact on philosophical and theological thought in this century. *God and Philosophy, The Presumption of Atheism,* and *Hume's Philosophy of Belief* are just a few of his most influential books. Professor Parsons, who teaches at Berry College in Mount Berry, Georgia, has just begun to contribute to the many briefs against the case for theism. His most recent books are *God and the Burden of Proof* and *Science, Confirmation, and the Theistic Hypothesis.*

On Professor Moreland's side of the courtroom are two theistic respondents, Drs. Dallas Willard and William Lane Craig. Dr. Willard is a professor in the School of Philosophy at the University of Southern California. He has written several articles and books, including *Logic and the Objectivity of Knowledge, In Search of Guidance,* and *The Spirit of the Disciplines.* Dr. Craig, who has two earned doctorates—one under British philosopher Dr. John Hick and the other under German theologian Dr. Wolfhart Pannenberg—is a prolific author and frequent lecturer in the areas of religion, philosophy, theology, and apologetics. His works include *The Kalam Cosmological Argument, The Cosmological Argument from Plato to Leibniz, Knowing the Truth about the Resur-*

rection, The Only Wise God, and *The Problem of Divine Foreknowledge and Future Contingents from Aristotle to Suarez.*

To say the least, our two philosophical lawyers and four assistants are well qualified to try the case for and against the existence of God.

The question could be raised, however: Is God the defendant here and are we the judge and jury? Or is it the other way round? If there is a God, how could He be the *defendant?* If there is *no* God, how could *He* really be a defendant? Thus, the metaphor of the law court with God as the defendant, with Dr. Moreland as God's defense attorney and Dr. Nielsen as His prosecuting attorney, would be rejected by both sides. But it may be a useful and memorable image to begin with.

After reading through the manuscript of this debate, I think it is one of the most lively and well-argued debates on God's existence that I have read or heard. (I have not read and heard them all, of course, but I have read and heard quite a few.) Compared with the famous Russell-Copleston debate, it has more existential bite and is less technical. Compared with the old Chesterton-Shaw debates, it has less wit but much more logic. May it be the first, not the last, in a long series of debates on this question.

What a revolution that would be! Just think of the consequences, both for individuals and for our civilization, if we progressed so far along this road that we worked our way back to the seriousness of Socrates or the logical debates of the medievals once again.

Pursuing great questions often leads to great answers. *Whichever* way this great question is answered, it is a great answer—an answer that changes the course of lives and civilizations.

PART I

DOES GOD EXIST?

The Formal Debate

J. P. Moreland

Yes! A Defense of Christianity

MODERATOR, DR. LOUIS POJMAN: Our distinguished philosophers are Professor J. P. Moreland and Professor Kai Nielsen.

Dr. Moreland was born in Kansas City, Missouri. He received his bachelor's degree in chemistry and his master's of theology at Dallas Theological Seminary, and he has a master's degree in philosophy from the University of California at Riverside, as well as a Ph.D. in philosophy from the University of Southern California. He has spoken on more than seventy-five college campuses. He has been on the staff of Campus Crusade for Christ, working in apologetics, and still works with this organization. He is a very versatile philosopher. His interests range from philosophy of science to medical ethics and, of course, philosophy of religion. He is the author of several articles and two books, the latter of which, *Scaling the Secular City: A Defense of Christianity,* is [available] in the back of this building.

Professor Kai Nielsen was born in Moline, Illinois. His education was at St. Ambrose College, the University of North Carolina, and Duke University. He has taught worldwide, including South Africa, Canada, and the United States. He was head of the philosophy department at N.Y.U. for a number of years and he is currently department head and professor of philosophy at the University of Calgary in Calgary, Alberta, Canada. Dr. Nielsen is an editor of the *Canadian Journal of Philosophy,* a past president of the Canadian Philosophical Association, and a fellow of the Royal Society of Canada. He is probably the most prolific philosopher in North America. He has authored more than 375 articles and eighteen books, including *God, Scepticism and Modernity, The Defense of Atheism, Marxism and the Moral Point of View, Ethics Without God,* and *Why Be Moral?*

Tomorrow Professor Moreland will give a talk "Why I Am a Christian" in Bishop 106 at 1 P.M., and following that talk, Professor Nielsen will give a lecture on "Equality of Conditions and Self Ownership," and that's a lecture in political ethical philosophy.

Now, our debate will last one hour; that is, the actual presentations will last one hour. Each speaker will speak twice, Professor Moreland going first. This will be followed by questions from you, the

audience. And during the question period, please come up to one of
these microphones. There are two microphones. Make your questions
as short and to the point as possible, and if possible you might want to
write them out for clarity's sake ahead of time. Please keep your questions under two minutes. After the question period, each speaker will
make a short closing statement.

Now will you join me in welcoming both our speakers to our University. [Applause]

MORELAND: Good evening. I am delighted to be here with you on this
occasion. That lover of children and pets, W.C. Fields, was once caught
reading the Bible. When asked what he was doing, his response was
equal to the occasion. He said, "Just checking for loopholes, my dear;
just checking for loopholes."

Well, perhaps you're here this evening just checking for loopholes,
but it could very well be that your presence signifies a good deal more
than that. Perhaps it illustrates the growing interest in rational theism
in the contemporary world. Three years ago a conference was held in
Dallas, Texas, which brought together over two hundred scholars from
Europe and the United States from a variety of disciplines, including
philosophy, the hard sciences, history, and sociology. The title was
"Modern Thought Turns to Theism." The participants met to show
how in the last fifteen years, a growing number of scholars have come to
believe their disciplines point to the existence of a personal God.

In my own field, philosophy, the developments have been quite
exciting for the Christian theist. On April 7, 1980, *Time* magazine
stated, "In a quiet revolution in thought and argument that hardly anyone could have foreseen only two decades ago, God is making a comeback in the crisp intellectual circles of academic philosophers."

Indeed He is. For example, the last decade has witnessed the
formation of the Evangelical Philosophical Society and the Society of
Christian Philosophers, and today there are at least eight philosophy
journals that exist to promote the rationality of Christian theism. These
facts do not show that God exists, nor do they, by themselves, show
that it is reasonable to believe that God exists. But they do dispel the
myth that belief in God is merely a matter of blind faith and that no
thinking person can believe in His existence. Such a belief I call ostrich
atheism; it is simply out of touch with the facts.

But why has there been a quiet revolution in rational theism? Is it
reasonable in today's world to believe that God exists? My answer is
yes, and the thesis I wish to defend is that it is rational to believe that

God exists. I do not mean that God's existence can be proved with mathematical certainty, but I do want to argue that there are good reasons for believing in God, and the believer is well within her epistemic rights in believing that God exists.

There are a number of arguments I could offer on behalf of my thesis. Take, for example, the argument for God based on the design in the universe.[1] In spite of David Hume, this argument has received strong support in recent years from astronomy, physics, and biology. Scientists are discovering that the universe is a finely-tuned and delicately-balanced harmony of fundamental constants, or cosmic singularities.[2] These constants are the numerical values assigned to the various facets of the universe, such as the rate of expansion of the Big Bang, the value of the weak and strong nuclear forces, and a host of other constants of nature.

For example, in the formation of the universe, the balance of matter to antimatter had to be accurate to one part in ten billion for the universe to even arise. Had it been larger or greater by one part in ten billion, no universe would have arisen. There would also have been no universe capable of sustaining life if the expansion rate of the Big Bang had been one billionth of a percent larger or smaller.[3]

Furthermore, the chance possibilities of life arising spontaneously through mere chance has been calculated by Cambridge astronomer Fred Hoyle as being 1×10^{40}, which Hoyle likens to the probabilities of a tornado blowing through a junkyard and forming a Boeing 747. Had these values, these cosmic constants which are independent of one another, been infinitesimally greater or smaller than what they are, no life remotely similar to ours—indeed, no life at all—would have been possible. The more we discover, the more it appears, as one scientist put it, "The universe seems to have evolved with life in mind."

The harmony of these features cannot be explained by mere chance. Says Paul Davies, theoretical physicist at Cambridge: "It is hard to resist the impression that the present structure of the universe, apparently so sensitive to minor alterations in the numbers, has been rather carefully thought out . . . the seemingly miraculous concurrence of these numerical values must remain the most compelling evidence for cosmic design."[4]

In biology, scientists have discovered that DNA molecules do not merely contain redundant order, but they contain what they call information.[5] They say that DNA can be transcribed into RNA, and RNA can be translated into protein. Now Carl Sagan, and this is one of the few times I agree with him, has made certain claims about the search for extraterrestrial intelligence, called SETI. According to Sagan, in that search all we need to do is find one message with information in it from outer space, and we will be able to recognize the presence of intelligence. We don't even need to be able to translate it; it is the presence of information instead of order that will tip us off to the presence of intelligence. Well, what is sauce for the artificial goose ought to be sauce for the DNA gander, and I argue that the information in DNA molecules is evidence of intelligence behind it.[6]

Or consider the arguments for God from the existence of moral value and meaning in life.[7] If God does not exist, it is hard to see how there could be any such thing as prescriptive, nonnatural morality. It just doesn't seem that the Big Bang could spit out moral values, at least not at the rate it spit out hydrogen atoms.

As one philosopher put it: "In a world without God, mankind could not be more significant than a swarm of mosquitoes or a barnyard of pigs, for the same cosmic process that coughed them both up in the first place will eventually swallow them all up again."[8] Even the late J. L. Mackie, perhaps the greatest atheist of our century, said, "Moral properties constitute so odd a cluster of qualities and relations that they are most unlikely to have arisen in the ordinary course of events without an all-powerful god to create them."[9]

A typical atheist response to all of this is to say there are no irreducible moral truths in the world or irreducible moral properties. What one must do is to "create" values or decide to adopt the moral point of view.[10] But it doesn't seem to me that the choice between Mother Teresa and Hitler can be likened, say, to the choice as to whether I am going to be a baseball player or a tuba player. Such a choice is not a rational one, and according to this response to the theistic argument, neither is the choice of adopting a moral point of view.[11]

Mention could also be made of the arguments from the exciting archaeological confirmations of much of the Bible;[12] the puzzling question of how mind or consciousness could have arisen in a world of only matter, and even if it did, how it could be trusted to give us truth about the world;[13] and the fact that millions of people claim to have direct experiences of a benevolent Creator.[14]

Rather than pursuing these issues, however, I would like to concentrate my remarks on two specific theses. Christianity maintains that (1) God created the universe from nothing a finite time ago, and that (2) Jesus of Nazareth is God's supreme revelation of Himself to mankind. I would like to argue for each of these in order.

Consider the first premise: *God created the universe from nothing a finite time ago.* This belief is rational in light of the philosophical and scientific support for it.

First the philosophical argument. It is impossible to traverse or cross an actual infinite number of events by successive addition. An actual infinite, what mathematicians call *aleph null,* $\aleph_0$ is a set of distinct things whose number is actually infinite. Infinity, plus or minus any number including infinity, is still infinity. This contrasts with a potential infinite which can increase forever without limit but is always finite.[15]

By contrast, an actual infinite has no room for growth and is nonfinite; that is, one of its subsets can be put into one-to-one correspondence with the set itself.[16] The impossibility of crossing an actual infinite has sometimes been put by saying that one cannot count to infinity no matter how long he counts. For he will always be at some specific number which could be increased by one to generate another specific number; and that is true even if one counted forever.

Now if one cannot cross an actual infinite, then the past must have been finite. If it were infinite, then to come to the present moment, one would have had to have traversed an actual infinite to get here, which is impossible. Without a first event, there could be no second, third, or any specifiable number of events including the present one. To get to the present moment by crossing an actual infinite would be like trying to jump out of a bottomless pit. Not only could one never complete the jump, one could never even get started; for to reach any point in the series, one must already have crossed an infinite number of points to get to that point, as Zeno's puzzles clearly showed.[17]

Put differently, suppose you go back through the events of the past in your mind. You will either come to a beginning, or you will not. If you come to a beginning, then the past is finite and my argument is settled. That would be the first event. If you had never come to a beginning, then the past is actually infinite; and as you go back in your mind, you never in principle could exhaust the events of the past. It would be impossible to traverse the past going backward in your mind.

Since time doesn't go backward but forward, and the number of events traversed is not a function of the direction of movement, this amounts to saying that the present could never be realized. But since it has been realized—after all, here we are—there must have been a first event, and this event must have been spontaneously generated by a situation that was immutable, unchanging, timeless, and free.

Now most of the experiences we have in life where an event is spontaneously generated without sufficient conditions prior to it occur by means of *agent causation,* or what we would call agent causes.[18] That is, you and I act everyday; we raise our arms; we do things. It seems reasonable, based upon agent causation, therefore, to say that the first event was spontaneously caused to be by a personal agent of some kind. The major alternative is that the first event popped into existence out of nothing without a cause, and that doesn't seem reasonable to me.

That there was a beginning to the universe is confirmed by two areas of science as well as philosophy. The first is the Second Law of Thermodynamics, which states that in a closed system the amount of energy available to do work is always decreasing. It can also be put by saying that the amount of disorganization, or randomness, increases toward a maximum. Applied to the universe as a whole, the Second Law states that everyday the universe becomes more and more disorganized. In other words, it is burning up. It will eventually die a cold death. The main implication of this is, as one physicist put it, "The universe cannot have existed forever. Otherwise it would have already reached its equilibrium end state an infinite time ago. Conclusion: The universe did not always exist."[19] Scientist Richard Slagel says, "In some way the universe must have been wound up."[20]

The Big Bang provides another argument. In 1929 Edwin Hubble discovered a phenomenon known as the red shift, which implies that space is expanding outward and that all bodies in space are growing apart.

These and other observations have led to the Big Bang theory, which has two key features. First, around 15 billion years ago, according to the theory, everything—space, time, energy—was all compacted into a mathematical point with no dimensions, and this exploded to form the present universe. In the words of Cambridge astronomer Fred Hoyle, "The universe was shrunk down to nothing."[21] So the Big Bang implies the universe sprang into existence from a state of affairs that has been described by some as nothingness.

Second, because of the density of the universe, there was only one initial creation, and there will be no contraction or further explosion in the future. There was only one initial creation, or first event. What is the atheist to do here? Oxford's Anthony Kenney has the answer. He says, "A proponent of the Big Bang theory, at least if he is an atheist, must believe that the matter of the universe came from nothing and by nothing."[22]

I would like to conclude by noting an observation by Robert Jastrow, director of NASA's Goddard Institute for Space Studies. Jastrow says, "For the scientist who has lived by his faith in the power of reason, the story ends like a bad dream. He has scaled the mountains of ignorance; he is about to conquer the highest peak; as he pulls himself over the final rock, he is greeted by a band of theologians who have been sitting there for centuries."[23]

Philosophically and scientifically, the belief that God created the universe a finite time ago is eminently reasonable.

The second proposition that I would like to defend is that *Jesus of Nazareth is God's supreme revelation of Himself to mankind.* Among other things, this claim hinges upon the truthfulness of His resurrection from the dead. I want to argue that the historical evidence for Jesus' resurrection is strong and belief in His resurrection is reasonable. At least four lines of evidence can be used to defend the historicity of the resurrection.[24]

First, *the time factor.* Let us consider the New Testament, not as an inspired book, though I believe it to be, but as a set of alleged historical sources about Jesus of Nazareth. We know He was most likely crucified in A.D. 33.[25] All New Testament scholars date the Gospels within the lifetime of eyewitnesses of the life of Jesus, and the latest they can possibly be dated is toward the end of the first century, from A.D. 70 on. In recent years there has been a growing number of New Testament scholars who date the Gospels from A.D. 40 to A.D. 70, including the late W. F. Albright at Johns Hopkins, the dean of American archaeology.[26] The bulk of the letters of the New Testament date from A.D. 48 to 64. This means that we have clear widespread testimony to a miracle-working, supernatural, resurrected Jesus no later than fifteen to twenty years after the events of His life.

In addition, the writings of the New Testament themselves contain statements, phrases, and hymns that are heavily Semitic and which translate easily back into Aramaic from Greek. These hymns are embedded in the epistles of the New Testament, and they existed prior to the New Testament because they are not spoken in characteristically Pauline language. As Martin Hengel argued, "These phrases and hymns present a miracle-working Jesus who rose from the dead, and they can be dated within the first decade of Christianity after the death of Jesus."[27] Further, there are good reasons for believing that the Acts account of the first preaching of the risen Jesus in Jerusalem just five weeks after His death is historically reliable.[28]

All of this means that a clear, widespread picture of a miracle-working, supernatural Jesus who rose bodily from the dead existed within a few weeks after His death, and at the latest within the first decade of the spread of Christianity. There was just not enough time for the facts of Jesus' life, death, and resurrection to be forgotten and replaced by a set of myths. A. N. Sherwin-White, a classical historian at the University of Oxford, has studied the rate at which myth replaced history in the ancient Near East. Sherwin-White argues, "Tests suggest that even two generations are too short a span to allow the mythical tendency to prevail over a hard historical core."[29] There is then not enough time between the deeds of Jesus and our earliest sources to allow for a high degree of myth making.

Secondly, *the empty tomb*. A large number of New Testament scholars hold that the New Testament statements that Jesus' tomb was found empty three days after His death are historically reliable. They do so for several reasons.

First, archaeological discoveries have verified the accuracy of the description of Jesus' burial and tomb and the plausibility of its location. Archaeologists have discovered tombs just like the ones that are described in the Gospels, in just the place in Jerusalem where Jesus is said to have been buried.[30]

Second, there were at least fifty tombs of holy men during the time of Jesus in Jerusalem that were sites of religious veneration. Thus, the location of Jesus' tomb would have been carefully noted by His followers in order to venerate Him after His death. But there is no evidence whatsoever that His tomb was ever a site of veneration.[31] This is explained by the fact that His tomb was empty.

Third, the Gospel narratives of the discovery of the empty tomb bear features of historicity. To site but one, the narratives tell us that women were the first to discover and witness the empty tomb.[32] Given the low social status of women then and the fact that they were not allowed to give legal testimony, it is highly probable that women were in fact the first ones to see the risen Christ. A fabricated account of the empty tomb would have used men, certainly not women. In fact, when Paul cites the resurrection formula in First Corinthians used to evangelize unbelievers, he leaves the women out, no doubt to keep unbelievers from stumbling on a peripheral detail which was culturally insensitive. The women are left in the Gospel accounts, however, to preserve a record of *"wie es egentlich gewesen ist,"* as it actually was, even though it was an embarrassment to them culturally.

Third, *the appearances of Jesus of Nazareth*.[33] The historical evidence indicates that on separate occasions different individuals and groups, one group of at least five hundred persons, saw appearances of Jesus from the dead. Even one of the most skeptical New Testament scholars, the late Norman Perrin of the University of Chicago, has said,

"The more we study the tradition with regard to the appearances, the firmer the rock begins to appear upon which they are based."[34]

I personally know of no New Testament scholar who denies that several of Jesus' early followers at least had a life-changing experience they believed to have been an experience of the risen Jesus. Many who deny that it was a real resurrection interpret these reported experiences as subjective experiences or hallucinations. But two objections refute this explanation. First, the variety and number of people seeing the appearances makes hallucination unlikely. Second, hallucinations do not create completely new thoughts, but they put together old thoughts.

Let me explain. The resurrection picture of Jesus is so out of touch with what was already in existence in Judaism that it is hard to explain how they [Jesus' followers] would have used a resurrection to interpret hallucinating experiences. According to Jewish belief at that time, there was to be only one resurrection, all at once. No one would be raised by himself; everybody was to be raised together. Second, the general resurrection was at the end of the world; there was no resurrection in history before the end of the world. Third, the resurrection was conceived of in crude, reanimating terms where the body parts were reanimated on the skeleton. Fourth, visions of people who were translated to heaven or raised were never given to groups. And fifth, the Messiah, according to first-century Jewish religious belief, was not a suffering servant who died or rose from the dead.

The point is that if they had hallucinations, they would never have thought to interpret those hallucinations as a resurrection. Already available in their culture was a ready-made genre—namely, translations to heaven or resuscitations. The fact that they interpreted it as a resurrection is hard to explain in light of their cultural beliefs.

Finally, *the origination of the Christian church* implies a resurrection. Why did Christianity begin? Where did it come from? What motivation did the early church have for spreading Christianity? Christianity didn't come from the stork. Christianity was a unique new movement. Without the resurrection, there is no adequate explanation for where it came from or how it got going.

For one thing, the church was not founded on loving your neighbor or doing good, but on spreading a message, the death and resurrection of the Son of God. But that message was so culturally unacceptable as to have little antecedent probability of success. If the early church was going to invent a message that would sell well and which was going to make them religious heroes, they did a horrible job. As one of the world's prominent New Testament scholars, Martin Hengel of Tübingen has put it, "To believe that the one pre-existent Son of the one true God, the mediator at creation and the redeemer of the world, had appeared in very recent times in out-of-the-way Galilee as a member of the obscure people of the Jews and even worse, had died the death of a common criminal on the cross, could only be regarded as a sign of madness."[35]

The resurrection of Jesus offers the best explanation for the incredible success of the early church. Without the resurrection there would have been no early church. Furthermore, it explains how a large generation of Jewish people (remember, most of the early Christians were Jewish) would have been willing to risk the damnation of their own souls to hell and reject what had been sociologically embedded in their community for centuries; namely, the Law must be kept for salvation, sacrifices must be kept for salvation, the Sabbath must be kept, nontrinitarian monotheism, and there is only a political Messiah, not a dying and rising one. How does a group of people in a short time span, a society, disenfranchise themselves from that into which they had been culturally indoctrinated for centuries and risk the damnation of their own souls to hell to follow a carpenter from Nazareth? The most reasonable explanation is there was something about that man that caused this change. He was a miracle worker who rose from the dead.

The resurrection also explains the motivation and endurance of the early Christians. The early disciples experienced a life of pain, physical and social abuse, and martyrs' deaths for their message. What kept them going? The question is even more pressing in light of their state of betrayal, fear, and disillusionment just after Jesus' crucifixion. What changed them and motivated them? The resurrection.

So strong is this point that recently an orthodox Jewish rabbi, a Jewish scholar of New Testament in Frankfurt, Germany, Pinchas Lapide, was converted to belief in the resurrection on strictly historical evidence. And he has written a book defending its historicity. Lapide writes, "How was it possible that His disciples, who by no means excelled in intelligence, eloquence, or strength of faith, were able to begin their victorious march of conversion only *after* the shattering fiasco of Golgotha?"[36]

Before concluding, let me point out that the miracles of Jesus rebut the argument that different world religions cancel each other out because they are all equally miraculous. This is simply not the case. No rival world religion has miracles attributed to its founder that are early and nonlegendary. Most [world religions] are simply ideologies or philosophical systems. The evidence for Jesus is different both in quality and quantity.

In summary, I have argued there are good reasons to believe that a personal God created the world a finite time ago. In addition to the arguments I cited at the beginning, I appealed to the philosophical argument against the possibility of traversing an actual infinite and the scientific arguments employing the Second Law of Thermodynamics and the uniqueness of the Big Bang, which make this proposition reasonable. I have also argued that Christ is God's unique revelation of Himself to mankind. This claim rests in part on His resurrection from the dead, which I supported by four lines of argument—the time factor, the empty tomb, the resurrection appearances, and the origin of the Christian church.

For these and other reasons one is well within his or her epistemic rights in believing that the Christian God exists. Thank you. [Applause]

Notes

1. Helpful treatments of the design argument are James E. Horigan, *Chance or Design?* (New York: Philosophical Library, 1979); A. C. Ewing, *Value and Reality* (London: George Allen and Unwin, 1973), 165–82; John Leslie, "Modern Cosmology and the Creation of Life," in *Evolution and Creation,* Ernan McMullin, ed. (Notre Dame, Ind.: University of Notre Dame Press, 1985), 91–120; "How to Draw Conclusions from a Fine-Tuned Universe," in *Physics, Philosophy, and Theology,* Robert John Russell, William R. Stoeger, and George V. Coyne, eds. (Notre Dame, Ind.: University of Notre Dame Press, 1988), 297–311.

2. Cf. Paul Davies, *God and the New Physics* (New York: Simon and Schuster, 1983), 164–189; John Leslie, "Anthropic Principle, World Ensemble, Design," *American Philosophical Quarterly* 19 (Apr. 1982), 141–50; John Leslie, *Universe* (New York: Routledge, 1989).

3. This point applies to any type of life and not just life that is present on earth. For something to be living, it must contain enough configurational complexity and information to ingest, excrete, and replicate, and such complexity is only possible in universes of a certain type.

4. Davies, *God and the New Physics,* 189.

5. See Charles B. Thaxton, Walter L. Bradley, and Roger L. Olsen, *The Mystery of Life's Origin: Reassessing Current Theories* (New York: Philosophical Library, 1984), 127–66; Herbert Yockey, "Self-Organization: Origins of Life Scenarios and Information Theory," *The Journal of Theoretical Biology* 91 (1981), 13–31.

6. This focus on informational specificity provides a way of seeing the inadequacy of an atheistic response to probability forms of the design argument. It is sometimes claimed, for example, that any deal of thirteen cards is as improbable as a perfect bridge hand since the same number of cards are involved in each case. Similarly, any arrangement of parts in a DNA molecule is equally improbable, provided, of course, that the number of parts is the same in all cases. But the two situations are not the same. The information required to produce some random, unspecified arrangement of n parts would be something like "produce some arrangement or other of n parts." But the information required to produce the specific structure of the DNA molecule (identified independently from the mere fact that this happened to show up) would require an incredible number of commands given in specific order. For more on this, see J. P. Moreland, *Scaling the Secular City* (Grand Rapids: Baker, 1987), 71-75.

7. See Robert Adams, "Moral Arguments for Theistic Belief," in *Rationality and Religious Belief*, C. F. Delaney, ed. (Notre Dame, Ind.: University of Notre Dame Press, 1979), 116-40; Ewing, 183-208; H. P. Owen, *The Moral Argument for Christian Theism* (London: Allen and Unwin, 1965); Basil Mitchell, *Morality: Secular and Religious* (Oxford: Clarendon, 1980).

8. William Lane Craig, *The Existence of God and the Beginning of the Universe* (San Bernardino, Calif.: Here's Life Publishers, 1979), 15-16.

9. J. L. Mackie, *The Miracle of Theism* (Oxford: Clarendon, 1982), 116.

10. For our purposes, we can agree to accept a widely embraced understanding of what it means to say that one has adopted the "moral point of view": one subscribes to normative judgments about actions, principles, and motives, one is willing to universalize one's judgments, one seeks to form his moral views in a free, unbiased, enlightened way, and one seeks to promote the good. Two things should be pointed out, however. First, this characterization is far too formal to provide anything even approximating a view of what the moral life looks like. For that, one needs a material definition of the good, the good life, the virtuous person, and so on. Second, it seems to me that when one adopts the moral point of view, along with some material content given to the good, then one implicitly behaves as though this view is really true—that is, that one's (individual or communal) notion of morality is discovered and not created. For more on morality and general conceptions of the good life, see Stanley Hauerwas, *Suffering Presence* (Notre Dame, Ind.: University of Notre Dame Press, 1986).

11. Rationality has two basic functions in a naturalistic cognitivist theory of metaethics. Reason functions first and foremost in a means/ends way— that is, given that I desire or will certain ends, then reason can help me find the most efficient means to those ends. Second, reason can postulate certain ends as "rationally desirable" in the sense that, given certain contingent facts about us as humans and given that we find ourselves working

within a set of contingent moral traditions or versions of human goods and the good life (e.g., Rawlsian primary goods—natural desires and wants that are "reasonable" to want whatever else one wants), these ends are desired by "normal" (nonneurotic) people. Unfortunately, neither of these senses of rationality has any connection to moral truth. But rationality is an honorific notion precisely because we believe that by being rational one is in a better position to have the truth. Thus, these natural notions of rationality cannot answer the question, "Why should I be moral?" where the "should" is a rational "should." For it would be possible for all "rational" (nonneurotic, unemotional, cool headed) human beings to desire something that is inconsistent with true moral facts. If this happened, it would not be "rational" to be moral. But a nonnatural notion of rationality does not have this problem. Given moral realism (there are irreducibly moral facts and moral truths correspond to these facts), one can have rational intuitive knowledge of synthetic *a priori* moral truths like "Mercy, as such, is a virtue." In this case, to adopt the moral point of view is to be rational, for it is to acknowledge the existence and knowability of true moral facts. For more on this, see Panayot Butchvarov, *Skepticism in Ethics* (Bloomington, Ind.: Indiana University Press, 1989), 5, 8–9, 36–39, 137–195.

12. For overviews of archaeological confirmations of the New Testament documents, see R. T. France, *The Evidence for Jesus* (Downers Grove, Ill.: InterVarsity Press, 1986), 140–57; Gary Habermas, *The Verdict of History* (Nashville, Tenn.: Thomas Nelson, 1988), 152–163.

13. A number of thinkers have argued that the reliability of the mind and senses is evidence that a designer designed them with the epistemic environment in mind. See John Hick, *Arguments for the Existence of God* (New York: Herder, 1971), 21–26; Ewing, 1778; Stanley L. Jaki, *Angels, Apes, and Men* (La Salle, Ill.: Sherwood Sugden & Co., 1983), 51–60.

14. There are two types of arguments for God based on religious experience: a causal argument and a direct perception argument. The former argues that certain effects (e.g., a changed life, spiritual power) are best explained by postulating God as the cause of those effects. This is an inference to the best explanation. The latter claims that religious perception is relevantly similar to sensory perception and both are frequently veridical. Here the claim is that, occasionally, God Himself is directly perceived in religious experience. For more on the two arguments, see Moreland, *Scaling the Secular City*, 231–240.

15. See ibid., 18–42, for a fuller explanation of this argument and a bibliography of other works relevant to it.

16. In finite sets (e.g., the set of numbers 1–10) a proper subset (e.g., the set containing 1–5) is always smaller in membership than the set of which it is a subset. But actually infinite sets (e.g., the set of all natural numbers) are

such that a subset, like the set of all even numbers, can have the same cardinality (number of members) as the set of which it is a subset. Stated simply, in finite sets the whole is always larger than any proper part. In infinite sets a part can equal the whole.

17. The real point of Zeno's paradoxes is that motion cannot even begin, much less be completed. Aristotle was the first to solve Zeno's paradoxes by distinguishing between an actual and potential infinite and claiming that motion between two points involved the latter and not the former. A good treatment of these paradoxes is Max Black, "Achilles and the Tortoise," *Analysis* 11 (Mar. 1951), 91–101.

18. On the nature of agent causation, see William L. Rowe, "Two Concepts of Freedom," in *Proceedings and Addresses of the American Philosophical Association* Supplement to Volume 61 (Sept. 1987), 43–64.

19. Davies, *God and the New Physics*, 11.

20. Cited in Craig, *The Existence of God and the Beginning of the Universe*, 65.

21. Fred Hoyle, *Astronomy and Cosmology* (San Francisco: W. H. Freeman & Co., 1975), 658.

22. Anthony Kenney, *The Five Ways* (New York: Schocken, 1969), 66.

23. Robert Jastrow, *God and the Astronomers* (New York: W. W. Norton, 1978), 116.

24. Cf. Moreland, *Scaling the Secular City*, 159–183.

25. Cf. Harold W. Hoehner, *Chronological Aspects of the Life of Christ* (Grand Rapids, Mich.: Zondervan, 1977), 95–114.

26. On the early dating of the Gospels, see Earle Ellis, "Dating the New Testament," *New Testament Studies* (July 1980), 487–502; John A. T. Robinson, *Can We Trust the New Testament?* (Grand Rapids, Mich.: Eerdmans, 1977), *Redating the New Testament* (Philadelphia: Westminster, 1976); Hugo Staudinger, *The Trustworthiness of the Gospels* (Edinburgh: The Handsel Press, 1981); John W. Wenham, "Gospel Origins," *Trinity Journal* (old series) 7 (Fall 1978), 112–34. Douglas Moo has replied to Wenham, and Wenham has offered a rejoinder to Moo in *Trinity Journal* (new series) 2 (1981), 24–36.

27. Martin Hengel, *Between Jesus and Paul* (Philadelphia: Fortress, 1983), 30–47, 78–96.

28. See G. N. Stanton, *Jesus of Nazareth in New Testament Preaching* (Cambridge: Cambridge University Press, 1974), 67–85.

29. A. N. Sherwin-White, *Roman Society and Roman Law in the New Testament* (Grand Rapids, Mich.: Baker, 1978), 190.

30. See William Lane Craig, *The Son Rises* (Chicago: Moody Press, 1981), 55–57.

31. See Edwin Yamauchi, "Easter—Myth, Hallucination, or History?: Part One," *Christianity Today* 4 (March 15, 1974), 4–16.

32. Cf. E. L. Bode, *The First Easter Morning* (Rome: Biblical Institute Press, 1970), 160–61.
33. For more on the resurrection appearances, see Moreland, 172–78.
34. Norman Perrin, *The Resurrection According to Matthew, Mark, and Luke* (Philadelphia: Fortress, 1977), 80.
35. Martin Hengel, *Crucifixion* (Philadelphia: Fortress, 1977), 6–7.
36. Pinchas Lapide, *The Resurrection of Jesus* (Minneapolis: Augsburg Publishing House, 1983), 68.

Kai Nielsen

No! A Defense of Atheism

2

POJMAN: Our next speaker is Professor Kai Nielsen.

NIELSEN: Thank you. It is tempting for the speaker who speaks second to comment on what the prior speaker did. But as you know, the way the thing is laid out, I'll have occasion to do that later, and I'll reserve that for then.

I should say initially that I suspect from what I've heard of my audience that a number of you will not be extraordinarily sympathetic to what I say. That doesn't bother me, but what does bother me is that I'm going to say some things that may offend some of you, and in honesty I don't know how I can avoid doing that. But I don't certainly mean it in a personally offensive way.

I am going to argue quite to the contrary to what Professor Moreland has been saying, and this is what will seem offensive to many of you, but I certainly don't intend it to be offensive. I am going to argue that for somebody living in the twentieth century with a good philosophical and a good scientific education, who thinks carefully about the matter, that for such a person it is irrational to believe in God.

Now I don't mean by that that I think I'm more rational than Professor Moreland or the rest of you. Rational people in my view can have irrational beliefs. I'm sure I have some. If I can spot them or they're pointed out to me, I'll reject them. I also mean this in a doubly hypothetical way. By that I mean that *if* my arguments are right—that is the first hypothetical—and *if* people do have a good scientific and philosophical education—you can have one without the other—that then they should come to see that it is irrational to believe in God. What I will do is provide an argument for that in just a moment.

All right. Is the Christian view of our world the true one? The Christian, of course, sees the world in the same way as others, but sees more besides. Part of this "more besides," but not all of it, of course, is that God exists. Does He?

That question, I first want to contend, is not as straightforward as it may seem. The standard view—I mean the standard view at present, among at least philosophers and a large number of theologians, though it is not a view that either Professor Moreland or I myself accept, but it is a very standard view—is that you can't prove that God does exist and you can't prove that He doesn't exist. Indeed, some will say you can't even successfully argue that it is more probable that He does exist or more probable that God doesn't exist. In debates concerning religion neither side has been able to win the day here.

This being so, the argument goes—this is, let me repeat, the standard view—the believer is not being unreasonable in continuing to believe, and the atheist is not being unreasonable in not believing in God. Reason, a thoughtful attention to our experience or the reflective use of our intelligence, will not settle matters here. Whether we believe or not, so the standard view has had it, is a straight matter of faith. There is no showing that belief or unbelief is the more reasonable, though it can be shown that both atheism and theism are reasonable views. What you can't do is show that one is more reasonable than the other. That is, by now, a very standard view. Philosophical theologians like John Hick or Terence Penelhum believe this—and indeed have given distinguished articulations of such views.[1]

Now the first thing I want to note is that this is a far cry from the grand tradition of natural theology. In the Middle Ages, Thomas Aquinas and Duns Scotus and William of Occam thought they could prove that God exists and that it is irrational to be an atheist or an agnostic. Now, that's a great distance from the standard view. The standard view is a rather modern invention. A Moslem philosopher that I know regards it as a kind of a revisionism of Christianity, or, for that matter, of Islam where it is so influenced.[2] And I take it that Professor Moreland, though he waffled a bit about this, doesn't have that standard view. He thinks that it is more probable that God exists than He does not, and in that sense you can give some kind of a proof of the existence of God. That is brave of him indeed because there are very, very few Christians, at least Christians who are philosophers, people of Thomist persuasions apart, who think you can do that. In my discussion later, I will come to some of his arguments for this.[3]

I reject the standard view as well. I think, as I said to you initially, that belief in God is irrational. That is, it is irrational for someone who has a good scientific and philosophic education. And I point out to you that I don't mean to say by this that I think that I'm more rational than Professor Hick or some religious person, because I remind you that rational people can have irrational beliefs. And what I'm maintaining is that belief in God for people in the twentieth century, not people at all times and at all places, with a good scientific and philosophic education, is irrational.

Now why do I say that? Why, in my view, is belief in God irrational?

Take a belief in a Zeus-like, anthropomorphic God. Such a belief is just plainly false and superstitious. Such a being is an odd kind of being, and there is no evidence for His reality. Moreover, anything that could be observed, as an anthropomorphic God could or in any way directly be detected, would not be the God of Christianity or at least of advanced Judeo-Christianity. As I think it was Kierkegaard who quipped, "God is not a great green parrot you can possibly see." But the anthropomorphic God, and anthropomorphic conception of God, is not incoherent; it's just superstitious to believe in such a god. But at least since the Middle Ages, and even earlier than that, religious people have long since, at least when they are reflecting about the nature of God, ceased believing in an anthropomorphic Zeus-like God, while continuing to believe in the God of developed Judaism, Christianity, and Islam. And it is this belief, a much far more ethereal conception of God, that I maintain is incoherent.

There are a number of arguments for that. But I am going to stick with just one, developing it in some detail. This is a dangerous strategy because it puts all your eggs in one basket, but it will allow me to develop one argument I take to be of vital importance. I'm going to use the opposite argumentative strategy from Professor Moreland. Professor Moreland gave you a battery of arguments. I'm going to give you one sustained argument principally. And if I have enough time, I'll give you some supplementary ones which will argue to the same conclusion.

Consider the problem about the reference of the word "God" or any alternative word in some other language with the same meaning. What does the word "God" refer to for Christians or for Jews?

Consider the sentence, "God made the heavens and the earth," as distinct from "Louis made pasta and cake." Consider those two sentences. What is "God" in this first sentence supposed to stand for, and how is the referent of that term to be identified? Compare this with "Louis." I can say "Somebody asked, 'Who's Louis?'" and I'll say, "That chap over there." That's what philosophers would call an *ostensive definition,* an extra-linguistic definition. I point out the reference of the term "Louis" by pointing to its referent. There is another way to give meaning to the term. I could say, "Well, the professor, one of the professors of philosophy at the University of Mississippi," or "the professor of philosophy at the University of Mississippi who studied Kierkegaard in Denmark," or "the man sitting on the platform with the dark glasses on." I could give you a number of intra-linguistic definitions, what philosophers call "definite descriptions," which identify who Louis is. So when I say, "Louis made pasta and cake," you can understand what would make that sentence true or false.

Now go back to the religious sentence, "God made the heavens and the earth." How do we know, as we said when we rejected the anthropomorphic conception, that anything that could be pointed to or literally seen or literally observed or literally experienced or literally noted wouldn't be God? It would be some kind of temporal something that you could detect; something limited. So God, unlike Louis [Pojman, the moderator of this debate], can't be identified ostensively, extra-linguistically.

Well, let us try to identify, try to establish what this God is that we speak of and concerning whom we try to use premises to prove His existence. Let us try to identify God by means of definite descriptions, that is, intra-linguistically. Suppose we say, "God is the maker of the heavens and the earth," or "The being transcendent to the world on whom all things depend and who depends on nothing himself," or "the being of infinite love to whom all things are owed," or "the infinite sustainer of the universe," or "the heavenly father of us all."

Now the difficulty with those definite descriptions, unlike the ones I used to identify Louis, is that with them, if you had trouble about knowing what was referred to by the word "God," you are going to be equally puzzled about "A being transcendent to the world." How would you identify that? Or "the being of infinite love to whom all things are owed?" How do you know what it would be like to meet such a being? What is it that you're talking about in talking about a being of infinite love? Or "The maker of the heavens and the earth," rather than "The maker of the pasta and the cake?" How would you know what that refers to?

What I'm trying to say is (and I don't say these expressions are meaningless; or that they are linguistic irregularities) that they are what philosophers would call problematic conceptions. Indeed, they are so problematic and so obscure that it turns out that we don't know what we are talking about when we use them. We have a kind of familiar pictorial sense that we know what we are talking about, but when we think very carefully about what these expressions mean, they are so problematic that we can't use them to make true or false claims.

Suppose someone says, "Look, Nielsen, you should know better than that. God, in Judeo-Christianity and Islamic religions, is the Ultimate Mystery." And that is almost definitional. A non-mysterious god might be the god of some form of deism, but it wouldn't be the God of Christianity. But, if we say definitionally, "God is the Ultimate Mystery," if we are puzzled about the referent of "God," we are going to be terribly puzzled about what is "the Ultimate Mystery."

What are we talking about there? We need to have some account of who or what we are talking about in speaking of God. Some minimal understanding is necessary even for faith to be possible.[4] If you have no understanding of those terms at all, then you can't take them on faith or take them on trust, because you don't know *what* to take on faith or you don't know *what* to take on trust. Nor could you use such terms in a premise. For something to be a premise in an argument, its terms must not be so problematic that we do not understand them. No matter how tight Moreland's arguments might be, he can't use them in premises if we don't know what they mean. But—or so I shall argue—we don't know what they mean.

Suppose we say, "Look, Nielsen, if you're so bloody empiricist, what you are going to do is rule out molecular biology too." We often explain biological phenomena in physical chemical terms. But the relevant chemical processes are unobservable. There is an important distinction to be made here. They are only contingently unobservable; there is no logical ban on the possibility of their being observed, even if we don't know what it would be like presently to observe them. And the same thing is true about physics. There is no logical ban; they are just contingently unobservable.

In the case of God, however, anything that could be observed would not be the God of Christianity. It would be the anthropomorphic Zeus-like god that it would be superstitious to believe in. One of the responses to this is to say, "Well, God isn't directly observable, but He is indirectly observable. You observe Him through His works and so forth and so on, through the design *in* the world and the like." This, I shall add in passing, is very different than the design *of* the world, if indeed there is design. You observe God, it is said, indirectly in His works. But it makes no sense whatsoever to say something is indirectly observable, if it is not at least in theory or in principle directly observable as well. Suppose I say to you, "There's a glass of water under this podium," or, better still, suppose I say, "There's a still over there." And you say, "How do you know there's a still?" "Well, can't you see the smoke coming up?" I respond. That is, many believe, pretty good indirect evidence for there being a still. Yet, even if it is not in reality terribly good evidence, still it is reasonable indirect evidence to there being a still there. But it is only indirect evidence at all, good or bad, because you know what it would be like to observe the bloody still, and to say, "Ah, yeah, that's what's making the smoke." That is plain enough, isn't it?

But there is no directly observing of God or directly noting His existence or personally encountering God. You can't encounter a transcendent being. (Think here literally of what you are saying.) And if so, then there is a logical ban on the very *possibility* of direct acquaintance with God. Being then parallel with the other cases, there can't be any indirect observation either. It just makes no sense to say you can indirectly observe something you have no idea of what it could even mean to directly observe.

Suppose one says, by way of counter argument, "But look, mathematical objects are unobservable. We need numbers to do mathematics, and we need mathematics to do science." That is, of course, perfectly true. We do need numbers to do mathematics, and we do need mathematics to do science. Still we need not reify numbers into queer Platonic objects. There is one group of mathematicians that does this, but a lot of them don't. There is no need to make such a reification.

But suppose, all the same, we do reify numbers; that is, objectify them as to some sort of queer objects. Let us, for the sake of the argument, allow this to be legitimate—something I wouldn't in fact allow for the moment. Let us, that is, read numbers Platonically, and talk of numbers being eternal, of their being mathematical objects. If we do so, we cannot now, it will be claimed, say that the concept of God is incoherent. Remember, my principal basis for saying that it is irrational to believe in God is that I believe the concept of God in developed Judeo-Christianity is incoherent. I would also have to say then that to believe that there are numbers is incoherent, and that is absurd.

We can, we are now allowing, think of eternal realities, namely numbers. But God is also said to be an infinite *individual*, an infinite *person* transcendent to the universe. Acknowledging that there are eternal realities, such as numbers, gives us no purchase on this. We have no understanding of what we are talking about when we speak of an infinite person or an infinite individual transcendent to the world. Numbers, after all, are types, and not tokens, not individuals.

Let me explain what I mean by that bit of philosophical jargon. Suppose there were a blackboard here, and I wrote down the number *2* three times. How many numbers are there on the blackboard? Well, normally you would say, "There's one number; that is, one type and three tokens, three physical representations of the word *2*." So that is the difference between the words *types* and *tokens*.

Numbers are, after all, types and not tokens, and they can be eternal objects, if you want to talk in that Platonic way. But we have no understanding of what it is for an individual, a token as distinct from a type, to be eternal, such that it could not *not* exist in any possible world. But God is supposed to be a person—an individual.

We compound the trouble when we speak of infinite individuals.

And remember, God has to be an individual, not a type. God is not a "kind" term. "God" does not refer to a kind of reality but supposedly to an utterly unique, infinite individual. My argument is that it doesn't make sense when you think it through. God is an infinite individual who created and sustained the world. And so even if numbers are eternal realities, and so we can give sense to eternal realities, we still haven't given sense to an individual, a token, being an eternal reality, to say nothing of giving sense to there being an infinite individual.

The definite description, "The infinite individual who made the world," is as puzzling as is God. Suppose it is said, "God's reality is *sui generis*. God just has a distinct reality which is different from any other kind of reality. It is not like mathematical reality; it is not like physical reality and so forth." But such talk of being *sui generis* is, I believe, evasive. Suppose I ask you to believe in *poy*, an utterly nonsensical term, a made-up word of mine. But I can't tell you what poy is. You can't in that circumstance, no matter how much you want to, believe in poy or have faith in poy. To do that, you would have to have some understanding of what poy is. Now what I'm trying to argue is when you really think through to what God is supposed to be, you will see that you have no more understanding of God, except as a familiarity in the language, than you have an understanding of poy. There's no way of conceptually identifying God that isn't equally problematic.

Remember I told you—I'm going to skip over some steps in the argument—that I have a number of additional arguments for this. No, I think I will and leave the others for later. Suppose someone says—I'll stick with this one line of argument—"God by definition is eternal." That's fair enough, but it may have been eternally the case that there are no eternal individuals or persons. In saying that God is eternal, we are not saying that there are any eternal individuals or persons. We are only saying that *if* there is a God, He exists eternally. But of course, there might not be; there might never have been any eternal individuals or persons. Eternally, it might have been the case that there are no eternal individuals.[5]

You need an argument to show that there must be an eternal individual or person. Professor Moreland tried to give one. To do that we must show that the very idea of there not being such a reality is self-contradictory. That seems at least to be either patently false or itself incoherent. To put it minimally, the notion of a logically necessary individual or person that is itself at best problematical.[6]

This being so, we cannot give coherent sense to the concept of God by that alleged definite description. It has been said, "Well, why couldn't I offer any of the following: 'God is a being which cannot not exist,' 'God is the being which exists in every possible world'?" But these are just alternative ways of speaking of a logically necessary individual or person, and it is this very notion that is so thoroughly problematic as to appear to be at least incoherent.

Let us go back, and I'm now about to finish, to our question at the beginning: Does God exist? If I am right in claiming that the concept of God in developed Judeo-Christian discourses is incoherent, then there can be no question of proving God's existence or establishing that He exists. Proof requires premises and conclusions. But if the concept of God is incoherent, it cannot be used in a premise purporting to prove that God exists. Moreover, it as well, and for the same reasons, cannot be used in a conclusion purporting to have been established by premises not employing the concept of God or other religious concepts. If the concept of God in developed Judeo-Christianity is incoherent, as I have argued it is, then arguments of the ontological type, cosmological type, or design type cannot possibly get off the ground. This being so, there is no need to consider their details. But these are the standard arguments for the existence of God. Moreover, if the very idea of there being a God of the requisite type for Judeo-Christianity is incoherent, no other argument can fare any better.

To worry this out a little bit, let me argue by analogy. Suppose I say, "All married bachelors are irascible. Jones is a married bachelor. Jones is irascible." Now that's a valid form, but it couldn't be a sound argument. Sound arguments are valid arguments with true premises, but if a premise is incoherent, then there can be no question of its being true. There is no need, if my argument is sound, even to look at the proof. Nothing could prove there is a round square or a married bachelor or that procrastination drinks melancholy. The very idea of such a thing is incoherent.

Before we go to the proofs or the evidence for God's existence, the believer must show that we know what we are talking about when we speak of God. And in closing, just one more thing. We, in some not very clear way, know our way around when we speak of God anthropomorphically, as we of course learned to use God-talk as children. That gives us the *illusion* that we understand what we are talking about when we speak of God. We are told that God is our *heavenly* Father, not a father like our real father, but our *heavenly* Father. And what's that? And eventually we move from anthropomorphic conceptions of God, which we do in some way understand, to nonanthropomorphic ones. When we engage in our devotions (if we do such things), the anthropo-

morphic ones reassert themselves and we feel confident that we understand what we are praying to, worshiping, and the like. But when we
reflect, we realize that neither our religious nor our intellectual im-
pulses will sustain the anthropomorphic conceptions. That way makes
religion into superstition. So we are driven, when we reflect, to ever
less anthropomorphic ones, but in doing so we pass over, unwittingly, in
the very effort to gain a religiously adequate conception of God, to an
incoherent conception.[7] We do so de-anthropomorphize that we no
longer understand what we are saying. Yet an anthropomorphic conception of God of any sort gives us a materially tainted God which is subject
to evident empirical disconfirmation in the more obvious anthropomorphic forms, made so pantheistic that religion is naturalized, made into
what in reality is a secular belief-system disguised in colorful language.
[Applause]

Notes

1. John Hick, *Arguments for the Existence of God* (London: Macmillan, 1971);
   Terence Penelhum, *Religion and Rationality* (New York: Random House,
   1971).
2. Shabbir Akhtar, *Reason and the Radical Crisis of Faith* (New York: Peter
   Lang, 1987). Note his powerful attack on what he calls the Christian revisionism of Hick and Penelhum. In saving Christianity, they undermine it.
3. John Hick, *Arguments for the Existence of God*. There is a sophisticated and
   fair-minded selection of the arguments pro and con and their relevance or
   lack thereof in Louis Pojman's *Philosophy of Religion: An Anthology* (Belmont, Calif.: Wadsworth, 1987), 1–90. See also pp. 441–489.
4. Kai Nielsen, "Can Faith Validate God-talk?" *Theology Today* 20 (July 1963);
   "Religious Perplexity and Faith," *Crane Review* 8 (1965).
5. See chapters 2–4 of my *God, Scepticism and Modernity* (Ottawa: University
   of Ottawa Press, 1989). See also my discussion of the ontological argument
   for the existence of God in my *Reason and Practice* (New York: Harper &
   Row, 1970).
6. Kai Nielsen, *God, Scepticism and Modernity*, 30–31, 51–66, 69–77.
7. Kai Nielsen, *An Introduction to the Philosophy of Religion* (London: Macmillan, 1982), 17–42.

A Christian's Rebuttal

MORELAND: Thank you, Dr. Nielsen, for your remarks. I'd like to center my comments on three or four different things.

First of all, consider Professor Nielsen's statement that God cannot be detected. It seems to me a little bit presumptuous and prima facie odd to say that 99.9 percent of the entire human race has literally not known what they were talking about when they used the word "God." As Professor Nielsen knows, a lot of people who have reviewed his books on his theory of the meaning of God-talk have not been particularly favorable; and though I may be wrong on this, I don't think the majority of contemporary sophisticated atheists follow him in this view. J. L. Mackie, for example, was quite willing to grant the intelligibility of God-talk.[1] In a debate I read recently involving Antony Flew, a leading atheist, he agreed that if Jesus of Nazareth did rise from the dead, it would make the existence of God more probable.[2] And it was at least intelligible to hold that such a thing was the case.

Second, I disagree with Professor Nielsen that God cannot be detected. I think that God can be detected in religious experience. I believe that there is a form of perception called numinous perception. People who study these sorts of things are even able to describe laws governing the nature of numinous perception.[3] And I find numinous perception to be very, very similar to sensory perception. I argue this in *Scaling the Secular City,* and I refer you to the last chapter in that book and to a very interesting article by Wainwright on the comparison.[4] These go into more detail than I can attempt right now.

But let me just say that I believe that God could be defined ostensively in religious experience, in awarenesses of a being who is holy, who is loving, wonderful, kind, and so forth. It is not the case, by the way, that the concept of God is only defined by ostension. I believe that it is possible to give content to the concept of God by inferring God as a theoretical explanation, very much as is done in science, contrary to what Professor Nielsen said.

Scientists do postulate theoretical entities, and they give theoretical terms meaning as they are embedded in theories and used to explain certain effects.[5] The term "electron" gets some of its meaning as such and such an entity to explain such and such an effect. It is interesting to me that two leading philosophers of science—Stanley Jaki who is a Christian and Bas van Fraasen who, I have been told, was not a Christian at the time that he wrote *The Scientific Image*, though I have heard that he has recently converted to Christianity, but I have not had a chance to check that out and I am not certain that this is true—both of these men believe that scientific realism, that is, the view that you postulate theoretical entities to explain effects in the world, utilizes a method for giving meaning to theoretical terms which is like the way Aquinas and other theists argue from effects to give meaning to the concept of God.[6]

Now Professor Nielsen disagrees with that, but I don't see that he has made his case. It seems to me that the type of argument where you give content to a causal notion which explains a set of effects is analogous in theological and scientific causal explanations. Van Fraasen and Jaki and others in the philosophy of science have agreed.[7]

Further, it is not true that theoretical entities in science are unobservable in practice but they could be in principle. Magnetic fields are not even observable in principle; neither is gravity, especially if you take gravity as a field rather than as an exchange of gravitons. Neither is energy, at least in its relativistic sense before it is frozen into matter. None of these things is observable in principle.

Let me say in addition that I think things like numbers do exist, but that is not the point. Professor Nielsen does not believe that numbers exist. I happen to believe they do, but whether he is or I am right on that, the point is that there have been a number of philosophers who have believed that one can have direct ostensive awareness of Platonic entities called numbers.[8] Further, you can be aware of types, not just the tokens. I have written a book on the problem of universals, and I disagree with Nielsen's view of types and tokens.[9]

Consider the property redness, for example. I take redness to be a Platonic entity called a universal. I can see redness even though redness is timeless. But redness, even though timeless and spaceless itself, can be instanced in a ball in my child's toy box. I can see the timeless, spaceless entity in so far as it is instanced, and I am not merely looking at the token. I am also looking at the type; I am looking at the entity redness itself.[10]

It seems to me then that it's possible to have ostensive knowledge of God. It's also possible to have knowledge of him as you infer a cause to explain a set of effects. I would further say that Jesus of Nazareth has caused the garden to have been visited. C. S. Lewis called earth the visited planet. Perhaps miraculous acts of God could be baptismal events, to use Kripke's phrase, and meanings associated with those events, for example, "God," could be passed on through salvation history in a way similar to a Kripkian ancestral chain view of reference.[11] Suppose that God has appeared to certain people in the past, the reference was fixed, and content given to the term "God." Salvation history could be the path in which fixity of reference was passed on through an ancestral chain very much like the way Kripke has talked about reference.

So I disagree that God cannot be detected. I believe that God-talk makes sense through ostension, through the fact that the garden has been visited by Jesus of Nazareth, through a very similar kind of meaning postulate as is used in science, and through analogy with myself as I reflect upon my own faculties and form a conception of God as a being who has intellect, emotion, and will.

What Nielsen has done is to commit what I call the centipede fallacy. If the centipede took long enough to look at his legs and figure out how in the world he walks, he would probably end up stumbling and falling. And philosophers are guilty of the centipede effect all the time. The centipede knows very well that he can walk, even though he can't give you all the details about how he does so. Most people know very well what "God" means, and they use it to refer, even if they cannot give you a complete theory of reference and meaning to explain this.

There is no philosophical topic of interest wherein philosophers are in universal agreement regarding how we talk about it or what its definition is. No philosopher to my knowledge has given a universally accepted definition of "knowledge." I couldn't for the life of me define "history." I'm not sure I could define "love"; I'm not sure that I could define to everyone's satisfaction what a number is. And I couldn't define to everyone's satisfaction what God is nor how I refer to any of these entities. Nonetheless, it does seem reasonable that I could know something about these things, whether or not I could give an exhaustive treatment of how those terms get meaning. We can know them truly without knowing them exhaustively.

Take design, for example. As I mentioned earlier, there are a number of examples of design. Richard Taylor gives the following illustration: Suppose you were driving on a train and you saw a sign on the hillside that said, "Wales in ten miles." Suppose that you knew that the wind had blown that sign together. If the sign had been put together by a purely nonintelligent random process, says Taylor, there would be no reason to trust the information conveyed by the sign.

Similarly, it seems to me that if our intellectual and sensory faculties were merely the result of the wind blowing, as it were, or a struggle for survival, there would be no reason to trust that they give us accurate information about the world.[12] All that would be needed for survival value would be consistency. If an amoeba saw as small an enemy that was really large, and a thing that was really small was seen as large, as long as it could see things consistently, it could survive, evolutionarily speaking. It would not need to have the truth or see accurately.[13]

As Alvin Plantinga has recently argued, the reliability of our cognitive and sensory capacities is most reasonably explained in light of the fact that they were designed to give us reliable information about the world.[14]

One more point about the historicity of the New Testament, and then I'll sit down. In my doctoral program, I was walking into the library one day, and I ran across a student who was reading the Septuagint, the Greek Old Testament. I went over to him and I said, "What in the world are you doing?" And he said, "I have a master's degree from Harvard in business, and I have a master's from UCLA in classics, and an undergraduate degree in classics from Harvard. I'm finishing my Ph.D. degree from UCLA in classics, and I was reading the Greek New Testament here recently." He was Jewish, and he went on to say, "I became a committed follower of Jesus of Nazareth. And I just wanted to come over here to USC because I knew there were Christian graduate students studying philosophy." I asked, "How did you become a Christian?" He said, "Dr. Moreland, I have studied myth most of my education. I know the earmarks of myth; that's all I study. My undergraduate training was in mythology; my graduate training has been in mythology. And I was practicing Koiné Greek reading the Gospel of Luke, and I got halfway through it, and as a Jew, I said, 'My God, this man really did these things. What am I going to do? This is history. It reads like history. It doesn't read like myth. I know what myth tastes like because all I do is read it, and that is not myth.'"[15]

I submit to you that there are earmarks of historicity in the New Testament that make it reasonable to believe that Jesus Christ is who he claimed he was, and the historical evidence that he rose from the dead seems to me to be persuasive. Thank you. [Applause]

Notes

1. J. L. Mackie, *The Miracle of Theism* (Oxford: Clarendon, 1982), 1–4. Mackie points out that we know from self-awareness what it is to be a person, and, even though we have bodies, there is no difficulty in conceiving of a person without a body, including a divine person. Regarding this strategy, theists as diverse as Leibniz and Calvin would agree. Mackie also argues that the main reason philosophers have denied the intelligibility of God-talk is that they accept a highly implausible verificationist theory of meaning. For attempts to clarify the concept of God and some of the attributes of God, see Richard Swinburne, *The Coherence of Theism* (Oxford: Oxford University Press, 1977); Thomas V. Morris, ed., *The Concept of God* (Oxford: Oxford University Press, 1987).

2. See Gary Habermas and Antony Flew, *Did Jesus Rise from the Dead?* Terry Miethe, ed. (San Francisco: Harper & Row, 1987), 3.

3. For works treating the development of numinous perception as well as the lawlike stages of spiritual growth, see Evelyn Underhill, *Mysticism* (New York: New American Library, 1955); Cheslyn Jones, Geoffrey Wainwright, and Edward Yarnold, *The Study of Spirituality* (Oxford: Oxford University Press, 1986), especially 17–24; Adrian van Kaam, *Religious Personality* (Denville, N.J.: Dimension Books, 1964). Still relevant is William James's classic work *The Varieties of Religious Experience*.

4. J. P. Moreland, *Scaling the Secular City* (Grand Rapids, Mich.: Baker), 231–240; William J. Wainwright, "Mysticism and Sense Perception," in *Contemporary Philosophy of Religion*, Stephen M. Chan and David Shatz, eds. (Totowa, N.J.: Rowman and Littlefield, 1982), 123–45; *Philosophy of Religion* (Belmont, Calif.: Wadsworth, 1988), 113–130.

5. Scientific realists (roughly, advocates of the view that scientific theories refer to entities in the world, and scientific progress is to be understood as growth in the approximate truth of our theories) often utilize a causal theory of reference to explain scientific terms and theories. See W. H. Newton-Smith, *The Rationality of Science* (Boston: Routledge & Kegan Paul, 1981), 148–182. A theoretical term, say "electron," is understood as "whatever causes a specified range of phenomena," and the phenomena are those for which scientists believe electrons are causally responsible. More content can be given to the theoretical term by viewing it (and the theory in which it is embedded, e.g., electron theory) as part of an analogy with something familiar. Thus, in ideal gas theory the unseen molecules and process are likened to billiard balls that undergo elastic collisions. In analogies of this kind, we often have no independent access to the unseen entities (molecules in this case) apart from the phenomena they cause and the model we construct (the billiard ball model). In this case we attribute to the unseen theoretical entities those properties required for that entity to

fulfill its explanatory function in the theory regarding the relevant range of data. See Rom Harre, *The Philosophies of Science* (Oxford: Oxford University Press, 1972), 168–83. So "electron" is understood as an entity that has such and such properties deemed necessary to explain certain effects. The term "God" can be similarly defined as that entity with such and such properties deemed necessary to create and design the world, to be a maximally perfect being, to reveal Himself in religious experience, and so on.

6. Stanley Jaki, *The Road of Science and the Ways to God* (Chicago: University of Chicago Press, 1978), especially pp. 80–95, 246–62, 314–331. Jaki's main thesis is that there are an epistemology and metaphysics in good science that are the same as the epistemology and metaphysics involved in natural theology. Bas van Fraasen, an anti-realist in the philosophy of science, agrees with this thesis but uses it to argue against scientific realism. See *The Scientific Image* (Oxford: Clarendon Press, 1980), 204–15. For a critique of van Fraasen, see Richard N. Boyd, "Lex Orandi Est Lex Credendi," in *Images of Science*, Paul M. Churchland and Clifford A. Hooker, eds. (Chicago: University of Chicago Press, 1985), 32–33.

7. For other comparisons between science and theology regarding methodology, language, testing, and so on, see Holmes Ralston, III, *Science and Religion* (Philadelphia: Temple University Press, 1987), 1–21; Edward L. Schoen, *Religious Explanations* (Durham, N.C.: Duke University Press, 1985), 81–120, especially pp. 101–110.

8. For an overview of different views regarding the ontological status of numbers, see Reinhardt Grossmann, *The Categorical Structure of the Word* (Bloomington, Ind.: Indiana University Press, 1983), 293–323.

9. J. P. Moreland, *Universals, Qualities, and Quality-Instances: A Defense of Realism* (Lanham, Md.: University Press of America, 1985).

10. This insight implies that there are several different senses in which one thing can be in another. A container "in" ("The milk is 'in' the glass") is not the only sense of "in" needed to make sense of the world. Thus, if a timeless, spaceless universal like redness can be "in" a spatiotemporal entity like a red ball, then I see no reason why God cannot be "in" a burning bush or a religious experience without God becoming a spatiotemporal entity, even if the senses of "in" are different in the two cases. If this is so, then God can be "present in" some revelatory event (e.g., a biblical miracle or a religious experience), and He could be known immediately and defined ostensively without somehow becoming spatiotemporal.

11. Cf. Saul Kripke, *Naming and Necessity* (Cambridge, Mass.: Harvard University Press, 1972), 91–97.

12. See A. C. Ewing, *Value and Reality* (London: Routledge and Kegan Paul, 1973), 177–78; John Hick, *Arguments for the Existence of God* (New York: Herder, 1971), 21–26; Stanley Jaki, *The Road of Science and the Ways to God* (Chicago: University of Chicago Press, 1978), 246–61, 282–287.

13. An evolutionary picture of an organism views it as a functional unit that receives input from its environment and gives output and advances to a new state ready to receive new input as it struggles for reproductive advantage. But such a functional view of organisms is inadequate. On this view, the teleological, goal-directed behavior of an organism is reduced to natural properties and capacities. These, in turn, are selected because of their function in reproductive advantage. But a given functional state defined in terms of input/output is compatible with a potentially infinite number of internal states of the organism. For example, two organisms can "see" red functionally if each can scan the same room and sort the same objects (e.g., separate the red objects from the rest). But this functional sorting capacity is compatible with the fact that one organism sees red objects as red while sorting and the other sees red objects as blue. This is called the problem of inverted qualia, and it shows that an organism does not need to see objects accurately to sort them. Now if an organism had systematic error (e.g., saw large objects as small and vice versa, felt warm objects as cold and vice versa) the organism could functionally win in a struggle for survival without accurately representing the world. Thus, truth obtaining faculties are not necessary for survival and such faculties are underdetermined vis-à-vis other internal capacities in light of the functional demands of survival. Thus, naturalistic evolutionary theory cannot adequately explain why our sensory and mental faculties can give us truth, and this lends support to a design argument for God based on the reliability of these faculties.
14. Alvin Plantinga, "Justification and Theism," (unpublished paper), 3–11, 14.
15. C. S. Lewis made a similar point in *Christian Reflections* (Grand Rapids, Mich.: Eerdmans, 1967), 152–66.

4 Kai Nielsen

An Atheist's Rebuttal

NIELSEN: I appreciate Professor Moreland's thoughtful remarks, and what I think I will do before I go to what he said himself in his initial remarks is to respond to some of the comments he has just made.

He wants to argue—it surprises me a bit—that he thinks God can be detected. You can have an ostensive definition of God. Now he says that even Antony Flew, whose views on religion are rather like mine, believes that Jesus of Nazareth was raised from the dead and that this would give us an ostensive definition of God, enabling us to give intelligibility to God-talk and would, if true, provide some evidence that God exists. I don't see how. Jesus, let us suppose—I don't know much about such things and to be perfectly frank, I'm not terribly interested in them—but let us just suppose it were the case that Jesus was raised from the dead. Suppose you collected the bones, and they together in some way reconstituted the living Jesus. Suppose something like that really happened. Suppose there were good historical evidence for it. I have no idea if there is or isn't; I suspect for anything like that, there isn't very good evidence, but let us assume there is. This wouldn't show there was an infinite intelligible being. It wouldn't give you any way of being able to detect if there is a God. It would be just that a very strange happening happened, namely, that somebody who died— or certainly appeared to have died—came together again as a living human being. It would not enable you to understand at all what you were talking about concerning an infinite individual. It would just be a very peculiar fact we hadn't explained and indeed lacked the scientific resources to explain. And the same thing is true of the familiar resurrection story.

When Moreland says that about 99 percent of the philosophers agree that God can be detected, I doubt that very much. But what they do say when they say that God-talk is intelligible, and I grant this, is that *anthropomorphic* God-talk is intelligible. Where the concept is sufficiently anthropomorphic, the concept is perfectly intelligible. Moreover, I've never said that God-talk is meaningless. I simply said that it is so problematic, when you get a completely ethereal God who is supposed to be an infinite individual transcendent to the world, that we literally don't know what we are talking about, though we have the illusion that we do.

Suppose, Moreland remarked, referring to the famous work of a very interesting man, Rudolph Otto, we advert to numinous percep-tions. But these were numinous feelings; they weren't perceptions in any ordinary sense. And they weren't the sort of thing that enabled you to observe or detect God. Religious experience doesn't enable you to detect God.[1] It is, of course, perfectly true that people have religious experiences, including mystical experiences. But that is a different matter. That is a matter of having certain feelings. Moreover, Buddhists have such experiences, but Buddhists don't claim to see God but Christians and Sufis do. It depends upon what religious framework you start with. Religious experience is a matter of feelings, and feelings are not a way of cognition. But even if religious experience were a form of cognition, it is so variously interpreted from religious tradition to reli-gious tradition that there is no good reason to believe it yields a direct knowledge of God.

Moreland talked today about scientific realism and potentialities and he referred to Bas van Fraasen, who by the way, has been a Dutch Reformed believer for years. He has always been religious, but even so it doesn't matter. His view is a very instrumentalist view of these things. It is hardly a matter of realism. The point is that when a theoret-ical entity in physics is an entity that could be real in the world, it is something that, like an electron or a neutron, is judged to be just very very very very very much smaller than some microscopic objects. In some cases, say that of a photon, we have no idea what it would be like to observe it or what we would have to observe to observe. We only see its traces. But still if it is really a minuscule particle in the universe, there can be no logical ban on the possibility of its being observed. If it really is part of the same universe as rocks and trees and grains of sand, it cannot be logically impossible to see it. It is, as the positivists used to say, in principle possible directly to verify that there are photons.

There are other notions, perhaps fields of forces, that may be the-oretical *constructions*. They may just be useful devices for talking about the world. They are not meant to point to things in the world that could be detected. Which of the conceptions of physics are which—which are constructs and which are real entities—is not for Moreland and myself to decide, but for physicists to decide, and physicists often disagree about this.

Moreland wants to give analogies to seeing God. He can, he tells us, see redness or types. He can't see redness; what he sees is vari-

ous red objects which have the characteristic redness. There's no seeing of redness and the like. He says, "Well, look, definitions are hard to
give by definite description." But to note problems here, he said, indicates that I committed the centipede fallacy. Well, I do not know exactly
or even inexactly what is involved here or whether it is even a kind of
fallacy.

He commits the more familiar Platonic fallacy. It is as difficult to
define "chair" as it is to define "knowledge," to give necessary and
sufficient conditions for all of those things and only those things which
are chairs. Nobody has been able to do that. We can identify chairs
perfectly well, and what he's referring to is that we do know what
knowledge is even though we can't define knowledge. But I'm saying
that for an entity as mysterious as God, some people think they understand and believe in its reality and some people don't. There are real
doubts, as is not the case, with chairs or with knowledge. Moreover, it
is impossible to identify God. If I can't define a chair, at least I can point
to one. But by contrast, to point out the God you can't define is impossible.

Moreland made an appeal to arguments for design. As far as I can
see, they only point at best to design *in* the world. They don't point to
design *of* the world, nor do they show that a personal infinite creator
created it. There could have been a number of creators, some of them
long gone. The same thing is true about actual infinities. The most, the
very most it could give him would be some *factually* necessary beings
or being. It wouldn't give him an infinite eternal God. It wouldn't be
able to link up with the Jesus of Nazareth who supposedly is the one
true God or at least the son of the one true God.

One thing about the historicity of Jesus. When I bring this out you
will see why I'm not much interested in it. What I read in Moreland's
book about his account of the historicity of Jesus is that he shows
clearly enough that it wasn't a myth that the Christian community tried
to purvey, rather they were recording what they actually believed happened. As I read that, it seemed a very plausible thing to say, though I
don't know what biblical scholars would say about it. But this shows us
nothing at all about Jesus being divine. It only shows us that some people thought he was.

One of the things he does about quoting authorities—he quotes
the ones on his side, not the ones on the other side, for the most part.
And that is an easy game to play. There are plenty of such authorities.

These matters are much more problematical about actual infinites
than he gives to understand. But even if his argument about actual infi-

nites would work, and I'm not sure that it does, again this would not get you to an infinite God. Even more seriously, it wouldn't get you to something that wasn't utterly naturalistic.

Finally, even if there is this historicity side, the point is that there is a historicity side to the other religions too. And if you want to say, "I'm going to accept my Christian faith on the basis of the revelations in the Bible and so forth," then it is natural to ask why the Christian ones rather than Jewish ones or Hindu ones and the like. Putative revelations are plentiful. How do you know that the Christian putative revelations are the genuine ones and not the Hindu ones? If you stick with claims internal to the Christian Bible, you go in a vicious circle.[2] Granting its historicity, Christianity makes a lot of claims that are beyond empirical check. Some of them are incapable of empirical check. So do all the other religious doctrines. Why the Bible rather than the Koran? Why the Bible rather than the canonical Buddhist texts? Why the Bible rather than the Hindu texts? Why the Bible rather than the religious revelations of other people? If you look at religion anthropologically, you will see that there are thousands of religions all claiming "The truth."

And just because there are more Christians than there are of any other religion doesn't prove anything. Suppose Hitler had won the war. First you would get rid of the Jews, then the Blacks (Christians and non-Christians), and then the Indians. After that cleansing is done, you start getting rid of the Christian whites until there is only a small sect of Christian whites left. Would that prove that the Christian message is any less true? Would it in those circumstances be less true because there weren't very many Christians about? So what I'm trying to say is there are thousands of putative revelations in the world. And as far as I can see, there is no more reason to rely on the Christian revelation than any of those others.

I ask you, why the Bible rather than the Koran? Why the Bible rather than any other historically extensive systems of faith? And do not say that really they are all saying the same thing because they do not. Buddhism is very different indeed from Christianity. [Applause]

Notes

1. C. B. Martin, *Religious Beliefs* (Ithaca, N.Y.: Cornell University Press, 1959); Ronald Hepburn, *Christianity and Paradox* (London: Watts, 1958); and Kai Nielsen, *Reason and Practice* (New York: Harper & Row, 1970), 195–203.

2. Kai Nielsen: *Philosophy and Atheism* (Buffalo, N.Y.: Prometheus Books, 1985), 145–158; "The Burden of Ideological Masks in *Ideologiekritik*: On Trying to View Faith Scientifically," *Metaphilosophy* (1991).

Closing Arguments for Atheism

5

NIELSEN: Well, I'd first like to say that I'm grateful to Professor More-land for the way he argued. I don't know whether you learned anything. Maybe we bored the hell out of you, but, speaking for myself, I found it an interesting discussion. I found he was thoroughly aware of the relevance of my arguments, and went back and forth with them. Maybe we all learned a little something. At least I did.

Now, to go to argumentation itself, take the part about the self-reputing statements about the universe. Suppose I say to you, "I'm a Calgarian." Suppose I then go on to say, "All Calgarians are liars." Do I say something which is true or false? The paradox is, if I say what is true, it is false. There are, however, well-known ways of getting around such paradoxes. Russell's theory of types is the best-known way. For my remark about the universe, I can do the same thing. So I don't think I'm trapped.

More importantly, I think there are three central issues that still need to be faced. Well, I mean there are much more, but there are three very central ones I want to face. They are things that I said very little about, mainly because I haven't thought about them for years since in 1968 I wrote *Reason and Practice* and tried to deal with them in some detail there. I dealt there with the classical arguments purporting to prove that God exists, and after that I put those things aside. Moreland, it seems, has a number of new arguments or variations from old arguments, and they are interesting. I include the ones from actual infinity, and strangely enough, the arguments from design. Richard Swinburne has recently argued for this, and John Mackie argues against it. But generally, in his line of argumentation, there seems to me something that he does that I think is questionable. It would also be questionable if I did the opposite on the other side. He talks about what science is showing now. What sort of evidence have you got for the probabilities of various things, appealing to scientific authorities? And I'm not saying bad authorities. But there is something very dangerous for a theologian or a Christian philosopher or, for that matter, for an atheist philosopher to use that strategy. Take, to illustrate, the Big Bang theory. I don't know much about this, but I gather that is the reigning theory in cosmology now. Years ago the kinetic states theory was the alternate operating theory. I'm not a physicist. I'm not a scientific cosmologist. I don't know which of the beliefs is more plausible apart from the implication they appear to have for religion. But if you rest your case on scientific evidence like this—highly speculative scientific theorizing—you make your religious claims very much hostage to changing scientific fortunes and even fashions. And you must realize, and take to heart, the fact that you can't second guess what physics will look like two hundred years from now, much less five hundred years from now.

At certain times I could have appealed to the kinetic states theory, and that would then have been the dominant theory, and it had different consequences for religion than the Big Bang theory. Now you can appeal to the Big Bang theory, for it is the reigning theory. Maybe, just maybe, though, I'm not at all convinced of this, you can begin to make some form of cosmological argument from it. But that is risky business. Scientific fads come and go, and the speculative fringes of science are very much subject to fads and very much subject to change. It is always very fallible. It always alters. It grows, but it alters. These cosmological theories are what Steven Toulmin, a philosopher of science, once called scientific mythologies.[1] They vary greatly, and they also are at the very speculative fringes of science, so we can be less certain about them. So it seems to me very very very risky indeed to center an argument for the existence of God, as Moreland does, on something that relies heavily on these speculative matters. The same, of course, would be true for arguments for atheism that relied on speculative cosmological theories.

We still have problems with the design argument. What does it mean to say, "The universe *as a whole* was designed"? There are difficulties, deep conceptual difficulties, in speaking of the universe as a whole. There are difficulties in discovering the design of the universe. Even the use of the word "design" cheats in a way. I don't mean deliberately cheats, but unwittingly cheats. You may only be studying order or regularity. From order and regularity you don't automatically get design. These are all old arguments; they are at least as old as Hume. And it seems to me those you need to take very seriously indeed.

There is the crucial argument about religious experience. What I think is undeniable is that there are religious experiences. Professor Moreland said, I think rightly, that I begged the question to say that they are all of the nature of feelings. It did seem to me when Otto described them, they sounded like feelings. But suppose we say no, they are numinous experiences? They are a form of non-sensory perception that we have. And maybe there is such a thing. It is certainly only an empirical truth to say the five senses are all we have. It *may* be an empirical falsehood. Maybe there is some kind of nonsensory or a special sensory direct awareness. But all that to the contrary notwithstanding, one of the things I would argue is there couldn't be a nonsensory awareness of an infinite eternal God transcendent to the universe. Moreland says that in Christianity God was immanent. That's one of the paradoxes of Christianity. How could God be both transcendent and immanent? It is self-contradictory to say that *x* is both transcendent to the world and in the world at the same time. And God, remember, is said to be an eternal, timeless reality.

I want to turn now to another point. If I were shopping around for a theistic religion, I would be much more inclined to be a Moslem or a Jew than a Christian because you wouldn't in those religions have such paradoxes. There isn't any immanence of God in Judaism.

So I still want to say that those people who try to argue that there is a direct awareness of God that gives you a kind of certainty that no philosophical argument can ever give are mistaken. But there is no reason not to think that there are religious experiences, but there's no good reason to think they are experiences of God.[2] If you use the causal argument to say, "I know from experience; I had these experiences and that leads me to postulate God," that is not a direct awareness of God. That is to argue for certain experiences and try your best to explain them by postulating God. There are, however, alternative ways of explaining those same experiences, including some purely secular ways. It's terribly unclear which of those ways are the best at explaining the phenomena.[3]

I, of course, don't believe this to be the case—but perhaps I am just being pigheaded. But suppose I'm wrong about the concept of God being incoherent and suppose Moreland is also right about the historicity of Jesus. Well, there's a historicity of Mohammed too. There is a historicity of Buddha. I return to the fact that there are many, many religions, many, many putative revelations.[4] Don't say they say the same thing. They don't. Any being that could be Christ—could be both man and God—for a Jew couldn't be God. No man, on his conception of things, could be God. That would be idolatry. That is not the sort of thing that God could be. And for the lesser vehicle in Buddhism, which is as old a religion as Christianity, there is neither worship nor God.[5] So I want to say, "Why Christianity rather than Buddhism?" "Why Christianity rather than Judaism?" They have their claimed revelations too.

How do you decide that a *claimed* revelation is a *genuine* revelation? And if we use reason, including empirical research to judge revelation, why then do we need revelation?[6] [Applause]

Notes

1. Stephen Toulmin, "Contemporary Scientific Mythology" in his *Metaphysical Beliefs* (London: SCM Press, 1957), 13–81.
2. C. B. Martin, *Religious Beliefs* (Ithaca, N.Y.: Cornell University Press, 1959). See also Kai Nielsen, *Reason and Practice* (New York: Harper & Row, 1970), 195–203.
3. Ronald Hepburn, *Christianity and Paradox* (London: Watts, 1958).
4. Ninian Smart, *A Dialogue of Religions* (London: SCM Press, 1960); *Reasons and Faiths* (London: Routledge and Kegan Paul, 1958).
5. Ninian Smart, *A Dialogue of Religions*.
6. Kai Nielsen, *Philosophy and Atheism* (Buffalo, N.Y.: Prometheus Books, 1985), 145–158.

Closing Arguments for Christianity

MORELAND: Professor Nielsen, when it comes to science, I state clearly in *Scaling the Secular City* that I don't rest the entire case on it.[1] I primarily use philosophical arguments. But let's face it, science has been used against Christianity. You yourself use science in your book on philosophy and atheism, to engage in reflective equilibrium, in formulating biological and sociological laws of human nature, and so forth. And I see no reason why, if science does lend support to Christianity, it can't be used as part of a general argument. Certainly the theories may be overturned in the future. But if you are going to say that, the same thing could be true for the theories that are used against Christianity right now. I would rather say that we've got to go with current theories, epistemically speaking, and the best evidence presently available. Some solid, current scientific theories seem to me to point to theism.

Regarding Christianity, your claim is simply false. Mohammed never claimed to be God, and he never claimed to authenticate his revelations by miracles. He is in his tomb; Buddha is in his tomb; Zoroaster is in his tomb; and so is Confucius. Jesus isn't. Jesus rose from the dead, and He authenticated His divine Messiahship by performing works that men couldn't do. The reason that I hold to the Christian revelation, as opposed to the Muslim revelation and others, is (apart from conceptual difficulties I find in those), I don't see enough evidence for them—that is, authenticating signs which demonstrate that they are revelations from God.

During his lifetime the great French philosopher, Jean-Paul Sartre, was a passioned atheist. According to the *National Review,* before his death, he made this statement, "I do not feel that I'm the product of chance, a speck of dust in the universe, but rather someone who is expected, prepared, prefigured, in short, a being whom only a creator God could have put here."[2]

Bertrand Russell, a very well-known atheist, had this letter that he wrote in 1918 put in the second volume of his autobiography. He said:

> Even when one feels nearest to other people, something in one needs obstinately to belong to God and refuse to enter into any

earthly communion—at least that is how I should express it if I thought there was a God. It is odd, isn't it? I feel passionately for this world and many things and people in it, and yet . . . what is it all? There *must* be something more important, one feels, though I don't *believe* there is. I am haunted. Some ghosts, from some extra mundane regions, seem always trying to tell me something that I am to repeat for the world, but I cannot understand the message.[3]

I am here to say that the message has come. Jesus Christ was the Son of God.

As a university student in 1968, I met Jesus Christ personally and He changed my life. I have had close to two decades of walking with Him and fellowshiping with Him and falling more and more in love with Him daily. He has given me a power for life that I did not know before, and I have had personal experiences of Him.

In addition to my own personal religious experience, I have offered some arguments for you to consider. I have cited a cosmological-type argument, I have cited the design argument, and I've made brief reference, though I've not gone into detail on them, to the moral argument, the argument from consciousness, religious experience, and the historicity of the New Testament. All of these factors, in my opinion, show that Christianity is reasonable and one ought to believe in it.

When one tries Christianity based upon these rational considerations, he can put Jesus Christ to the test and see if Christianity works out in his own personal life.[4] I have done this, and I have found that Jesus Christ has changed my life. This is an argument from religious experience that has meant a lot to me intellectually and personally, and I recommend it to you. Thank you very much. [Applause]

Notes

1. Moreland, *Scaling the Secular City*, 196, fn. 15.
2. Cited in the *National Review* (11 June 1982), 677.
3. Bertrand Russell, *The Autobiography of Bertrand Russell* (Boston: Little, Brown and Company, 1968), 125–126.
4. Two points need to be made regarding this recommendation. First, this is a type of theory confirmation similar to confirmation used in science. If a theory implies such and such data, then if these data obtain, the theory receives some degree of confirmation. Similarly, if Christianity is true, then the Christian faith implies that certain changes will occur in one's life if one

engages in certain activities—e.g., trusting in the substitutionary death and resurrection of Christ for salvation. For more on this type of confirmation in science and religion, see Holmes Ralston, III *Science and Religion* (Philadelphia: Temple University Press, 1987), 1–21; Douglas Clyde Macintosh, *Theology as an Empirical Science* (New York: Arno Press, 1980), 1–46; Patrick Sherry, *Spirits, Saints, and Immortality* (Albany, N.Y.: State University of New York Press, 1984), 31–63; George Schlessinger, *Religion and Scientific Method* (Boston: D. Reidel, 1982), 135–201; J. P. Moreland, *Christianity and the Nature of Science* (Grand Rapids, Mich.: Baker, 1989), Chap. 2. Second, this recommendation could be seen as a challenge along the lines of Pascal's Wager. For a delightful treatment of Pascal's Wager, which includes a discussion about the "burden of proof" issue between Christian theism and atheism, see Thomas V. Morris, *Anselmian Explorations* (Notre Dame, Ind.: University of Notre Dame Press, 1987), 194–212.

7

J. P. Moreland and Kai Nielsen

Questions and Answers

POJMAN: All right, now it's time for questions. I would just ask you to come to one of these two microphones and keep your question as short as possible. Address them to one of the two speakers, so both speakers will get a chance to answer each question.

QUESTION: This is for Professor Nielsen. In your *Ethics Without God*, you state that the existence of hospitals and concentration camps warrants the conclusion that God is not good, and I assume that you would say that it also warrants the conclusion that God does not exist. Since you claim that [the] theist is irrational in his use of the word "God," to what extent is your reasoning rational since, if set out formally, an argument based on the existence of hospitals and concentration camps, you would be required to use the word "God" in at least one of your premises, and since you've just argued in your first speech that the use of the word God is incoherent? What I'm asking is, Are you not limited then to the kind of reasoning that you gave in your first speech, and thus you would not be able to use arguments based on hospitals, concentration camps, etc?

NIELSEN: There are, I think, two responses to that, or at least two. One is that if the word "God" is used in an anthropomorphic sense, I'm not maintaining that it expresses an incoherent concept. And in those particular premises I could be using "God" in an anthropomorphic sense. Two, and perhaps more importantly, that this is a matter of argumentative strategy. I mean Professor Moreland might—though I'm sure doesn't believe that the concept of God is incoherent—well take it as a premise in arguing against me. Assuming the concept of God is incoherent, then such and such conclusions would follow. But it would be absurd to believe that. But then it is absurd, he could argue, to believe that the concept of God is incoherent. He would, that is, be making a *reductio* argument against me and that is a perfectly acceptable form of argument.

And that is basically what I was doing. I was saying, "Well, let us assume that it makes sense to speak of God—and, after all, it does make sense in a kind of pictorial way, and God-talk has linguistic regularities. We can't ask sensibly how much does God weigh or did God get divorced or is God red. Given ordinary linguistic regularities in English, I can form sentences with 'God' in them that are normal English. But they are sentences that I believe in an important way to be incoherent." But as I remarked, I set that aside for the purposes of this argument about God and morality. Maybe this God-talk is incoherent and maybe it isn't, but if the sentences are coherent, then such and such consequences follow. So it seems to me there is nothing wrong with doing that. I say to the Christian, "Let's assume, for this argument, your concept of God is coherent. If it is coherent, these untoward consequences follow."

MORELAND: I think the remark is a good one. If you are going to use a concept in an argument, the concept has to have some kind of meaning in order for you to know what premise, what inferences to draw from it in your *modus ponens* or *modus tollens*. If you're going to say, "If God, therefore *Q;* not *Q*, therefore not God," how do you know what to deduce from the concept of God unless it has some meaning for you? Further, I suspect that Professor Nielsen wasn't just using an anthropomorphic sense of God, but a more robust sense of God. Now I could be wrong about this, but I suspect he was using a conception of God which he had some understanding of in order to know effectively how to argue against it.

Now the simple fact of the matter is, that most philosophers of religion on either side of this question find these kinds of questions about God-talk just as boring as Professor Nielsen finds questions about the historicity of the New Testament. Again, I have already tried to give you my views about how God-talk gets meaning and accomplishes reference. It seems to me that there are some views of God that are logically incoherent, but no one has been able to prove that the Judeo-Christian concept of God is logically incoherent. So I would say that your point was well taken.

QUESTION: Dr. Nielsen, are you defining "God" as a figment—when I say "God," I mean an all-powerful, infinite being—are you defining that as a figment or a mirage or something of this nature?

NIELSEN: Well, it is obvious in what I said in my argument that I do. Because I believe it is incoherent, though I believe it started out from a coherent anthropomorphic notion. And I agree with Professor Moreland that there are coherent conceptions of God. The coherent ones, I believe, turn out to be superstitious and obviously false, entailing false beliefs.

Professor Moreland mentioned Professor John Mackie, who has a very distinguished book named *The Miracle of Theism*. In spite of the fact that I think it misses one very important thing, I think it is one of the most, probably the most, distinguished articulation of an atheistic point of view given in the twentieth century. Mackie, unlike myself, and like a philosophical theologian like Swinburne, thinks that religious talk is perfectly all right; we just want to know, to try to find out, whether there is a God.[1] And Mackie thinks there isn't very good evidence for the existence of God, and Swinburne thinks there is. And then there are atheists like myself and Antony Flew, who think that question cannot get off the ground because the concept of God in developed forms of Judeo-Christianity is incoherent.

And there are also so-called Wittgensteinian fideists like D. Z. Phillips and Ilham Dilman who think the concept of God is terribly problematic. Phillips is a minister, a Welsh minister. He thinks the concept of God is very, very problematic—quite possibly incoherent—but that you can give some very demythologized sense to it. But he recognizes that it is a difficult thing.

So there is division among philosophers of religion. There are atheists, like John Mackie or Wallace Matson, who think that it is just false that God exists. And there are atheists like me and Paul Edwards who think either that it is just false, where an anthropomorphic God is at issue, or incoherent, where the nonanthropomorphic one that has come to have hold in our religions is at issue.[2] But I don't think the religious tradition for a long time has been interested in the anthropomorphic one. So the important thing is to grapple with the problem of incoherence.

By the way, just to make a concluding remark about what Professor Moreland said. Look, suppose I say, "All married bachelors are irascible." I could also say, "Jim is a married bachelor; so Jim is irascible." Well, I can make logical mappings like this as much as I want. And you can understand them, even though all of us agree that the very concept of a married bachelor is incoherent. That we can make such logical inferences does not show the argument is a good one. It is a very bad one.

MORELAND: I'd like to take your question about whether belief in God is a figment in a slightly different direction, because I think there are probably questions on other topics that would be more interesting. I'd like to consider the figment-of-the-imagination question more in its Freudian and Feurerbachian conceptualizations, where the argument has been, roughly, that believers merely need a father figure, they are afraid, they project this idea of God outside themselves, and they proceed to objectify it or reify it and worship it.

I would like to say, and again I'm taking your question in a slightly different way, that this type of thing commits what is known as the genetic fallacy. It tends to fault belief in God, not for its own lack of rational justification, but for where it came from. As I said this morning in my lecture, it would hardly be appropriate to say that I can't know two and two is equal to four, because I learned it from my second grade teacher, Mrs. Fred, and she wasn't a very nice person. Further, as R. C. Sproul has pointed out, the biblical God is not the kind of a God that one would want to project.[3] One would want to project a much more tame being and not a being quite so holy, so demanding, so awesome as the triune biblical God.

Thus, if you were going to project a being and reify him outside your own mind, then you would be practicing an action the Bible calls idolatry. And the types of gods resulting from those projections would be much more in keeping with ones depicted and challenged in Isaiah and Jeremiah.

I would like to say, in addition, that if anyone is engaging in some sort of projection or defense mechanism, then a good case could be made that it might be the nontheist and not the theist. Let me tell you how this argument might go. Paul Vitz, who is a psychologist, I think at New York University, studied the lives of several atheists and he just came out with a book on Freud.[4] He concluded that most of them had bad relationships with their fathers, and, in fact, if anyone was not approaching the God-question fairly, then it was the atheist who desired to kill the father and who was afraid to have someone control his or her life.

Now I am not inappropriately substituting genetic arguments for rational arguments, but there is a place for genetic considerations as follows: Suppose two people are talking and one says, "Well, you're not seeing the evidence," and the other person says, "Well, you're not seeing the evidence." It is at this point I think that genetic considerations can be relevant. They are not the whole show, but they can be relevant. And in my view, I think that atheists define a much tighter control group than theists for psychologists to study.

Theists, and Christians in particular, have been converted from every possible kind of psychological background, every possible culture, and so on. And it seems the only thing that defines the control group is the fact that they claim that Christ came into their lives.

Atheists, I would be willing to predict if the study were done, would be much more easily placed in a uniform class. And I would be willing to bet that we could find psychological causes for atheism that might be plausibly argued as the causal factor contributing to their atheism and constituting the factor which unites the class of atheists. Again, I'm not recommending this as a knock-down argument. I'm not saying that it rests on genetic considerations only. They come in only in the conditions I specify, but I think this is one way to respond to the fictional type of question that you raised, and I wanted to take it in a slightly different direction.

QUESTION: Hello. I just have a question for Mr. Nielsen. Sir, my question is that a lot of your discussion concerning a concept of God being coherent or incoherent seems to suggest that the only two concepts of God allowable are a concept of God that is entirely anthropological, like Zeus, or a concept of God that's entirely ethereal. My question is, Is this indeed the concept of God that Christians and theists have, and does not a God who created man in His image, with a deliberate consequence of being able to communicate to Him in the realm of knowledge, as well as in all other realms, escape the consequences of your argument?

NIELSEN: I think that is a fine question. I think anthropomorphism admits of degrees. Something can be more or less anthropomorphic, just as something can be more or less irrational to believe. I took two; there are many, many concepts of God. But I took two, a plainly anthropomorphic one and a plainly nonanthropomorphic one.

It seems to me, though I could be wrong about this, that with the development of the Christian and the Jewish and the Islamic traditions that the God that is now believed in by most mainline Christians is a very nonanthropomorphic God. And that's why I stressed that. If one alternatively says, "Well, there is a God who reveals Himself to us and that notion isn't treated metaphorically but treated literally, then it does seem to me that you have to construe God anthropomorphically in some sense of "anthropomorphically." A colleague of mine, a Catholic theologian whom I greatly admire, Hugo Meynell, in writing an article called "Kai Nielsen's Atheism," for a *Festschrift* for Father Copleston, tries to argue that there are senses of "anthropomorphism" that are more legitimate than one I advert to. Perhaps there are; I haven't seen a clear articulation of that yet, but I don't want to rule it out *a priori;* it is quite possible. So I take the point of the question.

I'd like to say something just briefly about the business of projection. The reason I didn't bring in projection is that I, like Professor Moreland, believe the crucial thing we should argue about is not whether Christians are more neurotic than atheists or less neurotic and how they came to be this way, but we should try to find out what reasons we can give for or against religious beliefs. I think, however, that his view here is misplaced. My own view of the matter, though I am not a psychologist, is fairly simple. I know plenty of neurotic and fanatical Christians, and I know plenty of neurotic and fanatical atheists. One of the reasons I don't like going around to little humanist societies is that it seems to me that many of them are just the reverse side of sectarian Christianity. I've also known many sane and sensible atheists and many sane and sensible Christians. I think it would be very hard to tell which group is the more neurotic.

But I would like to say something about the actual use of projection. The really great thinkers who used it used it for much more reasonable purposes than what was discussed above. Take Sigmund Freud and his book, *The Future of an Illusion*. We know that he knew Hume's *Dialogues,* and we know he knew Kant. He had a good classical education and he studied philosophy with Franz Brentano. He said at one point in *The Future of an Illusion* that others can do better than he could in assessing the arguments for the existence of God. He was thinking of Hume and Kant. Freud plainly thought that they had shown them to be unsound arguments. He said that what he was trying to explain was why people so massively believe something which is so unreasonable to believe in. He presupposes the very point I am trying to argue for. He thought—and actually I agree with him—that that was a reasonable presupposition to make standing where we are in history. He then asked, quite reasonably, given that there are no good *reasons* for belief, what *causes* people so massively to believe in God? First you look for reasons, but where there are no reasons you look for causes. It is here where Freud's projection theory comes in.

Ludwig Feuerbach, from whom Freud took the projection theory, wanted to substitute a humanist perspective for a theological one. He wanted theology to become anthropology. He said, using a projectionist concept, look at all the attributes that man attributes to God. They are really attributes of perfect human beings, and we should transfer them back to their proper home. Theology should become anthropology.

This wasn't antireligious, you know. He wanted to cash religion out in human terms. That's very different from killing the father.

MORELAND: I'd like to publicly apologize to Professor Nielsen for the remark. You probably don't need an apology, but I'd like to say on behalf of the Christian community, that I thought the comment was very distasteful and out of place. The Christian community is an embarrassment to me sometimes because of the way it treats people who are on the other side, and I would like to say publicly, for myself, I have learned a great deal from Professor Nielsen's writing. He has represented to me a model of scholarship, and he's a very professional philosopher. I have found you to be nothing but cordial to me, and I very much appreciate your collegiality. You and I disagree deeply about the question of God, but I deeply respect you, and I think you respect me. And I'm sorry for that comment, and I certainly want to disassociate myself with that type of thing.

Now, in terms of this anthropomorphic business, again I want to get off this, simply because I think we're beating a dead horse here and it would be more interesting to talk about other things, but I'll say one more time that according to Christianity, it's really that man is theomorphic, not that God is anthropomorphic. The causation goes in the other way. God existed first, ontologically at least, and created human beings after His image.

Now based on that ontological causation and analogy, Calvin, for example, argued that it's possible for a person to have an awareness of God and to recognize Him and to build an ontological understanding of God based upon reflection of our own faculties. And the Thomistic type grounding of God-talk is that you base this on a causal relationship by means of what is called an analogy of intrinsic attribution. And you use only those concepts which can be removed from finite things and apply them to God. It is true that, according to this approach, God cannot be known or understood exhaustively; but he can be known truly because the Thomist use of analogy, based on the theomorphic grounding between God and us and creation in general, God can be known through what is called a univocal concept, by an analogy of predication, where the concept of, say, love means the same between us and God, but it's predicated differently of God, not in its meaning but in its extent, in its perfection.

In terms of the projection argument, and I think Professor Nielsen agrees here, I'm not using that as a knock-down argument, and I really wasn't trying to say that all atheists are neurotic and no theists are.

What I was saying was this: If two people are arguing and one says something like, "I don't think you're facing up to the evidence," and the other person is saying, "I don't think you are," then you need to keep arguing about the evidence. That's one thing to do. But another thing to do might be to say something like this: "Look, I think it's more plausible that the evidence is good, and it's just that you're not facing up to the evidence." Now what comes in at that point? How would you settle something like that? I'm not sure I have a full answer, but one way to do it would be to try to see if there were reasonable explanations for why the other person believed his view and denied what appeared to be clear evidence to the other person. In other words, one could try to give psychological reasons for why this other person is not seeing the evidence and is not using his noetic faculties correctly. This strategy would add another level to the debate.

I am saying that theists do not fit a neat control group. I suspect that you could find a constant causal factor of a psychological nature which explains why atheists do not read the evidence properly. Of course, the atheist can make the same charge against the theist. So now a new aspect of the argument emerges: Which side can offer a better account for explaining why, on its view, good evidence is not being seen by one whose epistemic equipment, as it were, is not functioning correctly, and what constant psychological factor appears to be causing the breakdown? But again, I'm not saying that one would lead out with this sort of thing. Rather, it would simply be part of an overall case.[5]

QUESTION: On the topic of religious experiences, Dr. Nielsen, you said that you cannot simply point to God as reference as you can point to Louis. And it's very much a claim of Christianity, I believe, that religious experience does just that. In fact, that the arguments from religious experience say the believer is justified from perceptive, non-sensory kind of experience. On what grounds do you reject this self-authenticating type of experience as making these individuals justified?

NIELSEN: The way I argue was the way it was argued years ago by C. B. Martin, another colleague of mine in his book, *Religious Belief*, and, I think, even more interestingly, by a Scottish philosopher, Ronald Hepburn in *Christianity and Paradox*, a book that unfortunately is not read much anymore.[6] They both argued that religious experience is enormously important. But they also argued, soundly, I believe, that it yields no knowledge of God. I rather closely follow them there.[7] I don't deny that there are religious experiences and they're humanly very important. Rudolph Otto was very good at describing the sort of circumstances that generate and sustain religious feelings. They are very real indeed, but they in no way are a ground for religious belief. They do not afford a special experience that gives us a knowledge of God. They are very fundamental religious experiences. People like Ninian Smart have argued they're quite various from culture to culture.[8] And I don't really have a view about that, but there is, especially within our communities, a distinct religious experience which I think Otto and Schliermacher, particularly Otto, put their hands on. Nobody denies that; it's a question of how to interpret it.

So there are two points. It's supposed to be an experience of God. I'm saying that can't be if God is in infinite individual transcendent to the universe. Because just think about what you mean by that term, and it should be evident to you that you just could not experience directly such a being. To go back to the anthropomorphic thing, you could only experience an anthropomorphic being. And that's religiously inadequate, for it is not the infinite transcendent reality of the tradition.

Suppose one says, "Look, look, look. I don't understand your fancy philosophic arguments. Maybe they're good; maybe they're bad. But I've experienced God, and I know it in a self-authenticating way." But Martin argued powerfully that the only models we have for self-authenticating experiences are things like headaches or sensations—that is, purely psychological realities. Suppose I say to you, "I've got a headache." That's what Wittgenstein called a first person, present tense avowal. Suppose you say, "No, you don't have a headache." Well, I have a kind of authority here on what I avow. As long as I understand the meaning of the word "headache," you can't gainsay me on this. Some philosophers, among them Armstrong and Mackie, have challenged this, but it still looks pretty strong that that looks like a self-authenticating experience, if you wish to use that vocabulary. So perhaps there are self-authenticating experiences. Not, of course, that I had a headache twenty minutes ago. I could be mistaken about that, but right now I have a headache, or express that I intend to go fishing on Saturday. Those things can be self-authenticating. But, let me repeat, what we have here are purely psychological realities. (If Armstrong and Mackie are right against Wittgenstein, the religious believer is even worse off, for then we have no good models for self-authenticating experiences.)

Those are all very private experiences which, though they are intentional and thus have *intentional* objects, are not experiences of some strange ontological realm. They are just psychological experiences, and they can't be used as a model for saying you have a self-authenticating experience of God. That is a more public claim, and then you are faced with the counter that it doesn't make sense to say such non-purely psychological experiences are self-authenticating. Suppose I say to you, "I know how to draw a round square," or "I have really experienced round squares." You know ahead of time that I'm giving what the Germans call *quatsch*.

MORELAND: Professor Nielsen said earlier that religious perception was merely feelings. And I think that that's question begging, frankly, because the same kind of objection could be raised, and has been raised, against more sensory modes of perception. It seems to me that David Hume is a good example here. According to Hume, the major way one distinguishes between impressions and ideas derived from impressions was the vividness of the feeling that one had about them. For Hume, impressions were not caused by the external world, whereas ideas were merely mental entities with no necessary connection to a mind-independent world. Thus, sensory impressions and ideas could be called "mere" feelings too.[9]

Further, I disagree with Nielsen's notion of God's transcendence. God is transcendent, but in Christian theology He is also immanent. And one of the modes of His immanency is in religious experiences.[10] Third, I don't agree with the propriety or accuracy of his use of the word "self-authenticating." My view of religious perception is an application of a more general epistemological strategy expressed by Roderick Chisholm.[11]Chisholm adopts an epistomological strategy called particularism.

What is particularism? This is the view that there are some things I can just know immediately without having to have a criterion for how I know them. And these items of knowledge occur in cases which cannot be likened to headaches. For example, Chisholm refers to knowledge of the past and memory. I know I had breakfast this morning, even though I might not have a criterion for how I know that. I know other minds exist, says Chisholm, even though I might not have a criterion for that. I know the external world exists without needing a criterion to justify that knowledge. Chisholm also argues that the same claim could be made for a sense of knowledge and a direct awareness of God.[12] So such an awareness is self-authenticating in that it is known immediately but not in the sense that it is immune to criticism. But there are a lot of knowledge claims that way, and I would recommend that if a person doesn't adopt particularism as a general strategy in our knowledge of the world, then one ends up either in a vicious infinite regress or in skepticism. I think that Chisholm's arguments on this topic are convincing.

So my point again is that in religious experiences God is, or can be, experienced immediately. I've had experiences like that myself. I also believe that there are some cases of religious experience that are not appeals to direct perception, but are rather what are called causal arguments.[13] This is William James's classic type of argument in *Varieties of Religious Experience*.[14] You postulate God's existence to explain a range of religious effects that are not adequately explained by other hypotheses. It seems to be that certain cases of answered prayer or certain examples of power fit this type of argument from religious experience.

In this regard, there's a book I'd like to recommend by Patrick Sherry called *Spirit, Saints, and Immortality*.[15] Sherry argues a type of causal argument from religious experience and says that, after all, it has been Christian theism which has produced heroes like Mother Teresa and others, who have gone around the world and who have reached out to people in great numbers and have performed supererogatory acts of heroism on behalf of God or humanity. He says that this provides evidence that the Christian faith is true, because of the Power that is postulated to explain the production of such heroes. Spiritual work has been done.

Now one could object to this by pointing out periods like the Crusades or the modern church where the church is *not* producing saints and heroes. A Christian theist could respond by pointing out that these are not good test cases for "authentic" Christianity. In order to keep from making this a question-begging counter-argument, I suggest the following: One should go to the New Testament, study the New Testament itself, and derive an hypothesis, independent of the actual practices of the church at any period of history which would state what spiritual practices, what model of spiritual growth ought to regularly produce transformed persons if God really exists.[16] One could then test this hypothesis to see if saints and heroes are, in fact, produced. And that would provide an empirical test that would lend some kind of confirmation to Christian theism.[17]

QUESTION: This question is directed to Dr. Nielsen. Dr. Nielsen, what are your views on afterlife, where there have been those who have claimed they have experienced either a heaven or a hell? If this is true, then there had to have been some ultimate being who decided how much wrong caused them to go to hell or how much right they did [which] caused them to go to heaven. There has to be some way to explain it.

NIELSEN: I'll say something that might surprise some of you. There's a famous Cambridge philosopher, John Ellis McTaggart, who was an atheist *and* believed in immortality.[18] There's no logical impossibility of believing that you survive the death of your body, even though you do not believe in God. I mean I don't happen to believe what McTaggart believed. So I neither believe in God nor the afterlife. But my point is that the two beliefs are not logically linked. I could be an atheist who believes that he will survive the death of his body in a godless world. The two beliefs are only linked traditionally. There's no logical connection between believing in the afterlife and believing in God.

Still you might think this is a kind of evasion. It isn't an evasion really. It just shows you that there are different notions. And then there are some Christians who do *not* believe in immortality. I was at a conference John Hick sponsored at Claremont and there's a book coming out published by Macmillan. There I have an article on immortality, the only extensive article I have ever written on this topic. There were lots of other people there who write on such matters, including a good number of Christians, professors of theology. Some claim they didn't want to have anything to do with the afterlife—neither bodily resurrection nor immortality. (They are different notions, by the way.)

So even within the Christian community belief varies. You might say, "Well, the true Christians all believe in an afterlife." Well, you have got to define what a "true Christian" is without begging some questions. It is a matter of sociological fact that people who call themselves Christians and take religion very seriously indeed differ about this, to say nothing about Judaism and the like.

Somebody might still say I'm not getting to the heart of the matter. Take the business that people go to heaven and hell and they will be damned. Well, I just don't think that's very plausible. I think that about the notion of bodily resurrection very nicely argued for in the Claremont conference I just mentioned by a very good Christian philosopher, Stephen Davis, who referred to immortality as nonsense, but accepted *a bodily resurrection*. You can make logical sense of the notion of bodily resurrection. It doesn't involve any dualist assumptions or anything else about immaterial spirits. Peter Geach argues this way too. There is just a resurrection of the body. That seems to me not incoherent, just unbelievable. There is no reason to believe in such a thing. It is like believing in Santa Claus or the Easter Bunny. But it is not something that is incoherent. It is a matter of scientific argument. I might turn out to be wrong.

It seems to me belief in immortality—a disembodied soul—has many of the same difficulties in it as a belief in an infinite nonmaterial person does. But I have been told that the really strong parts of the Christian tradition don't believe in immortality in that sense; they believe in bodily resurrection. That belief seems to me coherent but superstitious. So you have the choice between a coherent but superstitious belief, to wit, bodily resurrection and an incoherent belief, namely, immortality through eternal disembodied existence.

MORELAND: Well, C. J. Ducasse is another atheist who believes in immortality without God, but just because it is logically possible that one can believe in immortality and atheism, it certainly doesn't follow that immortality is equally plausible vis-à-vis atheism and theism.[19] It is logically possible that we're all brains in vats, but I don't think anybody is going to die for that belief. So I don't think you can make too much hay out of the fact that a few atheists believe in immortality or that immortality is logically consistent with atheism.[20]

Secondly, it is true that within Christendom you can find someone who believes practically anything, including Christian atheism. But I think a straightforward, common sense, honest understanding of the Christian faith would recognize that to be a Christian you'd be committed to some form of a personal afterlife. Now I quite agree with Nielsen that there is a debate among Christians between bodily resurrection and personal immortality of the soul. I do think, however, that a proper reading of the New Testament implies that dualism is true, not Platonic dualism, but at least the view that there is a substantial soul and it's distinct from the body. It infuses the body, but it is different—it has different properties from those characterizing matter, it is capable of disembodied existence, and it will be renunited with the body of the future.[21]

So the real debate does not center on personal immortality versus resurrection; it is really a debate between those who hold to personal disembodied survival followed by resurrection and those who merely hold to a bodily resurrection. I happen to hold to disembodied survival with a resurrection of the body in the future.[22] Apart from exegetical arguments and general arguments for dualism, I would cite after-death experiences as evidence for my view. I'm not certain what to make of these, but I'm not going to reject them *a priori*. A physicalist explanation of them is to claim that they are near-death, not after-death experiences. But this response doesn't explain the following: Allegedly there are cases where people have died, and in the period when they've been "gone," they have obtained knowledge of things that have happened two blocks away. It would have been very difficult for them to have known this type of information.

Now that sort of thing makes me stop. What I want to know is, Did those things really happen? And I would say that if they really did, it would be pretty tough to explain these cases on any kind of physicalist interpretation. Now I'm not saying these stories are clearly true, but if these kinds of cases can be established, then we have got something interesting to discuss.

QUESTION: Dr. Nielsen, you stated that you did not accept the standard tradition, which stipulates that you cannot prove or disprove God's existence. Then it seems that the weight of your argument rests on the meaninglessness of the term "God." Yet this seems oddly enough meaningless to exactly the same extent that postulating the universe simply came into existence [is]—a brute fact, as Bertrand Russell believed.

Where is your proof that atheism is more rational than theism? It seems that you have only given a persuasive case for the standard tradition; that is, both explanations are, in the final analysis, unable to claim a greater reasonableness over the other. You do not offer an explanation of the world; I suppose you would just claim that the world just is, brute fact, *á la* Bertrand Russell. But then, as I stated, this is about as satisfying as the alleged meaninglessness of the term "God." This is fine to cast doubt on theism; however, it doesn't very well prove that atheism is more reasonable than theism.

NIELSEN: I think, by the way, that is a very good question. And let me say that there are lots of people—Ronald Hepburn is a good example—who regard themselves as agnostics and not atheists.[23] They do so because they think that even about these arguments for incoherence that I make that they, while persuasive, are not decisive, but then they also believe neither are the arguments that go the other way. Some people would want to respond to such agnostics by saying, "But we have a clear sense of God." The agnostics would in turn respond that such believers can say nothing more decisive here. And we are left with something very problematical, so the more reasonable thing is to be just agnostic about matters of religious belief.

I think that is the standard position. It may be right. I tried to give arguments for why I think it is not, and I will stick by them. But remember, I said at the very beginning, when I asked you not to be offended when I say it is irrational to believe in God, that in saying that I am not so arrogant as to think that I have wisdom by the tail and know what the truth is and Professor Moreland doesn't. Ronald Hepburn doesn't think that my arguments are decisive, and he may very well be right.

These arguments are very difficult; they are very complex. As both Moreland and I know, they are much more difficult than we have been able to indicate. They are difficult on either side, and maybe agnosticism is the best thing. But agnosticism both for the believer and the unbeliever is a rather unhappy position to be in. People try to get something more definitive, and I tried to give you reasons which I think are good reasons, but I may be mistaken in thinking they are that. That is just meant to set the stage.

What about your specific things, your Russell things, about it being just a brute fact that we could come into existence and this being as problematical as belief in God? It seems to me to talk in either of these ways is a mistake. We should not try to treat the universe as if it were one big thing. When you speak of the universe, if you say that it is either finite or infinite or anything like that, you are treating it as if it were some kind of an entity. And that doesn't seem to me to make much sense.

And so then you say, "Well, why the universe? Did it come in with the Big Bang? Or was it in the steady state in the oscillating theory? What can we say about the universe as a whole?" I don't think we can say anything about the universe as a whole that is very intelligible. And so I don't think that those sorts of questions are conducive to salvation, or to clear thinking for that matter. And so when Russell says that it is just a fact that the universe exists, I think that is just a way of saying, if it makes any sense at all, that, as a matter of fact, there are various things in the universe that we are aware of, that we make predictions and retrodictions about them, that we are developing theories about them, all fallibilistic, all alterable, and so forth.

I want to get in something rather quickly about direct perception, to go back to something Professor Moreland said. I take, at least for discussion, his point that there is knowledge that is criterionless. It is not my way of talking, but I take the point. That is to say, I acknowledge that there are some things we are directly aware of without any *explicit* appeal to critera. If we couldn't be aware of them without any such appeal, we wouldn't be able to be aware of anything. For example, that you've got a pair of green pants on, I've first got to have an understanding of that, and then, with that primitive understanding, I could go on to develop a criterion. But I would first have to have instances of such knowledge before I could develop a criterion for what it was for you (or anyone) to have on green pants.

My point is that such particularism won't help out the person who talks about religious perception one bit, if it is direct perception. The causal perceptions that Moreland talked about, those are really the arguments for the existence of God, not arguments about being directly aware of God. But the claim made by the questioner is that there are direct perceptions of God that are self-authenticating. I want to argue that, criterion or no criterion, except for very limited things like headaches for the person who has them at the time he has them, there are no self-authenticating experiences. Take the simple statement that "You have a pair of green pants on." That statement may be a criterionless statement. Criterionless or not, it also may be false. So this direct knowledge, if we have it, which is criterionless, still doesn't give us any certainty. There is nothing, except perhaps the domain of the purely psychological (for example, headaches), that is self-authenticating.

MORELAND: Regarding criteria for testing the veridicality of religious experience, I don't want to go into this in detail, but in the last chapter of *Scaling the Secular City,* I state criteria that can be formulated, after one has had direct experiences of God, to offer further confirmation of their veracity.[24] Several people have studied these things and generated literature on this subject. You can read this literature for yourselves and decide if it makes sense and if it is rationally persuasive. But the claim that there have been no criteria stated for religious experience is simply not true.

Next, let us consider claims about the universe as a whole. I don't mean to make this a cheap debater's point here, but if you can't make any statements about the universe as a whole, then what Nielsen just said, "You can't make any statements about the universe as a whole," was itself a statement about the universe as a whole. It was a self-refuting type of statement. It's like saying there are no truths. Unless he meant "universe as a whole" as a mere unintelligible "blick" or "glip," that might have been what he meant. Maybe he can tell us about that in his summary speech.

Further, the arguments for design that I used don't need to take the universe as a whole because some of them take parts of the universe and argue for a designer for them. The point about cosmic singularities does take the universe as a whole in the sense that these are boundary conditions that are brute givens in science from which the universe unfolded. These are properties or features of the universe as a whole in the sense that they are ultimate, that they define the universe as it is currently.

I tried to argue that these features are so incredibly balanced that a minor alteration, greater or smaller, in a large number of these would have made any life whatsoever impossible. To have life you've got to have at least the chemicals necessary for an organism to ingest, to defecate, and to replicate itself. And whether that's oxygen or silicon-based or whatever, it's got to have a pretty high degree of specified complexity. There aren't too many windows through which the universe could come to have that sort of information, and that's part of the argument. And I'm saying that because there is information in the DNA molecule, I don't see any reason at all why that can't be some evidence that there was a mind behind the design of the DNA, if we agree that there is usually a mind behind some other kind of message. [Applause]

Notes

1. Antony Flew shows something of what is wrong with Mackie's and Swinburne's common assumption here. Antony Flew, "The Burden of Proof" in *Knowing Religiously,* Leroy S. Rouner, ed. (Notre Dame, Ind.: University of Notre Dame Press, 1985), 105–6, 112–14.
2. Kai Nielsen, *Philosophy and Atheism* (Buffalo, N.Y.: Prometheus Books, 1985); *God, Scepticism and Modernity* (Ottawa: University of Ottawa Press, 1989); Paul Edwards, "Atheism" in *The Encyclopedia of Philosophy,* vol. 1 (New York: Macmillan, 1967), 174–189; "Difficulties in the Idea of God" in *The Idea of God,* Edward H. Madden, ed. (Springfield, Ill.: Charles C. Thomas, 1968), 43–97.
3. See R. C. Sproul, *The Psychology of Atheism* (Minneapolis: Bethany, 1974).
4. Paul Vitz, *Sigmund Freud's Christian Unconscious* (New York: Guilford Press, 1988).
5. Parallel cases occur in ordinary sensory perception. Suppose Jones and Smith are both in the desert. Jones is standing beside the highway, and Smith is driving his car toward Jones. Smith looks at the road and claims to see water on the surface while Jones looks at the road and claims to see no water. In support of his case, Smith could cite the fact that he (epistemi-

cally) seems to see water—that is, he is being appeared to in a certain sensory way whereby he experiences a wet area in his visual field and, on this basis, he is inclined to believe that water is there. Jones could counter by claiming that he sees no such sensory qualities when he looks at the same location on the road. Both Smith and Jones claim that the other disputant is not seeing the evidence correctly. Now if we had a background theory that explains how it could be that Smith is appeared to in such and such a way, even though he is experiencing a mirage, then this genetic, causal explanation could be used to decide the debate in favor of Jones, even though it is logically possible that Smith is correct. This genetic, causal explanation would cite certain factors common to mirage-type experiences. In the atheist/theist debate, if one side could cite a common set of psychological factors that are present in advocates of the other side—e.g., defense mechanisms of repression, bad relationships with one's father, and the like—then these factors could be cited as evidence that the other side was being influenced by these factors in an epistemically inappropriate way. I suspect, though I cannot *prove*, that the class of atheists would be easier to group in this way than would be the class of theists.

6. C. B. Martin, *Religious Belief* (Ithaca, N.Y.: Cornell University Press, 1959); Ronald Hepburn, *Christianity and Paradox* (London: Watts, 1958).
7. See my discussion of religious experience in Kai Nielsen, *Reason and Practice* (New York: Harper & Row, 1970), 195–203.
8. Ninian Smart, *Reasons and Faith* (London: Routledge and Kegan Paul, 1958).
9. What is at stake here is different views about intentionality and the nature of feelings. Those who speak disparagingly about the epistemic value of feelings tend to view consciousness and its objects along Humean lines: consciousness involves simple sense perception and (perhaps) introspection. Feelings are merely mental entities or states (or for many today, physical entities, states, functional roles, or terms in "folk psychology") that occur in the self but which have no objects and are neither true nor false, appropriate nor inappropriate. A richer view of consciousness, feelings, and intentionality has been presented by those operating in the phenomenological tradition of Bretano and Edmund Husserl. According to this view (or family of views), feelings are ways of truly apprehending the world. For example, if I feel desire for some object, then this means that I see the object as desirable—that is, I attribute the property of desirability to the object and, perhaps, the second order property of goodness. Now, the object either does or does not have the property of goodness, and I can be right or wrong in seeing it as good. After all, it is possible to desire the wrong things. Similarly, numinous "feelings" can be intentional in the same way. Why should a criterion appropriate for perceiving physical objects (e.g., there must be a sensory quality to the perception) be used as a

standard of acceptability for other forms of perception (religious, ethical, rational) which have as their objects entities that are not colored?

10. Eugene Fontinell has argued that God can be immanent in one's field of consciousness in religious experience. He uses this fact to argue for the existence of an afterlife. See *Self, God, and Immortality* (Philadelphia: Temple University Press, 1986), 101–161. Unfortunately, he combines these insights with a process metaphysic that renders unintelligible my literal survival of death. This is because process metaphysics rules out a substantial self that can maintain literal sameness through change. See J. P. Moreland, "An Enduring Self: The Achilles Heel of Process Metaphysics," *Process Studies* 17 (Fall 1988), 193–99.

11. See Roderick Chisholm, *The Problem of the Criterion* (Milwaukee, Wisc.: Marquette University Press, 1973).

12. See Roderick Chisholm, *Theory of Knowledge* (Englewood Cliffs, N.J.: Prentice-Hall, 2nd ed., 1977), 132–34.

13. Cf. J. P. Moreland, *Scaling the Secular City* (Grand Rapids, Mich.: Baker, 1987), 231–34.

14. William James, *The Varieties of Religious Experience* (New York: The Modern Library, 1936; first published 1902).

15. Patrick Sherry, *Spirit, Saints, and Immortality* (Albany, N.Y.: State University of New York Press, 1984), 31–63.

16. See Dallas Willard, *The Spirit of the Disciplines* (San Francisco: Harper & Row, 1988).

17. On the general topic of theism and confirmation theory and how the latter fits into an evaluation of the former, see Richard Swinburne, *The Existence of God* (Oxford: Clarendon Press, 1979); George Schlessinger, *Religion and Scientific Method* (Boston: D. Reidel, 1982).

18. John Ellis McTaggart, *Some Dogmas of Religion* (London: Routledge and Kegan Paul, 1906).

19. C. J. Ducasse, *Nature, Mind, and Death* (LaSalle, Ill.: Open Court, 1951), 444–502.

20. For a defense of dualism and additional bibliography, see J. P. Moreland, *Scaling the Secular City*, 77–103.

21. For a biblical defense of dualism, see Robert Gundry, *Soma in Biblical Theology* (Cambridge: Cambridge University Press, 1976).

22. See J. P. Moreland, *Scaling the Secular City*, 235–240; cf. Gary Gutting, *Religious Belief and Religious Skepticism* (Notre Dame, Ind.: Notre Dame Press, 1982), 150–53; William J. Wainwright, *Philosophy of Religion* (Belmont, Calif.: Wadsworth, 1988), 113–130.

23. Ronald Hepburn, "Agnosticism" in *The Encyclopedia of Philosophy*, vol. 1, 56–59. I have discussed this historically, sympathetically but critically, in my *Atheism and Philosophy*, 9–31 and 55–104.

24. J. P. Moreland, *Scaling the Secular City*, 239–40.

PART II

DOES IT MATTER THAT GOD EXISTS?

The Debate Continued

Kai Nielsen

Ethics Without God 8

POJMAN: Good afternoon. We have the privilege of having the first series of meetings on questions relating to God and morality. There are some chairs back around there, and you can sit on the floor otherwise, I'm afraid, or stand.

The topic of this meeting is "Religion and Morality," or "Ethics With or Without God." And our two speakers are Professor Kai Nielsen, who will take the position of "Ethics Without God," and then Professor J. P. Moreland, who will take a position that shows an intricate relationship between morality and religion.

We are very privileged this afternoon to have two distinguished philosophers with us. Dr. Kai Nielsen is professor and head of the philosophy department at the University of Calgary in Canada. He received his doctorate in philosophy from Duke University, has been on many, many, many committees in the philosophical world, is known for his hundreds of articles and his several books, including *Ethics Without God*, which is relevant for our topic today.

Professor J. P. Moreland is currently Associate Professor of Apologetics and Philosophy at Liberty University in Lynchburg, Virginia. He received his doctorate in philosophy from the University of Southern California, and he has spoken on more than seventy-five college campuses. He also, before he became a philosopher, was a speaker for Campus Crusade for Christ in apologetics, and he still works in this area. He is the author of several articles and books; the most famous is his recent book which I am seeing all over campus. It's called *Scaling the Secular City: A Defense of Christianity*.

Now what we'll do is first Professor Nielsen will speak on ethics without God for about a half an hour, and then Professor Moreland will speak secondly for about twenty minutes, giving a response, giving his answer to Nielsen. Though I must say, Professor Moreland has not heard or seen Nielsen's speech, so he's going to do a lot of this ad-lib, and very, very graciously has accepted to do so. But he has some independent thoughts on the matter, I'm sure.

Will you join me in welcoming our speakers to Ole Miss?

NIELSEN: Well, thank you very much for having me here. I spent years in the South, and it's always a pleasure to come back.

Religious people frequently claim that to make sense of our lives and to define an objective basis of morality, we must believe in God. Is this so? And exactly what does this claim come to?

Now when I speak of "God" here, I intend to use the term in a traditional sense. If you simply mean by "God" *love*, then all atheists can be led gently into belief. I am not concerned here with those who use the term in such an eccentric sense. So when I speak of "God," I'm going to mean something that I think orthodox Christians, Jews, and believers in Islam all hold. So when I say it's necessary to believe in God to make adequate sense of morality or indeed to make any sense of morality, I mean by "God" the one infinite creator of all things, the one infinite, uncreated, eternal, personal reality transcendent to the world, who created all that exists other than Himself and sustains and protects all His creation. This in our culture is a very standard conception of God, and for good or for ill, that is roughly what I mean when I raise this question.

Now does the viability of moral beliefs depend on belief in God? This can be asked in at least two forms. The one form asks, or asserts rather, that to have any kind of coherent moral belief at all, one must presuppose the existence of God. Remember Martin Luther's famous remark, "There's no greater enemy of grace than the ethics of Aristotle." This tradition, I suppose, is more Protestant than Catholic, though it is surely not adhered to by all Protestants. Its famous contemporary formulators have been people like Emil Brunner or Karl Barth. But there is another form of religious ethics (I think a more moderate and plausible form) which says that any secular ethic is inadequate when compared with an ethic inspired or informed by theistic commitments. That form doesn't deny what is obvious anyway, that nonreligious people can be morally responsible, but it maintains that a through and through adequate account of morality would answer to the deepest needs that human beings have and that, this account maintains, would have to be an ethic with theistic commitments. Contemporary representatives of that rather more moderate view are Professor John Hick and my colleague Terence Penelhum.[1]

About the first view first, namely, the belief that to have any kind of coherent moral belief at all, you must believe in God—believe, that is, in God in the sense or roughly the sense I defined—I think that just the reverse is true. I think, that is, that you cannot even have a coherent sense, if indeed it is a coherent sense, of God that the Judeo-Christian-

Islamic traditions wish to have, at least as that has been developed, without at least some prior *moral understanding*. That, in short, to oversimplify, instead of morality requiring religion, the very possibility of even understanding the concept of God and in making a religious response presupposes some minimal moral understanding.

Now I just asserted that it is not the case that without God nothing matters. I'm not going to argue for that in this lecture. The basic line of argumentation for it, the sort of thing I've argued on numerous occasions, including in my *Ethics Without God,* is familiar enough. I suppose most of you are in some philosophy course, and I suppose you have read about theories of divine command morality. That is, moral theories which say that to know what is right, to know what is obligatory, even to know what is good, you have to know what God commands, God wills, God ordains. And *whatever* God wills and *whatever* God ordains, that establishes what is right and what is wrong. This is the divine command theory.

If that theory could be justifiably held, not in its modified forms, where it does not meet secular ethics head on and does not challenge in the above way secular ethics, but in its unmodified form, it could be a very powerful moral theory indeed.[2] It would yield some decisive decision procedures in ethics. These modified forms may be adequate for other purposes, but not as a kind of response to a secular morality. It is, in its unmodified strong form, as you see in Emil Brunner, where you simply determine what is right by knowing what God wills, that you get a deep challenge to secularism.[3] These accounts just assume that there is a God—it is just background assumption. That, they claim, settles what is right, no matter what it seems to human beings, no matter what our frail moral sense suggests. You must do it even if God orders you to kill your only son. If God orders you to do it, then it is right, no matter what He orders you to do. You would, no doubt, say He wouldn't give you such orders, but if He did, you would still conclude that it is the right thing to do because whatever is right and whatever is wrong is determined by what God wills. We don't have even to look at the content of His commands. You just have to know that they are His commands.

I want to say, to understate it, that that sort of ethic is clearly inadequate. It's wrong, God or no God, to torture little children just for the fun of it. What basis we have for making that confident moral claim is another thing, but we know, if we know anything, if we have any moral understanding at all, that that is wrong. And moreover, to understand what you're talking about, to understand that God, among other things, is a being worthy of worship and that God is said to be perfect, the perfect good, we need some logically prior understanding of those normative concepts. In order to understand that something is the perfect good, you have to understand what is good, and in order to understand that something is worthy of worship, you have to have at least some elementary criteria or understanding of what worthiness is, and that is *not* itself derived from God. Or to put the point more accurately, though rather more pedantically, though it may be derived in a causal sense— since everything comes from God—it is not derived in a justificatory or logical sense from God or a belief in God. Our understanding of these concepts is quite logically prior to any religious response.

This is the thing, if I develop it properly, as I do when I teach elementary ethics courses, that takes me about three classes. So I won't try it today. I'll just assert it, and if there are questions which come up in the discussion about this, I will respond to them. But what I want to do here today is examine what I take to be the more moderate sort of claim that doesn't say that an atheist has no moral understanding, which doesn't deny that there could be such things as secular moralities, but which contends they are inadequate when compared with a religious ethic. Again, let me remind you, I develop a critique of divine command theory as well as other religious moral theories in my *Ethics Without God* and *God and the Grounding of Morality*.

I want to take up the claim that argues, and sometimes with considerable force, that the best of religious moralities, though not all religious moralities, are far more worthy of acceptance than even the best of secular moralities. I say not all religious moralities, for, after all, there are brutal religious moralities and there are brutal secular moralities and there are stupid religious moralities and there are stupid secular moralities. But the best forms of religious moralities, the ones expressing most adequately the tradition or the common traditions of Judaism, Christianity, and Islam, the claim I wish to examine goes, are more adequate than any form of humanistic ethic. It is not that there can't be secular humanistic ethics, but the most adequate morality would be a religious morality. That is the sort of thing that I want critically to examine.

Many Christians argue this way, and from now on I'll just talk about Christians because I suppose most of you are Christians in this environment. (I have, by the way, no strong preference between Christianity and Judaism and Islam, but that's another issue. I suppose if I were shopping around, I'd rather be a Zen Buddhist than any of the above, but that's neither here nor there for this discussion. So let us just talk about Christians.)

Some Christians accept the fact that there are coherent secular moralities and that atheists can indeed be decent and principled people. They can even admit that secular moralities can have a justification of sorts, while still claiming that a morality informed by theistic commitments will be a much superior and more securely founded morality than any purely secular morality. What I want to do is argue that this claim is false.

Now I don't think this claim is *demonstrably* false in the way that I think the divine command theory is demonstrably false. I may, of course, be mistaken in thinking it is demonstrably false, but what I think goes on is the more moderate argument that you can give considerations, none of them decisive, for both views; I think, however, that considerations can be given that are cogent enough such that most people, if they reflect upon them very carefully in a cool hour, will come to say what I'm about to say. But I may, of course, be wrong in saying this. That is for you to make up your mind about in reflecting on the force of my arguments.

First, what grounds lead religious moralists to make such assertions? Why do they believe that a fully adequate religious morality would be a more adequate morality than any humanistic secular morality? Well, one of the claims, and an important one, is that religious moralities answer more deeply to our deepest human needs.[4] This, of course, goes with a background assumption—an assumption I am perfectly comfortable with—that an adequate morality is a morality that will meet human needs. It will not be a morality so concerned with rights and duties that it will ignore the importance of meeting human needs.

They will make claims, diversely expressed, something like this: Human beings everywhere are religious animals, religious beings, in need of rituals and saving myths. Even if the reference to "saving myths" means that there is no truth involved here, the claim might still be pressed. Moreover, myths could also be ways of indicating something which was true. But whether or not myths could be vehicles of truth or falsity, people need these big saving myths, the claim goes, with the framework beliefs that go with them. Without a belief in God and immortality, or at least a resurrection of the body (something that replaces immortality), our lives, the claim goes, will remain fragmented and meaningless and thus the deepest needs that we human beings have won't be answered.

A secular morality, they will say, can afford us no sense of providential care, while a Christian or Jewish or Islamic morality can. Recall that in the [Apostle's] Creed it speaks of "God the Father Almighty." God is a creator who is the source of care, protection, and moral guidance. We are, if our faith is strong, free of anxiety and fear. With a firm faith in God, we have the reassurance that if we will orient our will to God, we will be saved and that evil will not ultimately triumph and that our efforts will not be hopeless because the evil in the world is too much for us. In God we can find peace and a reassurance that all is not in vain.

Contrast this with how I have to respond, given my secular belief-system, when I reflect on the fact that 10,000 people will starve during the course of this day. (Just calculate, as you sit here, how many people will starve while I am giving this lecture.) All I can say about it, beyond expressing my anguish, is that we must work to halt this by struggling in a political-social way. While, if you're a believer, you could hate this, struggle against it just as much as I do, but you would also feel you have some awareness that somehow these struggles, especially when there is a sense of the struggles being defeated, are not in vain. In some ways that you as a religious person do not very well understand, it still is, appearances to the contrary notwithstanding, not all in vain. There's a kind of reassurance and peace religious people have—or so it is sometimes claimed—that no secular morality can offer. The Jew or the Christian or the Moslem can have a confident future-oriented view of the world, knowing that there is a purpose to life, that we are creatures of God, made for a purpose. There is, the belief goes, a purpose in which ultimately for all humankind there will be human liberation in a life of bliss. There is a hope there and a moral promise that no secular morality can match.

Now how should secularists and atheists respond to this? (I am, I should say parenthetically, something worse than this, for I am not only an atheist but a Marxian as well.) I will first tell you one response which I think is a bad one, and then I'll tell you what I think is a good response. The first one is not altogether bad, but it is question-begging and it smacks a bit of sour grapes.

It is the response I first heard when I took my Ph.D. at Duke. There was there a Freudian anthropologist who used to say about such things, "Look, we need to learn to stand on our feet as adults without behaving like children, relying on a father figure." Religious ethics, he contended, with its stress on providential care, infantalizes us. Instead of urging us to stand on our own feet as adult, autonomous, moral agents, it sets us on a search for a protective father figure.

I think myself that there is something in that, but only something. It is important to come to be able to stand on your feet, but after all, some religious people can—and do—learn to stand on their feet too. I mean, it's not just that God helps those who help themselves, but there is a sense within the Gospel tradition of both depending on God and being prepared to stand on your own feet too. So I think that that secular response, while having a grain of truth, is still a bit of sour grapes.

What do I think is important here? If I were arguing about the logic of divine commands—the first religious defense I mentioned—I would say to you, "Well, look, let's put aside all questions about whether God exists or doesn't exist. Let us argue that on another occasion. Let us just assume for the purposes of this discussion that God does exist and that the very concept of God is a coherent one. I want to still show you that even so the morality of divine commands won't work."

In the present argument about the comparative adequacy of a religious and purely secular morality, I don't think you can do that. And how you will go on here about a religious morality is not independent of what you believe about the truth-claims of religion. If you really believe that there is a God and that He has the attributes attributed to Him by the Christian tradition—I don't mean the most Neanderthal Christian traditions, but rather more like United Church Christian traditions in Canada or something like that—then there is considerable reason to take the religious morality as something added to the secular morality. It, moreover, plainly is something secular morality doesn't have. On the other hand, if you think, as I do, perhaps mistakenly, that belief in God is at its best problematic and deeply implausible, or if you thought like Kierkegaard that you had to crucify your intellect to believe in God, then the religious morality is going to be much less attractive. You can understand why people, if they have such an intellectual understanding of the world, would find it much less attractive. So the argument that is going on now, unlike philosophical arguments about divine command ethics, can't be made in independence of what you think about the reality of religious truth-claims. And that was not our present subject. But we need to recognize here that such arguments are relevant to the kind of argument that is going to be broached now.

To start the whole matter, suppose, just suppose, there are within religious traditions a lot of people who are sort of Barthian-Kierkegaardians. People, that is, who are extreme fideistic Christians.

They are extremely skeptical about the possibility of establishing anything about religion by the use of rational argumentation or investigation. Let us for now ignore the question of whether they are right about this. And yet, like Pascal, Kierkegaard, and Hamann, they think that if you do not believe in God, then everything goes down and so you need at least the saving religious myths, even though they may be very implausible myths as I think they tend to be. They even tend to agree with the secularist about this. You need to believe this, they maintain, in order to make sense of morality or at least to make the deepest sense of morality. And so they are going to say it is because of this that we are going to believe, in spite of the fact that it seems very implausible.

Now here I think you have to make trade-offs. And here I think the secularist could make a rather strong comeback. He can argue, and argue persuasively, that there is a lot more to morality that is quite independent of religious orientation. He can point out that there is a lot that is important about morality that holds quite apart from religious belief.

Let me spend the rest of the lecture dealing with this. In the first place, there can be purposes *in* life even if there is no purpose *to* life. So, if God exists, you were made for a purpose. And that itself poses problems about your autonomy. Such matters caused a lot of trouble for the Christian tradition, especially in the Calvinist tradition. But maybe there is a way of resolving this. That, at any rate, is not the issue I want to pursue here. What I want to stress is the point there can be purposes *in* life, even though there is no purpose *to* life. You have lots of intentions, interests, aims, goals, things that you care about, that, God or no God, remain perfectly intact.[5] If you love someone, whether there is a God or not, that love can go on. It remains intact. It might even be more intact, because if death ends it all, the love relationships between people in life are all the more precious because that is all there is in that respect. So that's perfectly intact, God or no God. Indeed, as I have just argued, it may even become more important.

If you have some life plan, if you want to be a doctor or a professor or a political radical, whatever you want to be, if there's something you want to do in this world, you can do that, God or no God. There are all those intentions, purposes, goals, and the like that you can figure out and find and can have. They are what John Rawls called *life plans*. You figure out what you want to do with your life. You can have all these purposes *in* life even though there is no purpose *to* life, so life doesn't become meaningless and pointless if you were not *made for* a purpose.

There can be small individual purposes, things like love, friendship, caring, knowledge, self-respect, pleasure in life. All of these things remain perfectly intact in a godless world. There can also be larger political and social purposes that you can struggle for. You can, in Camus's famous phrase, fight the plague, if you will. Even if you are skeptical about transforming the world, at least you can try to cut back some of the evil in the world, and sometimes you can succeed in some measure.

And all of this remains perfectly in place in a godless universe. You don't have to have a Kierkegaardian sense of sickness unto death where all worldly hopes are undermined because there is no purpose to life. There are these intact purposes in life, and they can be forged together in clusters to give you a coherent but still utterly secularist worldview. There are, that is, things that are worthwhile doing and having. It is worthwhile struggling to make a better world. Friendship, love, caring, all these things I mentioned remain intact in a godless world.

And morality in the terms of questions of justice and the like will still retain a point in a godless world. We need, in living together, a set of practices that work to adjudicate, in a fair way, conflicts of interests. That is in a simple way what justice is all about. We need a set of social practices which, when you get into a hassle with a colleague, let's say, or if one group gets in a hassle with another group, or suppose you and I get into a hassle about how long we're going to talk, we need some procedures rooted in social practices to fairly adjudicate those conflicts of interests. And those remain totally intact in a godless world. Justice hardly requires God.

Secondly, and rather more controversially, I think, a secularist can be a Kantian who can reflectively desire the kingdom of ends. What I mean by that big and rather pretentious phrase is that a secularist can believe that it's essential to morality that no person should be treated as a means only. This obtains for good people and bad people alike. The good of self-respect should be directed to everyone.

That conception is usually rooted in a religious worldview, but it needn't be. You can see if you reflect on the fact that probably one of our most fundamental goods as individuals is the good of self-respect. John Rawls took it to be the most fundamental of our primary social goods. But if I recognize this as a deep good for me, I also recognize that it's going to be a deep good for you. And while there are many differences between us, there is no relevant difference between us with respect to that. Moreover, if I judge this to be a fundamental good for me, I must, logically must, on pain of rejecting universalizability—that is, rejecting what is good for the goose is good for the gander—be prepared to recognize it for you too. So I can get to the good of self-respect on a purely secular basis, though it has come into our culture, of course, through a religious tradition. But validity is independent of origin.

It is worthwhile recalling that Kant developed this notion, though even as a very, very religious person, he justified his ethical beliefs on purely autonomous, nonreligious grounds. But it is no doubt true that he probably would never have come to have this belief in the kingdom of ends but for the fact that he grew up in a religious tradition. There is a thing called the genetic fallacy; in avoiding it we need to realize that the validity of a claim is independent of its origin. So even if things came out of our religious traditions, it doesn't mean that their present justification rests on these religious traditions.

We can also on a purely secular basis come to recognize things like the fact that human suffering is evil. And we can know that pain and suffering is bad if we can know anything at all, and we can come to recognize, without a recourse to God, that we have an obligation to relieve it.

There is a lot more to be said about this, but since I'm running out of time, let me shift to something else. The natural question to ask here is, "Yeah, so, Nielsen, you affirm all those things. You give expression to your deep moral commitment, but you, the bloody secularist that you are, need to explain to us on what basis, what foundation, do you make these affirmations. Aren't these just your personal preferences? Personal preferences you happen to hold, and if you had, after all, different personal preferences, you would have responded in different ways. Come clean. What foundations do you have?"

Well, I would say, like John Rawls and Norman Daniels, for those of you taking courses in ethics, that they rest on my considered judgments that I can fit into what I call wide reflective equilibrium.[6] What do I mean by that big mouthful? I mean that it seems to me that we must start in ethics from considered judgments, like we start from evidence in empirical matters.

Suppose somebody—for example, that fellow over there—is drinking a coke. Whether I have good grounds for believing it to be true would rest on my being able to observe it and, if skeptical, to taste it and so forth and so on. Science isn't just a matter of this, but it is very fundamentally this. Suppose I am skeptical and the chap offers me a taste, but it isn't coke at all but colored water. I drink and just taste that it's in fact water. So I use my senses in a perfectly standard way to test an empirical claim. By the senses you have a way of testing these things. Just as sensory experience is to science, so in morality we start with considered judgments or, if you will, intuitions, where nothing funny epistemologically is built into such talk. They are not, that is, synthetic *a prioris* or any bizarre thing like that. So you start with considered judgments and then you try to get them into a coherent pattern with everything else you know, with the best theories of the function of morality in society, with the best theories we have about human nature, and so forth and so on.[7] And you get this into a coherent package, and in the famous phrase of Otto Neurath, you rebuild the ship at sea. They are justified by putting them into a coherent pattern. And of course, in the process of doing that, some of them drop out.

But some of them won't drop out; not that there wouldn't be a logical possibility of their dropping out, but as a matter of brute fact, some of them will not, and by putting them into this coherent pattern, we will see their underlying rationale. Take something like "It is wrong to torture people." Some beliefs like that cut across cultures; they are not just "part of our tribe." To say it is wrong to torture people would probably never drop out in the reflective equilibrium. I can't realistically conceive of that ever dropping out. But in theory you could allow for the logical possibility of its dropping out. But that is not worrisome. It is *logically* possible that I might start to shrink right before you as well.

So you start with these considered judgments. You get them into a coherent packet with themselves and everything else we know; that's as much—indeed it's *the* only kind—of objectivity I think you can get in ethics. But I want to point out that the religious moralist is exactly in the same boat. He doesn't have any better or any worse objectivity. Because suppose he says, "We should love God," and then further suppose we ask the religious moralist, "Why love God? Why do, or try to do, the will of God? Why obey God's commands?" He basically would have to say, "Because God is the perfect good, and God with His perfect goodness reveals to us the great value of self-respect for people. He shows that people are of infinite precious worth." But even if you accept all this, you could go on to ask, "Why should you care? What difference does it make anyway whether people are of infinite precious worth?" Faced with such questioning, you will finally be pushed into a corner, where you say that "It is important to me that people be regarded as being of infinite worth because I just happen to care about people. It means something to me that people should be treated with respect."[8]

So the religious moralist as well has to rely finally on his considered convictions. So if that is too subjective a ground—that is, ground-ing things in considered judgments in wide reflective equilibrium—then both the religious person and the secular person are in the same boat, though he [the religious person] has all these cosmological claims he might appeal to in backing his moral judgments. Nonetheless, you can ask, "Why pay attention to these cosmological claims?" "It simply," you might respond, "rests on a judgment about the importance of truth." "Why should you," Nietzsche asks, "pay attention to the truth?" You might say, "It is what you ought to do—you must simply pay attention to the truth." So there are these deep considered judg-ments that underlie our moral response, and which we justify by getting them into coherent patterns with everything else we know. That es-capes a kind of relativism and subjectivity, though it doesn't give you an absolutism. If anybody is asking for any kind of form of absolutism, I think they're just kidding themselves. Critical modernity has knocked that out, and post-modernity doesn't even attempt to restore it. Abso-lutism belongs to a premodern view of the world.

Suppose somebody says, "Look, there's one thing you ignore. That simply is the fact that, after all, if there is a God and you don't do what He commands, you will fry in hell. This being so, you had better do what He commands so you won't fry in hell." I regard this as an utterly immoral response. It's just pure prudence masquerading as mo-rality. You want to say, "Look, look, I want to do what is right so I won't burn." But that is hardly a good moral reason for doing anything. It is, as I said, a purely prudential reason, which says very little about the morality of someone that says it. Indeed, if anything, it reveals the per-son's immorality.

I'm not saying that all religious moralists or even most religious moralists appeal to it. I only say that if you try to resist the kind of argument I made by arguing in such a way, as even as good a philoso-pher as Peter Geach did once, that that is a despicable sort of answer.[9] It simply substitutes prudence for morality.

Suppose somebody says, "All the same, there still are needs that a religious morality will answer to that no secular morality can." And that's true. But it also goes the other way around too. There are needs that a secular morality answers to that no religious morality can. And you have to make a kind of trade-off here. If there being a God really is highly implausible, I say, *if* because maybe it isn't, I haven't argued that in this lecture, though I do in the other one, then that poses prob-lems for the religious moralist. If it is highly implausible to believe in God or immortality, then a secular ethic becomes very attractive, particularly if you consider the line of argument I've been giving you with its appeal to considered judgment in the wide reflective equilibrium. This is true because you can see how many of the things that are in a religious ethic, Nietzsche to the contrary notwithstanding, that remain intact in a secular ethic. However, there is Sartre's worry that too many remain intact in a humanist ethic.

However, suppose alternatively that a belief in God is very plausible, then, someone might add, the believer has an additional reason for being a moral person, for treating fellow human beings with equal respect. The additional reason is the fact that God created all persons in His image as infinitely precious, destined to enjoy His fellowship forever. That, by a Jew or a Christian, can be added and that's a plus on the religious moralist side that the secular moralist doesn't have and can't have. And so then the question becomes, Which of these pluses count the most? But that judgment is not independent of your judgment about how plausible it is to believe in God.

But suppose that it isn't very plausible, just suppose. If that is so, one of the things that a secular morality can teach you is that you can give up a belief in God and immortality, but with that there will be a gain in moral integrity, and that is plainly not nothing. There is something to be said for a person who can hold steadily on a course without telling himself or herself fairy tales. Moral integrity, fraternity, and love of humankind are worth subscribing to without a thought to whether or not such virtues will be rewarded in heaven.

Notes

1. I develop these considerations in considerable detail in my *Ethics Without God* (Buffalo, N.Y.: Prometheus Books, 1989) and in my *God and the Grounding of Morality* (Ottawa: University of Ottawa Press, 1991).
2. Robert Merrihew Adams, "A Modified Divine Command Theory of Ethical Wrongness" in *Philosophy of Religion*, Louis P. Pojman, ed. (Belmont, Calif.: Wadsworth, 1987), 525–537.
3. Emil Brunner, *The Divine Imperative*, trans. by Olive Wyon (London: Lutterworth Press, 1974). Note particularly Chap. 9. Here, unlike in Adams, we get the full-bodied thing and it does definitely collide with my account.
4. John Hick, "Belief and Life: The Fundamental Nature of the Christian Ethic," *Encounter* 20:4 (1959), 494–516.
5. See the essays of Kurt Baier and Kai Nielsen in *The Meaning of Life*, E. D. Klemke, ed. (New York: Oxford University Press, 1981).
6. John Rawls, *A Theory of Justice* (Cambridge, Mass.: Harvard University

Press, 1971), 19–21, 48–51, 577–587; "The Independence of Moral The-ory," *Proceedings and Addresses of the American Philosophical Association* 47 (1974/75), 7–10; Norman Daniels, "Reflective Equilibrium and Archi-medean Points," *Canadian Journal of Philosophy* 10 (1980), 83–103; Kai Nielsen, "Searching for an Emancipatory Perspective: Wide Reflective Equilibrium and the Hermeneutical Circle" in *Anti-Foundationalism and Practical Reasoning,* Evan Simpson, ed. (Edmonton, Alberta: Academic Publishing, 1987), 143–164; "In Defense of Wide Reflective Equilibrium" in *Ethics and Justification,* Douglas Odegard, ed. (Edmonton, Alberta: Aca-demic Publishing, 1988), 19–37; "On Transforming Philosophy," *Dalhousie Review* 67:4 (Winter 1987/88), 439–456.

7. Kai Nielsen, "Teaching Moral Philosophy: Method in Moral Philosophy and the Influence of John Rawls," *Aita* 9.(1982); "Reflective Equilibrium and the Transformation of Philosophy," *Metaphilosophy* 20:3/4 (July/October 1989), 235–246.

8. Kai Nielsen, *Why Be Moral?* (Buffalo, N.Y.: Prometheus Books, 1989).

9. Peter Geach, *God and the Soul* (London: Routledge and Kegan Paul, 1969). For a judicious treatment of immorality, see Terence Penelhum, *Survival and Disembodied Existence* (London: Routledge and Kegan Paul, 1970).

MORELAND: To say something meaningful on this topic in fifteen minutes is roughly like trying to define the universe and give two examples. It's a difficult topic, and I'm not going to respond directly to a lot of the things Professor Nielsen said, since I was informed about this relatively late. Instead, I've got my own thoughts I'd like to share. Later I will interact with some of the things Professor Nielsen has said, and perhaps that will give you two different points of view on the subject about which you can ask questions.

To begin with, let me say that I do not hold to a Barthian-divine command theory. That is not my view. I part company with those theists who hold more extreme forms of voluntarism.

To push the boat off shore, let me begin by saying something about the genetic fallacy which Professor Nielsen mentioned. The genetic fallacy is the fallacy of faulting the rational justification of something because of where it came from. For example, it would be troublesome to me if you said that I can't know two and two is equal to four because I learned it from Mrs. Fred, my second grade teacher, and she was an evil person. That wouldn't be a very good argument to raise against my mathematical knowledge claim.

On the other hand, there are occasions where the origin of something does serve to count against it. Illustration: You're driving down a road, and you claim to see water in front of you. Your evidence for that would be experiences that you were having at the time, namely, experiences of a certain wetness down the road. However, we could have a relevant background theory to this claim that would tend to defeat it. Suppose that it happened to be in the desert, it was 95 degrees outside, and what was causing this to happen was light waves reflecting on the highway, and thus, you were experiencing a mirage. This background theory would give an alternate account of the causal origin of your experience of "water." This background theory would serve as a defeater. It would tend to defeat your claim that there really was water out there, and it would make more reasonable the belief that it was merely a mirage.

I think the very same thing is going on in the justification of morality. I don't know that Nielsen necessarily tried to do this, but many atheists say something like this: "Look, let's keep the world totally constant, remove nothing whatsoever, and then just assume God doesn't exist. Well, look here, God doesn't make any difference for morality."

Well, of course, if you stipulate by definition that you are going to hold the world constant and you're just not going to consider God, obviously, you've got two equivalent situations and appealing to God isn't going to make any difference. But this way of setting up the problem does not really bring into focus what most theists believe to be the relationship between God and morality. A better way to characterize the problem is to liken the atheist/theist debate about the nature and existence of morality to a situation where you are testing rival scientific hypotheses regarding a range of conceptual or empirical problems. Those of you who have had any study in confirmation theory know that if you have a range of phenomena to be explained, you try to determine which of two or more theories makes better sense or makes those phenomena more plausible, more reasonable, and less puzzling.[1] That to me seems to be the proper way to characterize the difference between a secular and a theistic morality.

On an evolutionary secular scenario, this is basically the most plausible current background theory. Human beings are nothing special. The universe came from a Big Bang. It evolved to us through a blind process of chance and necessity. There is nothing intrinsically valuable about human beings in terms of having moral non-natural properties. The same processes that coughed up human beings coughed up amoebas; there is nothing special about being human.[2] The view that being human is special is guilty of specieism, an unjustifiable bias toward one's own species. The same process that coughed us up is eventually going to swallow us up, and in fact there is a good chance we will evolve toward higher forms of life sometime in the future.[3] There is no point to history. There are no such things as non-natural properties or moral properties.[4]

Now, the question that needs to be asked is this: In a universe of that sort, what possible reason could be given for why I should be moral? Keep in mind, the question Why I should be moral? is not asked from within the moral point of view. It's not saying, "Give me a moral reason for being moral." It is asking, "Why as a part of my rational life plan, when I'm trying to consider the rational way I wish to live, why should I include in that life plan the dictates of morality?"[5]

Now, consider the following sentences: "Red is a color." "This ball is red." These are, at least, *prima facie* subject-predicate sentences. And they have ontological implications about the way the world is. If you believe that "Red is a color" is true, or that "This ball is red" is true, then you hold that there are certain entities which exist in the world, namely redness in this case, and perhaps what is called the second order, or higher order universal, color.

Similarly, consider the claims "Kindness is a virtue;" "Humans have value;" "Persons have value." Or, as Roderick Chisholm says, "Mercy as such is good."[6] In spite of what Nielsen says, these are synthetic *a priori* propositions. They are standard subject-predicate propositions, where at least on the surface, it seems like, just as "Red is a color" commits one to the existence of red and color, "Kindness is a virtue" commits one to the existence of kindness and virtue. "Humans have value" commits one to the existence of there being such a thing as human nature, which is not merely a biological natural kind, but has moral properties as well, as David Wiggins has argued.[7] "Mercy as such is good" commits one to non-natural properties that do exist and are part of the furniture of the universe.

Now the question for any view regarding the nature and justification of morality is this: Is that view adequate, and if so, what general metaphysical worldview must we embrace to render intelligible a particular conception of morality? Well, let me try to give you three answers to that question. As far as I can tell, the first one is not held by Nielsen. I think the second one is, and the third one would be a theistic answer.

The first answer I call the *immanent purpose view*. According to this view, the scientific account of the origin and nature of life is not all there is to the universe. In addition to natural properties, there are non-natural properties that exist as a part of reality. So there is such a thing as goodness. There are moral properties, value properties, and these things are, let's just say, Platonic forms. So why should I be moral? Well, because there are these things called moral properties that exist, and it's irrational to deny their existence.

What is the purpose of life? In this view the purpose of life involves trying to live for these intrinsically valuable states of affairs that can be realized in human life. For example, it's intrinsically valuable, according to the immanent purpose view, to have kindness, to achieve intellectual virtue and knowledge, to have wisdom, and so on. These would be states of affairs that are intrinsically valuable and worthwhile, and meaning in life comes from trying to embody these properties even though these properties themselves do not come from God. They're just there, that's all, part of the ultimate furniture of the universe.

I have several problems with this view. For one thing, to have these sorts of properties existing in a Godless universe would be odd and puzzling, to say the least. Now this isn't a knock-down argument, and I can only appeal to your basic intuitions on this question. But it does seem to me that to hold that moral properties, or non-natural properties, are modes of existence of an impersonal universe is less reasonable than seeing them as modes of existence of a personal universe.[8]

The late J. L. Mackie, who in my opinion may be the best philosophical atheist of this century, agrees with me on this point. And he made the following statement: "Moral properties constitute so odd a cluster of properties and relations that they are most unlikely to have arisen in the ordinary course of events without an all-powerful god to create them."[9] Mackie's solution is to just deny the existence of these properties. And he goes on to argue that all we can do is to create values subjectively; you just have to choose what you want to be.[10]

Many atheists have agreed with that. They've said there is no essence to man ready-made for him; there are no moral properties in the universe. What you choose to do is what you find worthwhile. I think we're a bit closer to Nielsen's view at this point, and we'll touch on this alternative in just a moment. So first of all, in light of the immanent purpose view, it seems odd that these properties would exist.

Second, let's grant that they do exist. It is nonetheless odd that they would have anything whatsoever to do with human beings. Why would these moral properties ever refer to or supervene upon a short-lived little cluster of creatures that were a result of a blindness process on a tiny dot hurling through space?

Two scientists, Barrow and Tipler, recently wrote a book called *The Anthropic Cosmological Principle*.[11] They believe that there are these moral properties and that there is something in the world which is intrinsically valuable. The thing that's intrinsically valuable, they claim, is an idealized form of DNA molecule that the evolutionary process will ultimately realize in the universe. All intermediate forms on the way to that idealized state are means to ends, not ends in themselves. So from amoebas to men, you have a means to the end of trying to realize what is really the good in itself; that's this idealized DNA molecule.

It does seem to me to be a bit anthropocentric for an advocate of the immanent purpose view to single out human beings in this process and say, "Oh my, isn't it interesting that the moral universe intersects with the physical universe at just the point where human beings emerged, or at least largely at the point where human beings emerged."[12] I, for one, don't know why, if the evolutionary process continues to go on, we won't find other forms of life years down the road which will have more value than we have, and we will stand to them as primitive life forms stand to us. So it seems odd to me that these properties would ever uniquely supervene upon human beings in the first place, and it would be hard to justify the claim that all are of equal moral value.

Third, it seems to me odd in the immanent purpose view of human beings that people could have one of the necessary preconditions for being moral agents in the first place. I believe it is important to have freedom of the will in order for there to be such a thing as human moral action or moral responsibility. And by freedom of the will I mean what Thomas Reid called agent causality.[13] This includes the notion of incompatibilism. I know that perhaps some of you here disagree with this view, but I for one do not believe that freedom and determinism are compatable because, for one thing, compatibilism is really determinism under another name. It reduces to a form of determinism, and it only shifts the causal factors from those outside the "person" to those inside the "person." And this shift doesn't leave any room for a real agent to act responsibly.[14]

If we are mere creatures of matter, or even if we have mental properties or events which interact via state-to-state causation, and this Platonic moral universe exists and supervenes upon humans, then the immanent purpose view still has this difficulty. It is hard to see how we could ever have the requisite freedom to be morally responsible. Physicalist Paul Churchland has made the following point: "The important point about the standard evolutionary story is that the human species and all of its features are the wholly physical outcome of a purely physical process. If this is the correct account of our origin, then there seems neither need nor room to fit any nonphysical substances or properties into our theoretical accounts of ourselves. We are creatures of matter."[15] If we are creatures of matter, it seems difficult to me to make sense out of how I could have freedom of the will. And that, I claim, is a necessary precondition for me even taking upon myself the moral point of view.[16]

For these and some other reasons I could mention, I find the immanent purpose view highly implausible and unlikely.

But there is a second view, and this is more in keeping with what I take Professor Nielsen to hold, at least it's in keeping with some of his writings. He may have changed his views. You can correct me if you have. I call this view *optimistic humanism.*

According to this view, there are no moral facts. There are no moral truths to be discovered in an old-fashioned correspondent sense of the word "truth." And we can't ground morality in any kind of sense of pure reason or rational deliberation without sentiment and without what he calls "wide reflective equilibrium." And remember, wide reflective equilibrium, as John Rawls uses it, is not just theory of epistemic justification; in other words, it's not just a theory of how we justify our beliefs. It is an ontological theory about what truth is. It is a coherence theory, not of justification only, but of truth. Reflective equilibrium *creates* our moral views; it does not merely justify them.[17]

Now one problem with a coherence theory of truth is this: You can have two coherent webs of beliefs that are both internally consistent. One of these systems of beliefs can say that *p* is legitimate and the other one can entail that not-*p* is legitimate. And according to a coherency theory of truth, both *p* and not-*p* would be correct. The standard objection against coherent theories of truth is that it removes the connection between propositions and a full blown, realist, mind- or theory- or language-independent world. You can have more than one system that's internally consistent; one can imply *p* and the other not-*p*. And according to that view, we would be in the position of saying both were true.

I might add as well that it seems to me that optimistic humanism tends toward formal autonomy-based ethics. Stanley Hauerwas at Duke has argued against such an autonomy-based ethic, because it reduces to a minimalist ethic wherein the good is ultimately what I competently and autonomously choose for myself, provided, of course, that I do not harm or offend others. This may be a necessary condition for an act of mine to be moral, but it is not sufficient; that the good is what I choose for myself is too empty. It is too formal to get us very far, and what we really need is a substantive theory of the good life. We require a substantive vision of the moral life to give content to formal principles of morality. And in my opinion, this substantive vision of the moral life is embodied in Jesus of Nazareth. Christianity does not leave morality at the abstract level of principles. Moral virtue and vision is embodied in Jesus of Nazareth and others in the Scriptures. According to a Christian view of the world, virtue properties exist and can be instanced in persons, and virtues and vices can be epistemologically distinguished.

But the optimistic humanist view will have none of that. There are no irreducibly non-natural properties, and we have to engage in a coherence reflective equilibrium where we create values by coherence. We don't discover them.

Second, why is it that someone should choose the moral point of view? As Nielsen has said elsewhere, choosing to embrace the moral point of view, vis-à-vis some form of private personal egoism, is arbitrary and subjective.[18] It is not a rational decision. One simply has to choose what kind of life he wants to live and make his choice.

Now consider what Nielsen claimed in his presentation. When he talked earlier, he said, "We have to choose our vision of life, and we can have plenty of things that we find worthwhile even if God does not exist."[19] Of course, the kinds of things he mentioned were the kinds of things that most people already know within theism are reasonable, like friendship, pursuing love, and so on.

The radical nature of this thesis, however, is that if there is no moral truth to be discovered and if I have to simply choose the moral point of view because that type of life is what I find worthwhile for myself, then the decision is arbitrary, rationally speaking. And the difference between, say, Mother Teresa and Hitler is roughly the same as the difference between whether I want to be a trumpet player or a baseball player. There is no rational factor or truth of the matter at stake. There are no moral truths that can be discovered to adjudicate between the two choices. I have to just decide my form of life.

This type of thing has surfaced recently in a book by James Rachels called *The End of Life*.[20] Rachels says that we don't need purpose in the sense of an over-arching objective purpose *to* life, but we can have purpose *in* life, as Nielsen says. And he means by that "subjective satisfaction," things that we find worthwhile to us.[21] Now if this is true, what's the difference, let's say, between becoming a doctor and feeding the poor, and sitting around pinching heads off rats or being a Sisyphus and pushing a rock up and down a hill, or giving your time to flipping tiddlywinks? There is no difference since each of these options could be satisfying and worthwhile to someone.

Or consider the case of a person called the Texas Burn Victim. There was a man who was burned in Texas named Donald C. Donald C. was burned in an accident; he was rehabilitated; but he was confined to a wheelchair. He could lead a normal life, only he was not able to be a ladies' man and go to rodeos, activities which were satisfying to him. He wanted to commit suicide. And according to James Rachels, he should have been allowed to do just that.

Why should he have been allowed to commit suicide? Because his life no longer had any point to it. Why didn't it have any point? Because he could no longer do the things that were worthwhile from his point of view. Well, what was worthwhile from his point of view? Chasing women and going to rodeos.

Now it seems to me that it's possible to trivialize your own life by giving yourself to things that are inherently trivial. If a person wanted to be the best male prostitute he could be, and if that was his subjective choice of how he wanted to live his life—that was his vision of the good life, as it were—it doesn't seem to me that the optimistic humanist view provides a sufficiently robust framework for criticizing that type of choice. Because, after all, a person could find trivial actions worthwhile from his perspective, and, therefore, this person's actions would be just as morally significant as the deeds of someone like a Mother Teresa who gives herself to helping other people. Nielsen has said time and again, and he's right, that atheists can in fact do good moral things. But what I'm arguing is, What would be the point? Why should I do these things if they are not satisfying to me or if they are not in my interests?

This is a serious problem. It does not occur within theism, but it does occur within the optimistic humanist version of atheism. If there is no human nature which has intrinsic moral value as Nielsen says elsewhere, the question can arise: "Here I am with my money. Why should I give it to help the poor instead of keeping it and having a little better life for myself?" Well, a response might be that doing morally virtuous acts is what it means to take the moral point of view. This means that you universalize your judgments, you treat others as ends in themselves and yourself as an end in itself, you seek to promote the good, and so on.

But the problem is, Why should I take the moral point of view? "Well, what if you were in his shoes?" the answer could come back. But you see, I'm not in his shoes. "Well, if you were in his shoes, you would want him to do the same to you." Yes, but the difficulty is, you're already operating from within the moral point of view, and my question is, Why should I adopt the moral point of view as a part of my rational life plan? That's the very thing at issue.

Furthermore, why should I care for future generations, or why should I give to help the poor? I happen to like mice. Why shouldn't I give my money to caring for mice instead of caring for the poor? Well, you might say, "Human beings have certain properties that make them more valuable than mice, let's say rationality." I don't know if Nielsen would make that response, but if someone did, there is a difficulty. Because, after all, some people are more rational than others. And does that mean that we ought to help feed, let's say, university professors, but not plumbers, because they have more of the property of rationality?

Well, one way to go at this is just to say it's egoistically better to adopt the moral point of view. After all, it's better to live in community with other people rather than live a nasty, brutish, short life, and so I give up some of my rights because it is in my self-interest to do so. I will be egoistically altruistic. I will do things for you out of an egoistic motivation and because of an egoistic justification.

Now, apart from the fact that this appears to be a contradiction to me—ethical egoism appears to contradict the moral point of view—this type of recommendation suffers from the very same objection that Nielsen himself has raised against the Christian notion of hell. He said if a person merely embraces God out of a desire to cover his cosmic rear end and to avoid getting flames on it, then he is guilty of egoism.

The very same thing seems to me to be true of someone who is saying, "Now I think I'll consider the moral point of view. Why should I adopt it? Well because it's in my best interest to do so. And in fact I will adopt the moral point of view except in those cases when it's not in my best interest to do so." It doesn't seem to me that optimistic humanism can offer a good reason why one ought not to do that, rationally speaking. The point is that on the optimistic humanist view, we now substitute subjective satisfaction for objective value and meaning.

I've offered two solutions. I don't have much time, so let me say a brief word about *Christian theism*. Christian theism is a background theory that makes the existence and knowability of morality more likely than does the background theory of atheism. Morality is more at home and less ad hoc in a theistic universe than in an atheistic universe. This is because God is a postulated entity who is Himself good. He has the property of goodness. Men are made in His image and to be a human being is to be a member of a natural kind that is not merely defined biologically, but is also defined in terms of moral properties. I have intrinsic value or worth as I reflect the intrinsic value of God and His worth.

Second, I believe that Christian theism helps explain the knowability of morality in a number of ways. I can't get into this much, perhaps in the question and answer period we can, but Christian theism helps make sense out of how my moral faculties could have come about in the first place. How is it that humans can have intuitional insight into the nature of morality?[22] God has created us to know moral values.

In summary then, Nielsen says something like this: "The theists are on a ship, and they claim there's meaning in life on this ship because there's a point at the end of the voyage. We are going to help lepers on the shore. So along the way we've got meaning because there's a goal we're heading toward that's meaningful. And furthermore, there's meaning in life and there's morality because we are ends in ourselves, because we have goodness in us, moral properties which reflect the moral properties of our creator.

"Never mind about that," he says. "Let's suppose that we are on another ship and call it the Titanic. The ship isn't going anywhere, just as long as it doesn't crash in the next few hours; let's let it crash, say, seventy years from now. I can still find plenty of things that are worthwhile from my point of view. I can visit these people in the sick bay of the ship. I can read Plato in the library of the ship, and I can do all kinds of wonderful things."

Of course, the problem is, Why should I do these things as opposed to, say, pushing a rock around the boat or spending my time staring at mice in my cabin quarters? It doesn't seem to me that there would be much difference. Furthermore, why should I worry about the people on this ship instead of, say, the mosquitoes, the orangutans, or some other life form? I am not denying, by the way, that theism has within itself a theory of animal rights. It does. But I am denying that human beings are on the same moral plane as animals. In the optimistic humanist view, it is difficult to see how you could make such a distinction.

Notes

1. This type of reasoning is often used in science and is called "inference to the best explanation." When two or more hypotheses can offer some type of explanation for a phenomenon, it still may be the case that one hypothesis best explains the phenomenon given the evidence available. The hypothesis does not logically entail the phenomenon (as would be the case if a covering law model of explanation were used—e.g., this copper rod expands when heated because all metal rods expand when heated; this copper rod is a metal rod; therefore, this copper rod expands when heated). Nor is the hypothesis a generalization formed by inductive enumeration (raven[1] is black; raven[2] is black; . . . raven[n] is black; therefore, all ravens are black). Regarding the presence of morality in the universe, a phenomenon best explained by theism, the argument is roughly that our common sense moral intuitions imply irreducible, nonnatural value properties, a correspondence theory of moral truth, and moral obligations that seem to require duties that often go against my own best interests. These features of morality are best explained by some form of theism (or Platonism, which I believe to be a form of theism) vis-à-vis a naturalistic world view.
2. While Nielsen is somewhat uncomfortable with this view, he has stated that it may be justifiable to, say, transfer an organ from a defective newborn to a higher primate who has a relatively normal existence. His point is that

there is nothing intrinsic about being a human being that gives humans intrinsic worth compared to animals. James Rachels has made the same point. According to Rachels, there is nothing special about being a human being. (He mistakenly makes this point by saying that there is nothing special about having biological life. But he begs a serious question here by identifying being a human with merely possessing biological life; but a human is a member of the natural kind "being human," which has moral and other nonbiological properties—e.g., normative rationality—so a human is more than a biological organism.) What is important, says Rachels, is that a living thing has a biographical life—that is, a living thing has desires, interests, goals, etc. that matter from its own point of view. Rachels goes on to argue that animals have biographical lives and certain humans do not (e.g., those in persistent vegetative states), and therefore, these animals are more important from a moral point of view than these humans. See James Rachels, *The End of Life* (Oxford: Oxford University Press, 1986). For a critique of Rachels, see J. P. Moreland, "James Rachels and the Active Euthanasia Debate," *Journal of the Evangelical Theological Society* 31 (Mar. 1988), 81–90, or my review of *The End of Life* in *The Thomist* 53 (Oct. 1989). See also, J. P. Moreland, Norman Geisler, *The Life and Death Debate: Moral Issues of Our Time* (Westport, CT: Greenwood Publishing Group, Praeger Books, 1990), chapter 4.

3. A number of issues are currently being debated in bioethics. One of them involves genetic engineering and screening. It may become possible to perfect various aspects of human beings and, for example, to produce more tall or blond people. Some ethicists believe that the morality of these activities turns on what kind of organism we want to be and whether people with certain features are more important and valuable than people without those features. This problem illustrates the difficulty with all attempts to ground moral value on some property or social utility that can be quantified—e.g., rationality, the capacity to communicate or have a self-concept, physical ability. These can be possessed to a lesser or greater degree. And if moral value accrues to a thing because it possesses one of these properties, then it is hard to see why genetically perfected future life forms would not be more valuable than present life forms, if future life forms possessed the relevant properties to a greater degree than present life forms. For that matter, the same problem arises with regard to, say, more intelligent people compared to less intelligent people. One can respond by saying that it is the capacity for the property that matters and not the amount of the property actualized (e.g., rationality). Unfortunately, this response will not work. Different people have different capacities for rationality. The only way this response can succeed is for it to claim that *all* humans equally possess, or ought to possess, these capacities or properties. But this move implicitly utilizes the notion of a natural kind, *being*

human, which gives intrinsic value to all members of this natural kind in virtue of membership alone, not in virtue of the degree that certain properties have been actualized. But this raises the question, Why is being a human being something morally unique and special? Christian theism answers this question by saying that humans are made in the *imago dei.*

4. It would be possible to be an atheist with regard to God but a Platonist with regard to moral properties. See Panayot Butchvarov, *Skepticism in Ethics* (Bloomington, Ind.: Indiana University Press, 1989). This view is what I call the immanent purpose view and will be discussed later. But for now it should be pointed out that most thinkers in the history of the West have seen a family resemblance between Platonism and theism; indeed, many have seen Platonism as a form of theism. See George Mavrodes, "Religion and the Queerness of Morality," in *Rationality, Religious Belief, and Moral Commitment,* Robert Audi and William J. Wainwright, eds. (Ithaca, N.Y.: Cornell University Press, 1986), 213–26.

5. If one accepts the "dictates of morality," one accepts the moral point of view—one subscribes to normative, moral judgments about actions, things (e.g., persons, the environment), motives; one is willing to universalize one's judgments; one seeks to form those judgments in a free, unbiased, enlightened way; and one seeks to promote the good. It should be clear that this understanding of the moral point of view is merely formal. It may, at best, give necessary conditions for something to count as moral, but it does not give much material content to the moral life itself, and it cannot serve as action guides for real moral decisions. Stanley Hauerwas has argued, persuasively in my opinion, that real moral dilemmas—e.g., the morality of "rational suicide"—cannot be decided without appealing to broad world view considerations that answer factual and moral questions such as: Is life a gift? What is the point of life, pain, suffering? What kind of community would value a profession like medicine? Do I exist as an atomistic individual with individual liberties only, or am I also a member of a moral community? Hauerwas goes on to argue that Christian theism gives morally and intellectually satisfying answers to these broad world view questions and, thus, provides material content to the moral point of view. See Stanley Hauerwas, *Suffering Presence: Theological Reflections on Medicine, the Mentally Handicapped, and the Church* (Notre Dame, Ind.: Notre Dame Press, 1986). Cf. Daniel Callahan, "Minimalist Ethics," *Hastings Center Report* 11 (Oct. 1981), 19–25.

6. Roderick Chisholm, *A Theory of Knowledge* (Englewood Cliffs, N. J.: Prentice-Hall, 2nd ed., 1977), 123–26. Cf. his *Bretano and Intrinsic Value* (Cambridge: Cambridge University Press, 1986); "Verstehen: The Epistemological Question," in *The Foundations of Knowing* (Minneapolis: University of Minnesota Press, 1982), 86–94. This last article discusses problems associated with our knowledge of other minds, and it is also a

good discussion of the fruitfulness of the notion of "intuitive understanding," which is the sort of rational capacity that is (or, perhaps, contra Kripke, *must* be) involved in our knowledge of synthetic *a priori* propositions.

7. David Wiggins, *Sameness and Substance* (Cambridge, Mass.: Harvard University Press, 1980), 152–89.

8. Cf. George Mavrodes, "Religion and the Queerness of Morality"; Robert M. Adams, *The Virtue of Faith and Other Essays in Philosophical Theology* (Oxford: Oxford University Press, 1987), 97–163.

9. J. L. Mackie, *The Miracle of Theism* (Oxford: Clarendon Press, 1982), 115. Mackie utilizes a "supervenience" relation to explain the way moral properties (e.g., intrinsic goodness) relate to natural properties (e.g., various properties constituting what it is to be human). Just as wetness supervenes upon hydrogen and oxygen when they come together in a certain way to form H_2O, so moral properties supervene upon natural states of affairs when they are structured in certain ways (e.g., the structuring of materials to form a human being). Recently, Panayot Butchvarov has questioned this use of supervenience and has argued that the relationship between goodness and certain states of affairs (e.g., knowledge, acts of kindness, happiness, and, perhaps, being human) is a genus/species relationship that obtains between higher and lower order universals. Thus, goodness relates to, say, friendship like color relates to redness or shape relates to triangularity. See Butchvarov, *Skepticism in Ethics*, 53, 59–81. Butchvarov's Platonist view does not affect my argument, however, for one can still ask why it is that (1) moral properties exist in the first place; (2) why the higher order universal goodness has being human, friendship, and so on as lower order universals; (3) why goodness and its lower order universals were ever instanced in the actual world (this differs from point one, for a universal can exist without being instanced in a particular—e.g., according to Platonism, redness could exist with the existence of red things); (4) why goodness (rationally) should be pursued when it is not in my self-interest to do so; (5) why humans could have the faculties necessary for intuitional knowledge of goodness and its determinate universals like friendship; (6) why we desire the good in the first place; (7) why the good is often within our ability to do. Though these questions are difficult for all world views, Christian theism does have the resources to answer them. But Platonism would seem to posit these features as brute givens in the world and leave it at that.

10. Elsewhere, Nielsen has argued that no ultimate rational justification can be given for adopting the moral point of view over a rational life plan that is lived according to some form of egoism. Nielsen claims that we must simply decide how we should act and what kind of persons we want to be. Reason does not help us here. See Kai Nielsen, "Why Should I Be Moral?

Revisited," *American Philosophical Quarterly* 21 (Jan. 1984), 81–91. The radical nature of this position is masked by our sociological and psychological milieu wherein we still feel that people will, in fact, choose to adopt the moral point of view, and we feel that when they do so, they have adopted a rationally superior way of life. But if Nielsen is correct, the feelings involved in this way of looking at the choice between egoism and the moral point of view will have to be revised. For the decision to be a Mother Teresa, an honest businesswoman, or a faithful father instead of a Hitler, a lying businesswoman, or a faithless father is not a rational decision at all. It is very much like the decision to be a Royals fan instead of a Cardinal fan, or to go to McDonald's instead of Burger King.

11. John Barrow and Frank Tipler, *The Anthropic Cosmological Principle* (Oxford: Clarendon Press, 1986), 658–77.

12. Christian theism does imply that animals in particular, and the environment in general, have value. But Christian theism also implies that humans have special significance in creation. However, in the absence of some form of essentialism coupled with the existence of irreducible non-natural properties (humans are members of the natural kind—humankind—which is constituted, in part, by moral properties), it is hard to see why (1) higher primates with biographical lives (interests, desires, etc.) are not more valuable than some defective humans; (2) advanced creatures on other planets (or superior creatures shaped by genetic engineering) would not be of more value than humans; (3) some humans with more of a given capacity, say rationality, are more valuable than those with less of that capacity. In this regard, see Helga Kuhse and Peter Singer, *Should the Baby Live?* (Oxford: Oxford University Press, 1985), especially Chapter 6. By the way, Ernst Mayr and other thinkers have argued that essentialism is incompatible with evolutionary naturalism. I am inclined to agree. Essentialism may be logically consistent with evolutionary naturalism (one can hold to both ideas without affirming a contradiction), but the latter does tend to count against the former. In my opinion, fundamental moral intuitions imply some form of essentialism, and thus, these moral intuitions provide external conceptual problems, which count against evolutionary naturalism. For more on the nature of external conceptual problems and scientific theory assessment, see J. P. Moreland, *Christianity and the Nature of Science* (Grand Rapids, Mich.: Baker, 1989).

13. See William L. Rowe, "Two Concepts of Freedom," *Proceedings of the American Philosophical Association* Supplementary Volume 61 (Sept. 1987), 43–64. Cf. Steward C. Goetz, "A Noncausal Theory of Agency," *Philosophical and Phenomenological Research* 49 (Dec. 1988), 303–316. Roderick Chisholm uses the term "immanent causation." See his *On Metaphysics* (Minneapolis: University of Minnesota Press, 1989), 3–15.

14. What is at stake here is the importance of the metaphysics of substance for

the mind/body problem. Agent causation is most compatible with a substance view of the self wherein the self is an immaterial substance with causal powers and which acts without prior states of the self constituting necessary and sufficient conditions to determine all of one's actions. For a good treatment of this view of the self as a substance, see Richard J. Connell, *Substance and Modern Science* (Notre Dame, Ind.: University of Notre Dame Press, 1988).

15. Paul Churchland, *Matter and Consciousness* (Cambridge, Mass.: MIT Press, 1984), 21.

16. I have argued elsewhere that epistemic responsibility (e.g., given such and such evidence, I ought to see that P is more reasonable than Q) and moral responsibility presuppose substance dualism, and that the existence of finite mental substances is best explained by postulating God as the cause of finite minds. This could be called the argument from the queerness of the mental. The existence of mental substances is odd if the world came about according to the standard naturalist story, but it is not odd if Christian theism is true. See J. P. Moreland, *Scaling the Secular City* (Grand Rapids, Mich.: Baker, 1987), 77–103.

17. See note 5 for more on this point.

18. Kai Nielsen, "Why Should I Be Moral? Revisited."

19. One is reminded here of philosophers like Sartre who use certain cases to illustrate the fact that we are totally free to decide what is the right thing to do and reason is of no help here. Thus, a man who is torn between going off to war to fight against the Germans vs. staying at home and caring for his mother is faced with a decision for which there is no right or wrong answer, no advice, nothing in advance to help him decide. But the case gets its intuitive appeal because it already has built into it a set of alternatives that we antecedently know to be fairly balanced moral options. The case would be far less persuasive as an illustration of the need to simply choose what to do or what kind of person to be if the choices were between, say molesting one's daughter for personal gratification vs. refraining from such an act. This choice is not an arbitrary one from a rational point of view. The second choice is morally correct, and if one does not recognize this, then one's moral knowledge is defective and, thus, one is not fulfilling one's epistemic duty if one does not see this. Human rationality includes the capacity to have moral insight regarding moral truths. Such a view of rationality may not be in keeping with a strictly naturalistic account of rationality (e.g., one can recognize means to ends, and there may be some ends all humans, in fact, desire given that they are not experiencing serious psychological problems). But why should we limit our view of human rationality to naturalistic rationality? Butchvarov notes that some philosophers dismiss this view of moral properties and moral rationality by "arguing" that it is somehow obsolete. He correctly points out that this

type of "argument" belongs in Detroit, not in philosophy. See Butchvarov, *Skepticism in Ethics*, 36.

20. Rachels, *The End of Life*, 35–59.

21. Cf. A. J. Ayer, *The Central Questions of Philosophy* (New York: Holt, Rinehart, and Winston, 1973), 233–35; Paul Kurtz, *In Defense of Secular Humanism* (Buffalo: Prometheus, 1983), 153–68.

22. Richard Swinburne has argued that the origin of the soul and the precise nature of its cognitive and sensory functioning are issues that lie beyond the bound of science and evolutionary theory to explain. See Richard Swinburne, *The Evolution of the Soul* (Oxford: Clarendon, 1986), 174–99. Swinburne's point could be applied with equal, and perhaps greater force, to the human capacity for moral intuition and knowledge. If such a capacity is a normative nonnatural one—that is, if humans have the ability for rational intuitive knowledge of certain moral truths, then it is hard to see how such an ability could even be defined by science, much less explained.

More Questions and Answers

10

POJMAN: Thank you, both of you. We have about twelve minutes or thirteen minutes for questions. I know both speakers would like to, or Dr. Nielsen especially being first would like to, respond to the last paper or talk, but we're going to just open it up to you. Please address your question to one of the speakers, or to both of them if you have a general question. Are there questions?

QUESTION: Dr. Nielsen, how would you respond to Dr. Moreland's statement about covering your cosmic theories?

NIELSEN: We might ask, rather more earthly, how would I respond about covering my cosmic rear end?

I found Professor Moreland's remarks interesting. There's a million ways I would want to respond, but I will limit myself to one very brief way. As he himself recognized but then seemed to forget, there is a great difference between asking the question, Why should I be moral? and asking a *moral* question.[1] A question like, Why should I be moral? is like asking, What's valuable about science? which is not itself a scientific question. Similarly when you ask, Why be moral? you can't give a moral reason or you beg the question. And so you have to give a non-moral reason.

And exactly the same problem emerges for the religious moralist when we, as I pointed out and Moreland didn't respond to, ask exactly the same question of the religious moralist. Why should you pay attention to the commands of God? In both cases, once you're outside of morality, the only thing you can give is a kind of prudential answer. But for me it is tremendously important, and I think he misses this, to distinguish the questions you ask as a moral being from purely prudential questions that might be asked outside of morality—might, that is, be asked even when we are not resolved to act or reason in accordance with the moral point of view. This remains so even if becoming a moral being is *finally* just a matter, as I am inclined to believe, of one having to commit oneself here.[2]

Finally, at a certain point, you have to commit yourself. I think the religious person and the secular person are in exactly the same boat. Once you've committed yourself, then the morality you adopt has a certain structure, and it's no longer just a matter of choice. There is nothing in my views, especially my views in the last fifteen years, which says that moral claims are just choices, like, say, for A. J. Ayer or Axel Hägerström. I said, like Rawls, that there is a set of considered judgments which are *our* considered judgments, not just mine but yours as well.[3] They're in our culture, though not just in our culture. We start with these considered judgments, and we try to justify them in wide reflective equilibrium. The ones we cannot get into such as equilibrium—that we cannot reflectively sustain—we reject.

By the way, neither Rawls nor I regard this as an ontological theory about what truth is. Rawls's book, a six-hundred-page book, if you look in the index, has no reference to truth.[4] We completely put aside all metaethical and ontological questions about the logical status of values. They may have those nonnatural properties. Moreland talks about them, but I think that is highly implausible. They may be more like Mackie's understanding, who takes them to be projections of emotional states. Both Rawls and I just put those questions aside. We're concerned with the justification of moral beliefs, practices, and principles, so we don't try to say what truth is, whether there's moral truth or anything. We say here's a bunch of moral judgments that a culture shares and that I may or may not share. And we see whether those fit together with everything else we know and match with our considered convictions.[5]

And I want to claim that's the most plausible kind of justification you can get in the domain of morality.[6] Moreover, there is nothing subjective, nothing individualistic, about it. The analogy with being on a ship that has to sink has little point. We have to die. But that doesn't make our present moral arrangements less meaningful or less objective. To even think in terms of that analogy is already to be into a religious point of view. I'm not talking about a ship that has to sink. Presumably, that is just a way of saying we have to die. But I'm saying that here and now we are moral beings. And how are we moral beings supposed to interact with each other? How do we make sense of our lives together? How do we justify doing one thing rather than another? These things can correctly and reasonably be deliberated on without any reference to religion at all.

Consider again the genetic fallacy. I have a great appreciation for religious traditions. Certain of our moral beliefs come out of religious traditions. Moreover, they might have not come to us in just the way they do but for our religious traditions. I am not saying you take away belief in God and everything remains intact for moral belief. Nietzsche and Sartre are right about that. Everything else isn't intact. But a lot is intact. Moreover, some things that are lost may not be such a bad thing to lose. And there, as I have shown, are gains in a purely secular ethic.

And so that morality *came* from religion, so what? That I learned that I shouldn't urinate in public from my grandmother, so what? The question is, Is there a good reason not to urinate in public? And there probably is a good reason not to urinate in public, and that's why I don't urinate in public.

MORELAND: Well, for one thing, I didn't use the genetic fallacy. I hope you're not claiming that I argued in that way.

NIELSEN: No. But you talked about it.

MORELAND: But my argument was not itself a genetic fallacy. Secondly, Rawls, whether he explicitly states truth in coherence terms or not, that's exactly what he means.[7] In Section 4 of his *A Theory of Justice,* where he explicitly goes over his notion of reflective equilibrium, he likens his views on morality to the views of Thomas Kuhn and Nelson Goodman.[8] For Rawls, issues of moral justification are similar to Goodman's notion of an internal metaphysical problem and to Kuhn's idea that rational justification is itself paradigm dependent.[9]

Now if you read *The Structure of Scientific Revolutions,* to my knowledge Kuhn only mentions truth once in the whole book.[10] So he doesn't use the word, but it is still possible to understand Kuhn as though he is talking about a coherence theory of what is real, or a coherence theory of truth, whether he uses the word truth or not. And the same point could be made regarding Rawls. In terms of your understanding of reflective equilibrium, the very same thing seemed to be implied by what you were saying.[11]

NIELSEN: Just one thing about this. Rawls explicitly says that he sets aside for this purpose questions of moral truth altogether because the notion of moral truth is problematic.[12] He can say what he needs to say about coherence and justification in ethics without making any commitments or assumptions about moral truth at all. I said this explicitly too. I don't say that it doesn't make any sense to say moral propositions are true. We are concerned with questions of justification. Because you see that there are difficulties with asserting that moral propositions are either true or false, we set such issues aside. We can say what we want about coherence without invoking a coherence theory of truth or any other theory of truth at all.

We could, of course, speak quite unproblematically of moral claims being true if all we meant in saying they were true was a rather emphatic way of reasserting them. (Philosophers call it the assertive redundancy theory of truth.) But if you mean something stronger, like there is a correspondence between moral sentences and reality, then we will have trouble. Suppose I say, "Snow is white." You know exactly what will establish the truth of that. Suppose I say, "Hitler was a vile man." It isn't quite so clear what that refers to. Still, perhaps it does refer to something. Maybe there are truth conditions for it. Rawls sets all those questions aside, and his appeal to Goodman is not an appeal to a coherence theory of *truth*. He explicitly says he will not give or appeal to any account of truth at all. It's very clear in his essays on Kantian constructivism. I take exactly the same turn. It should also be noted, in passing, that we should, as Alvin Goldman does, sharply distinguish between accounts of what truth is and epistemological questions about how we justify whether claims that so and so is true are reasonable.[13] All kinds of confusions emerge if we do not keep these questions apart. Coherence, as Goldman points out, is plausible as a partial account of how we justify truth claims, but it has no plausibility at all as an account of what truth is.

QUESTION: My question is to Dr. Moreland. How would you respond to Dr. Nielsen's statement that you said that any secular ethic is inadequate compared to a theistic ethic in the fact that I think he says that it is always morally wrong to torture little children even if God commanded it? Wouldn't you say it is unreasonable to say if God would ever command it, it would be okay to torture little children? Or would you say that if God commands it, it must be morally right?

MORELAND: I'm not a divine command theorist, so I don't hold the view like Nielsen correctly imputed to Barth and certain strong Calvinists who hold to rather extreme forms of voluntarism. This view implies that morality is merely grounded in God's will as opposed to His nature. You can see this in Descartes and others, that God could have made seven times seventy equal to twenty if He'd wanted to, and He could have made mercy as such a vice. That's not my view.

I think God's will is ultimately expressed in keeping with His nature. Morality is ultimately grounded in the nature of God, not independently of God. There is a Euthypro-type argument that Bertrand Russell raised against theism—namely, that for the theist, morality is either arbitrarily grounded in God's will or it's grounded in something outside of God. But this is a false disjunction. I think the tertium quid is that morality can be grounded in God's own nature. We obey God because He is good and loving.[14] Now, when I say that God is good, I'm not stating a tautology. Further, I would agree with Nielsen that you have to understand the meaning of "good" before you can ascribe it to God.[15]

But so what? That only grants there is a certain epistemological or conceptual order to moral knowledge that's different from the metaphysical order regarding the existence of goodness itself. I might have to look at a road map of Chicago before I can know where Chicago is, so the road map might be first in the order of epistemology, but Chicago has to exist prior to the fact of the road map. Similarly, God's goodness would exist prior to the existence of finite, derived goodnesses, though conceptually or epistemologically, I might have to understand what "goodness" means before I would be able to make a judgment that God is good.

QUESTION: Dr. Nielsen, are you an atheist because you can't find any concrete evidence for the existence of God?

NIELSEN: The short answer to that is no. The reasons that I became an atheist are something that took years. They are very diverse.[16] They are in part related to the fact that I don't think there is much plausibility connected with believing in the existence of God. Indeed, I believe that the very concept of God in developed versions of Judeo-Christianity is incoherent.[17] Part of the reason I believe that belief in God is implausible is that without recourse to God, we can make perfectly good sense out of our moral life, find meaning in life, and at certain junctures give meaning to life.[18] In this connection, there is another thing I would say vis-à-vis what Professor Moreland was saying. There can be larger purposes in life. I mean you can be a Marxist or a socialist or you could be all kinds of things. There can be larger purposes in life even if you're an atheist. I have lots of larger purposes. There are a bunch of connected things, things connected with what kind of a social world I would like to see us forge together, which are among the things which give meaning to my life.

The point about asking the question, "Why be moral?" is to point out that there is no way of showing that an individual who doesn't care about people or anything else and is willing to be a freeloader and an unprincipled jerk need not be acting irrationally or be making an intellectual mistake in so living his life. Kant thought that you could show that such a person was irrational, as distinct from saying what a religious person might say, "just sinful." My argument is I don't think you can show that. But some secular theorists think you can do just that, show that you, if you are through-and-through rational, will also be committed to the moral point of view. Kurt Baier is one such secular moralist and David Gauthier is another.[19] But I do not think there is any such intrinsic link between morality and rationality. At a certain point, morality just requires commitment and subscription.[20]

But I'm saying that once you're in morality, once you take a moral point of view, that is not a live option.[21] Just like it's not an open question once you're doing science to ask why pay attention to a well-conducted experiment. You may override its results for some reason, but you at least have to start off by paying attention to a well-conducted experiment.

POJMAN: We've time for one more question, I believe. . . . The question is essentially, Is one of the reasons secular people are moral is because God made the world the way it is to put a kind of moral inclination into people?

MORELAND: Okay, let me sort out a couple of questions real quickly. One, my argument was not primarily the claim that religious people are more moral than nonreligious people; though in my opinion, it has been primarily religious people who have gone to Third World countries and taken care of the poor and needy. And there's a good book by Patrick Sherry called *Spirit, Saints, and Immortality,* where he makes a similar claim. He offers a causal argument from religious experience, that Christianity has produced more people who have done heroic, supererogatory, and morally virtuous kinds of acts. Thus we must postulate some power or cause to explain this effect.

The real question I am trying to emphasize is this: How could there be such a thing as goodness and morality in the universe? In my opinion, a worldview is inadequate which implies that it is not irrational to be a moral monster or to be indifferent to the moral point of view by embracing, say, a rational life plan centered in some form of ethical egoism.[22] What kind of universe makes most reasonable the existence of objective morality?

And to me you cannot get away from the truth question, and I don't think that Rawls, Quine, or Kuhn adequately deal with the importance of truth for rationality. Just shaking hands via reflective equilibrium and saying, "I don't want to deal with truth," or accepting some redundancy theory of truth, is simply not adequate. For example, Carl Kordig wrote a recent journal article saying Quine's theory was self-refuting, because you can ask him, Is your theory true and normatively rational?[23]

Now in terms of how we know the specific content of morality, very roughly, I think you need to utilize insights of virtue theory, you need to adopt particularism as an epistemic strategy, and you also need to include some form of moral intuitionism.

Finally, if we step back from the issue of knowing the specific content of morality, and we consider the broader, transcendental question of how it could come about that human beings have normative, rational, truth-gathering faculties in general, as well as how humans came to have these faculties regarding moral knowledge in particular, then we have the makings of a design argument for God. It is this concept of rationality that, at once, justifies the claim that a moral egoist is irrational and provides an argument for God to ground the possibility of moral knowledge. Well, a lot could be said, but time is up. Thank you very much for having us.

Notes

1. For how these distinctions are to be drawn, see my *Why Be Moral?* (Buffalo, N.Y.: Prometheus Books, 1989).
2. Kai Nielsen, *Why Be Moral?*, 196–206.
3. How this is so is very well brought out toward the end of John Rawls's Dewey Lectures, "Kantian Constructivism in Moral Theory: The Dewey Lectures 1980," *Journal of Philosophy* 77 (1980), 560–572.
4. He also makes these matters very clear in his Dewey Lectures. Moreland badly misunderstands Rawls. He sees him as making truth claims he explicitly disavows.
5. John Rawls, "The Domain of the Political and Overlapping Consensus," *New York University Law Review* 64:2 (May 1989), 233–255.
6. Kai Nielsen, "Searching for an Emancipatory Perspective: Wide Reflective Equilibrium and the Hermeneutical Circle" in *Anti-Foundationalism and Practical Reasoning*, Evan Simpson, ed. (Edmonton, Alberta: Academic Publishing, 1987), 143–164; "In Defense of Wide Reflective Equilibrium" in *Ethics and Justification*, Douglas Odegard, ed. (Edmonton, Alberta: Academic Publishing, 1988), 19–37.

7. Cf. John Rawls, *A Theory of Justice* (Cambridge, Mass.: The Belknap Press of Harvard University Press, 1971), 17–22, 48–51, 432, 577–79.

8. Rawls explicitly compares his view with Nelson Goodman, who authored *Fact, Fiction, and Forecast* (Cambridge, Mass.: Harvard University Press, 1955), and W. V. O. Quine, in his *Word and Object* (Cambridge, Mass.: MIT Press, 1960), and his *Ontological Relativity and Other Essays* (New York: Columbia University Press, 1969). Rawls does not compare his views with those of Thomas Kuhn, as I thought he had, but he could have, since Kuhn's ideas of rationality and truth are in keeping with those of Goodman, Quine, and Rawls. All of them are against a foundationalist theory of epistemic justification, and all of them are antirealist regarding a correspondence theory of truth.

9. According to Kuhn, there are several epistemic virtues that a theory ought to embody if it is to be rational—e.g., simplicity, predictive success, empirical accuracy, and fruitfulness in guiding new research. But both the interpretation and the weighting of these virtues are paradigm dependent, and thus, there are no paradigm neutral criteria that can be used to adjudicate between different paradigms. Paradigms are strictly incommensurable.

10. Thomas Kuhn, *The Structure of Scientific Revolutions* (Chicago: University of Chicago Press, 2nd ed., 1970), 170. Here Kuhn dismisses truth, understood as correspondence with a paradigm independent world toward which our successive theories converge, as unhelpful.

11. Clear-headed coherentists have combined a coherence theory of epistemic justification (e.g., a proposition P is justified for person S if and only if P is a member of a set of beliefs which are maximally coherent for S) with either a correspondence theory of truth or a coherence theory of truth. For an overview of these issues, see Jonathan Dancy, *Introduction to Contemporary Epistemology* (Oxford: Basil Blackwell, 1985), 110–140. The reason for this is stated nicely by coherentist Laurence BonJour: "If finding epistemically justified beliefs did not substantially increase the likelihood of finding true ones, then epistemic justification would be irrelevant to our main cognitive goal and of dubious worth. It is only if we have some reason for thinking that epistemic justification constitutes a path to truth that we cognitive beings have any motive for preferring epistemically justified beliefs to epistemically unjustified ones. Epistemic justification is therefore in the final analysis only an instrumental value, not an intrinsic one." *The Structure of Empirical Knowledge* (Cambridge, Mass.: Harvard University Press, 1985), 8. Cf. 157–188. This point seems to have been overlooked by Nielsen and Rawls. Once rationality loses its connection with truth, there is no longer any point in preferring to be "rational." Rationality is an honorific notion precisely because we believe that in being rational one is in a better position to obtain the truth. For an application of this point to ethical justification, see Panayot Butchvarov, *Skepticism in Ethics*

(Bloomington, Ind.: University of Indiana Press, 1989), 5, 6, 9–10, 36–39, 137–160.

12. See John Rawls's Dewey Lectures.

13. Alvin Goldman, *Epistemology and Cognition* (Cambridge, Mass.: Harvard University Press, 1986), 142–161.

14. See Robert M. Adams, *The Virtue of Faith and Other Essays in Philosophical Theology* (Oxford: Oxford University Press, 1978), 128–163.

15. Cf. Alan F. Johnson, "Is There a Biblical Warrant for Natural-Law Theories?" *Journal of the Evangelical Theological Society* 25 (June 1982), 185–99. Johnson perceptively points out that in Genesis 18, Abraham is arguing with God over the fate of Sodom, and Abraham points out that it would be wicked for God to slay the righteous with the wicked. Now if "morally right" merely means "whatever God wills," then Abraham's argument would have been pointless, for he would be saying, in effect, "How can You fail to do what You will do?" This would replace, "How can You fail to do what is right?" So even Scripture itself recognizes that one can have a concept of rightness before one evaluates or receives some revelation from God. But this does not mean that the existence and nature of morality is not somehow dependent on God.

16. See my autobiographical remarks in *Atheism and Philosophy* (Buffalo, N.Y.: Prometheus Books, 1985), 33–40.

17. See Nielsen, *Skepticism* (New York: St. Martin's Press, 1973). See also my "Religion and Rationality" in *Analytical Philosophy of Religion in Canada*, Mostafa Faghfoury, ed. (Ottawa: University of Ottawa Press, 1982), 75–124.

18. Kai Nielsen, *Ethics Without God* (Buffalo, N.Y.: Prometheus Books, 2nd ed., 1989); "Religious Perplexity and Faith," *Crane Review* 8:1 (1965); "Linguistic Philosophy and The Meaning of Life," in *The Meaning of Life*, E. D. Klemke, ed. (New York: Oxford University Press, 1981).

19. Baier and Nielsen divide on this issue. See Kurt Baier, "Rationality, Reason and the Good" and Kai Nielsen, "Must the Immoralist Act Contrary to Reason?" both in *Morality, Reason and Truth,* David Copp and David Zimmerman, eds. (Totowa, N.J.: Rowman and Allanheld, 1985), 193–227.

20. Kai Nielsen, *Why Be Moral?* (Buffalo, N.Y.: Prometheus Books, 1989), 167–206, 284–300.

21. Kai Nielsen, *Why Be Moral?*, 83–97.

22. Cf. George Mavrodes, "Religion and the Queerness of Morality," in *Rationality, Religious Belief, and Moral Commitment,* Robert Audi and William J. Wainwright, eds. (Ithaca, N.Y.: Cornell University Press, 1986), 213–26.

23. See Carl R. Kordig, "Self-Reference and Philosophy," *American Philosophical Quarterly* 20 (Apr. 1983), 207–16; "Some Statements Are Immune to Revision," *The New Scholasticism* 25 (Winter 1981), 69–76.

PART III

WHAT DO OTHERS THINK?

Responses to the Debate

William Lane Craig

In Defense of Rational Theism

11

Having participated in eight years of high school and intercollegiate debating, I have a pretty fair idea of what makes for a good debate. The most essential element is something called *clash:* the sustained, head-to-head presentation of argument and counterargument by the two protagonists. Unfortunately, this is an element sorely lacking in this debate, and it is pretty evident whose fault that is.

An easy way of seeing this is to keep what debaters call a "flow chart" of the debate: on the left-hand side of a sheet of paper one makes an outline of Moreland's constructive speech, and to the right of that records Nielsen's responses, and then to the right of that Moreland's final rejoinder to Nielsen. Then one does the same thing with Nielsen's constructive speech. When completed, such a chart would make it abundantly evident by the blank space who clashed with his opponent and who did not.

It is thus necessary to keep in effect two flow charts on this debate because the participants are not debating a proposition, "Be it resolved that . . . ," but a question, "Does God exist?" If they were debating a proposition, one person would bear the burden of proof (the affirmative side) and the other would have merely to refute it to win (the negative side). But in debating a question, each advocate has to shoulder the burden of proof for why his answer is the correct one. Thus Moreland has to present a case for an affirmative answer to the question and refute Nielsen's objections to it, and Nielsen must present a case for a negative answer to the question and refute Moreland's objections to it. A flow chart will, as I say, make evident who better bore these responsibilities.

Moreland's Case

The following is my outline of Moreland's constructive case:

PRINCIPAL THESIS: *It is rational to believe that God exists.*

PRELIMINARY ARGUMENTS:
  1. Argument from design

    ——Delicately balanced harmony of cosmological constants
    ——Improbability of chance origin of life
  2. Argument from moral value and meaning in life
    ——Without God it is difficult to see how prescriptive morality is possible
  3. Archaeological confirmations of the Bible
  4. Argument from mind
    ——Origin and trustworthiness of mind
  5. Religious experience
    ——Direct experience of a benevolent Creator

MAJOR CONTENTIONS:
 I. *God created the universe from nothing a finite time ago.*
   A. Philosophical argument
     1. One can't traverse an actually infinite number of events by successive addition
     2. To get to the present moment, one would have to have traversed an actual infinite
     3. But the past has been realized
     4. So there must have been a first event
     5. This event must have been spontaneously generated by an unchanging, timeless, and free situation
      ——It is unreasonable to say the first event was uncaused
      ——Agent causation is a reasonable explanation
   B. Scientific confirmation
     1. Second law of thermodynamics
      ——If the universe had existed forever, then it should be in an equilibrium state
     2. Big Bang theory
      ——The universe originated from nothing
      ——There was only one initial creation

 II. *Jesus of Nazareth is God's supreme revelation of Himself to mankind.*
   ——This claim hinges on the historicity of Jesus' resurrection
   A. Time factor precludes replacement of history by legend
     1. Early dating of New Testament books
     2. Presence of early traditions in the New Testament
   B. Empty tomb
     1. Archaeology makes plausible the description and location of the tomb
     2. No veneration of Jesus' tomb, unlike others'
     3. Women discovered the empty tomb
   C. Appearances of Jesus alive
     1. No one denies the disciples' life-changing experience

2. Hallucinations are improbable
   ——Number and variety of people involved
   ——Hallucinations do not bring new ideas, but Jesus' resurrection was radically new

D. Origin of the Christian church
   1. Without the resurrection, where did Christianity come from?
   2. Without the resurrection, how could it have succeeded?
      ——Jews risked damnation by converting
      ——Motivation and endurance of early Christians

Final Note: No other world religion has non-legendary miracles attributed to its founder.

Analysis of Moreland's Case

How would I assess Moreland's case? To begin with, notice how modest Moreland's principal thesis is: It is rational to believe that God exists. He does not even claim that theism is probable or more rational than atheism. His thesis leaves it open that it is also rational to be an atheist. Just as during the 1950s it was rational for a physical cosmologist to hold to either the Big Bang or the Steady State model, so Moreland's thesis leaves open the possibility that atheism or theism is each a rational option. But having stated this very modest thesis, Moreland then proceeds to present a vigorous argument for Christian theism that tends to show that theism is rationally superior to atheism. It is probably for this reason that Nielsen accuses Moreland of "waffl[ing] a bit" on whether theism is on a par with or superior to atheism. Nevertheless, Moreland's strong apologetic for theism leaves open the possibility, in light of his thesis, that there are equally weighty arguments for atheism. The advantage of defending a modest thesis is that it is easier to prove; the disadvantage is that, at the end of the day, one hasn't proved very much. According to his thesis, Moreland's answer to the question, "Does God Exist?" is merely, "It is rational to hold that God exists;" but I suspect in light of his arguments that he really wishes to defend a stronger claim, for example, "It is more rational to hold that God exists than that He does not." Fortunately, as we shall see, Nielsen disagrees sharply with even the more modest claim, so that the possibility for real debate is on.

That brings us to Moreland's *preliminary arguments*. These are, unfortunately, for the most part so underdeveloped that they serve almost no function in the debate. Arguments 3, 4, and 5, for example, consist of only one sentence each (though arguments 4 and 5 are sub-

sequently developed in Moreland's rebuttal speech, and Nielsen fails to
say anything in refutation). Argument 3 from archaeology seems very
out of place here in any case, since it is normally part of what are called
"Christian evidences," not natural theology, and constitutes at best
only very indirect validation of theism.

Moreland does devote more time to the argument from design, or
the teleological argument. As he correctly notes, this classic argument,
once thought to have been decisively laid to rest by Hume and Darwin,
has come roaring back in recent decades due to scientific discoveries
concerning what F. R. Tennant called "wider teleology"—that is, the
complex and sensitive nexus of conditions that must be given in order
for the universe to permit the origin and evolution of intelligent life on
Earth. In the various fields of physics and astrophysics, classical cosmology, quantum mechanics, and biochemistry, various discoveries
have repeatedly disclosed that the existence of intelligent carbon-based
life on Earth at this time in cosmic history depends upon a delicate
balance of physical and cosmological quantities,[1] such that were any of
these quantities to be slightly altered, the balance would be destroyed
and life would cease to exist. Nowhere has this evidence been more
impressively compiled than in Frank Tipler's and John Barrow's *The
Anthropic Cosmological Principle* (Oxford: Clarendon Press, 1986), to
which you may profitably be referred. What scientists have found is that
when one considers universes like ours (that is, those worlds governed
by the same fundamental forces and having similar structural foundations), one discovers that life-permitting universes are wildly improbable, that in order for intelligent life to exist, the values of the fundamental forces and physical constants have to be precisely assigned
and arranged in certain apparently independent ratios.

To get a picture of this, imagine all possible universes similar to
ours as points on a page. If we color red those which permit intelligent
life and blue those which do not, in order for life to be probable there
would have to be more red points than blue, so that a small deviation
from a red point would still land one on another red point. But what
scientists have discovered is that the overwhelming majority of these
starting points are inhospitable to life. The page is a sea of blue with
only a few isolated points of red. The slightest deviation from a red
point lands one on a blue point. In Barrow's words, "If we were to
imagine a whole collection of hypothetical 'other universes' in which all
the quantities that define the structure of our universe take on all possible permutations of values, then we find that almost all these other
possible universes we have created on paper are stillborn, unable to

give rise to that type of chemical complexity that we call 'life.'"[2] He concludes, "The more we examine the other types of universe that the laws of physics appear to allow, so the more special and unusual do the properties of the actual Universe appear to be."[3]

We do not need to speculate, therefore, about universes governed by wholly different laws of nature or wonder whether life could exist in them. The point is that within the wide range of universes permitted by the actual laws of physics, scarcely any are life-permitting, and those that are require incredible fine-tuning of the physical constants and quantities. In fact, Donald Page of Princeton's Institute for Advanced Study has calculated the odds against the formation of our universe as one out of $10,000,000,000^{124}$, a number that exceeds all imagination.[4] Truly, this appearance of "wider teleology" cries out for explanation.

But that is not all. As Moreland correctly notes, even the presence of these finely arranged constants and physical quantities does not guarantee that life will arise. In fact, what scientists have discovered is that even given the necessary conditions of the wider teleology, the origin of life is fantastically improbable. Actually, Moreland understates the case. Hoyle's odds against the random origin of life, which Moreland refers to, were not one out of 10^{40}, astronomical though that is. Rather Hoyle and his colleague Wickramasinghe calculated the odds of the random formation of a single enzyme from amino acids anywhere on the earth's surface as one in 10^{20}. But that is only the beginning: "The trouble is that there are about two thousand enzymes, and the chance of obtaining them all in a random trial is only one part in $(10^{20})^{20,000} = 10^{40,000}$, an outrageously small probability that could not be faced even if the whole universe consisted of organic soup."[5] And of course, the formation of enzymes is but one step in the formation of life. "Nothing has been said of the origin of DNA itself, nothing of DNA transcription to RNA, nothing of the origin of the program whereby cells organize themselves, nothing of mitosis or meiosis. These issues are too complex to set numbers to."[6] In the end, they conclude that the chances of life originating by random ordering of organic molecules is not sensibly different from zero.[7] They feel forced, therefore, to posit the existence of some sort of Cosmic Intelligence in order to explain the origin of life.

Moreland's argument stops here; but he could have pushed it a notch further. For even given the random origin of life, the odds against its spontaneous evolution into intelligent life and into homo sapiens in particular is unspeakably improbable. As we have seen, one cannot really assign a numerical probability to this, but Barrow and Tipler try to set at least a lower boundary.[8] They begin by seeking steps in the evolution of homo sapiens, each of which is so improbable that before it would occur the sun would have already ceased to be a main sequence star and would have burned up the Earth. They come up with a minimal list of ten such steps, including such things as aerobic respiration, autotropic photosynthesis, an endoskeleton, and so forth. They calculate that the odds against the assemblage of the human genome are between $(4^{-180})^{110,000}$ and $(4^{-360})^{110,000}$! It is simply breath-taking.

Certain scientists—like Barrow and Tipler—try to mitigate this appearance of teleology in the universe, life, and man by appealing to the celebrated Anthropic Principle, which states that we should not be surprised at the unimaginable odds against our complexly ordered universe, for if it were not complexly ordered, we wouldn't be here to be surprised about it! But such reasoning is simply logically fallacious.[9] To illustrate: Imagine that you are brought before a firing squad of one hundred trained marksmen, each with his rifle aimed at your heart. The command to fire is given, you hear the deafening roar of the guns, and you observe that you are *still alive*, that all of the one hundred marksmen missed! Now what follows from this? You should not be surprised that you do not observe that you are dead, for if you were dead, you could not observe it. But you should be surprised that you observe that you are alive, in light of the enormous improbability that all the sharpshooters missed. In the same way, while it is true that we should not be surprised that we do not observe conditions in the universe that are incompatible with our existence (since if they were incompatible, we wouldn't exist to observe them), nevertheless we certainly ought to be surprised that we observe conditions in the universe that are compatible with our existence (in view of the enormous complexity and improbability of those conditions).

In fact, the only way to save the Anthropic Principle is to conjoin to it a fantastic metaphysical hypothesis called a "World Ensemble," according to which all physically possible universes actually exist. In some of these, life originates by chance, and we are in one of those universes. With regard to this contrived and bloated ontology, theism looks mild by comparison!

Moreland's second argument, based on moral values and meaning in life, rather drops out of this debate, but assumes center stage in Moreland's and Nielsen's second encounter. I shall therefore ignore it in this review.

In summary, then, in his preliminary arguments, Moreland effectively presents a teleological argument, broaches a moral argument, and mentions in passing three other arguments. These preliminary arguments are not well-integrated into his case, and the question arises whether his major contentions might not be restructured to incorporate them.

When we turn to Moreland's two major contentions, it seems clear that restructuring is feasible and desirable. For the second contention, that Jesus is God's supreme revelation to mankind, is not directly relevant to the topic of this debate nor to Moreland's principal thesis. His second contention concerns which brand of theism is true and argues for Christian theism on the basis of Christ's resurrection, a centerpiece of traditional Christian evidences. Once again, Moreland proves too much. The question at hand is whether God exists. Whether this be the God of Deists, Muslims, or Jews is irrelevant. Hence, Moreland's case would have been stronger had he dropped his second contention entirely and replaced it with a more detailed development of the teleological, moral, and other arguments.

Looking more closely at Moreland's arguments, we see that his contention *I*, that God created the universe out of nothing a finite time ago, is supported by a philosophical argument and two scientific confirmations. The philosophical argument is based on the impossibility of an infinite past and seems to be clearly laid out. But you may feel perplexed at Moreland's rather abrupt conclusion that the first event "must have been spontaneously generated by a situation that was immutable, unchanging, timeless, and free." How did he arrive at that conclusion? Moreland's terse remarks following this conclusion need to be amplified.[10]

As he points out, it is unreasonable to hold that the first event popped into existence out of nothing without a cause. A little reflection makes this clear. In absolute nothingness, not even potentialities exist, since potentialities are always lodged in something that is actual. For example, my wife and I have a potential third child; but where does this potentiality lie? Not in the child himself, who is simply nonexistent, but in the reproductive capacities of our actual bodies. But that means that if there was absolute nothingness—no matter, no energy, no space, no time, no God—then nothing could come to exist. There would not exist even the potentiality for the universe. Hence, it is metaphysically absurd to claim that something literally came out of nothing. There had to be a cause for the origin of the universe.

But then what kind of cause was it? It could not have been a physical cause, for physical things are constantly changing (at least at the molecular level). If Moreland's argument against an infinite regress of events is correct, the first cause would have to be unchanging and therefore timeless (since if there is no change, there is no time), at least *sans* creation. So the first cause must have been immaterial, unchanging, and timeless. Otherwise, it would not have been the *first* cause.

But now the question presses, How can a temporal effect (the universe) arise from an eternal cause? Why isn't the effect as eternal as the cause is? One can't say that at a certain moment in the finite past, something caused the first cause to suddenly produce its effect after its having lain dormant from eternity; for in an unchanging, timeless state, nothing is happening so as to move the first cause into action. Besides, such a suggestion only pushes the question back a step: for now the cause that moved the first cause is really the first cause, and we may ask why it suddenly sprang into action. How can a temporal effect issue from an eternal, unchanging cause?

Moreland's answer is *agent causation*. Since conscious agents are free beings—not wholly determined in their actions by antecedent and contemporaneous external causes—they can initiate effects which are novel (or as Moreland puts it, spontaneous), that is, not determined by external causal conditions. Hence, the only way to explain how the temporal universe could originate from an eternal cause is if that cause is a personal agent who freely wills to produce an effect in time. Thus, the cosmological argument defended by Moreland leads us to an immaterial, unchanging, timeless, personal, free Creator of the universe, in whose creative power lies the potentiality of the universe's existence.

Moreland then introduces two scientific confirmations of his philosophical case for a Creator: one confirmation is from thermodynamics, and the other from the Big Bang model. With regard to his thermodynamic considerations, Moreland describes the heat death of an ever-expanding universe. And, as he points out, even if the universe is sufficiently dense so that it will someday recontract, it still faces a thermodynamic heat death. As the universe recontracts, it will grow hotter and hotter until all the elements are dissolved and the whole of space-time reality coalesces into a single black hole coextensive with the universe, from which it will never reemerge. Although some theorists have sought to avert this fate by postulating that the universe could bounce back from a contraction to a new expansion phase, recent studies of the thermodynamics of a contracting universe confirm that reexpansion would not occur.[11] And even if it could, other studies have shown that due to entropy increase from cycle to cycle, the oscillating universe would expand further each cycle, so that as one traces the cycles back in time, the expansion radius of the universe becomes progressively smaller until one reaches a first expansion and the beginning of the universe.[12] In fact, astronomer Joseph Silk estimates on the basis of currently observed entropy levels that the present expansion could not have been preceded by more than 100 previous cycles.[13] Thus, thermodynamics confirms the origin of the universe in the finite past.

The second scientific confirmation Moreland appeals to is the standard Big Bang model, which postulates the origin of the universe in a singularity about 15 billion years ago. The singularity is a mathematical point which marks the boundary of space and time. It is impossible for the Big Bang to have any kind of physical cause because the singularity constitutes a discontinuity with any other realm of physical reality (other spacetimes?) which might be conceived to exist. Nothing can pass through a singularity into our universe. The universe literally came into existence out of nothing a finite time ago, according to the standard model.

As Robert Jastrow's book, *God and the Astronomers*, cited by Moreland, reveals, many scientists were (and are) deeply disturbed by this feature of the standard model, and not merely for scientific reasons. The celebrated Cambridge astrophysicist and mathematician Stephen Hawking admits that a number of attempts to avoid the Big Bang were probably motivated by the feeling that a beginning of time "smacks of divine intervention."[14] Hawking himself has proposed an alternative model to the standard theory in order to erase the singularity at the universe's origin. He is not at all reticent about what theological implications he sees in his new model:

> The idea that space and time may form a closed surface without boundary . . . has profound implications for the role of God in the affairs of the universe. . . . So long as the universe had a beginning, we could suppose it had a creator. But if the universe is really completely self-contained, having no boundary or edge, it would have neither beginning nor end. What place, then, for a creator?[15]

This conclusion has been trumpeted in the popular press.

But what the layman may not realize is that Hawking's model is based upon at least two metaphysical assumptions that disqualify it as a realistic theory of the universe.[16]

(1) *It presupposes the World Ensemble ontology.* Hawking's model is based on applying quantum physics to the universe as a whole in its earliest stage. In accordance with quantum indeterminacy, the universe

thus becomes indeterminate in its existence. On the standard Copenhagen Interpretation of quantum physics, there would therefore have to exist some Ultimate Observer which transcends the universe and which "collapses" its indeterminacy into a determinate state. In order to avoid this conclusion (which certainly smacks of divine intervention!), quantum cosmologists are forced to regard our universe as a fluctuation in a sort of superspace, in which all physically possible spacetimes are embedded. All universes are equally real, but we experience only the one we are in. It hardly needs to be said that this is a piece of speculative metaphysics no less objectionable than theism; indeed, I should argue, more objectionable because the reality of time is ultimately denied as all dimensions, temporal as well as spatial, are subsumed into superspace.[17]

(2) *It replaces real time with imaginary time.* Hawking's model depends on the mathematical artifice of using imaginary numbers (like $\sqrt{-1}$) for the coordinates of the time dimension. This is nothing new. In the 1920s Eddington used imaginary numbers for the time coordinate in discussing Einstein's Theory of Relativity. Eddington, however, recognized this as a "dodge" and immediately translated the theory back into real numbers.[18] But what Hawking does is refuse to translate the equations back into real numbers. We are thus left in his model with imaginary time. In this imaginary time, the cosmological singularities do not appear. But if one translates the equations back into real time, one discovers the singularities are still there. Hawking's model thus appears to be a piece of mathematical legerdemain. Hawking goes so far as to suggest that perhaps real time is "just an idea that we invent," while imaginary time is the actual time.[19] But apart from the disingenuousness of this suggestion, it has at least two problems.

First, imaginary time is physically unintelligible. No one has any idea what is meant physically when an imaginary number is assigned to the time coordinate.

Second, according to Hawking, imaginary time turns time into space. By assigning an imaginary number to the time coordinate, that coordinate becomes indistinguishable from spatial coordinates. But obviously time is not space; that is just bad metaphysics.

Hence, in my opinion, Hawking's model, based as it is on false metaphysical foundations, provides no plausible, realistic alternative to the standard Big Bang model.

Thus, modern cosmology points to the same conclusion as the ancient cosmological argument does—the universe had a beginning in the finite past. Once again, the demand for a cause of the beginning arises.

In Moreland's second major contention, that Jesus of Nazareth is God's supreme revelation of Himself to mankind, Moreland attempts to provide justification for a specifically Christian form of theism. He does so by focusing on the evidence for the historicity of the resurrection of Jesus. Unfortunately, he does not make clear the organic connection between Jesus' resurrection and His being the supreme revelation of God. Why shouldn't we just shrug our shoulders and say, "I guess dead men do rise from the grave after all?" Or why not view the resurrection as a genuine miracle, but not as one qualitatively different from, say, Old Testament miracles? It seems to me that a twofold answer may be given here. In the first place, Jesus' resurrection so exceeds the productive capacity of natural causes that it is plausibly identified as a miracle. That a truly dead man should come back to life in a transformed body so outstrips the relevant causal powers known to science and medicine that such an event is reasonably judged to be miraculous. If Jesus' resurrection were the product of purely natural causes, then its uniqueness in the historicity of humanity would become inexplicable. For these reasons, sceptics invariably attack the evidence for the occurrence of the resurrection; after all, it would be a rather desperate expedient to admit that the resurrection occurred and then try to write it off as a merely natural event.

In the second place, the religio-historical context in which Jesus' resurrection occurred supplies the key to its interpretation. Jesus' resurrection was not a bare anomaly. It took place in the context of and as the climax to His own unparalleled life and teachings. He came on the scene with the claim to stand in God's place as the object of faith and the agent of salvation, a claim for which He was crucified. God's raising Him from the dead is the divine *imprimatur* for those claims, as Wolfhart Pannenberg explains:

> The resurrection of Jesus acquires such decisive meaning, not merely because someone or anyone has been raised from the dead, but because it is Jesus of Nazareth, whose execution was instigated by the Jews because he had blasphemed against God.
>
> Jesus' claim to authority, through which he put himself in God's place was . . . blasphemous for Jewish ears. Because of this Jesus was then also slandered before the Roman Governor as a rebel. If Jesus really has been raised, this claim has been visibly and unambiguously confirmed by the God of Israel, who was allegedly blasphemed by Jesus.[20]

Taken in its religio-historical context, then, the resurrection reveals

Jesus to be who he claimed: the supreme revelation of God (Matt. 11:27).

As for the evidence supporting the historicity of the resurrection of Jesus, while one should avoid the exaggerated claims sometimes made on behalf of the evidence by popular apologists, still it must be admitted that an examination of the New Testament materials concerning the resurrection reveals that the historical foundations for that event are surprisingly secure.[21] Moreland's first line of evidence is not directly evidence for the resurrection as such, but rather for the historical credibility of the Gospel narratives as a whole and thereby indirectly for the resurrection as the event which constitutes the climax of each Gospel. Though not securing historicity in detail, this persuasive consideration does, it seems to me, make the Gospel narratives in their broader strokes historically trustworthy.

The next three lines of evidence relate more directly to the resurrection itself. Moreland provides three pieces of evidence in support of the women's discovery of Jesus' empty tomb. His explanation of the third of these is somewhat muddled, as it confuses the women's discovery of the empty tomb with Jesus' appearance to the women. But his fundamental point is persuasive: A late legend would surely have been framed in terms of the male disciples' discovery of Jesus' empty tomb; the fact that women, whose testimony was regarded as worthless, are the discoverers of the empty tomb is most plausibly explained by its root in historical fact.

Moreland actually omits some of the most persuasive evidence for the historicity of Jesus' empty tomb.[22] For example, the empty-tomb story is most probably part of the pre-Markan passion story and is therefore very old. This makes the significant accrual of legend quite unlikely. A confirmatory piece of evidence for this conclusion is the simplicity of the empty-tomb story itself, which shows almost no signs of legendary embellishment, in sharp (and sometimes amusing) contrast to the accounts found in second-century apocryphal gospels.

The next line of evidence concerns the disciples' experiences of postmortem appearances of Jesus alive from the dead. It may surprise the reader to learn that Moreland is entirely correct in his assertion that no New Testament scholar denies that these life-changing experiences really occurred. The real question is how these experiences are to be interpreted. Moreland provides two reasons why an explanation in terms of hallucinations is unlikely. With respect to the first, you need to understand that these experiences took place on several occasions over a period of time, under varying circumstances indoors and out, and not only to individuals but also to groups of people, and not only to believers but also to sceptics (Thomas), unbelievers (James), and even enemies (Paul). Moreland's second point is especially persuasive: Given antecedent Jewish beliefs concerning the intermediate state of the righteous dead prior to the final resurrection at history's end, hallucinatory experiences on the part of the disciples would have led only to their belief in Jesus' *assumption* into heaven, not to their belief in his resurrection from the dead. That latter conclusion requires further explanation.

A problem with the hallucinatory hypothesis is that the earliest Christians precisely distinguished between a resurrection *appearance* of Jesus and a *vision* of Jesus.[23] The church experienced ecstatic visions of Christ and knew that these were qualitatively distinct from the resurrection appearances. But this distinction undercuts the hallucinatory hypothesis, since hallucinations could at best be construed as belonging to the category of visions.

Moreland's final point concerning the origin of the Christian church needs, I think, refinement.[24] He is correct that no adequate explanation of the origin of the Christian movement is available which omits reference to the historical event of Jesus' resurrection, but it seems to me that Moreland has not formulated the argument correctly. By construing the point in terms of the movement's "incredible success" and "the motivation and endurance of the early Christians," Moreland leaves himself open to obvious counterexamples of movements which he must regard as not divinely initiated, such as Islam or Mormonism, but whose adherents demonstrated great motivation and endurance and which have been enormously successful. Therefore, his point should have been that the Christian movement could not have originated had the earliest disciples failed to believe in Jesus' resurrection. Without such belief, Jesus could only be regarded as a tragic failure, nay, worse: the crucifixion would have revealed him to be a heretic under the curse of God (Deut. 21:22–23).

But since the disciples did believe, the question becomes, How does one explain the *origin* of the disciples' unprecedented belief in this rabbi's resurrection from the dead? It can be plausibly argued that nothing in Judaism or paganism before or during the disciples' lifetime suffices to explain the origin of that belief. (Here Moreland raises some excellent points on the dissimilarity of ancient Judaism to Christian beliefs.) Therefore, the most plausible explanation is that the event of the resurrection itself lay at the foundation of the disciples' belief and the origin of the Christian Way.

Finally, the miracle of the resurrection is certainly unparalleled in other world religions, as Moreland points out. Any miracles that might be adduced in favor of a counter-Christian claim pale by comparison.

Nielsen's Refutation

Well, it appears that Nielsen really dropped the ball at this point. As one looks at his flow chart on page 155, one sees almost nothing but blank paper to the right of Moreland's arguments.

In response to the teleological argument, Nielsen asserts that Moreland's evidence shows only design in the world, not of the world. But what philosophically significant difference is this distinction supposed to capture? Moreland's point *1.a.* is certainly design of the world; and as for *1.b.*, to what cause is this complex order to be attributed? Nielsen doesn't even begin to address the issues. He complains that Moreland's argument doesn't show the Designer to be a personal, infinite creator. But the argument certainly proves Him to be personal, since He is a designing intelligence. As for being a creator, that is proved by the cosmological, not the teleological, argument. That there is one Designer-Creator is justified by the principle that one should not multiply causes beyond necessity. As for the attribute of infinity, I shall reserve comment until later. In his concluding statement, Nielsen belatedly introduces a new objection: It is somehow inappropriate to speak of the universe as a whole. But this objection is singularly unconvincing, since such parlance is commonplace in astrophysical cosmology. It must be admitted that Moreland does not rebut Nielsen's objections to the teleological argument; but those objections are so misconceived or underdeveloped that they fail to scathe the argument as originally stated. In summary, Nielsen fails to refute the conclusion that a personal being of enormous intelligence designed the universe and was responsible for bringing life into existence—a conclusion which certainly makes belief in God rational.

Furthermore, so far as I can see, Nielsen says nothing in response to Moreland's other preliminary arguments, except indirectly, in that the issue of religious experience comes up again in the context of ostensively defining God. I shall defer comment on that issue also until I discuss Nielsen's case. It seems to me, therefore, that Moreland comes out of the preliminary arguments with at least a strong design argument for theism.

What about Nielsen's response to Moreland's crucial contention *I?* His refutation here is even more paltry than his response to the teleological argument. He objects that the philosophical argument only proves some factually necessary being or beings, not an infinite, eternal God. But a factually necessary being is a being that is uncaused, eternal, incorruptible, and indestructible.[25] It is what many theists take God to be. Hence, Moreland has, by Nielsen's own admission, given reason to believe there exists an uncaused, changeless, eternal, timeless, incorruptible, indestructible, free, personal Intelligence who created and designed the world. Again, concerning the question of infinity, I shall comment shortly.

In response to the scientific evidence for the origin of the universe, Nielsen belatedly complains that it is "dangerous" for a theist to rest his case on scientific evidence because theories of science are constantly changing. I cannot help but smile whenever I hear this piece of fatherly advice proferred to theists by atheists. It seems that whenever people think that some scientific theory, such as Darwinian evolution or, more recently, Relativity Theory or Quantum Theory, contradicts theism or biblical doctrine, they eagerly jump on the bandwagon of science and proclaim another victory in "the warfare between science and religion." But the minute a scientific theory confirms the theistic view, people start jumping off the wagon, and we are apt to hear grave intonations about "scientific mythology" and how "very, very, very risky indeed" this line of argument is. Moreland's response is right on the money: (1) his case does not *rest* on science, but it is *supported* or confirmed by it; (2) the same uncertainty that attends scientific evidence for Christian theism also attends any evidence against it; (3) we have no choice but to go on what the best evidence now indicates, and that evidence supports theism.

Finally, Nielsen objects that the being proved by the cosmological argument doesn't "link up" with Jesus of Nazareth. Not only is this irrelevant, since the debate is on theism, not *Christian* theism, but Moreland's whole contention *II* is constructed to show that link-up. Nielsen's repeated question, "Why Christianity rather than _____?" completely ignores Moreland's arguments for *II*, as Moreland effectively points out. All Nielsen says in response to *II*. *A-D* is that it doesn't prove an infinite, intelligible being exists or give meaning to the term "God," which is a completely irrelevant objection that fails to understand the purpose of *II*.

In short, the debate over Moreland's case ends with Nielsen tacitly *admitting* the existence of a factually necessary, timeless, changeless, free, personal Creator of the universe, and the resurrection of Jesus Christ from the dead. In addition, Moreland has presented an argument for a cosmic Designer that is unimpaired by Nielsen's objections and has shown Christian truth-claims to be uniquely substantiated by evidence.

Why is Nielsen willing to give away so much? Why is his refutation so skimpy? The answer to those questions may come in Nielsen's repeated complaint that Moreland hasn't proven the Designer-Creator to be infinite. At first blush, this may seem bewildering. Why should Moreland have to prove that? Moreland has given us a being that corresponds to a core concept of God that is full enough to make any atheist squirm with discomfort. So what if he hasn't *proven* the Creator to be infinite? That doesn't show that He is *not*.

But as Nielsen's own case reveals, Nielsen thinks of infinity as an essential attribute of God. Therefore, on Nielsen's view, unless Moreland proves the Designer-Creator to be infinite, he has not proven the existence of *God*. If one says that perhaps the Designer-Creator is infinite (even if we can't prove it), then Nielsen will launch into his case that the concept of an infinite God is incoherent. Hence, the Designer-Creator must be finite. Accordingly, Moreland's view is, paradoxically, still atheistic!

Now Moreland could counter by denying that infinity is an essential attribute of God and therefore contend that his view is theistic. After all, it seems bizarre to label as "atheistic" a worldview according to which there exists a personal Creator who brought the world into being out of nothing and has revealed Himself in Jesus Christ. Indeed, it isn't even clear what Nielsen means by "infinity" in this context. At any rate, as theists use it, the term doesn't really specify any attribute of God at all but rather is a catch-all term, qualifying all of God's most theologically important attributes: *omni*potence, *omni*presence, *omni*science, and so forth. But for that very reason, I don't think Moreland would take this tack. The theistic arguments, even if successful, don't prove many of these "omni-" attributes, yet I feel certain that Moreland would say that any being would have to possess them to qualify as God.

But must Moreland prove that the Designer-Creator has all the essential attributes of God in order to make it plausible or rational that God exists? Such a demand is clearly unreasonable, for applied to even ordinary objects, it leads to scepticism. For example, an essential property of J. P. Moreland is "created by God." But then in order to prove that J. P. Moreland exists, we should have to prove that God exists! Besides, we have no idea whatsoever of what all the essential properties of anything are.

Perhaps we should say that it is rational to believe that something exists if (1) it is rational to believe that something exemplifying some of its key attributes exists, and (2) no good reason has been given to doubt that that thing exemplifies the remaining attributes as well. If one takes this line, then Moreland has not shown it rational to think that God exists until he has refuted Nielsen's case—that is, until he has shown that no good reason has been given to doubt that the Designer-Creator is infinite. Perhaps Moreland should follow Aquinas's lead in concluding simply to a Designer-Creator of the universe with the various attributes he has proven and then add, "And this is what everybody calls God." After all, Nielsen has given away so much that he has really put his back to the wall, for he must now prove positively that the concept of God is incoherent or else admit that Moreland has proven the rationality of belief in God's existence.

Analysis of Nielsen's Case

As I read him, Nielsen's loosely organized case runs as follows:

PRINCIPAL THESIS: *It is irrational for a well-educated person in the twentieth century to believe that God exists.*

MAJOR CONTENTION:
 I. *The concept "God" is incoherent*
  A. Anthropomorphic concepts of God are superstitious
  B. Theological concept of God is incoherent
   1. "God" fails to refer to anything
    a. One can't refer to God by ostensive definition
     ——Anything literally experienced wouldn't be God but would be temporal and limited
    b. One can't refer to God by definite description
     ——Such definitions are problematic and incomprehensible
     ——Concepts of eternal or logically necessary being are incoherent
   2. Responses to possible objections
    a. "God is mysterious"—one cannot have faith in or prove something we can't understand
    b. "There are unobservables in science"—they are only contingently, not in principle, unobservable
    c. "God is observable indirectly in His works"—something indirectly observable must be in theory directly observable, which God is not
    d. "Mathematical objects are unobservable"

——That assumes Platonism is true
——Number are comprehensible, but an infinite, transcen-
    dent individual isn't
(1) Numbers are types (not individuals)
(2) God is a token being (an individual)

Now the first thing to notice is that Nielsen's principal thesis is the
contradictory to Moreland's; theism cannot be both rational and irrational. But Nielsen's claim is also modest, for he leaves it open that atheism as well as theism may be irrational (which was the position of the
great sceptic Pierre Bayle, for example). Moreover, given his stringent
definition of "theism," Nielsen's argument, even if successful, leaves it
open that a personal Designer-Creator of the universe exists, who has
revealed Himself in Christ by raising Him from the dead.

Nielsen charges that the anthropomorphic concept of God is superstitious and the theological concept incoherent. Unfortunately, he
never clearly tells us what is objectionable in the theological concept;
he only states that we cannot understand it. We don't really know, he
claims, what we are talking about when we use the word "God" (cf. my
earlier discussion of "imaginary time"). We can try to give content to
this term by either ostensive definition or a definite description.

But ostensive definition fails because "anything that could be . . .
literally experienced . . . wouldn't be God." Now this seems to be a
audacious claim, since people such as Moreland claim to experience
God in a real way every day. How does Nielsen know that their experiences are not veridical? After all, they are *their* experiences, not *his*.
Because, he answers, what is experienced "would be some kind of
temporal something you could detect, limited." But how does it follow
that God is limited by being known by finite minds? He could be an
infinite Mind only partially experienced by us, and He could be thus
experienceable at any point in space and time. As for being temporal,
what is wrong with that? Perhaps when God created time He entered
into : in order to sustain relations with His creatures.[26] A great many
orthodox theists, such as Alvin Plantinga, Nicholas Wolterstorff, Richard Swinburne, Stephen Davis, and Alan Padgett follow the lead of Dun
Scotus and William Ockham in holding that God is temporal. Therefore,
we could make sense of "God" by saying, "I am referring to the being
whose personal presence and love I experience in prayer." This is precisely the point Moreland makes in his rebuttal.

At this point Nielsen's argument degenerates. Nielsen charges
that such experiences are not like direct perception of God because

incompatible religions have them. But this confuses the argument about ostensive definition with the argument for God's existence from religious experience. The fact of competing religious claims does not prove that the experiences of none of them refer to God or, in particular, that Moreland's does not.[27] Nielsen reasserts that there cannot be "a nonsensory awareness of an infinite eternal God transcendent to the world." But if God is temporal subsequent to creation and able to act causally at all points in space, what is the problem? I don't see any difficulty here, though it must be admitted that Moreland in his concluding statement is not at all successful in clarifying the muddy waters stirred up by Nielsen.

In any case, why can't an intelligible definite description be given for the term "God"? There seem to be two reasons given in Nielsen's discussion. First, such descriptions, while not meaningless, are "problematic" and "so obscure that . . . we don't know what we are talking about when we use them." But I must confess that I don't know what Professor Nielsen's problem is. I have a perfectly perspicuous idea of, to use his example, "the Maker of heaven and earth." And analytic philosophy of religion has helped give clear, coherent definitions to divine attributes such as eternity, omniscience, omnipotence, necessity, and moral perfection.[28] Philosophers have made it perfectly clear what they're talking about.

Indeed, Nielsen's objection serves to underscore the value of analytic philosophy of religion as a corrective to the mushy-minded thinking that reigns in Continental theology. There it is very true that the concept of God is so vague and undefined that neither we nor, I dare say, the theologians understand what they are talking about. But I'm afraid that Professor Nielsen is just out of touch with what is going on in contemporary analytic philosophy of religion.

At certain points Nielsen's argument seems to be that we don't know what "God" refers to because He is unobservable, which forces him into the patently false position that (1) unobservable theoretical entities in science are only contingently, not in principle, unobservable and (2) something which is indirectly observable must be in theory directly observable, points for which Moreland then jumps all over him. Nielsen's reply is fumbling and scarcely coherent. I think he wants to say that because certain theoretical entities exist in the world, they are observable in principle, but God is not because He transcends the world. But while there certainly is this difference between, say, God and neutrinos, it does nothing to prove, nor is it true, that certain theoretical entities are in principle observable. Therefore, on Nielsen's view, we should have to say that certain segments of science are as empty of content as theology.

In any case, isn't this business about "observability" wholly beside the point? "Unobservability" could actually be part of my definite description of God. Nielsen seems to confuse our ability to identify God via a definition with the practical problem of identifying Him in the sense of "finding" Him. Unobservability would create problems for the latter (especially if God wanted to hide and refused to reveal Himself), but it presents no problem at all for the former, semantic issue.

Later Nielsen seems to argue that the problem with a definite description for "God" is that we can't make sense of the concept of an infinite, transcendent individual. But why not? He asserts that we have no understanding of what it is for an individual to be eternal. But if numbers exist (here my sympathies are with Nielsen), then the number 7 is certainly an individual abstract object—and so are possible worlds, individual essences, and propositions. As for infinity, this is, as I said, merely a catch-all term describing God's maximal attributes, and Nielsen has not yet demonstrated any incoherence in the idea of a being who, say, knows only and all true propositions or is morally perfect.

But Nielsen seems to have a second reason for rejecting definite descriptions of "God": the concept of an eternal or logically necessary individual or person is incoherent. Perhaps this is just a restatement of the first point, but I take Nielsen to mean more than merely "incomprehensible," but "demonstrably internally contradictory." But what is the logical incoherence of a being who exists in every possible world? Nielsen just reasserts that an individual can't be logically necessary. But why not? Nielsen seems to know nothing of the work of philosophers such as Alvin Plantinga or Robert Adams which defends the coherence of this notion.[29] Similarly, Nielsen gives no reason to think that a person cannot be eternal, or timeless. But an infinite Mind, having no need to think discursively but enjoying an immediate intuition of all truth, could be timeless. Only if He were really related to other changing things would He need be temporal.[30]

In summary, though Moreland does not make all these points, he does show that Nielsen fails to prove either that God can't be ostensively defined by the believer in religious experience or that the concept "God" is any more problematic than theoretical entities in science or abstract objects in mathematics and metaphysics.

Conclusion

In conclusion, we have seen that the debaters take diametrically opposed positions on whether theism is rational. Moreland gives at least two persuasive arguments for a Designer-Creator of the universe. Nielsen more or less concedes these, but insists that theism, strictly speaking, has not been proved because the Designer-Creator has not been proved to be infinite. Indeed, he alleges, this cannot be proved because the concept of an infinite individual who created the world is incomprehensible and incoherent. But Moreland shows that Nielsen fails to prove that we cannot give intelligible content to the concept "God" by either ostention or definite description. Since Nielsen fails to carry his case and more or less concedes Moreland's arguments, then, on the principle that it is rational to believe that something exists if (1) it is rational to believe that something exemplifying some of its key attributes exists and (2) no good reason has been given to doubt that that thing exemplifies the remaining attributes as well, we must say that Moreland has successfully demonstrated that it is rational to hold that God exists.

Notes

1. Moreland improperly calls these ' singularities." A singularity is a point beyond which a world line in space-time cannot be extended.
2. John D. Barrow, *The World within the World* (Oxford: Clarendon, 1988), 360. I have adapted my illustration from Barrow's.
3. Ibid., 355–56.
4. See Dietrick E. Thomsen, "The Quantum Universe: A Zero-Point Fluctuation?" *Science News* 128 (3 August 1985), 73. To get some idea of how large this number is, consider the fact that there are only 10^{80} subatomic particles in the whole known universe!
5. Fred Hoyle and N. C. Wickramasinghe, *Evolution from Space* (New York: Simon & Schuster, 1981), 23.
6. Ibid., 30.
7. Ibid., 3.
8. Frank J. Tipler and John D. Barrow, *The Anthropic Cosmological Principle* (Oxford: Clarendon Press, 1986), 557–65.
9. For a more formal critique, see William Lane Craig, "Barrow and Tipler on the Anthropic Principle vs. Divine Design," *British Journal for the Philosophy of Science* 38 (1988), 389–95. See also John Earman, "The SAP Also Rises: A Critical Examination of the Anthropic Principle," *American Philo-*

sophical Quarterly 24 (1987), 307–17, and my reply in "The Teleological Argument and the Anthropic Principle," in *Rational Theism*, Wm. L. Craig and M. McLeod, eds. (Lewiston, N.Y.: Edwin Mellen, forthcoming).

10. See my discussion in my *The Kalam Cosmological Argument* (London: Macmillan, 1979), 149–53. Cf. also Stewart C. Goetz, "Craig's Kalam Cosmological Argument," *Faith and Philosophy* 6 (1989), 99–102; William Lane Craig, "The Kalam Cosmological Argument and the Hypothesis of a Quiescent Universe," *Faith and Philosophy* (forthcoming).

11. Alan Guth and Mark Sher, "The Impossibility of a Bouncing Universe," *Nature* 302 (1983): 505–506; Sidney A. Bludman, "Thermodynamics and the End of a Closed Universe," *Nature* 308 (1984), 319–22.

12. I. D. Novikov and Ya. B. Zeldovich, "Physical Processes Near Cosmological Singularities," *Annual Review of Astronomy and Astrophysics* 11 (1973), 401–402; P. C. W. Davies, *The Physics of Time Asymmetry* (London: Surrey University Press, 1974), 188; P. T. Landsberg, "Entropy in an Oscillating Universe," *Proceedings of the Royal Society of London* A346 (1975), 485–95.

13. Joseph Silk, *The Big Bang* (San Francisco: W. H. Freeman, 1980), 311–12.

14. Stephen Hawking, *A Brief History of Time* (New York: Bantam Books, 1988), 46.

15. Hawking, 140–41.

16. For a more in-depth critique, see William Lane Craig, " 'What Place, Then, for a Creator?': Hawking on God and Creation," *British Journal for the Philosophy of Science* (forthcoming).

17. See John A. Wheeler, "From Relativity to Mutability," in *The Physicist's Conception of Nature*, J. Mehra, ed. (Dordrecht: D. Reidel, 1973), 227; "Beyond the Black Hole," in *Some Strangeness in the Proportion*, Harry Wolf, ed. (Reading, Mass.: Addison-Wesley, 1980), 346–50. Cf. C. Misner, K. S. Thorne, and J. A. Wheeler, *Gravitation* (San Francisco: W. H. Freeman, 1973), 1182–83.

18. Arthur Eddington, *Space, Time and Gravitation* (1920; rep. ed.: Cambridge: Cambridge University Press, 1987), 48. Referring to imaginary time as one of those "illustrations which certainly do not correspond to any physical reality," Eddington wrote, "It can scarcely be regarded as any more than an analytical device" (Ibid., 181, 48).

19. Hawking, *A Brief History of Time*, 139.

20. Wolfhart Pannenberg, *Jesus: God and Man*, trans. L. L. Wilkins and D. A. Priebe (London: SCM Press, 1968), 67; idem, "Jesu Geschichte und unsere Geschichte," in his *Glaube und Wirklichkeit* (München: Chr. Kaiser, 1975), 92.

21. See William Lane Craig, *Assessing the New Testament Evidence for the Historicity of the Resurrection of Jesus* (Lewiston, N.Y.: Edwin Mellen, 1989).

22. Ibid., 351–78.

23. Ibid., 67–72, 382–94, 401–408.

24. Ibid., 404–18.

25. See John H. Hick, "God as Necessary Being," *Journal of Philosophy* 57 (1960), 733–34.

26. See William Lane Craig, "God, Time, and Eternity," *Religious Studies* 14 (1979), 497–503; Alan Padgett, "God and Time: Toward a New Doctrine of Divine Timeless Eternity," *Religious Studies,* Dec. 1989.

27. See William Alston, "Religious Diversity and Perceptual Knowledge of God," *Faith and Philosophy* 5 (1988), 442–43. He argues that the diversity of religious experience does not undermine the rationality of the Christian's claim because, even if his process of forming his belief is as reliable as you please, we have no idea of what a non-circular proof of this fact would be. You may also be profitably referred to Alston's "Referring to God," *International Journal for Philosophy of Religion* 24 (1988), 113–27, for a discussion of the issue raised by Nielsen. Alston argues that God may be referred to by direct reference or by a definite description.

28. On eternity, see Padgett, "God and Time"; on omniscience, Jonathan Kvanvig, *The Possibility of an All-Knowing God* (New York: St. Martin's, 1986), Chap. 2; on omnipotence, Thomas P. Flint and Alfred J. Freddoso, "Maximal Power" in *The Existence and Nature of God,* A. J. Freddoso, ed. (Notre Dame, Ind.: University of Notre Dame Press, 1983), 81–113; on necessity, Robert Merrihew Adams, "Has It Been Proved that All Real Existence Is Contingent?" *American Philosophical Quarterly* 8 (1971), 284–91; on moral perfection, Thomas V. Morris, *Anselmian Explorations* (Notre Dame, Ind.: University of Notre Dame Press, 1987), Chaps. 2, 3.

29. Alvin Plantinga, *The Nature of Necessity* (Oxford: Clarendon Press, 1974), 197–221; Adams, "Existence," 284–91.

30. For a discussion, see Craig, "God, Time, and Eternity"; idem, "God, Creation and Mr. Davies," *British Journal for the Philosophy of Science* 37 (1986), 163–75; William Alston, "Does God Have Beliefs?" *Religious Studies* 22 (1986), 287–306.

12 Antony Flew

The Case for God Challenged

The business of a commentator is to comment rather than to develop his own case[1] for or against whatever proposition is in dispute. So I will deploy a series of not always necessarily connected comments upon the contributions of Professor J. P. Moreland.

1. Moreland speaks of "the argument for God based on the design in the universe" and asserts: "In spite of David Hume, this argument has received strong support in recent years from astronomy, physics, and biology." But Moreland fails to make what is here the essential distinction: between, first, arguments to the conclusion that the universe as a whole is a product of design; and, second, reasons for contending that some particular feature of the universe cannot be explained naturalistically, and should therefore be accepted as resulting from some special, one-off, Divine intervention.

Fred Hoyle's calculations of "the chance possibilities of life arising spontaneously through mere chance" are presumably intended to sustain a conclusion of the second sort. To this, as indeed to any argument to a "God of the gaps," the best response is: first, to insist that before Darwin, "the chance possibilities of" all the innumerable forms of multicellular "life arising spontaneously" rather than through special creation must have appeared, far, far smaller still; and then, to recommend Richard Dawkins's quite brilliant exposition of the Neo-Darwinian account of biological evolution.[2]

What David Hume, I believe, succeeded in refuting was the first kind of argument to design; and it is this which Moreland believes "has received strong support in recent years from astronomy and physics." Suppose we assume that the fundamental laws and constants of physics are what physicists today believe them to be; then it is possible to show that, if the values of some, or perhaps any of, those constants had been appreciably different from what they now appear to be, then intelligent life—so far as we certainly know, represented only by our own species—or perhaps any life at all, could not have evolved. It appears that, as the great Duke himself said of Waterloo: "It was a damned nice, close-run thing."[3]

The result of such calculations could, I am prepared to allow, provide some premises for an argument to construction by some immensely powerful yet nevertheless still finite and limited Fabricator—a Being out of the same stable as the Demiurge of Plato's *Timaeus*.[4] But we are supposed here to be debating the existence of the God of the three great Mosaic traditions of Judaism, Christianity, and Islam. And this God is stipulated as possessing various characteristics, some of which are awkward if not downright impossible to reconcile either with one another or with undeniable and undenied features of the universe. More on this later.

Most immediately relevant is that, unlike that Demiurge, the Being now being hypothesized is the Creator. But, by the hypothesis, a Creator determines both the content of all laws of nature and the values of all physical constants. Again, by the hypothesis, this Creator sees the production of human life as an or *the* main object of the whole exercise. So, given omniscience and omnipotence, why bother with any so nicely and so ingeniously arranged mechanisms? Why not, in the forthright fashion of the God of the opening chapters of Genesis, create whatever is wanted immediately and directly, without any necessarily redundant intervening means?

The truth is that every evidence of design must always be, as far as it goes, "evidence *against* the Omnipotence of the Designer. For what is meant by Design? Contrivance: the adaptation of means to an end. But the necessity for contrivance—the need of employing means—is a consequence of the limitation of power. Who would have recourse to means if to attain his end his mere word was sufficient?"[5]

Of course, such objections can be met by insisting that "His ways are not our ways";[6] and that, therefore and notoriously, they transcend all finite understanding. But this, as Hume suggested in his refutation of this first sort of argument to design, is something that should have been remembered before any attempts were made to think outside the universe; rather than, as here, offered only in response to a troublesome objection.

2. In one of his most remarkable works, Aquinas argued that—although, of course, since it was *de fide* to believe that the universe had a beginning, a belief he himself held—nevertheless it is not a conclusion which can be established by natural philosophical reason and without benefit of divine revelation. Moreland is so imprudent as to disagree: "If one cannot cross an actual infinite, then the past must have been finite. If it were infinite, then to come to the present moment, one

would have had to have traversed an actual infinite to get here, which is impossible."

Oh dear! This argument assumes the very conclusion which it is presented to prove. For only if you set out from a temporal starting position infinitely far removed from the present would you have to "cross an actual infinite" in order to get where we are now. But to hold that the universe was without beginning and will be without end, precisely is to *deny* that the universe and time itself had a beginning (and will have an end). It is not to *assert* that it did, after all, have a beginning; but a beginning one actual infinite time ago.

3. Since I have fairly recently had my own extensive say in a similar debate on the alleged resurrection of Jesus bar Joseph,[7] and since we are not at present primarily concerned with the credentials of the Christian revelation, I shall not spend much of my present space on this topic. But two of Moreland's claims did cause me to raise my eyebrows. The first was "that we have clear widespread testimony to a miracle-working, supernatural, resurrected Jesus no later than fifteen to twenty years after the events of his life." The second was the contention that "a large generation of Jewish people" were "willing to risk the damnation of their own souls to hell" by rejecting traditional teaching.[8]

About that second point, it will be sufficient to mention two things. First, although it may well be that most of the first Christians already accepted before their conversion from Judaism what Darwin so rightly described as the "damnable doctrine" of eternal torment,[9] still Matthew tells us that there were also "the Sadducees, which say that there is no resurrection" (Matt. 22:23, KJV). Second, the new and rival doctrine was in any case enforced by similar threats.

It is, however, the first of Moreland's two claims that is so breathtaking to anyone familiar with evidential disputes about the prima facie miraculous phenomena of parapsychology (*nee* psychical research).[10] Even allowing that—for the reasons urged by my respected sometime Ancient History tutor Sherwin-White——"clear widespread testimony" can be dated to "the first decade of Christianity after the death of Jesus" instead of to "no later than fifteen or twenty years after," still it remains merely "clear . . . testimony" that certain events were widely believed actually to have occurred much earlier and that certain things were widely believed to have been taught much earlier.

All this is utterly different from the *immediately* recorded testimony of those who were themselves witnesses to the events or auditors of the teachings in question. Certainly the hard persons of parapsychology, although concerned with the alleged occurrence of phenomena considerably less far removed from all ordinary experience than raisings of the unequivocally dead or miraculous multiplications of food supplies, would give little weight even to eye-witness testimony, unless this had been recorded hours or days rather than months or years after the event. But in the present case we have no signed and sworn eye-witness depositions whatsoever, however belated; nor, as near as makes precious little matter, any directly relevant evidence at all from non-Christian sources. Most regrettably, any contemporary administrative or judicial records that were made must have been lost in the destruction of Jerusalem in A.D. 70.

If, as all professing Christians used to believe,[11] some once and for all revelation was made in Roman-occupied Israel in the early thirties of our era, then it might seem that, whether because of or despite the enormous rewards and penalties to be imposed for the revelation's acceptance or rejection, the Revealer was not overly (if at all) concerned that it should be easily or decisively identified as such. Moreland is, I think, therefore wise to put most weight upon the argument that only a physical resurrection could have "changed . . . and motivated" the despairing disciples. But then, if all or most of them had witnessed all the miracles recorded in the Gospels, including the raising of the not merely dead but already stinking Lazarus (John 11:39), why were they not hopefully awaiting some similarly spectacular further confirmation of the later recorded claims of Jesus?

4. My sometime philosophical colleague and political sparring partner Professor Kai Nielsen chose as his main line of attack the contention that the idea of God shared by the three great traditions of Mosaic theism is incoherent. That was, he recognized, a choice that "puts all your eggs in one basket." And a bold strategic choice it was. But to go ahead on this line of reasoning without first taking great care to show how some term or expression may be in some way immediately intelligible, while nevertheless remaining ultimately incoherent, was not so much bold as reckless. For it left him wide open to Moreland's objection against the oddity and presumptuousness of saying "that 99.9 percent of the entire human race has literally not known what they were talking about when they used the word 'God.'"

Since Descartes argued that his own (and hence, presumably, everyone else's) idea of God was innate and that it thus constituted, as it were, the trademark of our Maker,[12] it perhaps becomes relevant to point out that much of mankind has never had occasion even to entertain this idea. The first Jesuit missionaries in China, finding no native equivalent to European words for God, tried to make their message more acceptable to Confucians by misemploying the Chinese character which in translations from the *Analects* and other classics is always rendered "heaven."[13] This Jesuitical maneuver was in time, and quite correctly, condemned by the Pope as a misrepresentation of the faith that those missionaries had been sent out to spread.

a. To forestall Moreland's understandably forceful objection, Nielsen should surely have provided a few examples of expressions, which although certainly to some degree immediately intelligible, can nevertheless in the last analysis be shown to be either simply incoherent or otherwise unviable. He might, for instance, have made an extremely relevant reference to Leibniz. He contended—in his 1684 "Reflections on knowledge, truth, and ideas"—that, before the ontological argument could demonstrate the existence of God, it was first necessary to demonstrate that the concept of God as a logically necessary Being is coherent. To establish the possibility of immediate intelligibility masking ultimate incoherence, Leibniz provided a characteristically elegant demonstration of the incoherence of the idea of a highest conceivable speed.

Again, the Roman Catholic doctrine of transsubstantiation—which at one time heretics might have been burnt alive for rejecting[14]—has sometimes been most persuasively assailed as strictly senseless. For what could it mean to say that, while all the accidents of the bread and wine remain the same, the substances of the elements have been replaced? How indeed could any substance be identified save by reference to its defining characteristics?

b. Nielsen makes much of the problem of identification, yet, I think, still not enough. With those other famous and long-debated existential questions—"Are there in Loch Ness surviving members of some marine species previously believed extinct?" and "Are there Abominable Snowpersons?"—everyone knows, at least roughly, what would have to be discovered in order to justify emphatically affirmative answers. Certainly to set out upon a search for a or the so-and-so without any satisfactory prior specification as to how a or the so-and-so was to be positively identified as such would be an enterprise no more sensible, and much less entertaining than, "The Hunting of the Snark."

Certainly too, scientists hypothesizing supposedly explanatory entities would be expected to indicate, even if only rather vaguely, what testable consequences must follow if indeed there actually are any such things as the entities thus hypothesized. And furthermore, the very fact that, according to Nielsen, conventional wisdom maintains "that you can't prove that God does exist and you can't prove that He doesn't exist" should be revealed as suggesting what Hume systematically showed—that "God" must be disqualified for service as a term in any explanatory hypothesis.

5. At the beginning of his "Rebuttal," Moreland asserts: "I think that God can be detected in religious experience. I believe that there is a form of numinous perception. . . . And I find religious perception to be very, very similar to sensory perception."[15] In his "Closing Arguments for Christianity," he testifies to his own experience:

> As a university student in 1968, I met Jesus Christ personally and He changed my life. I have had close to two decades of walking with Him and fellowshiping with Him and falling more and more in love with Him daily. He has given me a power for life that I did not know before, and I have had personal experiences of Him.

a. I have to say that, as evidence for the truth of the religious beliefs that it is offered to support, Moreland's appeal to his "personal experiences" strikes me as absolutely grotesque. So, in hopes of thereby slightly softening the harshness of my rebuttal, I will approach it a little indirectly, by way of a consideration of his treatment in "Questions and Answers" of what are now normally called Near-Death Experiences (NDEs). He says, "I'm not certain what to make of these, but I'm not going to reject them *a priori*."

Moreland's mistake is to assume that anyone refusing to accept these experiences as evidence for the existence, detachability, and *post mortem* survival of an essentially incorporeal, substantial soul must thereby and necessarily be giving the lie to all claims to have had NDEs.

To appreciate why this assumption is false, we need to develop the fundamental distinction between two senses of the word "experience." In the ordinary everyday sense—that in which a farmer might announce his need for hands experienced in dealing with cows—anyone so experienced must have both knowingly perceived and possess some theoretical and practical knowledge of real, external world, flesh-and-blood cows. But in the peculiar, philosophers' sense—the private as opposed to the public sense—someone might truly claim to have enjoyed experiences of cows without that assertion entailing any actual perception of such ruminants. It would be sufficient to have dreamed of cows, to have suffered hallucinations involving cows, or merely to have had—without prejudice—"cowish" sense-data.

This fundamental distinction once firmly made, it should become obvious that we may consistently concede the complete honesty of witnesses in their testimony about their *private* experience, while nevertheless insisting that, construed as accounts describing or misdescribing their *public* experience, their testimony is—partly or mainly or even totally—mistaken. Perhaps, for instance, the patient tells us, quite truthfully, that while she was at death's door, she seemed to herself to be on some kind of trip. Perhaps too she even comes up with information, which she had no normal means of acquiring, about "things that . . . happened two blocks away."[16] We, however, presumably know that she was all the time lying on her hospital bed, apparently unconscious. So, since any information acquired by a disembodied soul could only be acquired "by ESP," the most economical response, applying Ockham's Razor, would be to say that she must indeed have acquired that illicit information by that putative meansless means but while still motionless in bed.

b. Turning now directly to the passage just quoted from Moreland, it would seem that we also need another distinction: between, on the one hand, the immediate operations and the direct influence of some individual; and, on the other hand, the effects upon other people of their own beliefs about that individual. I remember seeing in Moscow a poster proclaiming: "Lenin's words and Lenin's ideas live. He is an inspiration to millions."[17] It is quite clear that in saying that "He has given me a power for life that I did not know before," Moreland intends to assert far more about Jesus than Soviet propaganda was asserting about Lenin.

Had Moreland been a very much older man than he is and had he announced that in, say, 1918, "I met Lenin personally and he changed my life," there would be no problem about either the interpretation or the truth of that announcement. Since Moreland certainly believes that in the early thirties of the first century Jesus rose from the dead, I suppose Moreland's talk about his "personal experiences of Him" might now be construed in a similarly straightforward way—as claiming, that is, the same sorts of perceptual experience of the risen Jesus as were, it is said, vouchsafed to doubting Thomas. This interpretation, however, has only to be mentioned to be dismissed at once.

But now, what have we left? All that Moreland is entitled to claim, surely, is that he enjoyed overwhelmingly vivid experiences—experiences such that it seemed to him that he "met Jesus Christ personally," that he was "walking with Him and fellowshiping with Him," and so on. I do not doubt for a moment that Moreland did have such experiences. Nor do I have any hesitation in my further belief, which I presumably share with Moreland, that, had I been present when Moreland was having those experiences, there would have been nothing at all out of the ordinary available for either me or for any others present to perceive.

So how is the "Jesus" with whom Moreland is so convinced that he has been communing to be identified as such? By what warrant does Moreland think he knows that he has been, as it were, perceiving rather than hallucinating or exercising his imagination, and that his undoubtedly religious experiences have been of the public rather than the purely private kind? Until and unless we can have a satisfactory answer to these hard questions, the last word must rest with the man known to his contemporaries, not without reason, as "the Monster of Malmesbury." Thomas Hobbes wrote in Chapter 32 of his *Leviathan:* "If a man pretend to me that God hath spoken to him supernaturally, and immediately, and I make doubt of it, I cannot easily perceive what argument he can produce, to oblige me to believe it . . . To say he hath spoken to him in a dream, is no more than to say he dreamed that God spake to him."

6. Back in my Section 1, above, in distinguishing the likes of the Demiurge of Plato's *Timaeus* from the God of the great Mosaic traditions, I stated that the latter is defined as "possessing various characteristics, some of which are awkward if not downright impossible to reconcile either with one another or with undeniable and undenied features of the universe."

a. As an example of the former kind of awkwardness, consider the first clause of Swinburne's preliminary definition in his *The Coherence of Theism:*[18] "a person without a body (i.e., a spirit) who is eternal, free, able to do anything, knows everything, is perfectly good, is the proper object of human worship and obedience, the creator and sustainer of the Universe" (p. 1). Later Swinburne states that "Human persons have bodies: he [God] does not" (p. 51). Again, in the course of a discussion of "What it is for a body to be mine," Swinburne, having first listed various peculiarly personal characteristics, tells us that "we learn to apply the term 'person' to various individuals around us in virtue of their possession of the characteristics which I have outlined" (p. 102).

But if persons really were creatures *possessing* bodies, rather than—as in fact we are—creatures which just essentially *are* members of one special sort of creatures of flesh and blood, then it would make sense to speak of a whole-body amputation. Who is it, too, who is presupposed to be able to ask sensibly which of various bodies is his or hers? How is such a puzzled person to be identified, or to self-identify, save by reference to the living organism which he or she actually is?

As for Swinburne's assertion that we could, and even do, learn to apply the word "person" to "various individuals around us" by first learning how to pick out certain peculiarly personal characteristics and then identifying persons as creatures of the kind that possess these characteristics, it constitutes a perfect paradigm of the literally preposterous. For the manifest truth is that our only experience of any peculiarly personal characteristics is, and indeed has to be, of these as characteristics peculiar to that particular kind of creature we have first learned to identify as a mature and normal human being. The identification of such peculiarly personal characteristics therefore is, and must be, posterior rather than prior to the identification of members of the particular kind of creatures to which alone these characteristics can be and are normally attributed.

It should certainly be seen as at least very far from immediately obvious that talk of "a person without a body (i.e., a spirit)" is coherent and intelligible. For according to their ordinary, everyday understanding, person words—the personal pronouns, personal names, words for persons playing particular roles (such as "spokesperson," "official," "Premier," "aviator"), and so on—are words employed to name or otherwise to refer to members of a very special class of creatures of flesh and blood.

In this ordinary, everyday understanding—what other do we have?—incorporeal persons are no more a sort of person than are imaginary, fictitious, or otherwise nonexistent persons. "Incorporeal" is here, like those others, an alienans adjective. Putting the point less technically but more harshly, in Chapter 5 of *Leviathan* the incorrigible Hobbes maintained, "if a man talks to me of 'a round quadrangle;' or 'accidents of bread in the cheese;' or 'immaterial substances;' . . . I should not say that he was in error, but that his words were without meaning: that is to say, absurd."[19]

Swinburne thought to deflect the ferocity of such critical onslaughts by making the emollient point that no one has any business to argue, just because all the so-and-sos with which they happen themselves to have been acquainted were such-and-such, that therefore such-and-suchness must be an essential characteristic of anything which is to be properly rated a so-and-so (p. 54).

This is indeed perfectly correct. Incorporeality, however, is a very different kettle of fish; or more like no kettle and no fish. For to characterize something as incorporeal is to make an assertion that is at one and the same time both extremely comprehensive and wholly negative. Those proposing to do this surely owe it both to themselves and to others, not only to indicate what positive characteristics might significantly be attributed to their putative incorporeal entities, but also to specify how such entities could, if only in principle, be identified and reidentified. It is not exclusively, or even primarily, a question of what predicates these putative spiritual subjects might take, but of how they themselves might be identified in the first place and (only after that) reidentified as numerically the same through an effluxion of time.

b. The tension considered in the previous subsection was described there only as an awkwardness, not as an incoherence. That was because, while I would argue that there are insuperable obstructions to giving sense to talk of disembodied human persons, these perhaps can be overcome in the special case of God. The difficulties which I do *not* believe can be overcome are those of reconciling certain of the defining characteristics of the theistic God with undeniable and undenied features of the universe—in particular, those of being not only "perfectly good" but also "the creator and sustainer of the universe."

Joseph Butler's *The Analogy of Religion* famously proclaimed that "There is no need of abstruse reasonings and distinctions, to convince an unprejudiced understanding, that there is a God who made and governs the world, and will judge it in righteousness."[20] It ought to be, but it seems that it very rarely is, inescapably clear that to describe as perfectly just and good a Creator—who as such must be the ultimate sufficient cause of every action and every passion of every creature—must be, if that Creator is also said in any way to punish any of these creatures for what are in that Creator's eyes their perceived deficiencies, among other things, flatly contradictory. Of course, if the punishments are in their duration and intensity infinite, then the case must be—in the strictest and most literal understanding—infinitely worse.

The least inadequate earthly analogue to the relation between creatures and their ever-sustaining Creator has to be that of puppets to their puppet-master. Apparent conflicts between individual puppets or puppet factions are always and necessarily bogus; their course and outcomes being determined by the (offstage) puppet-master rather than by the pretendedly independent (onstage) puppets. For such a puppet-master to hold the puppets, whose every move he himself manipulates, responsible for those moves would be absurd, escaping further and heavier condemnation as a moral outrage only because objects of wood and cloth are necessarily impassable.

The introduction of this unlovely picture is bound to provoke indignation and protest. It constitutes, it will be said, the most monstrous misrepresentation of the way in which Christians think. For Christians believe that the Creator gave free will to those creatures who are made in His image. Therefore the least inappropriate picture, and the picture that certainly remains most widely preferred, is that of a Father and his children.

Such protests miss the present point. For the contention is, not that theists in the Mosaic tradition do always, or even often, think in this way, but that these are in truth, albeit widely unrecognized, the necessary consequences of doctrines to which traditional Christians are explicitly and categorically committed. Indeed, it is doubtful whether those who regularly and consistently thought of themselves as the puppet creatures of such a Creator could preserve their sanity. So, to support the actual contention about necessary consequences, consider what Aquinas said in the *Summa contra Gentiles:*

> . . . just as God not only gave being to things when they first
> began, but is also—as the conserving cause of being—the cause of
> their being as long as they last . . . ; so he also not only gave
> things their operative powers when they were first created, but is
> also always the cause of these in things. Hence, if this divine
> influence stopped every operation would stop. Every operation,
> therefore, of anything is traced back to him as its cause. (III, 67)

The relevant, uncomfortable implications of that final statement are spelled out fully in two later chapters:

> God alone can move the will, as an agent, without doing violence
> to it. . . . Some people . . . not understanding how God can cause
> a movement of our will in us without prejudicing the freedom of
> the will, have tried to explain . . . authoritative texts wrongly: that
> is, they would say that God "works in us, to wish and to accom-
> plish" means that he causes in us the power of willing, but not in
> such a way that he makes us will this or that. . . . These people
> are, of course, opposed quite plainly by authoritative texts of Holy
> Writ. For it says in *Isaiah* (26:12), "Lord, you have worked all our
> work in us." Hence we received from God not only the power of
> willing but its employment also. (III, 88–89)

Calvin, of course, and Luther too, maintained substantially the same position. We need, however, to take special note of Luther's insistence that this total divine control abolishes none of the familiar, humanly crucial differences. Thus in 1525, in his *de Servo Arbitrio*, he wrote: "I did not say 'of compulsion' . . . a man without the Spirit of God does not do evil against his will, under pressure, as though he were taken by the scruff of his neck and dragged into it, like a thief or a footpad being dragged off against his will to punishment; but he does it spontaneously and voluntarily" (II, 8).[21]

To his great credit, and in this respect altogether unlike Aquinas, the Reformer is appalled by the so pellucidly perceived implications:

> The highest degree of faith is to believe He is just, though of His
> own will he makes us . . . proper subjects for damnation, and
> seems (in the words of Erasmus) "to delight in the torments of
> poor wretches and to be a fitter object for hate than for love." If I
> could by any means understand how this same God . . . can yet be
> merciful and just, there would be no need for faith. (II, 7)

Asking "Why then does He not alter those evil wills wnich He moves?", Luther concludes, understandably if unsatisfactorily: "It is not for us to inquire into these mysteries, but to adore them. If flesh and blood take offence here and grumble, well, let them grumble; they will achieve nothing; grumbling will not change God! And however many of the ungodly stumble and depart, the elect will remain" (II, 6).

Had we been able to press Luther further, he would doubtless have referred us to a key passage from *Romans;*[22] one which probably was also in the mind of Hobbes when he wrote, this time in Chapter 31. "And Job, how earnestly does he expostulate with God, for the many afflictions he suffered, notwithstanding his righteousness. The question in the case of Job, is decided by God himself, not by arguments derived from Job's sin, but his own power." In the Authorized Version the key passage in *Romans* reads:

> Therefore hath he mercy on whom he will have mercy, and whom
> he will he hardeneth. Thou wilt say then unto me, "Why doth he
> yet find fault? For who hath resisted his will?" Nay but, O man,
> who art thou that repliest against God? Shall the thing formed say
> to him that formed it, "Why has thou made me thus?" . . . What
> if God, willing to shew his wrath, and to make his power known,
> endured with much longsuffering the vessels of wrath fitted to
> destruction; and that he might make known the riches of his glory

on the vessels of mercy, which he had afore prepared unto glory, even us, whom he hath called. (9:18-24)

Notes

1. I have in fact done this in *God and Philosophy* (London: Hutchinson, 1967; reissued in 1984 by Open Court of La Salle, Ill., as *God: A Philosophical Critique*), which may be supplemented by my *The Presumption of Atheism* (London: Pemberton/Elek; and Barnes and Noble, 1976; reissued in 1984 by Prometheus of Buffalo, N.Y., as *God, Freedom and Immortality;* see Part I).
2. *The Blind Watchmaker* (London: Longman, 1986; now available in Penguin paperback).
3. Since Moreland commends the work of the astronomer J. D. Barrow and the physicist F. J. Tipler, it is perhaps worth pointing out that, although their book, *The Anthropic Cosmological Principle* (Oxford: Oxford University Press, 1988), contains a ninety-five-page chapter on "Design Arguments," the authors nowhere associate themselves with any sort of natural theology. Indeed, they are so kind as to commend critiques of that enterprise composed by the present writer (pp. 104, 106).
4. For an interesting exploration of the possibilities of a design argument to a much more modest conclusion, compare the third of J. S. Mill's *Three Essays on Religion* (London: Longmans Green, Reader and Dyer, Third Edition, 1874).
5. Mill, *Three Essays on Religion*, 176-77.
6. Why not, by the way, Her; or—much better—Its? A Creator hypothesized as bodiless becomes conspicuously disqualified from having a sex or—as those indifferent to grammar nowadays prefer to say—a gender.
7. The debate was with Dr. Gary Habermas, and it has been published in *Did Jesus Rise from the Dead? The Resurrection Debate,* Terry L. Miethe, ed. (San Francisco: Harper & Row, 1987). Cf. also G. A. Wells, *A Resurrection Debate* (London: Rationalist Press Association, 1988), and John K. Naland, "The First Easter," *Free Inquiry* (Spring 1988), 10-20.
8. *De aeternitate mundi contra murmurantes*. These opposing murmurers were people who, unaware that Aquinas was destined to be canonized, suggested that his position was heretical.
9. See N. Barlow (ed.) *The Autobiography of Charles Darwin* (London: Collins, 1968), 87: "I can indeed hardly see how anyone ought to wish Christianity to be true; for if so the plain language of the text seems to show that men who do not believe, and this would include my Father, my Brother and almost all my best friends, will be everlastingly punished. And this is a damnable doctrine."

10. Cf., for instance, Paul Kurtz, ed., *A Skeptic's Handbook of Parapsychology* (Buffalo, N.Y.: Prometheus, 1985), and Antony Flew, ed., *Readings in the Philosophical Problems of Parapsychology* (Buffalo, N.Y.: Prometheus, 1987).

11. I insert this reservation in sympathy with Moreland's observation "that within Christendom you can find someone who believes practically anything." David Jenkins, for instance, who, shortly before his elevation to the Senior See of the Church of England, dismissed the physical resurrection of Jesus as "a conjuring trick with bones," thereafter had no hesitation in denouncing, ostensibly in the name of the religion thus so contemptuously and offensively repudiated, the policies of our present Prime Minister as "wicked."

12. See Part IV of Descartes's *Discourse,* and compare his *Meditations* III.

13. 'T'ien' in the Wade-Giles Romanization. In Pinyin this becomes the "tian" of Tiananmen Square, Beijing.

14. Could the source of the enthusiasm with which so many prominent clerics support the Communist-controlled African National Congress derive in some part from a hankering after the days when their predecessors burnt dissidents alive? (Heretics too were, in the South African idiom, "necklaced.")

15. A little later Moreland says: "I would further say that Jesus of Nazareth has caused the garden to have been visited." Is this a reference to my many times reprinted piece "Theology and Falsification?" If so, or even if not, should it not be explained?

16. For a fuller treatment of the evidential significance and lack of significance of NDEs, see Chapter 10 of my *The Logic of Mortality* (Oxford: Blackwell, 1987). It perhaps indicates a contemporary lack of interest in the question of a future life that these were the first set of Gifford lectures to be entirely devoted to it in over sixty years; and that so far, and so far as I know, they have been noticed only in three specialist quarterlies.

17. Flew, *The Logic of Mortality,* 122–23.

18. This is the work cited by Moreland in his first endnote in Chapter 3.

19. The reference to the "accidents of bread in the cheese" was, of course, an altogether characteristic sideswipe against the peculiarly Roman Catholic doctrine of transsubstantiation. Old-fashioned "No Popery!" Protestants should also relish a further comment from Chapter 16:

> The Egyptian conjurors, that are said to have turned their rods to serpents, and the water into blood, are thought to have deluded the senses of the spectators by a false show of things, yet are esteemed enchanters. But what should we have thought of them, if there had appeared in their rods nothing like a serpent, and in the water enchanted nothing like blood, nor like anything else but water, but that

they faced down the king, that they were serpents that looked like rods, and that it was blood that seemed water?

20. *The Works of Joseph Butler,* vol. I, W. E. Gladstone, ed. (Oxford: Clarendon, 1896), 371. See endnote 11, above, for information about the present occupant of the see which Butler once adorned.
21. *The Bondage of the Will,* translated by J. I. Packer and O. R. Johnston (London: J. Clare, 1957).
22. This, and that quoted by Aquinas, are by no means the only texts which he and Luther might have quoted to the same effect. They are all collected in Jonathan Edwards's *The Freedom of the Will,* Paul Ramsey, ed. (New Haven, Conn.: Yale University Press, 1957)—a powerful Calvinist polemic by the first major philosophico-theological talent to emerge within the territories of what were to become the United States.

Is There a Case for Christian Theism?

In his debate with Kai Nielsen, Professor J. P. Moreland argues in defense of the rationality of theistic belief. He puts it this way: "The thesis I wish to defend is that it is rational to believe that God exists. I do not mean that God's existence can be proved with mathematical certainty, but I do want to argue that there are good reasons for believing in God, and the believer is well within her epistemic rights in believing that God exists."

What are "epistemic rights"?[1] To say that I am within my epistemic rights in believing something is to say that I violate no epistemic duties in believing it. An epistemic duty is any duty I have with respect to the formation or holding of my beliefs. For instance, if I own a ship on which certain persons have booked passage, I have a duty not to form the belief "my ship is seaworthy" until I have thoroughly checked and ascertained that my ship is indeed seaworthy. If, on the other hand, I form that belief without adequate checking, and if the ship goes down with loss of life because it is not seaworthy, then I am just as responsible for that loss of life as if I had planted a bomb on the ship.[2]

In general, epistemic duties spell out our intellectual obligations.[3] These include such obligations as not to form our beliefs dishonestly (through self-deception, say) or irresponsibly (for example, by ignoring easily available contrary evidence). To say that I have met all such obligations in the formation of a specific belief is to say that I am within my epistemic rights in holding that belief and, hence, that my belief is *rational*.

Note that when we say that a belief is rational in this sense, we are not in any way endorsing that belief. We are merely saying that for some specific person or group of persons, this is an allowable or permissible belief. We are not saying that we regard that belief as true or even that we regard it as very plausible. Indeed, we are not making a judgment about the *belief* at all. We are making a judgment about the *believer*—namely, that he or she is guilty of no epistemic malfeasance in holding that belief.

It follows that the claim that the theist is within his epistemic rights in believing in God is a rather weak claim, and, in my view, is not terribly interesting philosophically. Consider an analogy: Suppose I have a colleague, a tough-minded, widely-published philosopher, who believes in reincarnation. Now I do not believe in reincarnation and see no reason to do so. I do not believe in souls, much less that they can be reincarnated. Does this mean that I necessarily regard my colleague as irrational insofar as he believes in reincarnation? Obviously not. I need not judge that he has formed his convictions in any sort of dishonest or irresponsible manner. On the contrary, I might know that he has formed that belief according to his best lights and only after a patient and thorough enquiry. Further, it is entirely possible that he holds his beliefs in a non-dogmatic way and has demonstrated a willingness to modify such beliefs when confronted by adequate argument or evidence. Hence, in saying that my colleague's belief in reincarnation is rational, I am in no way sanctioning his belief or indicating any degree of agreement with it.

Of course, there are *some* beliefs that I regard as so bizarre, so utterly groundless or contrary to well-known facts, that I have a hard time seeing how any intelligent, educated person could believe them. For instance, I don't see how any scientifically literate person could rationally hold that the earth is only six to ten thousand years old or that present species have not evolved from earlier species. In my view, any scientifically literate person who holds these or any of the other tenets of so-called "scientific" creationism has sacrificed intellectual integrity and is guilty of dereliction of epistemic duty.[4] However, I don't see such judgments, or any similar judgments about someone's personal character or intellectual integrity, as having much philosophical significance. Philosophy's concern is to investigate the credentials of a *belief*, not to pass judgment on the rationality or irrationality of *believers*.

From the above, I conclude that if Moreland and other theists want to claim no more than that they are within their epistemic rights in believing in God, atheists should not bother to belabor the point. After all, to say that theists are within their epistemic rights in believing in God in no way indicates that atheists are one whit less rational in not believing in God. Further, why should atheists be at all interested in convicting theists of irrationality? Atheists are seldom interested in gaining converts: They don't preach on TV, ring doorbells to proselytize, or visit school yards to hand out copies of the works of Bertrand Russell.

Further, to admit that theism can be a rationally held belief need not in any way diminish an atheist's opposition to fundamentalism, "scientific" creationism, Vatican views on sex and birth control, church sponsored homophobia and sexism, the crusade against abortion, etc.

With respect to such bigotry and obscurantism, atheists can still shout with Voltaire "Écrasez l'infâme!" Crush the infamous thing!

My only criticism of Nielsen and others who wish to convict theists of irrationality is to ask why they are willing to shoulder such a heavy burden of proof to refute a relatively minor claim. What possible philosophical interest is there in showing that some persons are or are not within their epistemic rights in believing in God? If someone claims no more for their position than that they violate no epistemic duties in believing it, the appropriate response is apathy rather than hostility.

I suspect, however, that Moreland's arguments are intended to defend a stronger claim than the above quote would indicate. After all, Moreland does not argue in the manner of Alvin Plantinga, the best-known defender of the claim that theists are within their epistemic rights in believing in God.[5] That is, he does not claim, à la Plantinga, that theism is a properly basic belief—a belief that can be rationally held even though no arguments, reasons, or evidence can be advanced in its favor. His method is to present arguments that seem to have as their conclusion the claim that theism is *true,* not merely that it is rational.

Indeed, these arguments, if sound, would meet the evidentialist challenge made by atheist philosophers such as Antony Flew, Michael Scriven, and Norwood Russell Hanson.[6] The evidentialist challenge confronts theists with the demand that they "put up or shut up"—that they shoulder the burden of proof in their debates with atheists by providing compelling reasons, arguments, or evidence in support of the claim that God exists. In the absence of such compelling support, argue the evidentialists, atheism wins by default. After all, "atheism" means simply the lack of belief in God (and not, as is commonly supposed, the *denial* of God's existence); the *lack* of a belief requires no justification unless there is some reason to *have* that belief.

Since Moreland's arguments seem designed to justify theistic truth claims (and not just show that theistic belief is rational), I shall construe his arguments as efforts to meet the evidentialist challenge and shall evaluate them on the basis of how well they do. Specifically, if Moreland's arguments fail on this basis, I shall take this as further evidence that the philosophical debate over the existence of God has been and is being won by atheists.

Moreland does not claim to prove God's existence with mathematical certainty. Presumably, then, his arguments are probabilistic in nature—that is, they aim to show that it is highly probable that God exists. However, such an aim immediately leads to intractable difficulties. "Probability" is a useful term in the context of everyday discourse, but when we try to specify its meaning with philosophical rigor, we run into enormous difficulties. Different philosophers have radically different interpretations of the meaning of the term.[7] Some see probability as the expression of a strict logical relationship between propositions. Others see it as a measure of the degree of strength with which we hold our beliefs. Another interpretation views probability as a measure of the relative frequencies with which events are to be expected.

It is very hard to see which of the interpretations of probability is applicable within the context of arguments for the existence of God.[8] Interpretations that equate probability with the strength of belief are clearly inapplicable. On such an interpretation, to say that God's existence is highly probable can only mean that someone believes it very strongly. However, such an assertion is merely a piece of biographical information and therefore has no polemical force in the context of philosophical debate. Further, since God's existence is not an event that occurs with a measurable regularity, the relative frequency interpretation is out. In order for the logical interpretation to work, there has to be some agreed-upon assignment of the so-called *a priori* probabilities. The *a priori* probabilities are those basic, underived probabilities from which all other probabilities derive. However, there is simply not enough common ground between theists and atheists for any agreement to be reached about the value of those *a priori* probabilities.

It seems, therefore, that before offering probabilistic arguments in behalf of God's existence, theists have the burden of specifying and defending the precise interpretation of probability they intend. Without such a specification, it is hard to grant much significance to claims about the probability of God's existence.

However, it would be too hasty to refuse to consider theistic arguments until theists have adequately spelled out their interpretation of probability. After all, it would be foolish to rule out an intuitively plausible argument just because it employed a notion of probability that is hard to spell out in terms of the standard interpretations. Hence, in the remainder of this essay, I shall consider Moreland's specific arguments.

Moreland's arguments fall into two sorts which I shall characterize as scientific and historical. His scientific arguments attempt to show that certain facts, or alleged facts, about the natural world reveal the designing hand of a Creator. His historical arguments contend that there is overwhelming evidence that Jesus of Nazareth was resurrected from the dead. I shall concentrate on the arguments I have characterized as scientific before turning briefly to his historical case.

A number of Moreland's arguments are expressed very tersely.

Since this essay faces rather strict space limitations, my rebuttals of these arguments will have to be similarly succinct.

Moreland mentions the recent efforts to refurbish the design argument by making reference to the "fine tuning" of the universe:

> Take, for example, the argument for God based on the design in the universe. In spite of David Hume, this argument has received strong support in recent years from astronomy, physics, and biology. Scientists are discovering that the universe is a finely-tuned and delicately-balanced harmony of fundamental constants, or cosmic singularities . . .
>
> For example, in the formation of the universe, the balance of matter to antimatter had to be accurate to one part in ten billion for the universe to even arise. Had it been larger or greater by one part in ten billion, no universe would have arisen. There would also have been no universe capable of sustaining life if the expansion rate of the Big Bang had been one billionth of a percent larger or smaller.

What exactly is the argument here? The tacit premise seems to be that a "finely tuned" universe is much more likely if there is a God than if there is not.[9] In other words, it is implied that the cosmic "coincidences" that make possible a universe such as ours are extremely improbable unless they are the product of conscious design. Presumably, the conclusion is that since a "finely tuned" universe does in fact exist, its existence strongly confirms the existence of a conscious Designer—that is, God.

It is hard to see that such an argument represents an advance over those criticized by Hume.[10] The argument turns on the claim that it is more likely that a finely tuned universe will exist on the hypothesis of theism than on the hypothesis of atheism. But it is hard to see how meaningful probabilities are to be assigned to either hypothesis, if, indeed, theism and atheism can even be meaningfully regarded as hypotheses. How can we know *a priori* what, if anything, God would be likely to create? After all, God is supposed to be complete and perfect within Himself, having no desires or needs. How do we know He wouldn't choose simply to bask in His own eternal glory? After all, any created thing would, by definition, be less perfect than God Himself. Would God have been any less good if He had chosen to create nothing?

Further, if God did decide to create something, why a *physical* universe? Why not hosts of purely spiritual entities? Surely, God's innermost purposes and intentions cannot be known *a priori;* indeed, it seems almost blasphemous to suggest they can. (Appeal to revelation is, of course, not possible here since to make such an appeal prior to establishing God's existence would hopelessly be question-begging.)

The assignment of meaningful probabilities upon the hypothesis of atheism is even more difficult. If atheism is correct, if the universe and its laws are all that is or ever has been, how can it be said that the universe, with all of its "finely tuned" features, is in any relevant sense probable or improbable? *Ex hypothesi* there are no antecedent conditions that could determine such a probability. Hence, if the universe is the ultimate brute fact, it is neither likely nor unlikely, probable or improbable; it simply *is*.[11]

Further, even if the universe were somehow improbable, it is hard to see on the hypothesis of atheism how we could ever know this. If we were in a position to witness the birth of many worlds—some designed, some undesigned—then we might be in a position to say of any particular world that it had such-and-such a probability of existing undesigned.[12] But we simply are not in such a position. We have absolutely no empirical basis for assigning probabilities to ultimate facts.[13]

It is this last fact that distinguishes cosmic "coincidences" from coincidences of the everyday kind, a distinction often missed by popular writers on these issues. For instance, the alleged improbability of the cosmic "coincidences" is often illustrated by comparing it to extremely improbable mundane situations—such as every gun jamming at once in a firing squad.[14] But such analogies are not apt. We have prior experience of rifles and their performance and, on the basis of that experience, we know how unlikely it is that, say, ten of them would simultaneously jam. We have no similar experience that would justify such an inference about the cosmic "coincidences" (unless, of course, these "coincidences" can be explained by some yet more fundamental *physical* principle—say quantum mechanics or Big Bang cosmology—and in that case, the explanation of these "coincidences" would be a job for science, not theology). Once this disanalogy is recognized, the "fine tuning" argument loses all of its intuitive appeal.

Moreland also mentions an argument based on biological data:

> In biology, biologists have discovered that DNA molecules do not merely contain redundant order, but they contain what they call information. They say that DNA can be transcribed into RNA, and RNA can be translated into protein. Now Carl Sagan . . . has made certain claims about the search for extraterrestrial intelligence,

called SETI. According to Sagan, in that search all we need to do is find one message with information in it from outer space, and we will be able to recognize the presence of intelligence. We don't even need to be able to translate it; it is the presence of information instead of order that will tip us off to the presence of intelligence. Well, what is sauce for the artificial goose ought to be sauce for the DNA gander, and I argue that the information in DNA molecules is evidence of intelligence behind it.

A natural first reaction to the above argument is to conclude that it rests on a pun. Surely, it seems, we are speaking metaphorically when we speak of the "information" in the genetic "code." Geneticists also speak of genes as "blueprints," but they clearly don't mean that if you looked at them closely, you would see little blueprints drawn up and laid out on a microscopic draftsman's table. "Blueprint" here is a metaphorical term that is employed to help explain what genes are and how they act. The same would appear to hold for the term "information" when applied to DNA. Hence, the above argument seems to turn on an equivocation between the literal and the metaphorical senses of the term "information."

However, some biologists take the notion of DNA as information quite literally. Consider the following striking passage from Richard Dawkins:

It is raining DNA outside. On the bank of the Oxford canal at the bottom of my garden is a large willow tree, and it is pumping downy seeds into the air . . . Not just any DNA, but DNA whose coded characters spell out specific instructions for building willow trees that will shed a new generation of downy seeds. Those fluffy specks are, literally, spreading instructions for making themselves. They are there because their ancestors succeeded in doing the same. It is raining instructions out there; it's raining programs; it's raining tree-growing, fluff-spreading algorithms. That is not a metaphor, it is the plain truth. It couldn't be plainer if it were raining floppy discs.[15]

Of course, biologists can misuse language the same as anyone else, but, for the sake of argument, let's not quibble over Dawkins's (and Moreland's) terminology.[16]

Suppose then that we are walking alongside the Oxford canal and we come across a floppy disk. Suppose further that at just that moment a fluffy willow seed comes floating by. Now, following Dawkins's usage, we would consider both to be packets in which information was encoded. However, whereas anyone would immediately recognize that the information in the floppy disk had an intelligent source, not everyone (certainly not Dawkins) would instantly conclude this about the willow seed. Why not? What is the *prima facie* difference between the two cases?

The difference is that unvarying experience shows us that the information in floppy disks always ultimately comes from intelligent sources. The information in the willow seed, on the other hand, comes from an unintelligent source—the willow tree. In fact, every living thing is a DNA factory. Nature is constantly producing new strands of DNA. Further, such processes, to all appearances, follow the impersonal, mechanistic laws of chemistry. There doesn't seem to be any foresight, planning, or contrivance in the process; all apparently occurs in conformity with the automatic, impersonal operation of natural law.

At this point, Moreland would be expected to make the following sort of objection: Yes, DNA is produced in nature by an automatic replicating process. Old strands of DNA split in half and new components line up with each half-strand until two new strands are produced.[17] All of this occurs in strict accord with the impersonal laws of chemistry. The point to note, however, is that each new strand of DNA had to come from a previous strand of DNA. The important question is not how DNA is presently produced in the natural world, but how DNA came about in the first place. It is the *origin* of DNA that needs to be explained in terms of an intelligent source.

In other words, Moreland might happily concede that, just as the program on a given floppy disk may have been copied through an impersonal electronic process from another floppy disk, so could new strands of DNA be replicated from old ones in a similarly automatic manner. However, we would expect the program on a floppy disk to ultimately have had an intelligent source, no matter how many times that program had been copied. Similarly, Moreland might argue, DNA must have had an intelligent origin, no matter how automatic its replicating procedure.

But what grounds could there possibly be for holding that DNA cannot have originated in a purely naturalistic fashion? Moreland mentions the famous analogy from Fred Hoyle: the likelihood of life arising spontaneously through mere chance is similar to the probability of a tornado blowing through a junkyard and forming a Boeing 747. The problem with this analogy is that it attacks a straw man. Proponents of the view that life arose naturalistically do not hold that the first DNA molecule arose, like the 747 from the junkyard, in a single step through a random shuffling of its constituent parts. Rather, they hold that the first DNA molecule developed from a slightly simpler molecule, which in turn developed from a slightly simpler molecule, and so on. Life developed through a process of *cumulative* evolution, not in one big leap.[18]

Further, each step in this process is controlled by orderly natural processes—not the vagaries of pure chance. Indeed, natural selection operates even at the molecular level, and natural selection, contrary to the obscurantist propaganda of "scientific" creationists, is the antithesis of randomness.[19] Geologist Cesare Emiliani employs the notion of natural selection at the molecular level in his reply to scientists such as Hoyle:

> Some scientists believe that life could not have evolved on earth because the earth is too young. According to them, even 4.6 billion years is too short a time to make all the various types of proteins and nucleic acids needed for even the simplest bacterium. These scientists, unfortunately, forget the extreme power of selection by the environment. Evolution was operating also at the molecular level: that is, early compounds that were not stable could not survive. The selection of suitable molecules by the chemical environment is analogous to the selection of suitable organisms by the natural environment. It just so happens that nucleic acids [like DNA] are very stable molecules.[20]

Additionally, it is the operation of natural selection at the molecular level that destroys Hoyle's and all of the other pseudomathematical arguments against the naturalistic origin of earthly life. With the environment operating to remove nonviable variations, the appearance of life on earth becomes a certainty rather than an extreme improbability. As Emiliani puts it: "Given the chemical and environmental conditions of the primitive earth, the appearance of life was a foregone conclusion. Only divine intervention could have kept Planet Earth sterile."[21]

Moving on, Moreland's main scientific argument concludes that God created the universe from nothing a finite time ago. I think that Moreland's argument can be set out in a semiformal way as follows:

1. Either the universe began a finite time ago or the universe has existed through infinite time. (premise)
2. It is not the case that the universe has existed through infinite time. (premise)
3. Therefore, the universe began a finite time ago. (from 1 and 2 by disjunctive syllogism)

4. If the universe began a finite time ago, either it was caused to come into existence or it came into existence uncaused. (premise)
5. Either the universe was caused to come into existence or it came into existence uncaused. (from 3 and 4 by *modus ponens*)
6. It is not the case that the universe came into existence uncaused. (premise)
7. Therefore, the universe was caused to come into existence. (from 5 and 6 by disjunctive syllogism)
8. If the universe was caused to come into existence, then it was created by God from nothing a finite time ago. (premise)
9. Therefore, the universe was created by God from nothing a finite time ago. (from 7 and 8 by *modus ponens*)

Now, the above argument is certainly valid, so its soundness depends on the truth of its premises. Let us begin with premise 2.

What reason is there to deny that the universe has existed through infinite time? Moreland's argument is a little hard to follow here, but I think it goes as follows: In order for the universe to have existed through infinite time, an actual infinite would have to be crossed, but, says Moreland, this is impossible:

> The impossibility of crossing an actual infinite has sometimes been put by saying that one cannot count to infinity no matter how long he counts. For he will always be at some specific number which could be added to generate another specific number; and that is true even if one counted forever. . . .
> Put differently, suppose you go back through the events of the past in your mind. You will either come to a beginning, or you will not. If you come to a beginning, then the past is finite and my argument is settled. That would be the first event. If you had never come to a beginning, then the past is actually infinite; and as you go back in your mind, you never in principle could exhaust the events of the past. It would be impossible to traverse the past going backward in your mind.

Now it certainly seems intuitively plausible to say that an actual infinite cannot be crossed. However, if the mathematics of infinity has revealed anything, it is that our intuitions are not very trustworthy when dealing with such topics. For instance, Bertrand Russell has suggested that it is a mere physical impossibility for a person to call out all of the finite numbers, provided that she takes only half the time for each as for its predecessor.[22] Similarly, mathematician Rudy Rucker imagines a mountain that is higher than infinity. However, says Rucker, climbers of this mountain could traverse an actual infinity of cliffs if they used a procedure he calls a "speed up": "The idea is to climb the first cliff in one hour, the next cliff in half an hour, the one after that in a quarter of an hour, and, in general, the nth cliff in $1/2^n$ hours. Since $1 + 1/2 + 1/4 + 1/8 + \ldots$ sums to 2, we see that after two hours our climbers have passed infinitely many cliffs."[23]

However, maybe Moreland only wants to claim that an actually infinite *time* cannot be crossed. For the sake of argument, let us concede, and this certainly seems to be the import of Moreland's above-quoted statements, that nobody can begin at time T and then pass through an actual infinity of time. But to say that the universe is infinitely old is *not* to say that the universe existed at some infinitely distant past T such that it had to pass through infinite time to get from T to the present. In other words, Moreland's above objections deal with the impossibility of beginning at a time T and then passing through infinite time. But to say that the world is infinitely old is *not* to postulate some infinitely remote T from which the universe had to pass through infinite time to reach the present. To say that the universe is infinitely old is to say that it had no beginning—not that it had a beginning that was infinitely long ago. Moreland's objections tell against the latter claim, not the former.

Maybe all that Moreland wants to argue here is something like this: "If the world has no beginning in time, an infinite series of events must have occurred. That is to say, before the present moment an infinite series must have been completed. But an infinite series can never be completed. Therefore the world must have had a beginning in time."[24]

However, to say that an infinite series can never be completed simply begs the question.[25] This statement rests on the assumption that however many members of an infinite series are taken, others will remain. Now it is certainly true that if any *finite* number is taken from an infinite series, other members will remain. However, a reason must be given why an *infinite* number of members cannot be taken from the series. In conclusion, there may be a hidden incoherence in the notion of an infinitely old universe, but Moreland has not shown one.

At any rate, the question of whether the universe could be infinitely old is, in the present context, a moot point. This is because Moreland's entire argument rests upon a false dilemma. The basic premise of Moreland's argument, that the universe either began a finite time ago or has existed through infinite time, overlooks a third possibility: the universe is finite but unbounded in time. It is precisely this last proposal that is defended by Stephen Hawking, generally considered the world's most brilliant theoretical physicist, in his book *A Brief History of Time*.[26]

From the physicist's point of view, the chief virtue of Hawking's proposal is that it avoids an undesirable consequence of the theory of general relativity. General relativity predicts that at the beginning of time the universe would have existed as a singularity—an impenetrable boundary at which all of the laws of physics break down. In such a circumstance it would be impossible for physics to specify the "boundary conditions" of the universe; the initial state of the universe would be unknowable. However, through the prodigious mathematical feat (employing such arcane concepts as "imaginary time") of combining quantum physics with general relativity, Hawking realized another possibility:

> The quantum theory of gravity has opened up a new possibility, in which there would be no boundary to space-time and so there would be no need to specify the behavior at the boundary. There would be no singularities at which the laws of science broke down and no edge of space-time at which one would have to appeal to God or some new law to set the boundary conditions for space-time. One could say: "The boundary condition of the universe is that it has no boundary." The universe would be completely self-contained and not affected by anything outside itself. It would neither be created nor destroyed. It would just BE.[27]

In other words, Hawking proposes that there was no absolute beginning of the universe and, hence, that the laws of physics apply to *every* point of space-time. In this case, it would be useless to ask whether the universe was caused or uncaused since it would not have begun at all.

However, to say that the universe had no beginning does not, on Hawking's proposal, imply that time is infinite. Time, in his view, is rather like a sphere. A sphere is finite in extent, but no point on that sphere can be considered an absolute beginning point. The Big Bang corresponds to the north pole of such a sphere. There is nothing special about the north pole of a sphere. It is a point on the sphere just like any other; the sphere does not have an edge or a boundary there. However, the north pole is a convenient point to start the lines of latitude and longitude which we use to locate other points on the sphere. Similarly, the Big Bang is just a point in space-time like any other, but it is a convenient point to begin our counting of time.

The upshot is that Hawking's universe has no need of a Creator. This point is expressed by Carl Sagan in his introduction to Hawking's book:

> This is also a book about God . . . or perhaps about the absence of God. The word God fills these pages. Hawking embarks on a quest to answer Einstein's famous question about whether God had any choice in creating the universe. Hawking is attempting, as he explicitly states, to understand the mind of God. And this makes all the more unexpected the conclusion of the effort, at least so far: a universe with no edge in space, no beginning or end in time, and nothing for a Creator to do.[28]

If there is nothing for a Creator to do, we had best follow Ockham's Razor and dispense with the idea.[29]

I think that Moreland's arguments illustrate some of the difficulties inherent in attempting to support theism with science. Science is unavoidably naturalistic—atheistic if you prefer. Science explains in terms of scrutable, independently testable entities that operate in accordance with knowable regularities. Supernatural beings, on the other hand, are essentially mysterious; claims made on their behalf are not independently checkable, and there are no "laws of supernature" governing their behavior.

Furthermore, "explanations" in terms of supernatural entities are inevitably *post hoc* and untestable. In other words, proponents of supernaturalistic theories can glibly account for things we already know, but they grow strangely silent when asked to predict something new— something that would allow their theory to be tested. With respect to theistic hypotheses, as Antony Flew showed in his famous falsificationist challenge, proponents of such hypotheses are very adept in finding ways to circumvent such testing.[30]

It might be added that the only prediction that *does* seem to be a legitimate consequence of some theistic hypotheses—that there will be no gratuitous evil in the world—appears to be quite false. The world is full of examples of apparently gratuitous evil, and, as I have argued elsewhere, proponents of theistic hypotheses have yet to devise an adequate theodicy to account for such ostensible counterexamples.[31]

The upshot of all this is that theistic hypotheses are contrary to both the spirit and the letter of scientific practice. Such hypotheses either are untestable or make false predictions. They specialize in *post hoc* "explanations" of a sort that abound in the various pseudosciences.[32] Finally, scientific hypotheses are always *tentative;* they are designed to be held only so long as they conform to the evidence. Proponents of the theistic hypothesis, on the other hand, are already sure that their hypothesis is correct; they only seek evidence to buttress a foregone conclusion. It is therefore an insult to science, and no help to theism, to attempt to argue for God's existence in this manner.

I would like to turn briefly to one of Moreland's other arguments. Moreland devotes considerable space to a defense of the claim that Jesus of Nazareth was miraculously resurrected. Again, I am curious to know just how much Moreland intends to prove with his argument. Is it intended merely to show that the Christian is within his epistemic rights in affirming that Jesus was resurrected? Is it intended to show that the atheist (not to mention the Jew, the Buddhist, and the Muslim) is *not* within his epistemic rights in denying that resurrection? On the other hand, does Moreland intend to argue for the *truth* of the resurrection while admitting that rational denial is possible?

As before, if Moreland is only maintaining the weakest of these claims, that it is rational for *Christians* to believe in the resurrection, I see no reason to belabor the point. Once again, however, Moreland's premises seem designed to prove a stronger claim. His arguments appear to have *apologetic* intent; they appear to be attempts to sway unbelievers. If Moreland has such an apologetic intent, it is odd that he launches right into historical argument without even a nod to the thorny philosophical problems that accompany such a venture.[33]

When a claim is made on the basis of human testimony, the believability of that claim is largely determined by the reliability of the testimony. For instance, it must be asked whether the evidence is unambiguous and not subject to a variety of conflicting interpretations. Similarly, it must be determined whether the alleged witnesses were of a sort that could be depended upon to provide truthful and accurate testimony. If the alleged witnesses are shown to be gullible, mendacious, or superstitious, or if their claims are ambiguous, or if the circumstances under which their observations occurred were not conducive to accurate observation (for instance, the alleged witnesses were under extreme emotional duress), the credibility of the claim will greatly suffer.

Now I certainly think that the claim that Jesus rose from the dead can be challenged by bringing into question the testimony of the alleged witnesses. For instance, the biblical scholar Reginald H. Fuller points out that the "appearances" of the risen Jesus mentioned by Paul in his famous formula from 1 Cor. 15:5-7 are characterized by the verb *ōphthē*, which has a meaning that is indeterminate between seeing with the physical eye and "seeing" with the eye of the mind or spirit.[34] In other words, it is not at all clear whether Paul is claiming that the risen Jesus was literally seen or whether he was "seen" in some spiritual sense. Given such ambiguity, it is highly questionable to interpret these verses as reliable testimony for the *physical* resurrection of Jesus.

Here, however, I would merely like to point out that the background or *a priori* probability of a claim is just as important as evaluating the reliability of testimony when it comes to ascertaining the credibility of a claim. It is very easy to illustrate the importance of background probability in assessing the credibility of claims made on the basis of human testimony. Suppose that saintly Mother Teresa, an irreproachable witness if ever there were one, announced that she flew to pick up her Nobel Peace Prize—not in an airplane but simply by flapping her arms. Surely there would be cause to disbelieve her (at least initially; if she followed that claim with an aeronautical exhibition, we might change our minds). The reason is that the claim that someone can fly simply by flapping her arms goes against everything we know, or think we know, about the capacities of human beings, the laws of gravity, the laws of aerodynamics, etc. Independently of Mother Teresa's testimony, we would rate the probability of the claim that she could fly by flapping her arms to be very, very low. In fact, that background probability would be so low that it would nullify Mother Teresa's testimony and make her claim unbelievable.

Now what applies to the claim that someone can fly simply by flapping her arms surely applies to the claim that a dead person can come back to life. Everything we know about what happens at death (irreversible tissue changes, etc.) plus the universal experience of the human race (with, so as not to beg any questions, the exception of the alleged witnesses of Jesus' resurrection) indicates that the dead stay dead. Hence, the background likelihood of a dead body returning to life must be extremely low.

Even worse, if it is claimed that an event is a *miracle*, then this event must have taken place contrary to a *true* law of nature. Now those who believe in God might have some reason to believe that God can and occasionally will overturn physical law. Hence, the background likelihood of such an event for them might not be so vanishingly small. For atheists, however, to say that an event is physically impossible means that it must have a background likelihood as low as any contingent event could have. After all, atheists do not believe in the existence of any Power behind nature that is capable of countermanding natural law. Hence, for an atheist to be justified in believing in a miracle on the basis of testimony, it must be the case, as Hume said, that it would be an even greater miracle if the testimony were false than if the event testified to occurred.

The upshot is that, with respect to the resurrection stories in the New Testament, it will be more reasonable for an atheist to believe just about *any* alternative scenario, no matter how improbable, rather than accept those stories at face value. As Sherlock Holmes said, "Eliminate the impossible and whatever is left, no matter how improbable, is the answer." Hence, all of Moreland's efforts to show the unlikelihood of alternative scenarios (mass hallucination, pack of lies, etc.) are beside the point. So long as such scenarios do not involve a physically impossible event, it will clearly be more reasonable for an atheist to believe one of them than to accept a literal resurrection. Hence, if Moreland's arguments are intended to have apologetic force, they fail in that purpose.

In conclusion, Moreland has not effectively argued for the truth of Christian theism. None of his arguments has the slightest force for those not already strongly inclined towards theistic belief. Hence, if Moreland's arguments are taken as efforts to meet the burden of proof in the context of philosophical debate, they must be added to the already long list of unsuccessful attempts.

What is the appropriate attitude of the atheist when confronted with yet another set of unconvincing arguments for theism? I think it must be the same as his attitude about claims made on behalf of the Loch Ness monster, UFOs, the Lost Continent of Atlantis, the Bermuda Triangle, and Bigfoot. These are interesting claims, but their proponents are perennially incapable of putting forward any good evidence for them. After years (in the case of theism, centuries) of such failure, it will not be surprising if such beliefs command little attention or respect. It might not be possible to *prove* such beliefs wrong, especially if their proponents are allowed unlimited room for *ad hoc* maneuvering. But those who would follow Hume's dictum that "the wise man proportions his belief to the evidence" will decline to harbor such beliefs.

Notes

1. The notion of rationality as having to do with epistemic rights and duties is developed at length by Alvin Plantinga in "Reason and Belief in God" in *Faith and Rationality,* Alvin Plantinga and Nicholas Wolterstorff, eds. (Notre Dame, Ind.: University of Notre Dame Press, 1983), 29–39.
2. The example given is an adaptation of the one that opens W. K. Clifford's classic essay "The Ethics of Belief" in *Lectures and Essays,* Leslie Stephen and Frederick Pollock, eds. (London: Macmillan and Co., 1879), 177–211. This essay is a brilliant exposition of the nature of epistemic duties and a vigorous challenge to theists to perform those duties.
3. More precisely, epistemic duties spell out *prima facie* intellectual obligations. As Alvin Plantinga notes, there are situations in which other duties might override the duty to check our beliefs as carefully as we normally should (see Plantinga, "Reason and Belief in God," 33).
4. The most careful and comprehensive critique of creationism is Arthur Strahler's exhaustive study *Science and Earth History* (Buffalo: Prometheus Books, 1987). The two best shorter critiques are Douglas Futuyma, *Science on Trial* (New York: Pantheon Books, 1983), and Philip Kitcher, *Abusing Science* (Cambridge, Mass.: MIT Press, 1982). Ongoing critiques are provided in the journal *Creation/Evolution,* Frederick Edwards, ed. This journal can be ordered by writing Creation/Evolution, 7 Harwood Drive, P.O.Box 146, Amherst, N.Y. 14226-0146.
5. See Plantinga, *Faith and Rationality,* 73–82.
6. See Antony Flew, "The Presumption of Atheism" in *God, Freedom, and Immortality* (Buffalo: Prometheus Books, 1984); Michael Scriven, *Primary Philosophy* (New York: McGraw-Hill, 1966), Chap. 4; Norwood Russell Hanson, "What I Don't Believe" in *What I Do Not Believe and Other Essays,* Stephen Toulmin and Harry Woolf, eds. (Dordrecht, Holland: D. Reidel, 1971).
7. The best elementary discussion of the various interpretations of probability is found in Wesley C. Salmon, *The Foundations of Scientific Inference* (Pittsburgh: The University of Pittsburgh Press, 1967), 65–96.
8. Alvin Plantinga argues that proponents of the probabilistic argument from evil face this difficulty when they try to argue that evil is evidence against the existence of God. See Plantinga's "The Probabilistic Argument from Evil," *The Philosophical Quarterly* (1979), 1–53. As Moreland observes, what is sauce for the goose is sauce for the gander. Hence, it must be pointed out that theists face the same set of difficulties when they try to provide probabilistic arguments in favor of God's existence as atheists face in providing probabilistic atheological arguments.
9. It is the consequence of Bayes's theorem (called the "relevance condition" by confirmation theorists) that a given piece of evidence *e* confirms a hy-

pothesis *h* if and only if *e* is more probable on *h* than on not-*h*. Hence, where *h* is theism and not-*h* is atheism and *e* comprises all of the "finely tuned" features of the universe, the "finely tuned" features of the universe confirm theism if and only if those features are more likely if God exists than if God does not exist.

10. An excellent exposition, analysis, and defense of Hume's case against the design argument is found in J. C. A. Gaskin, *Hume's Philosophy of Religion*, 2nd ed. (Atlantic Highlands, N. J.: Humanities Press Intl., 1988), 11-51.

11. Maybe the real issue here is whether the natural universe or God is more likely to be the ultimate brute fact. Richard Swinburne in *The Existence of God* (Oxford: Oxford University Press, 1979) argues that God is more likely to exist uncaused than the natural world. For a rebuttal of this view, see Chapter 2 of my book, *God and the Burden of Proof* (Buffalo: Prometheus Books, 1989).

12. This is essentially the argument given by Hume in Part II of the *Dialogues Concerning Natural Religion*. See the Norman Kemp Smith Edition (New York: Macmillan, 1986), 149-150.

13. Swinburne, in his *The Existence of God*, argues that the criterion of simplicity allows us to assign probabilities here. For a rebuttal, see Anthony O'Hear, *Experience, Explanation, and Faith* (London: Routledge & Kegan Paul, 1984), 116-17.

14. I have taken this example from George Greenstein, *The Symbiotic Universe* (New York: William Morrow and Co., 1988), 89.

15. Richard Dawkins, *The Blind Watchmaker* (New York: W W. Norton & Co., 1987), 111.

16. I am assuming that Moreland is not implicitly *defining* "information" in terms of having an intelligent source. This would beg the question against Dawkins and others for whom the term does not have such an implication.

17. There are many excellent books that tell about DNA and its replicating process. The two that are the most fun are Israel Rosenfeld and Edward Ziff, *DNA for Beginners* (Writers and Readers Publishing, 1983) and Larry Gonick and Mark Wheelis, *The Cartoon Guide to Genetics* (New York: Barnes and Noble, 1983).

18. Dawkins has an excellent discussion of the nature of cumulative evolution in his *The Blind Watchmaker*, 43—74.

19. See Futuyma, *Science on Trial*, 114-131.

20. Cesare Emiliani, *The Scientific Companion* (New York: John Wiley & Sons), 149.

21. Emiliani provides an example that vividly illustrates the efficacy of a selection procedure:

To show how efficient natural selection can be, imagine that you want to have the entire Bible typed by a wild monkey. What are the chances that such a monkey, typing at random, will come up with the Bible neatly typed without a single error? The English Bible (King James translation) contains about 6 million letters. The chances of success, therefore, are 1 in 26 to the 6 millionth power, as there are 26 letters in the English alphabet. This is equal to 10 to the minus 8,489,840. I wouldn't exactly wait around. Suppose, however, that I introduce a control (the environment) that wipes out any wrong letter the monkey may type. Typing away at one letter per second and assuming an average of 13 errors per letter (half of 26), the monkey will produce the Bible in $13 \times 6,000,000$ seconds = 2.5 years. Not only that, but you are *mathematically sure* that the monkey will produce the Bible within that time and without a single error. If you want your monkey to work only 8 hours per day with Saturdays and Sundays off and with two weeks vacation per year, you will have your Bible in 10.8 years. In any case, what is utterly impossible has suddenly become not only possible but certain. (*The Scientific Companion*, 149)

22. This illustration is mentioned by James Thomson in his article "Infinity in Mathemathics and Logic" in *The Encyclopedia of Philosophy*, vol. 4, Paul Edwards, ed. (New York: Macmillan, 1967), 188.

23. Rudy Rucker, *Infinity and the Mind* (New York: Bantam Books, 1983), 69.

24. This is a paraphrase of Kant's first antinomy given by Frederick Copleston in his *History of Philosophy*, vol. 6 (London: Burns and Oates, 1960), 287.

25. Thomson, "Infinity in Mathematics and Logic," 188.

26. Stephen W. Hawking, *A Brief History of Time* (New York: Bantam Books, 1988), 115–141.

27. Hawking, *A Brief History of Time*, 136.

28. *Ibid.*, p. x.

29. Of course, Hawking's proposal is not accepted by all cosmologists. However, other cosmologies offer no more comfort to theists than does Hawking's. *Contra* Moreland, many of them see nothing unreasonable in the notion of the universe orginating uncaused out of nothing (indeed, quantum physics makes it entirely feasible). See, for instance, Victor J. Stenger, *Not by Design* (Buffalo: Prometheus Books, 1988).

30. Antony Flew, "Theology and Falsification" in *New Essays in Philosophical Theology*, Antony Flew and Alasdair MacIntyre, eds. (New York: Macmillan, 1964), 96–99. Nearly four decades after its first publication, Flew's challenge remains pertinent and powerful. Those who wish to establish theism on a scientific or quasi-scientific basis still have the onus of specifying what observation, experience, experiment, or occurrence would lead them to reject their hypothesis. Their consistent failure to do so remains the best reason for refusing to regard theistic hypotheses as in any sense on par with scientific ones.

31. See the final chapter of my forthcoming book *Science, Confirmation and the Theistic Hypothesis* (New York: Peter Lang, 1990).

32. For a fine survey of the fallacies of hypothesis confirmation, see Ronald N. Giere, *Understanding Scientific Reasoning* (New York: Holt, Rinehart, and Winston, 1984), 151–176.

33. The classic statement of these problems is, of course, Hume's essay "Of Miracles," Section X of his *An Enquiry Concerning Human Understanding*. One of the best editions of this work is the one edited by Antony Flew (La Salle, Ill: Open Court, 1988). Bayes's theorem is a helpful tool here also. Anyone interested in the relationship between Bayes's theorem and miracle claims should consult Bruce Langtry's "Miracles and the Principles of Relative Likelihood," *International Journal for Philosophy of Religion* 18 (1985), 123–31.

34. Reginald H. Fuller, *The Formation of the Resurrection Narratives* (New York: Macmillan, 1971), 30.

Language, Being, God, and the Three Stages of Theistic Evidence*

I begin with a plea of "not guilty" to Professor Nielsen's charge that my belief in God is an irrational belief. I do live in the twentieth century, I have been given a passably good philosophical and scientific education, and I have thought carefully about the matter of the existence of God. According to him, "for such a person it's irrational to believe in God." Since he does not here spell out what he understands by an irrational belief, it is not clear how to develop a reply. But I must say that upon due inquiry, I am not aware of any true propositions which strictly imply that God does not exist, or of anything that confers significant improbability on His existence. So far as I have been able to determine, no falsehood can be deduced from the assumption of His existence, and that assumption itself is not meaningless or *logically* inconsistent. I have been and remain open to evidence, from Professor Nielsen or someone else, on these points, some of which will be considered shortly. I cannot say that I have a sound proof, in the strict logical sense, of the full-fledged deity in which I have come to believe, but I can point to a number of things which make a lot more sense on the assumption of such a deity. And I do believe that there is very good evidence for the existence of a being with *some* of His essential attributes—evidence that has not been successfully contested by those on Professor Nielsen's side. So it seems to me, at least, that my belief in God is not irrational, though, of course, I myself may still be a wildly irrational person.

Nielsen's Case Against God's Existence

Before turning to the one argument which Nielsen presents to show belief in God irrational, a few general comments on the logic of the issue will hopefully cast light on why the discussion proceeds as it does. We are concerned with an existential proposition, and it is very difficult to

---

*I am greatly indebted for comments on an earlier draft of this paper to David W. Edwards, Doug Geivett, Gregory Jesson, Brendan Sweetman, and Duane Willard, who do not necessarily agree with the views here expressed.

prove a negative existential proposition that does not involve a highly restricted universe of discourse, as certainly the one at issue here does not. Suppose you want to prove there are no green crows. All it takes is one green crow in order to show that the proposition, *There are no green crows,* is false. On the other hand, you can examine many crows and find them all black without being in a position to judge whether or not there are any green crows anywhere else. We will need to introduce some general considerations—for example, all crows that exist are within a certain distance of this tree, or the number of crows there are is *n*—before our examination of particular crows can begin to suggest there are no green crows. There *may,* after all, be many galaxies that have many planets inhabited by crows, and some of these crows *may* be green.

A similar point needs to be made with regard to the proposition, *There is no God.* It is a negative existential, and looking for God here or there, finding or proving *this* not to be God and *that* not to be God, does nothing to budge it one bit toward or away from the status of knowledge or even of justified belief. To make any headway at all with the atheist's project, we will have to settle on some *general* considerations that will provide a structure within which particular facts may evidentially count for something. For example, take the general consideration that if God exists, suffering will not be allowed. Given this, the particular fact of this child being sexually abused by a drunken relative gains evidential significance for the existence or nonexistence of God. But then, of course, we have the task of securing the truth of this particular general consideration. A notoriously difficult undertaking!

The atheist's case will, then, depend on certain "general considerations." She may decide to go right for the jugular vein and say, for example, that in order simply to exist or *to be,* anything must have a certain character—for example, that of a particular event or entity at a place and time, like this auto accident or that apple or atom or force field. (I conjecture that in fact something close to this is what Professor Nielsen has in mind, though of course he couches it in more contemporary terms.) *Naturalism,* which attempts to link existence itself to (physical) causation plus space/time location, is much favored by the contemporary mind. A theory of *being* thus might serve as the general background for atheism. But that has not worked out very well, and so for the last two centuries the "general consideration" invoked is more likely to have something to do with knowledge or language. And that is certainly the case with Professor Nielsen.

He boldly puts all his money on one horse. An act of great

courage—or desperation? The general consideration from which he operates has to do with language. His claim is that statements about a God of the Hebrew/Christian/Islamic variety are "linguistic irregularities." He does not say that they are *meaningless,* no doubt because he knows that game has already been played out, with his side losing. Rather, he holds that when you speak of an immeasurably vast person of love and intelligence who produced the physical universe, your statements are "so problematic and so obscure that it turns out that we don't know what we are talking about." We may have a feeling that we do know, he allows, "but when we think very carefully about what these expressions mean, they are so problematic that we can't use them to make true or false claims."

It is far from clear what he has in mind. In fact, his position looks awfully like warmed over Logical Positivism with superficial disclaimers. Does Neilsen mean that God-talk *does* refer to God or something, but we can't know what it is that it refers to? That our statements *are* true or false, but we just can't know which? That there *is* a reference for the term "God," but we somehow can't get our minds around it? Or, is he saying that there is no reference here, and hence no possibility of either truth or falsity? His discussions indicate to me that he means the latter, though his language is ambiguous. If so, he is adopting the *heart,* at least, of the old Logical Positivist position that statements about God have no truth value and hence no logical relations. Belief in God is, then, *a*rational—not subject to canons of rationality; not *ir*rational and somehow offensive to canons of rationality. Like a duck or a doorknob, belief in God isn't made of the right stuff to be irrational. It can't stand in any kind of logical relation. Thus, he says, Moreland cannot use terms for God in premises of an argument "if we don't know what they mean." (Why isn't this the same as being meaningless?)

If Nielsen does mean to say that the references, the truth or falsity, the logical relations, and all the rest, are really *there* in the God-talk but are just inscrutable, he should say so, and then go on to explain what it is about *these* references which makes them so different from other references—for example, those in his "Louis made pasta and cake" case. In fact, when he comes to discuss ways of establishing reference, which seems to be the same for him as identifying objects, he only discusses intra-linguistic and ostensive identification. His claim is that "God, unlike Louis, can't be identified ostensively, or extra-linguistically," and that intra-linguistic devices, especially definite descriptions, also don't succeed in picking God out. You can't see God in the way you see Louis, and when it comes to definite descriptions like "the maker of heaven and earth," "How would you identify that?" he asks. "How would you know what that refers to?" And we are supposed to reply that, of course we could not identify that, and thus could not know it. And this is supposed to imply that the concept of God is "incoherent," and that is supposed to show that it is irrational to believe in God. "Remember, my principal basis for saying that it is irrational to believe in God is that I believe the concept of God in developed Judeo-Christianity is incoherent."

Now we don't know what reference is for Nielsen, and it is not clear what he is saying about it. I wonder how he would reply to the following argument: Reference itself cannot be ostensively defined, and it cannot—at least in any generally acceptable way—be individuated by definite description. (There are plenty of people today who would agree with that!) Therefore, the concept of reference is incoherent, and his (and our) beliefs about it—including the ones upon which his reasons for atheism here depend—are irrational.

Certainly any post-Kripkian or post-Derridian thinker must be slow to accept empirical ostention and definite description as the only means of establishing reference. Possibly reference is something that, at least in certain cases, just emerges at a certain point in the development of language. The overly simple quasi-positivist models, which, it seems to me, lie back of Nielsen's remarks, surely cannot do justice to the actual performances of language. But one must be cautious in this area. The disagreements of philosophers about meaning are scarcely less striking than the disagreements people have about God. It is a well-known fact that we cannot agree on the nature of meaning. Indeed, we cannot even agree on what a theory of meaning is supposed to do. So it certainly is surprising as well as unconvincing when we find a leading atheist thinker staking his whole case on general considerations about meaning.

We should also point out that Nielsen's atheism is of a curious variety indeed. If what he says about the word *God* is true, then any claim that God does *not* exist is just as "incoherent" as the claim that He does. Atheism is therefore incoherent, and therefore is just as irrational as theism. This is additional evidence that he is merely restating the position of Logical Positivism. It is no accident, I'm sure, that he invokes Rudolph Carnap at the end of his talk; but Carnap, and *his* Logical Positivism frankly embraced, even insisted upon the incoherence of atheism as well as theism.

Now there are multiplied millions of human beings who believe they have had a direct experience of God, or who think that certain definite descriptions—for instance, the person who created the world or met Moses on the Mount, the God and Father of our Lord Jesus Christ—work perfectly well. These people are not always philosophically unsophisticated. John Locke, a Christian theist and an empiricist philosopher of considerable ability—who, however, was neither a Sensist nor a Positivist—carefully elaborated both how an empiricist can account for ideas of infinity (*Essay on Human Understanding*, Bk. 2, Chap. 17) and can, from one's own existence and from nature, argue for the existence of an infinite God (*Essay*, Bk. 4, Chap. 10). Nielsen surely owes such people a bit more than the suggestion that, "Well, they *think* it all makes sense, but it *really* doesn't." Perhaps these people, many of whom are just as rational, informed, and broadly experienced as he is, think it makes sense because it does make sense. In any case, it's only 'tis against 'taint until we can operate from an acceptable theory of "making sense," which Nielsen certainly does not provide.

He does say that his argument is "that it doesn't make sense when you think it through . . . [that] God is an infinite individual who created and sustained the world." But I don't believe he really advances an argument here, as distinguished from some rather vague assertions about meaning, which is based on no plausible theory. What exactly is the argument that "God" is "incoherent" in his sense, such that statements containing it are neither true nor false? I confess I can't find in his remarks given here anything worthy of the name "argument." Actually, that may well be too much to require of a popular lecture. But perhaps he could help us out in his final remarks for this volume by just indicating the premises and showing how they imply that statements containing the word "God" are neither true nor false. It would be especially useful to be shown how the "incoherence" of "God" in Nielsen's own sense—whatever that is, exactly—entails or renders probable the non-existence of God. Or, more generally, how an ontological conclusion can be validly deduced from *any* linguistic fact.

Three Stages of Evidence for God's Existence

But does the case for the positive thesis of the existence of God fare any better? I believe it does, and along certain lines stated by Professor Moreland. However, the overall argument as I would develop it is not one which in one stroke, from one set of true premises, purports to establish or render plausible the existence of Jehovah, understood by Christians to also be the God and Father of our Lord Jesus Christ and referred to in Islam as "Allah." Rather, the plausibility of theism, as I shall henceforth simply refer to it, emerges in three stages. These stages are not three separate arguments or "ways," each of which, supposedly, bringing you to the *same* logical point. Three unsound arguments are not to be expected by their collective force to prove a conclusion which they cannot establish by themselves. Nor do the earlier stages establish conclusions which, in a straightforward manner, serve as premises in the later stages. Instead, what is shown or evidentially supported in the earlier stages only determines a framework of possibilities within which the considerations of the later stages are carried on. For example, the first stage shows that there actually exists something which *might* be God in some more conventional sense.

What then, are the three stages? It is extremely hard to discuss the relevant issues without getting involved in many age-old entanglements that in fact have nothing to do with the case one is arguing. I shall, accordingly, avoid much of the traditional terminology in what follows and attempt to narrowly restrict myself to precisely those considerations upon which the evidence for theism, as I see it, depends. We begin with a *demonstration* that the physical or natural world recognized by common sense and the "natural" sciences is not the only type of thing in existence: that there concretely exists, or at least has existed, something radically different from it in respects to be discussed. By a "demonstration" I mean a logical structure of propositions where the premises are true and they logically imply or entail the conclusion when taken together.

Stage One: The Physical World

The argument at stage one proceeds from *the nature and the existence of the physical*. Confusions, quibbles, and philosophical exercises—pointless and otherwise—aside, it is true that there is a physical world, and we do know that this is true. Further—although the nature of that world may ultimately be a profound mystery or turn out to have some deep kinship with what we call the mental or spiritual—there are some things about its general character which we also know to be true. One of these is: *However concrete physical reality is sectioned, the result will be a state of affairs which owes its being to something other than itself.*

This, I submit, is something which we know to be true of the general character of things in the physical world. (And, of course, anyone should feel free to submit a case of a physical state of which this proposition is *not* true.) Now it is, certainly, an extremely complex proposition, and, if we begin to take it apart, we will surely be led to many things we do not know and possibly do not even understand. But this proposition has that in common with nearly all of the truths which we know best, both in ordinary life and in science. One of the things which I hope might be clear at this point in humanity's intellectual development is that degree of simplicity or complexity in an object that has no automatic significance either for being or for knowledge. It should be equally clear that the inability to say *how* we know something does not imply that we do not know it—although it is always appropriate to raise the question of the "how" whenever someone claims to know something, and some appropriate kind of explanation is usually required.

Now any *general* understanding of the dependencies of physical states would require something like Aristotle's well-known four "causes." Restricting ourselves to the temporal order, however, we find, among other things, that every physical state, no matter how inclusive, has a necessary condition in some specific type of state which immediately precedes it in time and is fully existent prior to the emergence of the state which it conditions. This means that for any given state—for example, Voyager II being past Triton—all of the necessary conditions of that state must be over and done with *at* that state or *at* the event of which the state is the ontic residue. The series of "efficient" causes, to speak with Aristotle, is completed for any given event or state that obtains. *At* the state in question, we are not waiting for any of these causes to happen, to come into being.

Moreover, this completed set of causes is highly structured in time and in ontic dependence through relationships which are irreflexive, asymmetric, and transitive. Thus, no physical state is temporally or ontically prior to itself, and if one, *a*, is prior to another, *b*, *b* is not prior to *a*. Further, if *a* is prior to *b* and *b* to *c*, then *a* is prior to *c*. This rigorous structure of the past is eternally fixed, and it specifies a framework within which every event of coming into existence and ceasing to exist finds its place. Most importantly for present interests, since the series of causes for any given state is *completed*, it not only exhibits a rigorous structure as indicated, but that structure also has a first term. There is in it at least one "cause," one state of being, which does not derive its existence from something else. It is self-existent.

If this were not so, Voyager's passing Triton, or any other physical event or state, could not be realized, since that would require the actual completion of an infinite, an incompletable series of events. In simplest terms, its causes would never "get to" it. (As in a line of dominoes, if there is an infinite number of dominoes that must fall before domino *x* is

struck, it will never be struck. The line of fallings will never get to it.)
Since Voyager II *is* past Triton, there is a state of being upon which that
state depends but which itself depends on nothing prior to it. Thus,
concrete physical reality implicates a being radically different from itself: a being which, unlike any physical state, is self-existent.

This completes the *demonstration* in our first stage of theistic evidence. To sum up: The dependent character of all physical states, together with the completeness of the series of dependencies underlying
the existence of any given physical state, logically implies at least one
self-existent, and therefore non-physical, state of being: a state of being, or an entity, radically different from those that make up the physical
or "natural" world. It is demonstrably absurd that there should be a
self-sufficient physical universe, if by that we mean an all-inclusive total-
ity of entities and events of the familiar or scientific physical variety. Of
course, we could, like Spinoza, prepare to treat the universe itself as
having an essentially different type of being from the physical, but then
we would be conceding our point.

It is common to hear in response to this argument the assertion
that there just *cannot* be a self-existent being, but it is very uncommon
to hear any very strong reason for the assertion. Professor Nielsen
comments on the "incoherence" (once again) of a logically necessary
individual, and I want to side with him in rejecting such a being. But I
have said nothing so far about a logically necessary being. Only that,
relative to the character of the physical world, it is logically necessary
that there be something the existence of which does not derive from
other things. So far as my argument goes, there is no reason why this
should have to be a being logically necessary in itself—although, of
course, I recognize there has been a lot of discussion about such a
being in the history of our subject, and I do not discount that discussion
as wholly pointless.

A more serious and perhaps more "common sense" objection to
my position, but one that is, I think, answerable, is contained in the
child's question, "Mommy, where did God come from?" (He's just
been told that God made trees and clouds, you know.) In our terminology: "Where did this self-existent being come from?" And the answer
is that He (She, It) didn't come *from* anything because He didn't *come*
at all.

One will have trouble with that answer only if one has already assimilated existence to *physical* existence. Then and only then does the
perfectly general question, "Why is there something rather than nothing?" make sense—because it is assumed that the "something" refers

only to the physical. Without that assimilation, the answer is, "Why shouldn't there be something—some existant or being?" And it turns out there is no good reason to suppose that everything that exists resembles physical existents in coming to be "from" something other than themselves. It should be pointed out that such a supposition, in any case, directly begs the question of God's existence—that is, it assumes that since all being is physical, there could be no spiritual reality such as God. For you certainly could not know that all reality is physical if the question of God's existence is yet to be decided. Efforts in the history of thought to tie the *concept* of being to that of the physical have proved resounding failures, it seems to me, although certain epistemological *programs*—for example, "Science is restricted to the physical (to physics and its derivatives), so 'knowledge' and therefore (!?!) being is restricted to the physical"—are still widely favored. The lack of a conceptual connection between being and the possibility of knowledge continues to plague such programs, as it has most philosophers from Hume and Kant to our time.

One has, I think, to go through a conceptual turn-around in general ontology somewhat like the one Newton executed for physics. Aristotelian physics made motion problematic and rest unproblematic. The question then was, "Why is there motion (here, or there, or at all) rather than rest?" Newton saw that motion was no more problematic than rest. What had to be explained was *change* from motion to rest, or conversely. Similarly, in general ontology one has to understand that existence is, in general, no more problematic than non-existence. Existence isn't somehow "harder" or inherently less likely than non-existence—unless, once again, we are obsessed with *physical* existents, which, because of their specific nature as dependent beings, *are* admittedly always more or less hanging on by the skin of their teeth and inevitably tending toward disintegration. (Aristotle, in his theory of motion, seems to have been obsessed with "forced" motion, such as donkeys pulling carts and persons hauling water out of a well.)

In fact, there are two interesting (by no means philosophically unproblematic) candidates other than God for the status of self-subsistent being or something similar: universals (Plato's "forms") and free human actions. With reference to universals, the question of origin in time does not arise, since they—as distinct from their exemplifications—are not temporally located at all, and since they lack any sort of adjacency or contiguity with other entities which would make sense of their being "produced" by them. Free actions also, it has been argued, involve at least an element of self-subsistence, lacking in their nature as free actions a sufficient, but not (at least on some accounts) necessary, condition.

Finally, it will be objected by some that, though the series of causes for any physical state is finite, the first physical event or state in the series could have come into existence without a cause—could have, in short, originated "from nothing." Many discussions today seem to treat the "Big Bang" in this way, though of course that would make it totally unlike any other "bang" of which we have any knowledge. "Big Bang" mysticism is primarily attractive, I think, just because "the bang" has stepped into a traditional role of God, which gives it a nimbus and seems to rule out the normal questions we would ask about any physical event. *That* "bang" is often treated as if it were not quite or not just a physical event, as indeed it could not be. But what then could it be? Enter "scientific mysticism." And we must at least point out that an eternally self-subsistent being is no more improbable than a self-subsistent event emerging from no cause. As C. S. Lewis pointed out, "An egg which came from no bird is no more 'natural' than a bird which had existed from all eternity" (*God in the Dock*, 211).

Now I am prepared to grant Hume's point that there is no logical contradiction in the supposition that something could come into existence without a cause. This, however, does not entail that Locke was wrong in his claim that "man knows by an intuitive certainty, that bare nothing can no more produce any real being, than it can be equal to two right angles" (*Essay*, Bk. 4, Chap. 10). There are, after all, general laws about how every type of physical state comes about. If we keep clearly before our minds that *any* "something" which comes into existence (including a however big "bang") will always be a completely specific type of thing, then we see that for that "something" to originate from nothing would be to violate the system of law which governs the origination of things of its type. To suppose that an apple, for example, could come into existence without any prior states upon which it depends for its existence is to simply reject all the laws we know to hold true of apple production. They are no longer laws. And it is not a matter of discovering further *conditions* under which apple-laws apply, for the hypothesis is one of no conditions whatever. The counter-intuitiveness of this is, I imagine, what Locke is referring to, and I certainly agree with him if it is. But even if it were neither self-contradictory nor counter-intuitive to suppose that something originated without a cause, the probability of it relative to our data would be exactly zero. There is, so far as I know, not a single case of a physical state or event being observed or otherwise known to originate "from nothing." And if anyone has observed such a thing, I am sure that our leading scientific journals and societies would like very much to hear about it. In fact, the idea is an entirely *ad hoc* hypothesis whose only 'merit' is avoidance of admission of a self-subsistent being—which it achieves precisely by claiming an entity of a type which in every other case is admitted to be dependent; to be, "just this once," itself self-subsistent.

Something which originates from nothing is precisely self-subsistent. It is dependent on nothing and exists in its own right. The editors of the Time-Life book *Cosmos* (published in 1989) gravely remark that "no one can say with certainty why the universe popped out of the void" (p. 13). They, along with many sober cosmologists who ponder this question, seem oblivious to the fact that in the nature of the case there can be no *why* for its "popping out," since it is precisely the *void,* the "empty," out from which it popped. (There is nothing to be uncertain about.)

Of course there are many other points of interest and disagreement to be discussed with reference to my first stage argument. It doesn't prove that there is only one self-subsistent being. It doesn't show that the uncaused being or beings which lie at the foundation of the world-causal series still exist—though, certainly, we would like to know of any reason, beyond the mere empty logical possibility which might be offered, for them ceasing to exist. (Admittedly, their not being dependent and contingent in the sense of physical states and events does not immediately imply inability to dissipate themselves in some fashion.) Finally, this argument does not show that the self-subsistent first cause is a person.

All of this I cheerfully grant. Nevertheless, from the viewpoint of the atheist's enterprise, we now have an ontologically haunted universe. It is haunted by unnerving possibilities. If I am right, there has got to be something more than the physical or "natural" universe, and something obviously quite different in character—though also essentially related to it, for from this "something more" the physical universe ultimately derives. If this is established, it is not clear to me that very much of a point is left to atheism, which in the contemporary world surely draws most of its motivation from a desire to *tame* or *naturalize* reality, all hope of which is now lost. (Again: If I am right.) Of course many important points about the exact character of this "more and different" aspect of the universe are still left to be determined. In particular, religion as a human institution and certain kinds of gods, can be effectively attacked by the atheist. But the theist is concerned with this no less than the atheist, and perhaps even more so. Early Christians were sometimes called atheists by the Romans whose gods the Christians denied. Later, Christians called Spinoza an atheist. And so forth. But I think there is an obvious sense in which the atheist in the current, standard philosophical understanding can never feel comfortable in a universe which supplements the physical in the manner demonstrated by my first-stage argument. The *possibility* of there being a God, even in the full theistic sense, has now become significantly more substantial. There is an ontological "space" for it to be realized which just would not be there in a strictly physical universe.

Stage Two: Design

The second stage in my development of the case for theism corresponds to what has traditionally been called the teleological argument, or the argument *to* design. The latter is the correct designation for what I take to be the essence of the point here. Many will be astonished at the suggestion that teleology actually has nothing at all essentially to do with the case, and has in fact only resulted in an incredible amount of confusion and arguing beside the point on both sides. Theists have, I believe, brought this upon themselves by fixing upon such striking cases of order as the human eye or the degree of inclination of the earth's axis in relation to the possibility of life on the planet. But, especially since the emergence of evolutionary theory, they in so doing open themselves up to massive and sophisticated, though often logically quite misguided, 'rebuttals'—every case of which purports to show how the cases fixed upon by the theist at least *could,* with *some* degree of probability, have originated, come into existence, by a lawlike process from a pre-existing condition of the physical universe *without* assistance from what one recent practitioner of this routine smugly calls "a Great Spirit in the sky with a tidy mind and a sense of order" or "A blessed miracle of provident design" (Richard Dawkins, *The Blind Watchmaker: Why the Evidence of Evolution Reveals a Universe without Design* [New York: Norton and Co., 1986], 43–44). The "rebutters," with almost no exceptions, quite conveniently manage to forget that evolution, whether cosmic or biological, *cannot—logically* cannot!—be a theory of ultimate origins of existence or order, precisely because its operation presupposes the *existence* of certain entities with specific potential behaviors and an *environment* of some specific kind that operates upon those entities in some specifically ordered fashion. It is characteristic of the thoughtlessness and ignorance which plagues the discussion of these issues that Darwin's book *On the Origin of the Species by*

Means of Natural Selection is often thought, by theists as well as anti-theists, to be an explanation of the origin of life and of living forms generally, when of course nothing was farther from Darwin's own mind. (I hasten to add that I am not suggesting that the contributors to this present discussion have fallen prey to any such misunderstanding!) Let us say quite generally then that *any sort of evolution of order of any kind will always presuppose pre-existing order and pre-existing entities governed by it*. It follows as a simple matter of logic that not all order evolved. Given the physical world—however much of evolution it may or may not contain—there is or was some order *in it* which did not evolve. However it may have originated (if it originated), *that* order did not evolve. We come here upon a logically insurpassable *limit* to what evolution, however it may be understood, can accomplish.

We should pause to notice that the order from which cosmic and biological evolution takes its rise must have been one of considerable power and complexity, since it provided the basis of cosmic and biological evolution. Evolution itself is a process that exhibits order of stunning dimensions, diachronic as well as synchronic, especially if given the scope customary among anti-theists. That specific type of structure found *in* evolution did not itself come about *through* evolution, any more than, as Liebniz pointed out, the laws of mechanics were instituted by the laws of mechanics. It is important to take note of this, because some partisans of evolution hold before us the image of being without order as that from which being with order emerged. Thus we find Dawkins, in the book mentioned above, discussing the non-random arrangement of pebbles of various sizes on an ocean beach. Clearly, the pebbles seem sorted and arranged. But, as he points out, this "arranging was really done by the blind forces of physics, in this case the action of waves. The waves . . . just energetically throw the pebbles around, and big pebbles and small pebbles respond differently to this treatment so they end up at different levels of the beach. A small amount of order has come out of disorder, and no mind planned it" (p. 43). Big Bang mysticism is, I find, usually accompanied by an "order out of chaos" mysticism.

After letting him enjoy a small moment of triumph, we can only say to this highly qualified scientist: "You gotta be kidding! No mind (directly) planned it, but nothing whatsoever 'has come out of disorder' in this case." Such an interaction of the waves and the pebbles is a perfectly orderly process, even if our comprehension of that order can only be statistically expressed. Moreover, *we* know for sure that *Dawkins himself* knows this. What afflicts him at this point can be very simply described: He is in the grip of the romanticism of evolution as a sweeping ontological principle, bearing in itself the mystical vision of an ultimate *Urgrund* of chaos and nothingness of itself, giving birth to the physical universe—which is all very fine *as* an aesthetic approach to the cosmos, and vaguely comforting. But it has nothing at all to do with "evidence of . . . a universe without design," as the dust jacket of his book suggests.

So at this second stage we have a challenge to offer the atheist which is similar to the one of the first stage. At the first stage we said that the probability, relative to our data, of something (in the physical universe, at least) originating from nothing was zero, and we invited the atheist to find one case of this actually happening, to raise the probability a bit above zero. Now we urge him to find one case of ordered being—or just being, for, whatever it is, it will certainly be ordered—originating from being without order.

Over against this challenge, we point out that the force, the power to convince, which most people seem to feel in the face of the existing physical order surrounding us undoubtedly comes from the simple fact that we all have experience—perhaps even a quite direct, first-hand experience—of order entering the physical world from minds, our minds as well as from those of others. Not as if the physical world were totally disordered before we produced our inventions. Of course it is not. We have no experience of *ex nihilo* creation, and the second stage of theistic evidence does not aim to establish such creation. But, to go back to Paley's classical example of finding a watch in the wilderness, we clearly know that the order that is in a watch first presented itself to the human mind without being present in physical reality, and only because of that did it later emerge within the physical world. We know that locomotives, bridges, and a huge number of other things exist in the physical world *because* the "design" for them previously existed in a mind. Some *person* designed them. Only the kind of scepticism that gives philosophy a deservedly bad name can suggest otherwise. That is why if we stepped on an apparently uninhabited planet and discovered what, to all appearance, was a branch of the May Company or Sears—or even a coke bottle or a McDonald's hamburger wrapper—it would be both psychologically impossible as well as flatly irrational in the light of our available data to believe that they came into existence without a design and a mind "containing" that design. The extension of this conclusion to cover eyes, DNA structures, and solar systems, by appropriate modifications of premises, is only slightly less coercive.

That, surely, is why David Hume, in the "Introduction" to his *The*

Natural History of Religion, states, "The whole frame of nature bespeaks an intelligent author; and no rational enquirer can, after serious reflection, suspend his belief a moment with regard to the primary principles of genuine Theism and Religion." And he puts in the mouth of Philo, at the end of his *Dialogues Concerning Natural Religion,* the somewhat more modestly formulated conclusion *"That the cause or causes of order in the universe probably bear some remote analogy to human intelligence."* Now I am aware of the carefully weighted meaning which Hume assigned to these words, and, indeed, I accept them in that meaning as an adequate formulation of the results of my stage two. But it is necessary at the same time to insist that he really did mean what he did say in these two passages. (I take Philo to speak for him.) Hume was a minimal or stage-two theist. He believed that the physical universe rationally required a mind or mind-like being as its source, and for the reasons I have indicated above. His further views, to the effect that the world offers no rational support for the full-blown God of Christian theism, do not diminish this one bit.

We should occasionally think about the fact that all of the "great" philosophers—the ones which, up to very recently, all of the better graduate programs in philosophy thought you had to know something about before professional respectability could rest upon you (Plato, Aristotle, St. Augustine, St. Thomas, "St. Occam," Descartes, Spinoza, Liebniz, Locke, Berkely, Kant, and Hegel)—accepted either second stage theism or (Spinoza, Kant, Hegel) something stronger. Kant, who along with Hume is generally credited among professional philosophers with destroying any possibility of significant theistic evidences, said that "belief in a God and in another world is so interwoven with my moral sentiment that as there is little danger of my losing the latter, there is equally little cause for fear that the former can ever be taken from me" (*Critique of Pure Reason,* B 857). At the very least, he held, it is impossible to prove "that there is no such being and no such life" (B 858). His belief was that if the moral life is possible, there is "another world," the "intelligible world," which alone makes the moral life possible. And he indeed believed the moral life to be possible. So here is an argument which, to his own mind, secured the existence of a person-like transcendental being with *its* world. That it is in some sense a "moral argument" does not mean that it is not as logically serious as any other argument. Kant did not regard the moral world as nebulous or non-existent in the contemporary manner.

Now I do not cite these great philosophers as authorities on the points here at issue, though it is about time that the actual role of authority in professional philosophy and in the intellectual world generally got a candid and thorough reexamination. (There's a whole lot of faking going on.) It is just that the general impression that philosophers—especially the "real" ones—are explicit or closet atheists, needs occasionally to be brought over against certain historical facts. And the often suggested idea that, if Aristotle or Descartes or Locke had only lived today, they too would have been atheists, needs to be faced with the challenge to point out exactly what it is that we now know or can do that would have modified the arguments upon which they based their theism. (I have even heard it suggested that these philosophers were just hypocrites and only seemed to accept theism from fear of their society!)

So what do we have at the second stage of theistic evidence? We have established that not all order is evolved, and that relative to our data, there is a probability of zero that order should emerge from chaos or from nothing into the physical world. In addition, we have experience of order emerging from minds (our minds) into the physical world. Under the limited conditions of human existence, we know what this is like and that it does happen.

Now what is the effect of all of this? Certainly no demonstration of God in the full theistic sense. But, similarly as with stage one, the possibility of there being such a God has become significantly more substantial. The existence of something significantly like Him has been given some plausibility, and the theist may now invite the atheist to show why the self-existent, mind-like entity of minimal theism—the God of the philosophers, shall we call Him—could not in reality be the same as the subject of praise and prayer and devotion in religion—the "God of Abraham, Isaac and Jacob." There is now a somewhat broader ontological "space" for the God of religion which would *not* be there in a universe without "design."

Once we are clear about this, we return to the more familiar cases associated with the "teleological" argument, some of which were discussed by Professor Moreland. The intricate cases of adaptive order found about us in the world are said by the atheist to have resulted from trillions of tiny increments of order. ("We do the difficult immediately," the U.S. Marines say. "The impossible takes a little longer.") That *is* logically possible, once we free it, as discussed above, from the logical confusions and sweeping ontological pretensions which have encumbered the idea of evolution. On the other hand, once it becomes clear that order is not self-generating and all instances of it could not have originated from evolution, and in the light of the fact that order does (at least in some limited sense) upon some occasions actually enter the physical world from the mind, we would want to know exactly why—given all of this—we should rule out some fairly direct role of "larger minds," shall we say, in the production of eyeballs and planetary orbits. And the theist, for her part, must take seriously the question of "how" such a role is to be conceptualized—lacking interesting responses to which the whole idea of "creation science" must remain as vacuous as it is today. That is a tough assignment. But it may be that *human history*, the realm of action and personality, more readily exhibits a direct role of larger minds in the course of worldly events. And that brings us to the third stage of theistic evidences, as I understand them.

Stage Three: The Course of Human Events

In this third stage we look at *the course of human events*—historical, social and individual—*within the context of* a demonstrated extra-naturalism (stage one) and of a quite plausible cosmic intellectualism (stage two). Thus human life is to be interpreted within the ontological space of the actualities, with their attendant possibilities, hewn out in stages one and two. Further things which we know about some minds (ours) and their creations at least put us in position to face the atheist with an urgent "Why not?" and to test the basis of any knowledge claims she may make about cosmic minds in relation to human history and experience. We know, most importantly, that human minds standardly create for a purpose, and that they retain an active interest in, feel intimately invested in, what they create—and all the more so the greater the originality or "creativity" involved. Intervention in human affairs by God need not, as in deism, be regarded as a sign of imperfection in the original creation. (Another factory recall?) Creation *might*, after all, be an ongoing affair with God, including what is usually called "redemption" in the language of theology. Intervention appropriately conducted could plausibly be seen as a loving will to communicate and to help, or to secure the purposes in creation, which is at least not radically foreign even to personality as we know it under human conditions. And, given all the preceding, we would like to know why the same *should not* be true of cosmic intelligence—all the while unequivocally conceding that we have not demonstrated it to be true or even strongly probable. While unexcluded possibilities do not imply truth or probability, they are nonetheless relevant to rationality.

More important in our third stage than these rather speculative extensions of minimal theism toward a more full-blown personal God is the examination of the actual course of human history and the actual contents of human experience to determine, as honestly and thoroughly as possible, what can and what cannot be understood in terms of "natural" events verifiable within objectively established methodologies of science. These methodologies are to be distinguished, as clearly as possible, from philosophical speculations about them, of course. But, to put it simply, we should always assume that particular events and experiences *might* be scientifically understood; and the theist should usually, if not always, give any benefit of any honest doubt to the naturalist in any particular question of fact (though, I think, not in matters of philosophical speculation). If there is anything to what the theist believes, we surely can afford to be generous.

But we must also be thorough, and we have every right to require the same of our atheist co-investigators and to ignore their objections if they refuse. Faith is not restricted to religious people, nor is blind prejudice and dogmatism. The atheist who can't be bothered to pay serious attention to the facts claimed for religious histories and religious experience is twin brother to the churchman who refused to look through Galileo's telescope because he *already knew* what was and was not to be seen. Of course the way is often paved for this in the life of the individual atheist by an equal prejudice and dogmatism on the theist side. Also, the (hopefully) sound argumentation laid out in stages one and two above may have been dismissed because it was presented as proving the existence of the God of religion, when it obviously does no such thing. Thus the individual atheist may recognize no context of possibilities within which the miraculous events of religious history and the experiences of sainthood and the devout can be taken seriously for the purposes of knowledge.

So I completely agree with Professor Nielsen's comment, at the opening of his "Rebuttal," that the resurrection of Jesus from the dead, even if *he* stood by and saw it happen, "wouldn't show there was an infinite intelligible being." He knows there are lots of weird things in the world, and, as he says, "It would be just that a very strange happening happened." (So what else is new in a universe where nothing bangs big and order 'congeals' out of chaos?) Jesus himself, according to the record, agrees with us on this matter. In the story he told of Lazarus and the rich man (Luke 16), the self-indulged rich man asked Father Abraham to send Lazarus back to warn his brothers of their fate in Hades, saying that "if someone goes to them from the dead, they will repent!" But Abraham replied, "If they hear not Moses and the Prophets, neither will they be persuaded, though one rose from the dead" (vss. 30–31, KJV). (You can imagine the fine, witty actions and comments to be heard around the dinner table had Lazarus reappeared on the scene! Just think how Monty Python or Bill Cosby or Woody Allen would do it, and you've got it. Abraham didn't fall off the turnip truck.)

Jesus' approach to these matters was, I believe, expressed in His statement: "Ye believe in God, believe also in Me" (John 14:1, KJV). That's the right order. The religious ideas, history, and context in back of His life as an Israelite, *together with* his own teaching and action and character, provided for those who absorbed themselves in them something close to a *logical* demonstration, *not* of the existence of Jehovah, which was never in question for them, but of His specific nature. And *this* is third-stage work. It will have no epistemic weight whatsoever except within an appropriate historical context or within some other arrangement which for the individual settles the first- and second-stage questions. Of course, occasionally some people will just be overwhelmed by a historical or personal event. But a philosophically thoughtful person will never be convinced, much less someone operating from prejudice—even if she decides that she "had better give in to God"—unless she has found some intellectual satisfaction on stage-one and stage-two issues, which clearly the Bible for its part presumes is quite accessible and important (see Ps. 19; Rom. 1:19–20).

Historical events and individuals—real or imagined, rigorously reported or mythologically elaborated—do in fact provide the specific content for beliefs about the gods of religious devotion. But it is *always* a mistake—regretfully very common, I'm afraid—to simply place the weight of proving the existence of God upon them, although they may always serve as appropriate points of challenge to dogmatic unbelief and although they in fact will lead some people to belief in God. It is the task of theistic evidences at stage three to subject these contents to appropriate rational tests to determine, so far as possible, the more specific nature of the mind-like causal ground of the physical universe. There is no reason whatsoever why recognized religious activities, such as prayer, ritual, and meditative practices, should not serve along with rational analysis, experimentation, and historical research to that end. In every domain, the subject matter ultimately must determine the suitability of the methods for its study.

My own conviction is that a properly worked out inference in terms of "the best explanation"—"best" in the full light of the results of stages one and two—will show it quite plausible that some extranatural mind or minds of roughly the full theistic variety are causally present in human events; that there is "a power working for righteousness," as Matthew Arnold called it, at work in human history and available for interaction with individuals under certain circumstances. The real force backing such a conclusion can never be felt in the abstract; it only comes from the patient, highly motivated examination and comparison of details, which simply can't be engaged in here—and really can't be done *for* another person. But, to nevertheless speak generally, the existence of the Jewish people and of the Christian church, when one goes into the fine texture of the history, personalities, thought, and experience which make them up, seems to me by far best explained by the existence of, roughly, the type of deity that Christians and Jews, among others, worship. I by no means suggest that God is responsible for everything in these traditions, nor do I restrict the action of God in history to them alone. Indeed, if He is the sort of being they themselves present Him as, then He is present with and makes Himself known to all peoples. Every religious culture and experience should be deeply respected—even if not adopted and even if regarded as mistaken in important respects. Christians above all *should* know of God's habit of turning up in the wrong company, where according to the official view He absolutely *could not* be. What further inferences are to be drawn from this is another matter: one which must be handled with the utmost care. But the partisan of one religion must extend the same generous openness and hopefulness to the practitioners of other religions as he would want them and the atheist to extend to himself. The rule, "Do unto others as you would have them do unto you," also extends to inquiry with others.

A Concluding Word

I have attempted in these pages to clarify some points about the structure into which theistic evidences must be arranged if they are to be properly appreciated. Failure to understand the limitations and the interrelations of what I have called the "three stages" of theistic evidences seems to me a great hindrance both to philosophical treatment of the question of God's existence and to the individual's efforts to come to terms with what is, after all, a major issue in dealing with life. Given the very best possible exposition, theistic evidences never replace a choice as to what kind of universe we would have ours to be, and a personal adventure of trust, which involves living beyond what we can absolutely know. Nevertheless, I believe that the structure of evidence outlined—in spite of its far too simple discussions of the nature of the physical, causation, order, etc.—indicates that the basic doctrine of God present in the historically developed theisms of the major world religions is most likely true and is certainly capable of being rationally accepted. With that much secured, and yet mindful of the vast amount we do not know about that God, we here give the last word to Philo (Hume):

> . . . the most natural sentiment, which a well-disposed mind will feel on this occasion, is a longing desire and expectation, that heaven would be pleased to dissipate, at least alleviate, this profound ignorance, by affording some more particular revelation to mankind, and making discoveries of the nature, attributes, and operations of the divine object of our faith.

Possibly this prayer has already been answered.

PART IV

WHAT WOULD THE DEBATERS SAY?

Some Closing Arguments

J. P. Moreland
Atheism and Leaky Buckets: The Christian Rope Pulls Tighter

15

In these final remarks, I propose to do two things: respond to the major criticisms raised against me and summarize my understanding of some of the central issues in the debate about the existence of the Christian God.[1] Regarding the contributions by Professors Willard and Craig, I am in agreement with the vast majority of what they say, and our approaches to these issues are similar. There are minor points of disagreement among us, but I will forego comment on those points because they are relatively insignificant compared to my differences with Keith Parsons and Antony Flew, and because space considerations warrant focusing attention on the latter. I appreciate the thoughtful contributions by these two thinkers, and I will try to give helpful, albeit brief responses to their main points.

Keith Parsons

In my view, Parsons raises five main objections, which I will discuss in the order they are presented.

Epistemic Duties and Rights

Parsons complains that my statement that a believer is in his or her epistemic rights in believing that God exists is merely a two-fold claim: (1) about the believer (the believer formed his beliefs honestly, holds them openly), not about the belief itself; and (2) that belief that God exists is rational, not an endorsement that the belief is true. For these reasons, such a claim is supposed to be a philosophically boring assertion for which "the appropriate response is apathy rather than hostility."

Unfortunately, Parsons' understanding of my assertion is so confused that he appears to be chasing windmills. For one thing, even if a theist grants that all he or she means to affirm about belief in God is that one is rational in holding that belief, this claim is hardly uninteresting. Given the rampant scientism and physicalism in current intellectual circles and the concomitant attitudes toward religion, such a position is far from boring. Having spoken on more than one hundred college campuses, I can only marvel at Parsons' assertion that atheists are not interested in convicting theists of irrationality and are not interested in gaining converts. Parsons' boredom may say more about him than about the issue itself.

But more importantly, his view rests on a number of confusions about the nature of epistemic rights and duties. He appears to be guilty of a failure to make a use/mention distinction regarding a claim to be in one's epistemic rights in holding to a belief. Such a claim is not mentioning rationality itself, but is using rationality to focus on the truth of the belief asserted to be rational. This is the standard way to understand an assertion to be in one's epistemic rights. Epistemologists as diverse as coherentist Laurence BonJour and foundationalist Roderick Chisholm understand epistemic rights and duties as instrumental: they are intimately connected with the truth of what is asserted and the degree of rationality for a truth claim.[2] My opening remarks in Chapter 1 make clear that this is how I meant to be understood. The important point is this: Even though a belief can be false and rational, a claim that a belief is rational is still a claim that the belief is true (and believed so *because* it is rational), and not merely a claim that it is rational simpliciter.

Parsons also confuses one way of understanding epistemic duties and responsibilities with the whole subject matter itself. He seems to take the moral analogue of virtue theory or utilitarianism to exhaust the philosophical study of epistemic duties and responsibilities. He does this by focusing his sole attention on how a person holds a belief (e.g., openly) or on the moral utility of holding a belief (see his ship illustration). He also seems to equate the assertion that one is in his or her epistemic rights in believing in God with the view that belief in God is properly basic.[3] Even if these are legitimate aspects of or approaches to the study of epistemic rights and duties, they surely do not exhaust these matters, and it should have been clear to him that my views on these are not those he criticizes.

I cannot resist one more point. If Parsons is so adamantly against focusing on the rationality of persons as opposed to their beliefs, why does he criticize creation science by attacking creation scientists? His problem with the former is that the latter fail to hold their theories tentatively. But even if this were true—and it is not[4]—it is at best only a point about the impropriety of believers and not of their beliefs. Parsons is loathe to accept such points. He fails to be consistent here.

What, then, do I mean when I claim to be in my epistemic rights in believing that God exists? To borrow Chisholm's terms, I mean that the proposition p—God exists—is at least probable and, more likely, epistemically in the clear or beyond reasonable doubt.[5] If theism is the view that believes p, atheism the view that believes not-p, and agnosticism the view that withholds p or is counterbalanced with regard to it (doesn't accept p or not-p), then to say that p is probable is to say that theism is more reasonable than atheism. To say that p is epistemically in the clear is to say at least that agnosticism is not more reasonable than theism. On the other hand, we can go further: To say that p is beyond reasonable doubt is to say that theism is *more* reasonable than agnosticism. My own view is that theism is beyond reasonable doubt, but I do not need this stronger position to make my case against atheism.

Burden of Proof

Parsons says that the burden of proof is on the theist, and in the absence of compelling (!) evidence, the atheist wins by default. He defines "atheism" as a lack of belief in God and not the denial of God's existence.

How does burden of proof figure into questions about God's existence? Let us continue to assume the usual understanding of atheism (atheism is the positive assertion that God does not exist) and comment on burden-of-proof issues between atheism and theism. Later I will comment on Parsons' definition of "atheism," which I take to be "agnosticism."

In general, burden-of-proof arguments in philosophy are unprofitable because they are often question-begging and they degenerate into mere assertions or, worse, emotive utterances. In the context of theism and atheism, burden-of-proof assertions are extremely problematic. For one thing, a number of different issues can be distinguished. For example, there is a difference between becoming a theist (atheist) and remaining a theist (atheist). We tend to be epistemically conservative, and usually there is a burden of proof present in *changing* one's views not present in *maintaining* one's views.

Second, there is a difference between being justified in holding a belief and being able to justify that belief to someone else. If I consider whether or not I am appeared to redly, then I may be justified in a belief by merely attending to the self-presenting state itself. My belief is, as it were, innocent until proven guilty. But I may sustain a burden of proof in convincing *you* that I am being appeared to redly. The rationality of religious experience could be similarly understood.

Third, there is a difference between being rationally justified in a belief and being in a debate situation. One could be rationally justified in believing a proposition is true without a burden of proof to justify that belief to someone else before that justification is legitimized. But in a debate, burdens of proof depend on the structure of the debate. If the debate is about an affirmation—"God exists," or "God does not exist"—then the person who affirms the affirmation bears the burden of proof, not the person who denies it. On the other hand, if the debate is over a question—"Does God exist?"—then the person who answers yes and the one who answers no *equally* bear the burden of proof. My debate with Nielsen was a debate about a question, Does God exist? and there was equal burden on each of us.

Thus, since there is no simple, single burden-of-proof issue, general claims about burden of proof are naive and simplistic.

Tom Morris has pointed out another problem with the claim that atheists win by default because of a general presumption towards atheism.[6] Imagine I am seated in an office. The thought occurs to me that a large boa constrictor is also in the office. So I make a thorough inspection but find nothing. My appropriate stance is not to continue to affirm the existence of the snake or be agnostic, but to positively deny that such a snake exists. This response, however, is only appropriate *after* I have decided that I am epistemologically well situated regarding the matter under consideration—that is, that my senses are reliable, I know what I'm looking for, I look in all the right places, and so on. But, Morris continues, this is not what is going on with claims about theism and atheism. Here it may be the case (and most theists believe it actually to be true) that one's noetic faculties are not functioning in a religiously neutral way—we are biased. Further, there simply *is* evidence for God's existence, while none existed to support the boa constrictor's presence.

Therefore, burden-of-proof assertions or claims that one should withhold judgment on an issue come into the picture, *after,* not before, these other considerations. And the appropriate focus is on the evidence itself and the proper functioning of our noetic faculties, not on burden-of-proof assertions.

The fact is that both theism and atheism involve positive assertions. The theist claims that God exists. The atheist makes the positive assertion that God does not exist, or asserts that some class of objects (such as physical objects) exists and that objects in that class *are the only things that exist*. Either way, the atheist makes a positive assertion just like the theist, and no general burden exists on just one side or the other.[7]

What Parsons calls atheism is really an expression of agnosticism. So understood, his claim about burden of proof is just the benign recognition of what it means to say a belief is counterbalanced: if the rational situation for p is the same as that for not-p, then one should withhold judgment either way. But, contrary to what Parsons claims, this is not a victory for atheism—it's a draw between atheism and theism. Furthermore, a state of withholding belief is justified *after* the evidence for and against the proposition is evaluated, so the issue should focus on that evidence. Finally, it is epistemically irresponsible to say, as Parsons does, that one needs *compelling* evidence for a belief before one is rational in accepting the truth of that belief. Surely if the evidence for a proposition is better than the evidence against it, one should accept the proposition, even if the evidence on its behalf is not compelling—that is, overwhelmingly conclusive. We rightly embrace the validity of any number of propositions which often lack the support of compelling evidence—for instance, "President George Bush probably won't raise taxes during his first term of office," or "Smoking causes cancer."

In my opinion, what is really going on with Parsons' claim is this: "burden of proof" is an expression of two deeper issues—(1) epistemological methodism, which is roughly the view that I must have criteria for p before I can know (or be rationally justified in believing) p; and (2) an unfairly high standard of the rationality of such criteria (they must be compelling), which I doubt that Parsons, or most rational people, apply (or ought to apply) throughout their intellectual life. I will return to these points toward the end of this chapter.

The Fine-tuned Universe and Probability

Parsons criticizes my argument regarding the delicately balanced presence of cosmic constants in the universe as evidence for a Designer. His main point is that such an argument requires assigning probabilities to theism vs. atheism, that such probabilities should be expressed along the lines of Bayes's theorem, and that it is virtually impossible to assign prior probabilities to atheism or theism.

Unfortunately, Parsons misrepresents the inductive formulation of a design argument by reducing it to an argument using probabilities. If there were any place that such a reduction should work, it would be science, not philosophy. But even in science induction cannot be reduced to probability theory. After surveying unsuccessful attempts to do so in nineteenth-century philosophy of science, Larry Laudan observed that "When the more recent history of probabilistic induction is told, . . . we will see a similar story of a tradition generating far more problems than it resolves and often substituting formalistic elegance and a preoccupation with technical minutiae for a sophisticated analysis of the modes of scientific inference."[8]

The same point could be made more strongly regarding Parsons' treatment of my design argument. Such an argument can be understood as a simple argument from analogy or as an inference to the best explanation, where neither involves probability considerations or a Baysian approach to confirmation.[9] The real point of my design argument is twofold. First, certain phenomena (for example, the nature of cosmic constants) are highly unlikely, surprising, and without explanation if they resulted without originating in a mind, because they bear features that apparently point to a mind responsible for their existence. Second, recent developments in science have shown the variability of these constants to be incredibly small. This was an empirical discovery, and one that could have gone the other way. Thus, the precise nature of these values as preconditions for life needs explanation.

Two hypotheses are being judged for their ability to explain these facts. The atheistic account can provide no reason for expecting the arrangement that yielded life to come about, other than the mere fact that it was just the one that happened. The atheist cannot simply assert that some arrangement or other had to occur, for this is an improper characterization of the situation. The theist, on the other hand, is not asking what the chances are that some arrangement or other would occur. He or she is asking what the likelihood is that a particular "deal of the cards" would occur where this particular "deal" is made more understandable by the hypothesis of theism, Christian theism in this case. The world view of Christian theism makes the occurrence of life likely as a part of its overall hypothesis. The concurrence of the particular factors necessary for the emergence of life with those predicted by Christian theism is to be compared with the emergence of those factors necessary for life against the backdrop of the atheist hypothesis, which does not make any particular arrangement more likely than any other.

When scientists discovered that the factors necessary for life were delicately balanced and yet actually happened, their discovery was already predicted and explained within the framework of Christian theism, and their discovery in turn tended to confirm Christian theism. For the atheist, however, no outcome is antecedently more probable or more predictable than any other outcome. Thus, the occurrence of these cosmic constants along with the emergence of life must remain happy, unexplained coincidences for the atheist.

Furthermore, the notion of probability can be used here, contrary to what Parsons claims. It is wrong, even on the assumption of atheism, to say that the universe (I presume Parsons means here the values of the cosmic constants—for instance, the rate of expansion of the Big Bang, the mass of a proton, and so on) is neither likely nor unlikely, but simply is and that's all there is to it. Counterfactual situations were possible, and the notion that these values could have been otherwise is neither unintelligible nor particularly problematic. Scientists themselves often claim that a number of other possible values for these constants could have been obtained and, thus, the values in the actual world need explanation which theism provides.

Finally, it is possible, even though not necessary, to construe my argument along Baysian lines. Richard Swinburne and William J. Wainwright take this approach.[10] For example, Wainwright says apparent design forces a choice between two possibilities:

D: An intelligent and powerful mind is the cause of the apparent design.
N: No supernatural reality underlies natural processes.

Even if the prior probability of D is low compared to N (which need not be granted), Wainwright claims that the probability of design on the designer hypothesis is 1 (that is, given a Designer, there will be design in the universe), and its probability on the naturalistic hypothesis is intuitively quite low (that is, given the naturalistic hypothesis, the presence of design is unlikely).

What is wrong with this argument? Parsons' objection fits a pattern: Because we cannot formulate here precise and all-embracing criteria prior to our argument, we cannot know anything at all about design and its role in arguing about atheism and theism. But this is epistemological methodism again, coupled with a "compelling argument" requirement, which is problematic in its own right (to be discussed in the final section) and is less reasonable than Wainwright's presentation of the argument above.

Finally, I want to anticipate and answer one more objection to my design argument. It is not explicitly formulated by Parsons, but his allusion to Hume suggests it, and it is often raised in this context. Hume and his followers have objected to the design argument by claiming that we should not be surprised by the apparent design in the universe (e.g., the values of the constants) because we should not have been here to discuss the matter if the world had not been one with apparent design in it. The factors are necessary for people to be around to puzzle over them.

But two things are wrongheaded with this objection. First, it misrepresents the argument. The advocate of the design argument is not holding the existence of human knowers constant to compare two alternative routes to get to them, one with apparent design and the other chaotic. Rather, the comparison is between (1) a universe with apparent design that makes human knowers possible and actual and (2) a universe without such apparent design and any life. As atheist J. L. Mackie put it:

> There is only one actual universe, with a unique set of basic materials and physical constants, and it is therefore surprising that the elements of this unique setup are just right for life when they might easily have been wrong. This is not made less surprising by the fact that if it had not been so, no one would have been here to be surprised. We can properly envisage and consider alternative possibilities which do not include our being there to experience them.[11]

Mackie's statement serves, not only as a clear response to Hume, but also as an indication of how inappropriate it is for Parsons to identify atheism as a view which denies talk about alternative possibilities. Mackie would not have sided with Parsons on this. And if Parsons wants to claim that atheism entails or supports the notion that the universe just is, then he needs to argue this, not merely assert it.

The second problem with Hume's objection is this: Before recent scientific discoveries, it could have turned out that life would have been possible, given a wide range of values for various cosmic constants. But this was not what was found. So the precision and balance of these factors demands an explanation even more than would have been required if it had been discovered that wide ranges in those values were consistent with the occurrence of life. By implying that this is a pseudo-issue, Hume (and Parsons) fails to account for this increased demand in explanation.[12]

Problems with the Kalam Cosmological Argument

Parsons raises a number of objections against the kalam cosmological argument. For instance, he argues that it is possible to traverse an actual infinite by successive addition. He offers two examples of such a task, one from Bertrand Russell and one from Rudy Rucher. But the examples fail to be convincing for two reasons.

First, they are examples of potential infinites, not actual infinites. A potential infinite is a series that can increase forever but which is always finite and is such that no time n is reached where a subset of the tasks completed at n can be put into one-to-one correspondence with (made equal to) all the tasks completed at n. For example, suppose someone started counting 1, 2, 3, 4, . . . , one could count forever but never reach infinity. As one continued counting, he would be forming a potentially infinite series of numbers, which would increase one number at a time but would remain actually finite. If he kept counting for six hours, he would count twice as many numbers as those he had counted in the first three hours.

An actual infinite is not a series but a set, and it is a set such that it has a denumerable subset (a set is denumerable if and only if it can be put into one-to-one correspondence with the set of all the natural numbers), or put differently, can be put into one-to-one correspondence with one of its proper subsets. In other words, part of the set can be made equal to the whole set. For example, if set A has all the natural numbers in it and set B has all the even numbers in it, then A and B are the same size, even though B is a part of A. Since the kalam argument involves the impossibility of traversing an *actual* infinite (which would be required to reach the present moment if the past were beginningless), then the series involved in Parsons' examples, being potential infinites, are irrelevant.

Second, his examples involve postulating an infinite series of temporal moments to explain how the infinite series of tasks can be completed. So, even if Parsons thinks his examples involve traversing actual infinites, his examples merely shift the problem from traversing one infinite to traversing another—hence, the same problems I raised apply to the new infinite.[13] An appeal to a time above time does not solve the traversing problem; it merely postpones it.

But Parsons has another objection to the kalam argument. It is one raised by Flew as well. They claim that I have assumed what I am trying to prove: my argument pictures a beginningless universe as a universe with a beginning time T, infinitely far away, from which the present moment must be reached. But, they claim, a beginningless universe has no beginning, not one infinitely far away.

But this is a gross misunderstanding of the kalam argument. The defender of the kalam argument does not assume a beginning time infinitely far removed from the present. It is those of us who defend the kalam argument, not the likes of Parsons and Flew, who take seriously a beginningless universe and the actually infinite past involved in such a universe. Parsons and Flew seem to think a beginningless universe involves an indefinite past, not an actually infinite past.

Actually, it is precisely the lack of a beginning that causes most of the problems in traversing the past to reach the present. If there were no beginning, then reaching the present moment would be like counting to zero from negative infinity $(n, \ldots, -3, -2, -1)$. Counting to positive infinity from zero $(0, 1, 2, 3, \ldots, n)$ involves the same number of events as does counting to zero (the present moment) from negative infinity. The number of events traversed is not a function of direction, and the latter task is as problematic as the former—not because both allegedly involve starting from some point (the former has such a point, the latter does not), but because of the impossibility of traversing an actual infinite by successive addition.

Further, coming to the present moment by traversing an infinite past is worse than counting to positive infinity from zero, because the former cannot even get started. It is like trying to jump out of a bottomless pit. The whole idea of getting a foothold in the series in order to make progress is unintelligible. Take any specifiable event in the past. In order to reach that event, one would already have to traverse an actual infinite, and the problem is perfectly iterative—it applies to each point in the past.

By the way, this was a major point of several of Zeno's paradoxes. He was not merely trying to show that one could not finish crossing an actual infinite, but that one could not even begin moving, because the problem of crossing was perfectly general and iterative. Aristotle solved Zeno's paradoxes, but only by distinguishing between an actual and a potential infinite and by showing that if the former were involved in those paradoxes, Zeno would be correct, but in fact, only potential infinites were involved.[14]

Finally, Parsons raises the objection that the kalam argument presents a false dilemma, and he cites Stephen Hawking's book as support for his objection. Professor Craig has adequately refuted this contention in Chapter 11, and I refer you there. I conclude, then, that neither Parsons nor Flew has given us reason to abandon the kalam argument.[15]

Miracles and the Resurrection of Jesus

Among Parsons' objections against the resurrection of Jesus, one appears to be central.[16] Reminiscent of Hume, he says that the prior probability of miracles is so small that an incredible amount of evidence would be required to believe it; furthermore, in the case of the resurrection of Jesus, one ought to believe the lesser miracle involved in even an improbable naturalistic alternative instead of believing the resurrection actually happened.

However, Parsons' skepticism is unconvincing. For one thing, in spite of protests to the contrary (see his caveat about Mother Teresa's "aeronautical exhibition"), his approach really boils down to an attempt to treat all events/data as natural, come what may. But this is to adopt a question-begging naturalism irrespective of the evidence for a particular case. It becomes a Procrustean bed that could never allow a miracle *even if* one actually occurred.

Second, it is generally recognized that this Humean-type approach overstates the case.[17] The blunder in such reasoning is that of arguing from the rarity of a given type of event to the fact that such events do not occur or that it is never reasonable to believe that they occur. But rare events or singularities frequently occur, and if there is good evidence for such an event, it ought to be believed. For example, it has been argued that if we were to accept the Humean criteria of evidence and apply it to the life of Napoleon Bonaparte, we would have to disbelieve in Napoleon's existence. Just because it is true that most events are not resurrections, it does not follow that no events are.

Third, when you assess some particular thing (say, an event or object), you try to place that thing in a class and use evidence we have about that particular class. You do not bring evidence to bear on your assessment from an irrelevant class. Piling up more and more evidence that cats are unfriendly is irrelevant to assessing a case of whether or not to believe that a particular dog is unfriendly. Miracles claim to be events in the class of supernatural events, so how is evidence about natural events relevant? The point is that, with miracles, evidence evaluation and classification are bound up together with the former being dependent upon the latter.

Consider a parallel case. Dudley Shapere has argued that science focuses on domains—classes of related items united by common features taken to be relevant to classification.[18] As science progresses, judgments about how to delineate domains change, and this in turn changes what is and is not taken to be relevant evidence. For example, during the period of 1828–1850, the problem of accounting for Brownian motion (the random motion of microscopic particles—for instance, tiny particles visible through a microscope that dart about in the surface of a beaker) was unsolved. Individual scientists classified the phenomenon differently as a biological, chemical, optical, electrical, heat-theory, or mechanical problem. Suppose scientist A argued that Brownian motion could not have properties A-F because it was a biological phenomenon, and biological phenomena do not have A-F. Suppose scientist B believed that it did have A-F, and thus, Brownian motion could not be biological. The relevance of general statements about biological phenomena to Brownian motion come into the picture after the phenomenon in question is classified. If further study of Brownian motion itself had showed that it was a biological phenomenon, then general statements about biological phenomena would again enter the picture.

Applying this insight to, say, the accounts of Jesus' resurrection, prima facie justifies one in classifying it as an alleged supernatural event which, in turn, requires that evidence for its evaluation not be drawn from evidence from another or naturalistic domain. The event must be studied on its own terms, and classification cannot be used as a Procrustean bed.

Finally, Parsons misunderstood my use of the resurrection in the debate. I did not use it as evidence for theism (although I am open to the use of miracles as confirmation of theism itself), but as evidence for *Christian* theism. Therefore, if we have other arguments that tend to support theism, then the prior probability of miracles is not what Parsons takes it to be, and the question really becomes, Which form of theism is the most rational? My use of miracles in general, and the resurrection in particular, is designed to refute queries (like those of Nielsen), which ask Christian theists why we should believe the Bible as opposed to, say, the Koran. Thus, general arguments for God, salvation history, and the life and predictions of Jesus Himself provide an interpretive grid and an explanation for the resurrection, and the resurrection tends to confirm Jesus' interpretation of salvation history (and, perhaps, theism itself).[19]

Antony Flew

My remarks on Flew's essay will be briefer than those in the previous section because Flew's contribution is shorter than Parsons', he raises fewer points, and I have already treated some of Flew's points in conjunction with my discussion of Parsons' arguments.

Flew and the Design Argument

Flew distinguishes design arguments that involve the universe as a whole from those that focus on some particular feature of the universe. His complaint against the latter is that they are inappropriate "God-of-the-gap" invocations which only cover our ignorance.

But here his view is simply false. For one thing, he fails to consider the difference between efficient causes and final causes. Just because science can explain something in terms of efficient causes, it does not follow that a complementary explanation is unreasonable in terms of final causes or in terms of an analogy with human artifacts. Regardless of whether one does this in terms of Tennant's wider teleology or in terms of some specific phenomenon in the world with apparent design, two complementary descriptions can be given of that phenomenon, and the one used in the design argument is not a cover for ignorance of efficient causes.

Second, some particular features of the universe (such as the existence of beauty in the world, the applicability of mathematics for both the description of the world and the discovery of descriptions of the world, signs of providence, the aptness of our sensory and cognitive faculties as truth-gatherers from our epistemic environment) are outside the bounds of science. Thus, an appeal to a particular feature of the universe in a design argument need not be viewed as an attempt to cover our scientific ignorance.[20]

Regarding the design of the world as a whole, Flew is prepared to allow that such an argument can support some form of theism but not the full-blown theism of Christianity, Judaism, and Islam. But the latter is consistent with the former, and the proper response to the design argument is not the one Flew offers but a realization that the design argument is not intended to support, say, Christian theism, all by itself. Thus, one should search further to see if there is more evidence that fills out and supports the best version of theism. Here the other arguments for God and biblical revelation complement the design argument.[21]

Arguments from Religious Experience

The next point I want to take up is Flew's view of religious experience.[22] He seems to think (1) that such experiences are merely private,

(2) that at best they only prove that people have experiences, not that there is a religious object causing those experiences or being accurately described from them, and (3) that there are no criteria for distinguishing veridical experiences of the risen Christ from, say, hallucinations.

In order to answer these charges, we need to distinguish two different ways religious experience is used to confirm the existence of God. First, there is what can be called the *causal argument*. Here a person or community cites a range of phenomena (changed lives, providential care, answers to prayer, the production of moral and spiritual saints, heroes, and communities), which require explanation, and God is postulated as a cause that explains those phenomena. This type of argument finds its classic expression in William James's *Varieties of Religious Experience,* where he argued (among other things) that real effects require real causes and that the spiritual effects present in religious experience cannot be adequately accounted for apart from the existence of God.

Three things need to be noted about this argument. First, the structure of the argument is precisely parallel to causal explanations in science that are realist in nature.[23] Second, there is nothing particularly private about this kind of argument. The postulated cause—God or a theoretical entity like an electron—is not private. Third, the strength of this type of argument depends on whether the theistic explanation is as good as or better than (depending on your view of burden of proof) alternative hypotheses. The relevant lines of assessment cannot begin with a naturalistic reductionism. Rather, one must start with a detailed exegesis of the New Testament (here I am arguing for Christian religious experience) to surface criteria for appropriate cases to be studied. From this a model of spiritual nurture and formation must be derived, and that model must be tested for its ability to produce the relevant effects. Moreover, the nature, intrinsic power, and duration of these transformational effects must be compared to effects produced by naturalistic causes. Nothing Flew says even remotely touches this type of argument.

The second way to use religious experience as confirming God's existence is through the *direct perception* argument: In sensory modes of experience, if it epistemically seems to someone that x is F (that is, I am inclined to believe that x is F because of the way x looks to me), then in the absence of defeaters of that claim, the principle of charity states that I am justified in believing that x is F. Furthermore, *sensory* modes of perception bear a close analogy to *religious* modes of perception, and thus, the same epistemic posture applies to the latter. The key to the argument involves the claim that there is an analogy between sensory and religious modes of perception. I have tried to justify this analogy elsewhere and cannot go into that justification here.[24]

How does the direct perception argument fare in light of Flew's objections? Consider the privacy of experiences of God. One's view of the privacy of experience has little to do with religious experience per se. Rather, it will be dependent on one's overall analysis of consciousness and intentionality.

If a philosopher takes intentionality to be a relation, he or she will be a representative dualist like Locke (I do not see chairs or God, but only chair-experiences or God-experiences as the direct objects of my awareness). In this case, religious experiences are private, but so are sensory experiences, and there is nothing especially problematic about the former.

If one takes intentionality to be a monadic property, he or she will be a direct realist like Thomas Reid (I directly perceive chairs and God). This is my view. But in any case, the objects of religious experiences are no more private than are the objects of sensory experience, unless of course, one likens them to pains which are (allegedly) not noetic in that pains (allegedly) do not have objects. But this is question-begging. It fails to treat mystical experiences and claims based on them in their own terms. If this is Flew's view, he needs to argue it, not merely assert it.

Second, consider Flew's claim that if an unbeliever were present during a religious experience, he or she would not experience anything, and thus, the experience must be private. This is a hopeless argument. For one thing, it often happens, especially during religious awakenings, that large groups of people spontaneously and simultaneously have the same religious awarenesses. This is easily explainable if the object of those awarenesses is public and identical in each field of intentionality that is epistemically well situated.

This leads to a second point. An unbeliever's lack of awareness can be explained, not by denying the public nature of the object of awareness, but by showing that the unbeliever does not meet the perceptual requirements epistemically relevant to perceiving the object. It does not count against the public nature of my claim to see a red apple that someone next to me does not see that object if she is color blind, has her eyes shut, is daydreaming, or looking in the wrong direction. Similarly, how is it relevant if Flew does not experience God if he is not meeting the epistemically appropriate conditions for such an awareness—conditions such as seeking God, progressively embodying virtues like repentance, contrition of heart, and the like?

One cannot respond that the relevant conditions are different in the red apple and God cases, because the relevance of the conditions should be appropriate to the object itself. One should not take epistemic conditions for perceiving physical objects and force those conditions on other kinds of objects.[25] Similarly, one cannot respond by claiming that sensory modes of perception are more predictable than are religious modes of perception, and thus, the latter are suspect. Criteria of appropriateness, predictability in this case, should be patterned after the object, not vice versa.

For example, if the physical objects of ordinary perception behaved in a capricious way—say, they popped in and out of existence, randomly changed spatial locations, shape, and color—then predictability would not be a good test for a veridical sensory perception. The God of Christian theism is not an inert physical object but a living, acting person, and thus, perceptions of Him will not be as predictable as those of relatively inert, passive, physical objects.

Finally, two things can be said regarding criteria for testing religious perception. First, one can know some things by aquaintance without having criteria beforehand, even though one may need to know linguistic rules before one could report those experiences to another person. Second, several criteria have been formulated that can be used to judge between veridical and nonveridical cases of religious perception. I have listed them elsewhere, so suffice it to say here that Flew's demand for such criteria has already been met.[26]

God and Human Freedom

Finally, Flew raises problems regarding the compatibility of the God of Christianity with human freedom. According to Flew, while a number of believers may deny that there is a problem here, nevertheless, the existence of the Christian God has as a *necessary consequence* the denial of human freedom. Humans become mere puppets in the hands of a Puppet Master who is "the ultimate sufficient cause of every action and every passion of every creature."

Now I must admit, I find this objection, coming from the pen of a thinker of Flew's stature, simply incredible. Where is his argument? All one finds is a few statements about sufficient causes and sustaining causes coupled with a string of quotations. But let us waive this point, and move to the issue itself.

For one thing, a large number of thinkers (I am not among them), atheists and theists alike, embrace compatibilism as a position on how to view freedom and determinism. Compatibilists claim that an acceptable version of moral responsibility can be worked out while embracing some form of determinism. Again, I do not agree with this view, but that is not the present point. What is at issue here is simply that the Christian theist who is a compatibilist is not in a more problematic position than, say, an atheist who is a compatibilist. Whatever difficulties there are with a theistic view of compatibilism are shared by compatibilists in the atheist camp.

But Flew is making a stronger claim here. He is asserting that Christian theism entails determinism. The only argument he gives for this dubious thesis is that God is a sustaining cause and, therefore, He must determine all the actions of all His creatures. But how does that follow? There is a clear distinction between God as a sustaining cause and God as an efficient cause. The former refers to the activity whereby God holds things in existence throughout their duration. An efficient cause is the means which produces an effect. It seems clear that God could sustain some entity in existence without being the efficient cause of that entity's effects in the world. For example, God could sustain me in existence but not cause me to be mean to my wife. I am the one who performs the acts against my wife; God is the one who sustains my existence during my actions, but He does not cause me to perform those actions.

Furthermore, many (and perhaps, most) Christian theists hold to a full-blown, libertarian view of freedom because, among other things, they believe that God is free in this sense, and part of what it means to be made in God's image is that humans exercise agent causation, libertarian freedom, and true creativity. Several models of divine sovereignty, foreknowledge, and human freedom exist.[27] It is hard to see how anyone could claim that no possible world exists wherein at least one of these models could describe a realizable state of affairs.

Aside from this fact, however, the theist does not even need to specify a model before he or she is rationally justified in believing the truth of both the existence of God and the libertarian freedom of humanity. One could have reasons for both propositions and be rational in believing both of them, without knowing in whole or in part how they fit together.

But things are even worse for Flew. He desires to preserve libertarian freedom, but such freedom is actually more compatible with theism than with the more defensible versions of atheism—versions that are physicalistic or scientistic in orientation. To see this, one must realize that the existence of full-blown freedom in certain creatures has metaphysical implications that are "danglers" for most versions of atheism. Freedom presupposes agent causation—agents that have the capacity to exercise their causal powers spontaneously for various reasons. But agent causation seems to presuppose substance dualism, and it is precisely the existence of finite, substantial souls or minds that is hard to explain if scientistic/physicalistic versions of atheism are true.

In this regard, it is instructive to observe how atheists handle the mind/body problem. Most of them are physicalists, believing that the human body and mind are both physical/material entities. Some, on the other hand, are willing to venture into event or property dualism. But these versions of dualism either involve epiphenomenalism (the belief that the body produces what we call the mind or mental states) or state-state causation (for example, a mental state such as a desire for coffee causes other mental states to obtain) or a bundle theory of the mental self. In all three cases (physicalism, epiphenomenalism, and event or property dualism), agent causation, and thus, libertarian freedom, are denied.

For example, physicalist philosopher Paul Churchland claims that since atheistic evolution adequately explains the emergence of homo sapiens, then there is "neither need, nor room, to fit any nonphysical substances or properties into our theoretical account of ourselves. We are creatures of matter."[28]

D. M. Armstrong, another physicalist philosopher, agrees:

> It is not a particularly difficult notion that, when the nervous system reaches a certain level of complexity, it should develop new properties. Nor would there be anything particularly difficult in the notion that when the nervous system reaches a certain level of complexity it should affect something that was already in existence in a new way. But it is a quite different matter to hold that the nervous system should have the power to create something else, of a quite different nature from itself, and create it out of no materials.[29]

In summary then, freedom turns out to be a problem for the atheist, not for the theist. The atheist not only cannot adequately account for it, but he also ends up denying it—if he accepts physicalist versions of atheism. Contrary to the atheist, the theist can accept, explain, and embrace human freedom. So I conclude that far from being an enemy to the theist, libertarian freedom is actually an ally.

Concluding Remarks

Let us back away from these specific arguments and gaze at the broad landscape. Throughout the preceding pages, Nielsen, Parsons, and

Flew have approached various questions from a similar epistemological point of view, which appears to involve two things.

First, we have been told repeatedly that we cannot know the meaning of the term "God," that we cannot use "God" as a referring term, that we cannot accept that such-and-such an event is a miracle, that we cannot know whether a given inductive argument is a good one without first knowing how it is we know these things (for instance, without first knowing what "probability" means). This approach is called epistemological methodism, and it usually includes three theses: (1) of the two main epistemological tasks—knowing or rationally believing the truth and avoiding falsehood—the latter takes precedent over the former; (2) one should adopt a nonheuristic attitude towards skepticism—the notion that the burden of proof is on the one claiming knowledge, and the view that if skepticism is logically possible, then the skeptic wins by default; and (3) one must have a criterion for how it is that one knows something before one can claim to know it.

However, methodism is bankrupt as an overall position in epistemology for at least two reasons. First, there just are some things that I simply know without having or needing criteria for how I know them. Second, methodism leads to a vicious infinite regress of justification, for one can always ask how it is that someone knows a given criterion, and the methodist must answer that this is possible only if a criterion is given for the first criterion.

I am an *epistemological particularist*. Criteria are important for an overall theory of knowledge, but I know some things without needing criteria for that knowledge: that I can refer without knowing how I refer; that a certain inductive argument is a good one without having a detailed theory of how I am using probability; that the resurrection of Jesus, if it in fact happened, would be a miracle.

Nielsen, Flew, and Parsons seem to couple methodism with a second feature: One cannot be rationally justified in believing in God (or, perhaps, in the meaningfulness or referential use of "God") unless one has compelling reasons for that belief or unless one exhaustively knows the item in question. I doubt if these colleagues would agree to this charge, but I invite you to investigate their style of argumentation in detail, and if you do, I think something like this is usually lurking in the background.

But again, this epistemological notion is unacceptable. One can know the truth about something without having exhaustive knowledge of that thing. Furthermore, there are several degrees of rationality, as Chisholm and others have demonstrated, between being counterbalanced regarding some belief and having "compelling" reasons for that belief. Indeed, I doubt that Nielsen, Flew, or Parsons apply their severe standard of rationality throughout their intellectual lives. If they don't apply it elsewhere, they should not do so when it comes to questions surrounding God's existence.

Where does this leave us? Craig, Willard, and I are among those Christian theists (one could hold that belief in God is properly basic and still see arguments for God as additional, confirming proofs) who believe that a number of phenomena find their best explanation by the belief that God exists and those phenomena confirm the truth of that belief, e.g., the beginning of the universe from an immutable state of affairs, various kinds of design, the existence of consciousness, the trustworthiness of our noetic faculties, the existence of moral and aesthetic properties, religious experience, and so on. We also believe that good arguments exist for choosing Christianity as the most rational form of theism. Among those reasons are arguments from philosophy, science, history, archeology, prophecy, the internal testimony of the Holy Spirit, and the power of authentic manifestations of the kingdom of God.

These phenomena are danglers (i.e., unexpected and unexplained phenomena) for the atheist, and he or she must grant them as brute, albeit queer, givens in the universe or deny that they really exist or reduce them to naturalistic phenomena or hold that the evidence against God from, say evil, is sufficiently strong to overturn the evidence for God. I do not think these strategies work, and I have tried to give at least some reasons why I think this way.

It is sometimes claimed that theistic arguments are like leaky buckets. If you add more and more leaky buckets to one another, you still don't have something that holds water. Similarly, if you add one weak argument for God to another, you do not have a case that holds water. But this claim is wrongheaded. For one thing, I have tried to show that the theistic arguments are not weak. Second, even if each argument fails to be convincing on its own, together they can be convincing. In a trial, each isolated piece of evidence may be insufficient to warrant a conviction, but conviction could be justified when all the evidence is taken together.

Finally, the leaky bucket metaphor is the wrong one. A rope metaphor is more appropriate. Just as several strands make a rope stronger than just a few strands, so the many-stranded case for God is made stronger than would be the case with only a few strands of evidence. Leaky buckets don't help each other because they are related to one another in a chain. Later buckets do their work in light of earlier buckets. If someone uses a number of leaky buckets to catch the water from other leaky buckets, no matter how long the chain of leaky buckets grows, she will never retain even a single bucket of water. Later buckets will not help earlier ones do their job more effectively if all the buckets leak. But strands of rope work independently of each other. Similarly, the various arguments for God from cosmology, morality, religious experience, miracles, and the like relate to one another independently, not linearly.

Obviously, one book cannot deal with all the aspects of a question as complex as the existence of God. But the preceding pages have suggested several lines of investigation for treating the question, and in my view, the arguments contained herein strongly suggest that the God of Christian theism is, indeed, the one in whom we live and move and have our being.[30]

Notes

1. My original understanding of the topic of the debate was over the question of the existence of the Christian God. That is why my presentation proceeded in two steps: arguments for a personal God followed by arguments that Christianity is the most reasonable form of theism.
2. Cf. Roderick Chisholm, *Theory of Knowledge*, 2d. ed. (Englewood Cliffs, N. J.: Prentice-Hall, 1977), 14–15; Laurence BonJour, *The Structure of Empirical Knowledge* (Cambridge, Mass.: Harvard University Press, 1985), 7–8.
3. Even if this equation were correct, Parsons still misrepresents advocates who hold that belief in God is properly basic. For example, are we really to believe that Plantinga is merely asserting that believers are rational in believing in God but not asserting that the belief itself is true?
4. Parsons' remarks about creation science are wide of the mark for two further reasons. First, there are creation-scientists who do hold their views tentatively, and there are scientists in other areas who hold their views dogmatically. Thus, he is factually mistaken. Second, he confuses and conflates two different senses of objectivity and two different senses of one's "right to be sure." One can lack psychological objectivity (be biased) but still be epistemologically objective (e.g., by presenting evidence and arguments that are publicly assessible). So even if creation-scientists lack the former, they need not lack the latter, and the latter is more relevant to epistemological considerations. Further, one can have the right to be sure regarding a belief in two different ways: one can dogmatically assert one's

belief and refuse to look at further evidence, or one can have the right to rely on the truth of the belief in explaining things and in forming other beliefs. Mature religious believers embrace this second notion of the right to be sure, but Parsons focuses on the first one.

5. See Roderick Chisholm, *Theory of Knowledge,* 3rd ed. (Englewood Cliffs, N. J.: Prentice-Hall, 1989), 8–17. These terms are slightly different from the ones he uses in the second edition of this book.

6. Thomas V. Morris, *Anselmian Explorations* (Notre Dame, Ind.: University of Notre Dame Press, 1987), 194–212, esp. 202–210.

7. For more on burden-of-proof issues, see Scott A. Shalkowski, "Atheological Apologetics," *American Philosophical Quarterly* 26 (Jan. 1989), 1–17.

8. Larry Laudan, *Science and Hypothesis* (Dordrecht, Holland: D. Reidel, 1981), 200.

9. For brief treatments of different forms of design arguments, see J. P. Moreland, *Scaling the Secular City* (Grand Rapids: Baker, 1987), 43–75; William J. Wainwright, *Philosophy of Religion* (Belmont, Ca.: Wadsworth, 1988), 48–58; A. C. Ewing, *Value and Reality* (London: George Allen & Unwin, 1973), 165–82.

10. See Richard Swinburne, *The Existence of God* (Oxford: Clarendon Press, 1979), 133–51; Wainwright, *Philosophy of Religion,* 55–57.

11. J. L. Mackie, *The Miracle of Theism* (Oxford: Clarendon Press, 1982), 141. Cf. John Leslie, "Modern Cosmology and the Creation of Life," in *Evolution and Creation,* Ernan McMullin, ed. (Notre Dame: University of Notre Dame Press, 1985), 94–107; *Universes* (New York: Routledge, 1989).

12. Parsons makes two further complaints. First, he says that we can only know that something is not a coincidence in those cases (e.g., several guns jamming in a firing squad) where we have had prior experiences of the cases at hand. But this is simply false. We can and often do notice analogies between cases we have observed and new cases of which we have no prior experience. Our ability to extend our reasoning by analogy to new cases is on what the analogy form of the design argument tries to capitalize. Furthermore, we have uniform experience that highly complex arrangements of wholes that have parts exhibiting information or specified complexity come from minds. Thus, in the case of DNA, uniform testimony should lead us to see a mind behind the information in DNA.

This leads to Parsons' second complaint. He thinks my use of information is problematical. Since I believe in the existence of intentional qualities (e.g., concepts, propositions, and other meanings), then I do not believe that information is literally in a DNA molecule, but then, neither do I believe that such information is literally in a physical sentence. However, there are incredible analogies between sentences and DNA, which modern biology has surfaced, and these analogies need an explanation. See Michael Denton, *Evolution: A Theory in Crisis* (London: Burnett Books, 1985), 233–343; Percival Davis and Dean H. Kenyon, *Of Pandas and People* (Dallas, Tex.: Houghton, 1989), 41–76.

One final point. Even if we grant Parsons' point about probability calculations, and multiply probabilities of each small step toward the formation of DNA, the probabilities would still be astronomically small. But we need not grant him this point. The probability of a molecule forming can be based on entropy calculations (especially configurational entropy which measures the aperiodic complexity of nucleic acids and protein), and entropy is a state function whose value is independent of the path used to reach that value. See Charles Thaxton, Walter Bradley, and Roger Olsen, *The Mystery of Life's Origin* (N.Y.: Philosophical Library, 1984), 127–43, 218–19.

13. Max Black has shown that the difficulty with traversing an actual infinite is not related to having enough time. See his "Achilles and the Tortoise," *Analysis* 11 (March 1951), 91–101.

14. Actually, though my argument does not rely on this insight, a beginningless universe could involve the existence of an event which has receded infinitely far into the past. But since this is absurd (it involves traversing an actual infinite by successive addition), it would be another way to show that the universe had a beginning. In a beginningless universe, the cardinality of the number of events in the past is $\aleph_0$, but the ordinality could easily be $\omega^* + \omega^*$ (. . . , -3, -2, -1, . . . , -3, -2, -1) when we remember that we are dealing with actual events in the real world and not with mere mathematical abstractions. We can number the events of the past any way we wish. But in this case, there would be an infinite number of events which have receded infinitely far into the past—an absurd conclusion if there ever was one.

15. Craig's rebuttal of Hawking involves taking an antirealist attitude towards Hawking's model of the universe. I think Craig is right here. I have argued elsewhere that even if one is a scientific realist, generally speaking, then it can still be appropriate to adopt an antirealist attitude toward a particular scientific theory, especially when a realist interpretation conflicts with significant external conceptual problems for that theory while an antirealist interpretation does not. See J. P. Moreland, *Christianity and the Nature of Science* (Grand Rapids: Baker, 1989), 202–211. This is what we have in Hawking's model, and Craig's appeal to antirealism does not entail an overall approach to science which is antirealist.

16. For issues involved in taking a miracle to be "contrary to a true law of nature," see Richard Swinburne, *The Concept of Miracle* (N.Y.: St. Martin's Press, 1970), Chap. 3.

17. Cf. George Mavrodes, "Bayes's Theorem and Hume's Treatment of Miracles," *Trinity Journal* 1 (1980), 47–61.

18. Dudley Shapere, "Scientific Theories and Their Domains," in *The Struc-*

ture of Scientific Theories, Frederick Suppe, ed. (Urbana, Ill. : University of Illinois Press, 1977), 518–65.

19. Thus, Parsons' analogy between Mother Teresa and Jesus' resurrection is inadequate. If she had an overall lifestyle of doing miraculous deeds, could predict some of them herself, did miracles that had religious significance (not silly things, like being a flying nun, which resemble the ridiculous deeds related in the Apocryphal gospels) and which fit into an overall flow of salvation history, and which were witnessed by a number of people who were willing and able to tell the truth and had little to gain and much to lose in lying or being inaccurate (e.g., losing their lives and, in their own minds, incurring damnation), then we would have a closer analogy to Jesus' resurrection. Here the epistemic situation is quite different than the one involved in Parsons' straw man of a flying Mother Teresa.

His caricature teaches an important lesson: *atheists have often failed to grasp the importance of detailed features of actual cases that theists believe to be miracles.* When detailed investigations replace vague generalities, cases like the one offered by Parsons fail to be genuine counterexamples and indicate a misunderstanding of the issue.

20. Even in cases where an appeal to God competes with a strictly naturalistic explanation of a phenomenon, say regarding the origin of life, the theist is not using a God-of-the-gaps argument to cover his ignorance. He or she is pointing to an explanatory hypothesis that has positive evidence in support of it—for example, analogies between first life and human artifacts, in comparison to a naturalistic explanation wherein the gaps are getting worse, not because of what we don't know, but precisely because of what we do know (e.g., that macromolecules show no appreciable preferred reactivity, which rules out equipossibilities in probability calculations, that the early earth's atmosphere was oxidizing).

21. Flew's assertion that the presence of contrivance (or what theologians call secondary causes) is evidence against omnipotence is just that—an assertion. He gives no real argument for it. Why does the use of means imply a limitation of power? Those theists who are essentialists hold that in conceiving a possible world, God also conceives laws grounded in the essences of the items in that world. God could choose to use secondary causes in that world as a means of honoring His own creation or, more importantly, as part of what He was doing in creating in the first place.

Further, Flew seems to use an efficiency model in conceiving of God's activity in the world (i.e., an omnipotent being will be efficient and that involves using primary causality, not secondary causality). But this model is inadequate for at least two reasons. First, God had other reasons for His activities other than efficiency, such as play and creativity. Second, efficiency is a notion that is only applicable if we presuppose a situation where there are limited resources, and this is precisely what is *not* granted in the case of an omnipotent God.

22. Flew's section on historical issues is, in my view, the weakest part of his contribution. For a stronger presentation of his views with rebuttals, see *Did Jesus Rise From the Dead?* Terry L. Miethe, ed. (San Francisco: Harper & Row, 1987).

23. Thus, one may object to causal arguments from religious experience because one adopts an overall antirealist standpoint, say like the one adopted by Bas van Fraasen. This would move the line of debate to the adequacy of this position as an overall epistemological strategy, a discussion which is outside the bounds of our present discussion. However, one thing should be mentioned. If one adopts this overall position and uses it as an argument against causal explanations of religious experience, then one cannot turn around and use science, realistically construed, as an argument against theism. One cannot have it both ways, unless, of course, realist causal explanations are allowed in science but not in religion. But this would be question-begging.

24. See J. P. Moreland, *Scaling the Secular City* (Grand Rapids: Baker, 1987), 234–40.

25. A parallel case in ethics further illustrates the point. Ethical nonnaturalists such as G. E. Moore argued that goodness was a nonnatural property which could be directly intuited. Naturalists argued against Moore by denying that they had the relevant intuitions. But nonnaturalists (and Moore himself) were looking for the wrong thing: an intuition of a first order property. If goodness is a second order property of first order properties (say a property of pleasure, acts of love, and so forth), then goodness could be intuited in the same way other second order properties are intuited (say shape, color, taste, and so on), and not as first order properties (e.g., being a triangle, redness, sourness, and so on). These latter are intuited by means of sensory experiences, and the former are arguably not. It is wrong, therefore, to argue that we do not have intuitions of second order properties such as goodness because alleged intuitions of them do not have features appropriate for intuitions of first order properties. It is one thing to claim that we do not have intuitions of second order properties, but it is another thing altogether to support that claim by applying an inappropriate criterion derived from intuitions of first order properties and forced on claims about intuitions of second order properties. The same point applies to intuitions of God and physical objects.

26. J. P. Moreland, *Scaling the Secular City,* 239–40.

27. Cf. William Lane Craig, *The Only Wise God* (Grand Rapids: Baker, 1987). For other models, see *Predestination and Free Will,* David Basinger and Randall Basinger, eds. (Downers Grove, Ill.: InterVarsity Press, 1986).

28. Paul Churchland, *Matter and Consciousness* (Cambridge, Mass.: MIT Press, 1984), 21.
29. D. M. Armstrong, *A Materialist Theory of Mind* (London: Routledge & Kegan Paul, 1968), 30.
30. I wish to thank David Beck, Norman Geisler, Gary Habermas, and Phil West for their helpful comments on an earlier draft of this chapter.

Defending Atheism Again: Remarks on God and Coherence

I

Before I turn to the criticisms of my theistic critics, I want to make some general remarks about the character of our deliberations and their possible import. As I made clear when I agreed to enter into the exchange with Moreland, I never took it to be a debate, great or otherwise, but to be an attempt at an inquiry after the truth about the existence of God. I viewed it, and continue to view it, as an attempt by a theist and an atheist to argue their beliefs here (as well as expressing their doubts and misgivings) and to probe each other in an attempt, as far as this can be done in a popular forum, to get at the truth of the matter (whatever that comes to) without trying to score points or to use the tricks of a debater. Truth was what we were after and not winning or the taking of a partisan stance. Whether religious or not, we most certainly should not be True Believers, more interested in our *cause* than in *truth*. It is the True Believer who is the real enemy of philosophy and intellectual integrity in general.[1] To achieve this, of course, is easier said than done; over a topic as close to our hearts as religion, it is very difficult to escape partisanship. Objectivity and impartiality do not require neutrality or indifference; they can ride tandem with conviction. But the former are essential in the search for truth.[2] Yet, with strong convictions, something common to all the participants in this "debate," it is hard to attain the requisite impartiality—and no doubt some of us some of the time failed. But our very vocation as intellectuals requires this impartiality. It was in this spirit I entered into "the debate." And I take it that this was true of the others as well. Otherwise, the whole thing would be a farce, a kind of silly sideshow.

The object of the exercise should be to try to ascertain what we should say and believe about God. (1) Can we prove that God exists, at least in the sense that we can show that it is more probable than not that God exists? (2) Can we show (alternatively) that it is reasonable to believe that God exists such that even a well-informed, philosophically and scientifically sophisticated contemporary person does not act unreasonably in believing in God, or, stronger than that, is it the case that, everything considered, it is more reasonable for such a person to believe in God than not?[3] (It is vital to see that (1) and (2) do not come to the same thing. Number (2) might simply show that, everything considered, it is more reasonable—without proofs—to be a person of faith than not.) (3) Is (alternatively) the very concept of God in developed forms of Judaism, Christianity, and Islam so problematic as to make belief in God unreasonable or at least a mistake for anyone who clearly sees that problematicity? (4) Is belief in God (to trot out a still further alternative) so necessary for us for our lives to make sense that, problematic though this concept may be, or ill-grounded or ungrounded (they are not the same thing) as our belief in God may be, we must simply accept a belief in God on trust in order to make some sense of our fragmented lives?

Questions (2), (3), and (4) present *live* options for me. Number (1) does not. I think, rather conventionally for a philosopher in our time and place, though *perhaps* too easily and too complacently and *perhaps* even mistakenly, that (1) has been reasonably decisively settled in the history of thought by the combined arguments of the skeptic David Hume and the fideistic Christian Immanuel Kant, or at least by some of the rational reconstructions of what are essentially their arguments given by some contemporary analytical philosophers.[4]

To proceed as Moreland does, or indeed as do Swinburne, Willard, and Craig, gives me a weary feeling of *déjà vu*. And reading the responses of Parsons and Flew reinforces that feeling and strengthens my conviction that the feeling is appropriate; for they show what I suspected, namely that Moreland gives us, in a scientistic and unfamiliar idiom, *essentially* the same classical arguments that were criticized so powerfully by Hume. It is little more than warmed-over stuff in a scientistic vocabulary. No step forward at all has been made toward establishing that God's existence is more probable than His nonexistence.

To the extent the reasonability of belief in God is tied to being able to give evidence for God's existence, Moreland's apologetic or philosophical efforts tend to show, given the way he conducts the argument, that belief in God is not very reasonable. Parsons' arguments in this volume and in his *God and the Burden of Proof* are a particularly effective supplementing of Mackie's.[5] But this leaves the options behind questions (2), (3), and (4) entirely intact. It provides conceptual space for the fideistic Christian and for those Christian philosopher-theologians, like John Hick and Terence Penelhum, who do not think we can prove either deductively or inductively that God exists, but who believe that faith can still be shown to be a justifiable option in our contemporary world.

It is here, I believe, where the serious debate should be conducted between belief and unbelief and not over the proofs for the existence of God. It is a very serious defect of this volume that it has no such Christian representative. The lack of such a representative seriously weakens the case for religion and skews the direction of the debate in an unfruitful way. Moreland and I stand too far apart for discussion between us to be fruitful. (The same is true for Craig.)

Moreland thinks there is nothing problematic in the concept of God and immorality, that a conservative version of orthodox Christianity is plainly plausible, that we know what it would be like to give a probabilistic proof for the existence of God, and that recent developments in scientific cosmology and biblical studies gives us strongly confirming evidence for the existence of God and the traditional Christian conception of Jesus. I, in turn, find these latter beliefs so patently absurd, so incompatible with what we have gradually learned in the last two hundred years, that I can hardly bring myself seriously to consider them. I should have been arguing with someone like Terence Penelhum, D. Z. Phillips, Hendrick Hart, or even William Alston, but not with Moreland. And he should not have been arguing with me, but with either a less conservative Christian or some skeptical philosopher-scientific cosmologist or someone like Parsons. As it stands, we are like ships passing in the dark. Only with Willard—whose essay is sensitive, sophisticated, and probing—did I feel the slightest intellectual bond among the Christian contributors to this volume. (Respect for persons is another matter entirely.[6]) A debate—where it is not a sideshow—to be fruitful must have some common ground.

II

I hardly had a debating strategy in mind (*pace* Craig), not caring about debate at all, but I did have a conception about how to conduct the argument and that was not to argue on Moreland's terms but to keep the argument focused on what I took to be essential—namely, on the question of the coherence of the concept of God and on whether we need, or indeed even should have, religion to make sense of our lives and give our moral beliefs a tolerably objective rationale. This, as Flew and Willard point out, is a risky strategy, but it also has the virtue of getting straightaway at what is central (or, so as to not beg any questions, at what I believe to be central) in the "debate" between believers and nonbelievers, both of whom have been touched by modernity and perhaps by postmodernity as well. (What may be a bad debater's strategy could be a good idea in the search for truth.) *If* I am mistaken about the claim of incoherency, the argument can always retreat to the arguments about God and the basis of morality—arguments which are not at all tied to the incoherency claims—and even to the rather tired arguments about proving the existence of God, which are effectively criticized by Parsons and Mackie. (I think that if you put together Richard Robinson's *An Atheist's Values,* my *Ethics Without God,* and Mackie's *The Miracle of Theism,* you get a formidable case for atheism argued out on the above mentioned rather traditionalist grounds.)

I have, some twenty years ago in my *Reason and Practice,* explicated and critically discussed the standard proofs for the existence of God.[7] As I read Moreland's book and then listened to him, and read Craig as well, I could see nothing but the old discredited arguments presented in a new rather scientistic vocabulary. Like Willard, I do not see that the various arguments from scientific cosmology and evolutionary biology contribute anything except confusion when they are turned to the topic of God and the establishing or disestablishing of His existence. He shows how believers can reasonably accommodate Darwinian conceptions and the Big Bang. (He appropriately refers to "Big Bang Mysticism.") And Parsons shows how atheists can accommodate the kind of scientific considerations Moreland adverts to (and, in effect, to the ones Craig adverts to as well). Moreover, in talking about design arguments, the mistaken nature of Moreland's appeal to probabilities is well demonstrated by Parsons. In all these cases there are logically prior considerations—considerations Aquinas and Scotus, Hume and Kant, could have discussed—which are the decisive considerations. More generally, we should be wary of putting much weight in such discussions of scientific cosmology. That is a wildly speculative part of physics not immune from bad philosophy and veiled, or not so veiled, theological or atheological assumptions uncritically held. Here, as Stephen Toulmin has pointed out, scientific mythology is rife.[8]

I made remarks to this effect in the discussion, which Craig badly misunderstands. In conducting my critique of religion, I have never relied on claims that science disproves religion. This is so, even when I discuss the design arguments in *Reason and Practice.* My warning was for *both* sides to be very cautious in their appeal to science, and my claim was that the key considerations were antecedent to the full flourishing of a scientific culture, though not antithetical to it. Paradoxically enough, given that they are very conservative orthodox Christians, Moreland and Craig, though not Willard, are caught up in the pervasive scientistic ideology of our culture—indeed I think more pseudo-scientific than scientific—which one would think their worldview would immunize them from. (Here they could profitably study Jürgen Habermas.[9])

In Willard's case, by contrast, we get a straightforward, clear argument that concrete physical reality implicates a being radically different from itself: a being who, unlike any physical state, is self-existent. There the argument turns on the claim that if this were not so, to explain how anything can be brought into being and be sustained, there would have to be the actual completion of an infinite series of events. But why? That treats an infinite series as if it were a very long finite series. Treating it as such, it is recognized that to give the *completed* series of causes for any event you like, you have to go very far back—infinitely far back—and that of course is impossible.[10] While this may be true of a very long finite series, it is not of a genuinely infinite series. If the series is really infinite, there trivially can be no completing the series, but for such a series, all we need say is that for any state of affairs, there is a (in principle at least) stateable state of affairs A such that when A occurs, B will occur, or when events of type A occur, then events of type B occur. We can, that is, in principle at least, specify the onsetting conditions of events of type B. We just resolutely stay, segment by segment, in the causal network. To the question, Do we give *all* the onsetting conditions? the answer should be that we can in optimal circumstances get all we need to explain why B occurs and to accurately predict when events of type B will occur.

Craig badly misunderstands, in discussing arguments for the existence of God, my response to Moreland. I do *not* more or less concede the argument for the Designer-Creator. I make a couple of fairly standard criticisms of it—Flew gives variants of them in his paper—and I take that, *perhaps* too easily, to be sufficient. For, as I remarked initially, this seems to me as dead an issue as the issues of Logical Positivism seem to Craig and Willard or to Alvin Plantinga. Then, trying (vainly it turns out) to turn the argument to a more profitable ground, I consider—*for the sake of continuing the argument and only for that*—what follows *if* that argument is conceded. (This is a familiar enough philosophical tactic. Craig, given his extensive philosophical training, plainly should know that.) I then point out that even with that concession, it will not get us to the God of Judaism, Christianity, and Islam. This is hardly "more or less to concede the argument."

Many, many reflective Jews and Christians will agree with me that no proof—in any plausible sense of "proof"—of the existence of God is likely, and some will say even possible. A considerable number will add that such a proof is not necessary for religious belief, and some few will even add that none is desirable.[11] They conduct their case for religious belief differently and sometimes powerfully indeed, as we see in Georg Hamann, Søren Kierkegaard, and in Alasdair MacIntyre during his fideistic period. I wanted an argument against the existence of God to be general enough to touch both those chaps as well as more rationalistic Christian philosophers. To touch, if you will, both Aquinas and Luther, though plainly, I think, the Luther sorts are on far stronger ground: they carry with them less bad philosophy—for example, less speculative metaphysics. Aquinas, who was a very great philosopher indeed, could still be seen from our vantage point, and standing on his shoulders, but on the shoulders of Hume and Kant as well, to be doing some bad philosophy, to be going at things in a very mistaken way. It isn't that what he did he did badly, but *what* it was that he did was mistaken. Luther was not one-twentieth the philosopher Aquinas was (indeed, in a way he was not a philosopher, though he did have a good scholastic training), but he was far more perceptive about religion than Aquinas. But that aside, I argued in my discussions *to* incoherence and *from* morality and the meaning of life. These arguments apply against the full range of theists from the rationalistic sorts to the fideists. If the concept of God is really incoherent, then we know *ahead of time before even considering the arguments* that there can be no proof of the existence of God, for no premise or no conclusion with "God" in it could be true (a requisite for a sound argument), since the term is of an incoherent concept. (If a concept is really incoherent, it is plainly illegitimate.) We could also *not,* if that really is so, just take God humbly on faith, for you can only have faith in X if you have some understanding of X. But, if X is incoherent, then you cannot understand X at all, and thus you cannot understand what it is you are suppose to have faith in, to take on trust. If I tell you, "Trust wornt," and you ask me, "What is wornt?" and I say, "Never mind, just trust wornt," you cannot comply no matter how much you want to. Only if you have some understanding of God can you accept God's word humbly on faith. But if the concept of God is incoherent, you can have no understanding of God—there is literally nothing to understand—and thus you cannot have faith in God.[12]

III

However, is the concept of God actually incoherent? Craig and Willard, and Moreland as well, think that my argument is very weak here. Craig and Willard do not content themselves with asserting that, but deploy careful arguments against me, which it is essential that I successfully respond to if my argument is to stand. The burden of proof here is, I believe, quite definitely on me. (The burden of proof is often very difficult to establish in philosophy, but here it seems to me I should assume it.) There is a further reason—a reason independent of the quality of their arguments—for believing that the burden of proof rests with me, and that has to do with the recent history of the sociology of the philosophy of religion that Moreland, Craig, and Willard all advert to. In current debate, as distinct from debate say of twenty years ago, Flew and I (along with Paul Edwards) stand virtually alone in arguing that the concept of God in developed theism is incoherent. Parsons does not argue that way, nor did Mackie in his masterful *The Miracle of Theism*.

Most people now who trouble to argue for atheism—there are many atheist philosophers (often closet atheists) who couldn't be bothered—claim to have little trouble with the meaning of "God"; they just think it is fairly evident that there isn't one. I think that their being quite so confident, if it is well motivated, rests on a sense—sometimes a rather inchoate sense—that there is something fishy about the concept of God. There *can* no more be a God than there can be witches. E. P. Evans-Pritchard, in spite of his belief that it was quite rational for the Azande to believe that there are witches, remarked casually that, of course, there plainly could be no witches.[13] Yet throughout his life he remained a Roman Catholic. There are not a few nonbelievers who feel about God the way Evans-Pritchard felt about witches. As most of us believe that there not only are no witches but that there cannot be any, so some, thinking a little about the mysterious concept of God, conclude, equally firmly, that there cannot be a God. Is it just dogmatism in both or either case? If you are a believer, whence the confidence that there cannot be any witches *and* the confidence that there is—perhaps even *must* be—a God? Why are the two notions, in this respect, not rather in the same boat?

I think this return on the part of people like Mackie and Parsons to firm confidence in the intelligibility of God-talk is a retrograde move (though it is all right sometimes as an argumentative strategy). The conviction emerging during the ascendency of positivism was that God is taken to be a very mysterious, scarcely intelligible, utterly other reality to which (a) one just might, as a knight of faith, commit oneself with fear and trembling or (b) instead be agnostic about (perhaps anguishedly agnostic about), as Ronald Hepburn is, or (c) as with atheists such as myself and Flew and Edwards, as a conception, which one might reject as a conception, so mysterious as to actually be incoherent. The question then becomes, Does such a stance in all its considerable variety answer more adequately to religious sensitivities than does a rationalistic stance? The former captures, I believe, a sense of the mysteriousness and the otherness of God, a sense of the strangeness of these conceptions. Even religiously it is more adequate than the rationalistic conceptions of Moreland and Craig, which treat God like a theoretical entity in an explanatory scheme and then prepares for disputation about whether or not such an entity actually exists, assuming all along that we have a good sense of what we are talking about, the only serious question being as to whether we can be quite sure whether that entity actually exists. (They hasten to add, lest we get jitters, that we can be sure.) This is enough to make poor Hamann or Kierkegaard turn over in their graves. (And they are hardly more tender-minded, to gesture back to Peter Kreeft's Introduction, than Moreland or Craig. Who is tender-minded and who is not is harder to make out than Kreeft seems, at least, to realize. Is Pascal or Luther more tender-minded than Augustine or Aquinas? It would be foolhardy to claim so.)

The way it is put now under the new rationalistic dispensation—though not always so flat-footedly as Moreland and Craig put it—makes it sound like it plainly is the case that we know well enough what it would be like for God to exist—He very well could exist—only we do not know if He *actually* does, so we better carry out some investigations and find out if He does. (Again, think of Kierkegaard's scathing irony at something like that.) This makes God sound far too much like the Loch Ness Monster to capture the reflective religious sensitivities of those who are trying to believe in at least a partially ineffable Ultimate Mystery in whom we stand deeply in need.[14] It utterly forgets John Wisdom's warning against treating the existence of God as if it were an experimental issue.[15] In this way, as in others I have noted, Moreland's and Craig's accounts are thoroughly scientistic. My objections here, paradoxically enough, are not only logical but *religious*. I am mildly offended by such scientism. I am, if you will, an atheist in favor of religious sensibilities that are adequate to their object (to use a bit of philosopher's jargon). But in philosophy of religion circles, at least in Anglo-America, the philosophical *Weltgeist* has not gone with me here, so the burden of proof seems at least to be on me. (But perhaps not; it just may be that fashions have changed. And they, of course, could change again.)

I want to say one further thing before I turn to the demanding business of argument. The core of any philosophical endeavor, no matter how important, is to place the argument in a proper philosophical narrative. Craig's and Willard's arguments are both very dismissive of mine. They think that I have not done my philosophical homework and perhaps give to understand—though I am not sure of that—as well that I am rather blinkered by partisan passion. (Others, not me, will have to be the judge of that. I can only try to be scrupulously honest while not being utterly bland.) But their arguments are not flippantly dismissive but careful and reasonably sustained and stay, for the most part, on the logical point. They have helped me see that arguments that I had thought to be decisive—and still think (perhaps blinkeredly) to be decisive—are less obviously so than I thought. (No doubt I should have been aware of that; it is in the nature of the game for philosophical arguments. But that is something Moreland should take to heart as well.) They have pushed the argument along generally, though not invariably, in a constructive way, and we should be grateful to them for that. Certainly I am.

IV

Now to the arguments. I maintain that in mainline Judeo-Christianity, God is conceived to be an infinite individual, transcendent to the world (the universe). This individual (putative individual) is both thought to act in the world and to be transcendent to the world. I maintain that a being cannot, logically cannot, at one and the same time, act in the world and be transcendent to the world. So, in this way, the concept of God is incoherent. It is incoherent in another way as well. God is said to be an individual (a person) but also to be infinite. (Paul Tillich would never talk that way, but that is another ball game.) But if something is an individual, it must be distinct. It must, that is, be distinguishable from other individuals and thus must be finite. An infinite *individual* is a contradiction in terms. So in another way, the concept of God is incoherent. Further, "God" is supposed to be a referring expression. If a term functions referentially, it must in theory at least be possible to say *what* it refers to.[16] (If this be positivism, make the most of it.) But where "God," as it is in developed Judaism and Christianity, is used nonanthropomorphically, we cannot say what "God" refers to. We cannot teach "God" by ostension—by pointing to Him—for anything we could point to or so identify would not be God. It arguably would be a material reality (if that isn't pleonastic), but God cannot be (except for Mormons) that. If God were so identifiable, He necessarily would be a discrete, limited (possibly material) reality, for otherwise He could not be picked out so that He could be identified and ostensively taught. But the God of modern Judeo-Christianity (if there is one) could not be like that. Such a God—a God of ostensive teaching—could not be transcendent to the world, for anything that could be pointed out and thus identified would be in the world.

"God," as I remarked above, is meant to be a referring expression, and of such an expression, we must be able to ask *what* it denotes (stands for). But we cannot show what "God" stands for by ostension (by ostensive definition, through pointing and similar devices). However, the meaning or use of referring expressions can also be taught intralinguistically by definite descriptions.[17] But the alleged definite descriptions used to teach the meaning of "God" are at least as problematic as the term "God" itself. "The infinite individual transcendent to the universe" we have already argued is a contradictory conception. Other definite descriptions such as, "The creator of the universe out of *nothing*" and "The maker of the heavens and the earth" are as troublesome as "God." If we do not know what it would be like to identify "God," we are going to be equally at a loss as to how to identify "The maker of the heavens and the earth" or "The creator of the universe out of nothing." What it is to make something out of *nothing* is utterly obscure. If we have trouble, as Willard rightly claims we do, with Big Bang mysticism producing something out of nothing, we should have trouble here too. Trying to teach the meaning of the word "God" intralinguistically, we chase ourselves around the web of equally obscure mutually defining words and phrases expressive of very problematic concepts indeed. Because of reasons of this sort, we have good reasons for believing that the concept of God in developed Christianity is incoherent. (Trinitarian conceptions plainly make for added troubles— troubles a Jew or a Moslem will not have. But let us stay with generalized theism.)

Craig argues in response that even if in some sense *being infinite* is an essential attribute of God, Moreland need not appeal to it in his proof of the existence of God, for if we applied that criterion to proofs of the existence of ordinary objects, it would absurdly lead to skepticism. *Suppose* it is an essential property of a human being that she has an innate capacity to master languages. Thus in order to prove that Elizabeth Anscombe *exists*, we would have to prove that she has that innate capacity. But that is absurd, and it is equally absurd in the God case.

But this response entirely misses the structure and force of my argument. I was arguing that an alleged essential (defining) property of God, namely *being infinite*, was logically incompatible with another essential property, namely *being an individual*. If they are essential properties and are, as I claim, incompatible, then no God can exist to be either proved or accepted on faith. Craig must show that one or another of these properties are not essential properties or that they are not incompatible. But he does nothing of the kind. His above argument doesn't even address itself to what is at issue, much less show that I have made a mistake. He does not address himself to that issue but simply evades it.

Craig further argues that my argument could be circumvented if we would simply drop "infinite" and stick instead with God conceived as a "personal Designer-Creator of the universe out of nothing." That, of course, takes away something that has been thought, and not without reason, to be essential to the Christian conception of God. (It is like getting around the problem of evil by no longer taking *being omnipotent* to be an essential property of God. That game has been played.) But, Craig could respond, the conception of God has changed before and perhaps it can change again. But even *if* we let this go, for the sake of the discussion at least, we still have the other half of my challenge—that it is incoherent to speak of an individual acting in the world who is transcendent to the world. Something cannot both be in the world and transcendent to the world at the same time. If, we say in response (and thinking rather materialistically) that a little bit is in it and the rest beyond, then that thing is not transcendent to the world because it is in it, even assuming we understand what "transcendent to the world" means. (We have, in any event, enough understanding of "transcendent" to see that such a being could not be transcendent to the world.) Moreover, how can something be in and out of the natural order at the same time? What does all this talk *mean?* It is important to try to be very literal and not rest content with metaphors. To say it is all a profound mystery is just to throw up our hands and give up. But to speak of a "Designer-Creator of the universe" seems to imply at least a being transcendent to the universe, and it is there where we get something so terribly problematic that we have at least a good candidate for incoherency.

Craig also tries to fault me on my claim that "God" cannot be taught by ostension. My claim here just amounts to, Craig would have it, a dogmatic denial on my part that Moreland's claimed religious experiences are really experiences. Moreland, recall, claims that he has experienced God in a real way every day. Here Flew's criticism of Moreland is very much to the point. Moreland, in a confessional mood, tells us, embarrassingly, that he has "met Jesus Christ personally and He changed my life." Suppose, analogously, I tell you that I have experienced the harsh winters of Alberta personally and this has changed my life. This claim doesn't rest just on my say so and doesn't hold independently of where I have been and what I say and of what others experience and how they are situated. We have something here which is plainly inter-subjectively testable. But Moreland's claim does not seem to be at all like that. He is not saying anything about being in Galilee at the time Jesus was wandering around. And he doesn't seem to be saying anything that is checkable in an ordinary way as my claim would be that I saw Trudeau yesterday at the Brentwood Shopping Mall. So it doesn't appear that Moreland is making an experiential claim in anything like the standard way, where it would plainly count as an evidential claim. He is rather speaking of experience in another way, a way that appears at least to be evidentially worthless, because it is plainly not publicly testable as my two plain experiential claims are. He is rather claiming "a private publicly untestable experience" where we really have no way of actually sorting out whether the experience is an experience of actually meeting Jesus, imagining one did, hallucinating Jesus, dreaming one met Jesus, just thinking that one met Jesus, and the like.

We can accept all right Moreland's honest avowal that he had some such feelings or other and that he thinks on the basis of these feelings that he met Jesus. Flew appropriately remarks that "All that Moreland is entitled to claim . . . is that he enjoyed overwhelmingly vivid experiences; experiences such that it seemed to him that he 'met Jesus Christ personally,' that he was 'walking with him and fellowshiping with him,' and so on." Flew continues, again appropriately, by remarking that he doesn't "doubt for a moment that Moreland did have such experiences." But Flew is also equally confident that Moreland would agree with him that had he [Flew] "been present when Moreland was having those experiences, there would have been nothing at all out of the ordinary available for either me or for any others present to perceive." That is not like seeing Trudeau in the shopping mall or experiencing Alberta winters. That is to say, this would not be at all the case for my experiential case about Alberta winters. There would, had Flew or Moreland been there for those winters, have been plenty for them to say of a confirming or disconfirming sort. And what they said would be perfectly inter-subjectively testable.[18]

This contrast shows that what Moreland is talking about is a *purely subjective psychological phenomenon*. The only thing it is evidence for is something about the state of Moreland's mind or perhaps (indirectly) of how he got in that state. In short, we are only talking here of something which is of psychological relevance. It tells us nothing about whether he met or could have met Jesus Christ, the son of God. (Jesus is somehow construed not just as a man but, as God's Son, as somehow Himself God.) However, even if we try to treat it as an ordinary experiential claim, assuming (I do not know how) that in some way we can get around these difficulties, it still cannot do any evidential work. Moreland could not have met a bodiless, infinite individual who is transcendent to the world any more than Nielsen could have drawn a round square, whistled a noiseless tune, or felt the color of heat.

Even if we agree, following Ockham and Scotus, that God (*pace* Aquinas) is temporal subsequent to creation and able to act causally at all points in space, we still have problems with the *direct* perception of God. We have some understanding of what it would be like for some strange material being to come into our field of vision, but we are also supposed to understand, in the Jesus case, and this is essential for understanding, that it is God or God's son we are experiencing, that He be infinite and transcendent to the universe. But no sense has been given to those terms. This being so, we can have no understanding that it is God—temporal or nontemporal—that we are experiencing, rather than some cosmic but utterly anthropomorphic Mickey Mouse.

At this point, Craig turns from argument to dogmatic counter-assertion and makes, as well, a confession of faith. He simply asserts that he has a "perfectly perspicuous idea" of "the maker of the heavens and the earth." This means, I suppose, that he is very clear about what it means to make the universe and to make it out of *nothing*. But that is indeed remarkable. Plainly, Craig has a little (to understate it) explaining to do. Most, including considerable segments of the religious tradition itself, have not found these things easy to understand. He also simply dogmatically asserts without argument, what is surely rather questionable, that "analytic philosophy of religion has helped give clear, coherent definitions to divine attributes like eternity, omniscience, omnipotence, necessity, moral perfection, and so forth." Some useful work has been done here by analytical philosophers, and some useful work was done in the Middle Ages as well, but to claim that in either case or in both together the decks have been cleared is either just pure dogmatism or naïveté. Controversy and puzzlement has, not unsurprisingly, continued. Craig sounds—again his scientism coming out—like he is reporting on the amount of smog around Los Angeles or the amount of damage caused by the San Francisco earthquake.

Craig thinks he has detected certain unfortunate positivist residues in my claim that we do not know what "God" refers to because God, even in principle, is unobservable. But if I stick with what he regards as such a positivist dogma, I not only—or so he claims—rule out God, I rule out physics and molecular biology as well. And that is surely a *reductio* of my position. Not wanting to do anything crazy like that, I must, so the claim goes, backtrack: do the same *volte face* the positivists did years ago. Some years ago—and I repeated it in this

debate, though in a truncated form—I developed a position in response
to such claims of which many (among them people of rather different
philosophical and religious or nonreligious persuasions) have been, to
put it minimally, rather skeptical and which Craig thinks is "patently
false." Given that so many have thought it wrong—some just obviously
wrong—I have grown wary of it. After all, why should it be me against
the world? (Here I should remember Cromwell's advice, "Think, in the
bowels of Christ, that you may be wrong.") Nevertheless, I have yet to
hear what I could make out to be a good argument against it (though
again here I may be blinkered), so I will restate it and face Craig's arguments against it such as they are.

In an attempt to avoid my arguments about ostensive definitions of
God and direct perceptions of God, many have said that God is *only*
indirectly observable. I have responded by arguing that if something is
indirectly observable, then, for "indirectly" to qualify "observable," it
must after all be at least conceptually (logically) possible for it to be
directly observed as well. There can, that is, if it is indirectly observable, be no *logical* ban on directly observing it; it cannot *in principle* be
only indirectly observable. If it were, then "indirectly" it would lose its
descriptive force, but then "indirectly observable" in that context
could make no sense. But it might, that notwithstanding, very well be
the case that we have at present no idea how to directly observe it. I, of
course, have no difficulty with that. Still, that is not to rule out the
logical possibility of doing so. However, with God, unlike with electrons
or even neutrinos, there is a conceptual ban on directly observing Him.
Anything that could literally be observed would not be God. (That
among other reasons is a reason why Moreland could not meet Jesus
Christ, the son of God, any day, let alone every day.) But then, for the
above reasons, it makes no sense to speak of indirectly observing Him
either. There is, however, no conceptual (logical) ban on observing theoretical entities, such as an electron or even something like a neutrino,
as long as they are construed as being part of the furniture of the universe and not as logical or scientific fictions. Sometimes, of course,
there are good theoretical-cum-empirical reasons why we cannot directly observe them, but their being so observed is not ruled out in
principle, while it is so for God. There is no logical ban on their being
observed. If certain entities exist in the world but are only just very
much smaller than entities that are directly observable, then there can
be no *logical* ban on observing those smaller entities, *no matter how*
much smaller they are. The theoretical entities of the natural sciences
(where they are *not* viewed as logical fictions, useful heuristic devices
of the natural sciences) are like that, but God is not. But then God is not

indirectly observable either. There is, in short, no conceptual space for indirect observation without allowing the *logical* possibility of direct observation as well. God, in no way, is an observable entity. (Again Kierkegaard would turn over in his grave at the thought of "religious people" with such preoccupations.)

Craig does not respond to that argument which he regards, as I have remarked, "as patently false," but contents himself with asking, Why should unobservability matter anyway? It might be, as I actually think it is in developed theistic religions, part of the definition of God that He be unobservable. Anything that could be observed wouldn't be God. But, Craig asks, So what? There is, he maintains, no problem because of this of the sort I have been talking about concerning the identifying of God via a definition (a definite description); there is, Craig claims, just the *practical* problem of actually finding Him.

But Craig is way off the mark here. If the definite descriptions used to define "God" are all in terms of observables, how does this give us a sense of what it would be like for there to be an *in principle* unobservable reality? And if definite descriptions, as they actually do, also make reference to unobservables themselves (in principle unobservables), then we have the problems all over again that made us turn to the verbal definitions because ostensive definition was unavailable. We have unobservables all along the line and do not know how to secure reference. This is just a rather more empiricist way of expressing the problematic nature of the whole web of related concepts which are suppose to give referential sense to God, or at least to God-talk of a nonanthropomorphic kind, but do not actually secure such reference.

I have also argued that a logically necessary individual or a logically necessary being is incoherent in the sense of being a contradiction in terms. If X is a being or an individual, it can never be self-contradictory to deny that X exists. This is simply Hume's old point. To this Craig responds that we can very easily indeed give sense to the idea of a logically necessary being by saying a logically necessary being is a being that exists in every possible world and that there is no incoherence in a being existing in every possible world. This sounds sensible, and perhaps is. But if this means, as it seems at least to, that the being exists in every logically possible world, then that in turn means that we cannot conceive of that being not existing. But for any being—any being you like—it is possible to conceive of its nonexistence, of its not existing. But it could in turn be claimed that this not being so just is the possibility of a being existing in all logically possible worlds. But then that too, if that is what is meant, must be an incoherent notion, for if something is a being, it is possible at least to conceive of it as not existing. There cannot be *a being* which cannot—logically cannot—not exist. Only *propositions* are logically necessary. For every X, if X is a being, it is possible to assert not-X. This being so, there cannot be a being which exists in every possible world.

It might in turn be responded that we can plainly conceive of a being existing in every possible world. So my essentially Humean claim must, as Norman Malcolm thought, be a philosopher's dogma.[19] However, it may not be so obvious when we are thinking of logically possible worlds that we can conceive or not conceive. But I think a better answer is that the sense in which we can conceive of a being existing in every possible world—whatever that exact sense is—is not equivalent to trying to conceive of a being whose nonexistence is inconceivable: a being that is an individual yet of which, when it is asserted that there is that individual, that it would not make sense logically to deny that that being actually existed. (Moreover, if we describe a being as an eternal individual—an odd description—we can always perfectly sensibly ask whether there actually are any eternal individuals. The denial that there are is not self-contradictory even if there are eternal individuals. That then would be a brute fact about the world and not a logical truth.) But we can always make such a denial. Or can we? *Perhaps* things are less decisive here than is usually thought. But here I think the burden of proof lies with those who would deny the "Humean dogma." Arm waving about modal logic will not help.

However, even if this argument is somehow mistaken, we are still not in a good position to make sense of the very idea of there being an infinite individual transcendent to the world who made the world out of nothing. "Infinite individual," "transcendent to the world," "made the world out of nothing" are all very opaque, problematic concepts.

Let me turn now to Willard's *generally* thoughtful and hard-hitting critique. Willard—and this is where he is not thoughtful and is only irresponsibly hard-hitting—asks a number of questions right at the start of his critique of my argument for the incoherency of the concept of God, which would have been obviated if he had had the slightest acquaintance with what I have said in any of a number of books and articles. Relying entirely, as he seems to have, on an unedited transcription of the debate, it is understandable that he would be puzzled. But it would have taken very little to unpuzzle him on at least some of these issues.[20] (The same is true for his worries about my characterization of atheism.)[21] This is sad, for his essay is a subtle and an important one, and it raises a number of very probing and significant points. It is too bad he had to intermesh this with red herrings. What I do say, as can be seen from the above, is that when our God-talk is of a nonanthropomorphic God, "God" makes no reference—indeed, we do not even know what would count as its securing references—and there is no possibility of truth or falsity for "God exists" and the like. This is a kind of atheism (if you will, a deeper kind of atheism), a kind Susan Stebbing noted long ago in discussing A. J. Ayer, which rejects a certain conception of God, not because it is false that there is such a God, but because such a conception is incoherent.[22] Stebbing argues (plausibly, I believe) that this is even a more deeply probing atheism than the traditional kind because instead of denying the truth of "God exists" and the like, it denies that such a sentence could possibly be used to make a true statement, where "God" is used nonanthropomorphically.

I am not (*pace* what Willard claims) saying that God-talk is a string of linguistic irregularities. (That is plain from what I have written and is just a matter of public record. Willard has no excuse at all for being confused about that.[23]) I argue instead that God-talk, though sometimes not theological-talk (some of Paul Tillich), has its plain linguistic regularities and, in spite of them, God-talk is so problematic as to be incoherent. We often do not understand what we are saying when we speak of God as can be revealed from even a superficial probing of some of our essential attributions of God. Some are contradictory or otherwise unintelligible. I do not (*pace* Willard) deny that there are logical relations between different bits of God-talk. But this does not ensure intelligibility, for this is true of plain nonsense too. If procrastination drinks melancholy, then it drinks, and it does not drink happiness. The word "meaningless" that Willard bandies about covers too many things to be useful here. Plainly in *some sense* we understand God-talk or we could not play the language-games we do with it. I, as my discussion of Wittgenstein and Wittgensteinian fideism has made evident, have been at pains to stress that.[24] But when I say we do not understand what we are talking about, that we do not know what we are trying to say, I mean, as is clear enough from the context, that we do not know what it would be like for "God" to successfully refer, given what we say "God" means, and we do not understand what it would be like for "God exists" or "God created the heavens and the earth" to be either true or false or even probably true or false. We are at a loss as to what we are asserting or denying here. Maybe I am mistaken about this, but it is plain enough what I am asserting.

Willard thinks this is warmed-over Logical Positivism, but, while it owes a lot to Logical Positivism, which in turn owes a lot to traditional empiricism, it does not make the characteristic claims of Logical Positivism—namely, to claim to a sharp distinction between empirical propositions and analytic ones, or to argue that an utterance only has cognitive meaning if it is at least in principle empirically testable and it does not claim (as Rudolf Carnap did) that all meaningful discourse must be recastable in an empiricist language. In my view, not all was dross in Logical Positivism, and I use some of its least challengeable conceptions in a way that I believe is unexceptionable and free of what was in effect an empiricist metaphysic. My arguments above about reference, however, do not depend on the verification principle or on any attempt to construct an empiricist language.[25]

Willard complains that I do not have a *theory* of reference and a *theory* of meaning. Without such theories, he claims, we do not know what we are talking about here. My response is that, as Wittgenstein in effect taught us, we can often pick out meaningless or incoherent utterances without a *theory* of meaning. Indeed, if we could not do this, we would not even be able to construct a theory of meaning. Similarly, we can determine whether certain terms do or do not make successful reference without a *theory* of reference. After all, we are masters of our own language, and we can, without anything as complicated as a theory, reflect on it. It is quite possible that we will have done all the philosophical work we need to do with meaning (use) or reference—assembled all the reminders we need—before we are even in a position to construct a theory of meaning or reference. And if that is so, it is not so terribly clear why we need a theory of meaning or of reference at all or why we need a philosophy of language. My intuitions, clearly, go with Ludwig Wittgenstein here rather than with Michael Dummett.[26]

I assumed that we establish reference either by ostention or by definite description. Willard thinks this is an "overly-simple quasi-positivist model which . . . cannot do justice to the actual performance of language." It may very well be the case, he argues, that reference "is something that, at least in certain cases, just emerges at a certain point in the development of language." Perhaps something like this is so. Wittgenstein has taught us to be wary of simple generalizations, though what Willard is talking about is so vaguely characterized that little can be made of it as it stands. I did make the assumption that Willard refers to. But it seems at least an innocent enough one. For plain cases of referring expressions, this does seem to me how we do secure reference. But I do not have a theory committing me to the belief that these are the only ways to secure reference. They do seem to me ways in which we characteristically proceed, but they may not be the only ways. If Willard has in mind some other way, let him (a) trot out an example and show how it works and (b) show how it helps us understand what "God" refers to. But he doesn't even gesture in that direction. His remarks here come to arm waving.

Willard pertinently raises the following objection to my account, an objection Antony Flew, usually my ally in these matters, also raises. Multiplied millions, the objection goes, use God-talk and think it makes perfectly good sense. There are language-games embedded in English, French, and the like in which much of this talk is perfectly nondeviant. (There are, that is, linguistic regularities in which "God" is used.) People who understand God-talk recognize immediately that "Yesterday it rained God" is nonsense and that "God weighs ten tons" is not something religious people would say. The latter sentence is not even good blasphemy. It isn't exactly nonsense, but it approaches it. And "God loves humankind" and "God created the heavens and the earth" are just unexceptional bits of the language-game Christians play using God-talk. (I could play-act being a priest and use it quite nondeviantly.) I stressed this some time ago in, among other places, my *An Introduction to the Philosophy of Religion*. But I argued there (and elsewhere) that though in our ordinary language there is a use for God-talk, just as there once was a use for witch-talk and goblin-talk, that when we look at God-talk even moderately carefully, we will come to see that, after all, it is incoherent—its central claims are either such as we can know that they could not be true in any possible world or, alternatively, that they are such that we have no understanding of what would establish, with any probability at all, their truth or falsity. Given their incoherence, there is no point in a la Moreland, Swinburne, or Craig, trying to give proofs, evidential or otherwise, for God's existence. Until we understand the truth-conditions for "There is a God" or "No God exists," we cannot intelligibly set about trying in any sense to prove that God exists. For whatever curious phenomena we think is established on the basis of the Big Bang or whatever, we do not know, and moreover cannot know, that the phenomena we have established on that basis warrants belief in God. If we do not understand what we are talking about in speaking of God, we will not understand whether inferences we make from such data lead to God. (This is a form of atheism. That this is so, and what is being claimed here and its import, is completely missed by Willard. But this is not invincible ignorance on his part, for he would not have missed it if he had even read either the article on atheism in the *Encyclopedia of Philosophy* or the article on atheism in the most recent edition of *Encyclopedia Britannica*.[27] These articles, hardly arcane, make it plain that atheism should not be defined as saying that

God exists is false but as a more general belief that rejects belief in God for a number of reasons, including the reason that the concept of God is incoherent. This is perfectly plain in my books, as it is in the writings of Paul Edwards or Antony Flew. Willard has simply not here, in the most elementary way, done his homework.)[28]

However, let me return to the central point here. It is, to say the least, surprising for me to claim that God-talk is incoherent or, in the way specified, unintelligible, when so many people think they understand it and when it plainly has standard (nondeviant) uses in many of our natural languages (English, Swedish, French, German, and the like). This is the point both Willard and Flew pertinently raise. (Flew, of course, is one of the atheist philosophers who claims the concept of God is incoherent.)[29]

Surely the burden is again on me, and I have shouldered it in a whole series of books from *Contemporary Critiques of Religion* (1971) to *God, Scepticism and Modernity* (1989). I gestured at the argument in Chapter 2 of this present volume, though I could do little more than that there. (I repeated a core of it, meeting Willard's request, at the beginning of this essay.) It is not essentially different from the onslaught that Flew and a host of others have made on dualistic talk about mind/body. Dualistic uses of mental terms are pervasive in our natural languages, Flew claims, but there are good reasons for thinking such talk incoherent all the same. This can be seen to be so when we look carefully into what is being said when such talk is deployed. I have tried to do the same thing for a thoroughly nonanthropomorphic conception of God and have stressed as well that should believers use "God" thoroughly anthropomorphically, so that God is taken to be a kind of Zeus, then belief that there is a God is intelligible but just straightforwardly false and obviously so. But the anthropomorphic talk makes rough sense. We get something to believe in that is intelligible but superstitious. But believers—or at least most of them—have for a very long time moved away from such anthropomorphic thinking.[30] As they make their God more ethereal, they imperceptively get to a point where their concept becomes—or so I claim—incoherent. (The move away from anthropomorphism is likely to be gradual so that the step from sense to nonsense may very well go unnoticed.)

This—as Rudolf Carnap argued long ago—is the key to the widespread conviction on the part of believers that their talk makes sense.[31] God-talk came into our stream of life as an anthropomorphic affair— God is our Father in heaven—and, in these homely employments, made rough sense. This is still the way we learn it as children, and it is still the images that have a hold of us when we pray, sing the praises of God, engage in ritual, and the like. This gives us a strong conviction that we understand what we are talking about when we use God-talk. But very early on, and increasingly pervasively, through the nineteenth and twentieth centuries, religious thinkers felt the utter inadequacy and indeed religious inappropriateness of such anthropomorphic talk of God.[32] Moreover, belief in God, so anthropomorphized, plainly became a superstition. So there was a move away from such a conception, a move that not infrequently pushed itself to a conceptionalization of God as an Ineffable Wholly Other, an Ultimate Mystery, a Pure Thou that was not at all an it and the like.[33] With such moves, step by step, for religiously understandable motives, and, of course, unwittingly, the conceptualization of God shifted from a conceptualization that yielded a false belief in the existence of God to one that yielded an incoherent belief. This has led, in a way rationalistic Christian conservatives such as Plantinga, Craig, Moreland, and Willard ignore, to all sorts of demythologizations on the part of Christian and Jewish thinkers. (I think in various ways these demythologizations are unsuccessful, as I try to show in my *God, Scepticism and Modernity,* but they are certainly understandable in view of the evident vulnerability of orthodoxy.)

So I have argued briefly here (and in detail and carefully elsewhere) that the concept of God in developed Judaism, Christianity, and Islam is incoherent, and I have as well given an account of why it should seem to so many, in spite of my not terribly arcane arguments, to be coherent. (Flew, by the way, completely misses this later point.) My critics, as far as I can see, have not touched my arguments for the incoherency of the concept of God or shown that my account (my narrative, if you will) of why God-talk should so pervasively be thought to be at least relatively unproblematic is, after all, just a convenient just-so story for me—a philosophical fable in the service of a militant secularism. Perhaps it is and perhaps my arguments for incoherency are unsound, but nobody, at least in this volume (unless I am utterly blind), has done much in the way of showing that this is so.

V

Willard appropriately enough begins his essay by remarking: "I begin with a plea of 'not guilty' to Professor Nielsen's charge that my belief in God is an irrational belief. I do live in the twentieth century, I have been given a passably good philosophical and scientific education, and I have thought carefully about the matter."

Keith Parsons, arguing for the atheist side, also wants to disassociate himself from my claims about the irrationality of religious belief. (This claim about irrationality needs qualification and interpretation, which it will subsequently get here and as I have given it as well in my previous writings.) Parsons thinks that that claim is unnecessary in a defense of atheism.

I tried at the very beginning of my talk in Chapter 2 to defuse such expected and perfectly understandable reactions by making it clear that I was not claiming that I or Flew or Parsons was more rational than Moreland or Craig or Willard. A lot more would have to be known about what we are like as individual persons to make any such claims. Moreover, the type information that would be relevant would probably have precious little to do with our views on religion or philosophy. It would be both arrogant and silly for me to make any such claim, and I made it clear at the outset that I was not making that claim. I had nothing even remotely like that in mind. Yet I wish to stick to my guns here and to defend (*pace* Parsons) the claim that I actually do make about irrationality. So a little explaining is in order. I can best do that by quoting from some remarks that I made in the final chapter of my recent (1989) *God, Scepticism and Modernity*. The first set of remarks indicates what I take a religiously appropriate conception of God to be, and they in effect also reveal why I think Moreland's and Craig's conceptualizations of God are so *religiously* deficient. I also articulate there the core of my claim about the incoherence of God-talk and show the link between that and my claims about the irrationality of religious belief.

> In arguments between belief and unbelief which are at all informed it is agreed by almost all parties that religious claims are paradoxical and that, if there is a God, he is indeed a very mysterious reality. The God of developed Judaism, Christianity, and Islam, whatever else that God is supposed to refer to, is supposed to refer to an Ultimate Mystery. God is supposed to be the Incomprehensible Other, the Ultimate Mystery whose mysterious reality is beyond all ordinary knowing. A God who was not such an ultimate mystery would not be the God of Judaism, Christianity, or Islam.
>
> This alleged ultimate reality, at least in tolerably orthodox versions of these sister religions, is taken to be a personal creative reality in the form of an infinite and eternal individual who exists beyond the bounds of space and time, and who, without ceasing to be infinite, transcends the world. This is what, most essentially, "God" is taken to refer to in such religions. What in

the essays in this book as well as in my *Philosophy and Atheism* and elsewhere I have probed is whether we have any good reasons at all for believing that there actually exists such a reality or whether it is even reasonable for us, standing where we are now and knowing what we know, to believe that such a reality could exist.

I reject such a religious belief—the fundamental religious presupposition of these religions—because it seems to me that we have no good reason for believing that such a reality exists or indeed even could. It is not just that we cannot decide whether we can be justified in believing in such a reality and thus naturally gravitate toward agnosticism. Rather—or at least so I argue—the most reasonable thing for us to do is to reject such a belief because at best the probability that such a reality exists is of a very low order and at worst such a belief is so problematic as to justify the claim that God, so conceived, connotes an illegitimate concept—an ersatz concept, if you will—that could never have an actual application because what we are saying in speaking of God is actually incoherent. Moreover, it seems to me that when we examine the matter carefully, we will come to see that the worst case scenario from the point of view of religious belief is also the more likely case.

Such a rejection is, of course, a form of atheism. And it is that atheism that I try carefully to characterize and defend in *Philosophy and Atheism*. I argue there, and in this volume as well, the strong thesis, some might even say the offensive thesis, that we cannot come to have a sufficient understanding of such perfectly orthodox talk of God such that the reality to which "God" purports to refer could be the object of a religious commitment that is both clear-headed and informed.

What I have sought to worry out and what seems to me to be plainly a central issue for a nonevasive consideration of religion, at least in cultures such as our own, is whether sufficient sense can be made of the key religious conceptions of the dominant religions of our culture to make belief in God a live option for a reflective and concerned human being possessing a reasonable scientific and philosophical understanding of the world we live in, or whether some form of atheism or agnosticism is the most nonevasive option for such a person. My argument has been that belief in God should no longer be a live option for us standing where we are and knowing what we know.[34]

What I am saying is that *if* we twentieth-century people, standing where we stand and knowing what we know, come to a proper under-standing of the concept of God in developed forms of Judaism, Christianity, and Islam, we will find it impossible to believe in God: we will find belief in God to be irrational. But what is important to see here—and this should take away any offense my remarks might otherwise cause—is that this claim concerning irrationality is entirely dependent on my claims about the incoherence of the concept of God being at least approximately correct. If either (a) they are not that or (b) they are so arcane that they would be difficult for a person with a tolerably good philosophical and scientific education to grasp, then my claims about the irrationality of religious belief are not justified. But (a) is an abso-lutely essential condition for me. The person who feels offended or (perhaps) threatened by my remarks about irrationality should concen-trate on criticizing (a). If (a) is not justified, he is (perhaps) home scot-free. But if (a) is justified and (b) as well, he plainly should agree that *his* religious belief is irrational and that he is being irrational in continuing to believe in God. (This does not, of course, mean he is being irrational in other respects. Most, perhaps all, of us have some irrational beliefs.)

Now I want to cite a second passage which brings out very clearly, I believe, the meaning and rationale of my claim that for us—we twentieth-century intellectuals—belief in God is irrational. I develop the point near the end of *God, Scepticism and Modernity* in response to a perceptive critic, Béla Szabados.

I turn now to Professor Béla Szabados's criticisms. Strong, tendentious philosophical claims require, to have any reasonable force, strong arguments. My claim that belief in God is in our time irrational for a scientifically and philosophically sophisticated per-son is just such a strong and, to put it minimally, contentious claim. Indeed it is a claim to which not a few would take exception and some, no doubt, will find it offensive. Szabados does well to focus critical attention on that claim, for, if it is to be persuasive, it must be very well supported indeed. I do not know whether I have done anything more than make a start at providing that support or if such support can in fact be sustained. It surely would, to under-state it, not be unreasonable to be wary of that claim. But, that to the contrary notwithstanding, it does seem to me, everything considered, the correct claim to make, so I will stick by my guns and, facing Szabados's objections, continue to argue, though with a full sense of my fallibility here, that such belief is irrational.

However, I should first make a disclaimer, for if my views here are misunderstood, as they might be by a careless reader or, more easily and more understandably, by someone who simply hears them, they could rightly be dismissed with contempt. I am not claiming that all or even most Jews, Christians, or Moslems are irrational. That is just too grossly *parti pris* and too absurd to even be worth considering. Indeed, it would be a silly form of hubris, as if I were claiming I am more rational than Professor Hart or claiming that such paradigm Christian philosophers as John Hick, William Alston, Terence Penelhum or Hugo Meynell are irrational or less rational than I am. Anyone who knows them—and they are tokens of a familiar type—knows that such a claim is absurd. Béla Szabados does not, of course, think for a moment that I believe anything like that, but my plainly contentious claim might be confused with that absurd claim. So I make the disclaimer and append an explanation.

What I am claiming instead is that, if my analysis of the concept of God is on the whole well-taken and non-arcane—belief in God is irrational for a philosophically sophisticated and scientifically knowledgeable person in our cultural space, standing where we stand now in the twentieth century. I am *not* saying the religious believer is irrational—he may or may not be, just as the atheist may or may not be irrational; what I am saying is that, if the believer is a twentieth-century person, with a good scientific and philosophical education, his or her belief in God is irrational if what I say about God is so. It is the *belief* for such a person and not the person himself that I am claiming is irrational. And there is no hubris or exaggeration in that claim, though the claim may well be false or unproven (as Szabados believes) or perhaps even incoherent.

To claim that reasonable people can have some irrational beliefs should be little more than a commonplace. Indeed, if our criteria for a reasonable person are so strong that, if a person is properly said to be rational it could not be the case that he had any irrational beliefs, then the class of rational people would most certainly be empty. Freud gives a partial explanation why, but, Freud or no Freud, it is as evident as can be that manifestly reasonable people not infrequently have a few irrational beliefs. My suit is not to convict the Christian of irrationality but to show that a key framework-belief of his is an irrational belief for him to hold if my analysis of the concept of God is non-arcane and near to the mark, and if he lives now in a society such as ours and has been educated in the way I have specified.[35]

My claims about the irrationality of religious belief are *doubly hypo-*

thetical. They depend on the approximate correctness of my analysis of God-talk and they depend as well on their being sufficiently nonarcane to be readily graspable by properly qualified people. Both of those conditions are satisfied, I believe (perhaps mistakenly), and if I am right in that, then I am also justified in believing that belief in God, in the sense and under the conditions specified, is irrational. Offensive or not, I stick by that until someone shows that in one way or another I have made a mistake here.

Finally (*pace* Parsons), I want to argue that it is important for believers and unbelievers alike to ascertain, if they can, whether belief in God and religious belief more generally are or are not irrational and to not remain content with the weak claim that believers or atheists are within their *epistemic rights* in believing what they believe. Parsons is right against Plantinga that this claim about epistemic rights is a trivial claim.[36] What is important instead for both believers and unbelievers to ascertain (if they can) is what they should believe (everything considered) in this domain. (This is not, by the way, a closet rationalism. It is not to make reason sovereign—whatever that means—for it *may* be the case that *non*rational—not irrational—factors will, and indeed even should, be decisive here.) What she does not want to have, if she is a reflective and reasonable person, is a belief that is *irrational*. So it is important to make as sure as we can that belief in God (or, for that matter, atheism) is not irrational.

VI

I want, in concluding this essay, to gather a few fugitives in response to remarks made by the other participants. Here is the miscellany of fugitives:

1. Willard thinks that "it would be especially useful to be shown how the 'incoherence' of 'God' in Nielsen's own sense—whatever that is, exactly—entails or renders probable the non-existence of God." My claim for the incoherence of God attempts to show that the concept of God (depending on exactly how God is conceived) is either self-contradictory (like a round square) or so problematic that we do not understand what it would be like for the claim "There is a God" to be either true (probably true) or false (probably false). If the former, there could not be a God any more than there could be a round square or a married bachelor. So the truth of that claim entails the nonexistence of God. If the latter, the existence of God is extremely improbable, for we

have no idea of whether "There is a God" is true (probably true) or false (probably false) or even any idea of how we could go about finding out which claim is the more likely to be true. This, in some strict sense, may not render the existence of God improbable—the order of being is different than the order of knowledge—but it surely means that we are and can be in no position to claim that God even probably exists or that we even understand what it would be like for God to exist.

2. I want now to consider a point that emerges out of a consideration that Willard raises in the context of his very interesting and reflectively intelligent effort to establish a case for the plausibility of theism. He remarks that it is necessary but not sufficient to do so to *demonstrate* (emphasis his) "that the physical or natural world recognized by common sense and the 'natural' sciences is not the only type of thing in existence: that there concretely exists, or at least has existed, something radically different from it." I realized, in reflecting on his important discussion there and not being convinced by his subtle attempted demonstration, that there is a self-existent reality distinct from physical reality, that I plainly think, in contrast to Willard, that existence should be assimilated to physical existence. Indeed, just as Hägerström argued that contingent existence is pleonastic, I would want to argue for an assimilation so strong as to make contingent physical existence pleonastic.[37] I have, perhaps in a wildly metaphysical moment (something not characteristic of me), the tendency to believe (not being a Platonist about numbers) that that is the only kind of existence there can be. I do not know how to argue for it, but I just *think* it is somehow plainly so. I cannot imagine seriously entertaining anything else. Yet Willard, and he is not alone as I am not alone in my physicalist beliefs, thinks he can demonstrate the opposite. That seems to me so implausible that if an argument to that effect looked good, I would certainly, rather than *right off* accept it, for a very long time indeed probe it to see if I could find what I expect to be most certainly an error of reasoning. I expect religious people would—and not unreasonably—do the same thing in trying to resist any proof, if there can be one, that physical existence is all there is. I expect there are deep down "animal" (in Wittgenstein's sense) convictions about what is reasonable to believe here. *My arguments for atheism do not depend on my physicalist assumptions, and to not lose sight of this is vital to remember in this discussion.* Yet I think that physicalism goes naturally with atheism and underlies many (though not all) the atheist's underlying convictions that he is right. Willard, as any theist must, rejects physicalism, though, as he is well

aware, it is not at all sufficient to carry him or us to God. Even a dualist, as I pointed out in Chapter 2, could consistently be an atheist.

Can we prove or (more plausibly) make one view more plausible than the other? Can we present any non-question-begging arguments here? I do not know. Sometimes in my more historicist moments (when the influence of Richard Rorty weighs heavily with me) I think nonrational factors determine things here, and which conceptions one accepts just depends on which *Weltbild* one was conditioned into. We just have different (in Wittgenstein's sense) framework beliefs here with no non-question-begging arguments either way. This historicist view, as I have argued in my various discussions of Wittgensteinian fideism, is more devastating to theism, at least where it is linked to the traditional religions, than to skepticism concerning religion (if not to atheism), for it is Christianity, after all (and its sister religions make similar claims), which proclaims incautiously that Christ is the Truth and the Way. If everything is *Weltbild*-dependent and there are just various *Weltbilden*, as a matter of fact there are, *with no way of assessing their comparative adequacy*, then nothing is left of that proud Christian claim. But I too, though less urgently, would like to know whether my physicalism, as George Santayana thought, rests, when really pushed, on animal faith. I hope and expect that a little more in the way of argument for and against physicalism can be churned up so it can be seen that one thing is more reasonable to believe than another. But that may be my illusion. My central point here is that this historicism or perhaps even relativism is more worrisome for the Christian than for me, for it is the Christian, after all, who proclaims that Christ is the Truth and the Way. I am not saddled with any such absolutism.

3. Willard, in his criticisms of scientists who, like Richard Dawkins, attempt to refute design arguments, remarks that what these "rebutters" with almost no exception quite conveniently manage to forget is that evolution, whether cosmic or biological, *cannot*!—logically cannot—be a theory of ultimate origins of existence or order, precisely because its operation presupposes the existence of certain entities with specific potential behaviors and an environment of some specific kind that operates upon those entities in some specifically ordered fashion. But this in turn conveniently forgets the arguments against our ability to give explanations for the *"ultimate* origins of existence or order." We can, as Bertrand Russell and A. J. Ayer argued against Father Copleston in their famous debates and as Paul Edwards systematized and extended in his article "Why" in *The Encyclopedia of Philosophy* (vol. 8,

296–302), never give successful explanations *of such scope*, though we can and do for various purposes give all sorts of explanations of a more limited scope.[38] There may very well be, as Russell quipped to Copleston, no explaining the sorry scheme of things entire. It is simply utterly uncritical thinking to just believe that there must be, or even likely is, explanations or theories of such type available to us. It is one thing to say that every physical event has an explanation; it is another thing again to say that there must be an explanation of the *ultimate origin* of things, and indeed to assume that there is an ultimate origin of things to be explained, or believe that there must be if only we could find out what it is or that we even can know what we are asking for here when we ask for such *ultimate* explanations. That there *must* be such a principle of sufficient reason operating *here* is certainly a very questionable and question-begging thing to believe. This may be another sign of what Fredrich Waismann called the irrational heart of rationalism.[39] It, strangely enough, afflicts rationalist believers such as Plantinga and Swinburne and the Christians writing in this volume but not more fideistic believers—and it is not a disease that afflicts me. Historicism does not seem to me a terrible threat, though I am curious about (a) whether it is the more plausible way to look at things and (b) about how we could decide (a), if we could decide it.

4. Willard quite properly remarks, "The atheist who can't be bothered to pay serious attention to the facts claimed for religious histories and religious experience is twin brother to the churchman who refused to look through Galileo's telescope because he *already knew* what was and was not to be seen." That is just the right thing to say about the debate between belief and unbelief, for, at the very least, the choices are, in a culture such as ours, sociologically speaking, live options. But, as a general principle, it is not so evident as Willard seems to think as to what, no matter what the context, is the reasonable attitude here. Must the reasonable atheist, or theist for that matter, pay serious attention to Mary Baker Eddy, to *The Book of Mormon*, to the Moonies, or to Flat Earthers? Life is short and it is impossible to investigate everything. It seems at least to be the most reasonable policy— knowing the little about them that most of us do—to just reject them out of hand using the scant information we have. (We have to know *something* of the content of what they say, but it is just at *that content* at which we balk. But we have precious little of the rationale that goes with those claims and, moreover, unless we are just idly curious, we do not want to search out that rationale.) These views surely do not get a

fair kick at the can. There are, I would guess, some closet atheist physicalist philosophers who feel about Christian belief like most of us feel about Christian Science. Are they obviously unreasonable or blind dogmatists? Are we blind dogmatists if our mind is shut against Mary Baker Eddy? I think answers are not as easily forthcoming here as Willard gives to understand. It is not—I admit—a practical problem for us, since Christianity is a live cultural option in our society, and as responsible intellectuals, whatever our personal beliefs about what is profitable to argue about, we must be prepared to argue such matters. But it does not settle the issue of principle, which may be more troublesome than is usually thought, particularly when combined with the historicist considerations of point 2 above.

5. Craig is perfectly right in saying that it is "absurd to claim that something literally came out of nothing." *If* the universe had an origin, it indeed had to have a cause. But the absurdity is to think the universe had, let alone had to have, an origin or that it even makes sense to talk that way. The temptation, as I point out, to think this way comes—and this is something quite prior to science—from thinking of the universe as a thing or an entity—only a very, very big thing or entity—and then to ask naturally enough about its cause. But "the universe" is just an umbrella term for all the events, processes, things that there are. It is not itself a label for anything. It is just a way of speaking compendiously of all those things, but it is not a name for some mysterious additional thing or entity that might have either had an origin or failed to have an origin, that might have popped into existence with a Big Bang. (Something coming from nothing, that is Big Bang mysticism!)

To this Craig responds lamely that scientists talk about the universe as if it were a thing. But that only teaches us, as Wittgenstein, MacIntyre, and Toulmin have made us aware, to be on guard for bad incoherent philosophy sneaking unwittingly into certain scientific accounts.[40] Scientific cosmology is a fertile place for that. Unguardedly naïve here, certain people (including some philosophers) are enthralled by the latest article in the *Scientific Monthly* or the latest popularization of these matters by some scientist slumming, as it were, on holiday and doing what is very likely to be some bad philosophy. Instead of giving in to this, we should carefully sort out genuine experimental results in the science in question from the bad metaphysics or ideology that has gotten embedded in it. Craig naïvely, and Moreland as well, takes all that cosmological talk at face value and resurrects in a new scientific garb cosmological arguments long since decisively refuted. We get the sense that something new is going on here when nothing is.

6. Moreland makes an illicit analogy between "God" and a theoretical term such as an "electron." Moreland follows reasonably enough a fairly standard scientific realist account in the philosophy of science, an account that utilizes a causal theory of reference to explain scientific terms—terms that refer to entities in the world.[41] Such a term—"electron" is a familiar enough example—is understood as referring to whatever causes a specified range of phenomena. Often, as a matter of fact, we have no independent access to the unseen entity (in this case the electron) apart from the phenomena (objects, processes) it causes and the model we use to talk about them. We attribute to the unseen theoretical entity the properties necessary for the entity to fulfil its explanatory function in the theory (in this case electron theory) in reference to the relevant range of phenomena to be explained. So we understand an electron as an entity that has such-and-such properties deemed necessary to explain certain effects. "God," Moreland tells us, can similarly be defined—utilizing a causal account of reference— "as that entity with such-and-such properties deemed necessary to create and design the world, to be a maximally perfect being, to reveal Himself in religious experience, and so on." But "God," Moreland to the contrary notwithstanding, is very unlike a theoretical term of physics such as "electron." We can use a causal theory of reference for "electron" because an electron, though a very, very small entity, is in the same physical causal network as the macroscopic entities it causally explains (the explaining here comes to showing one to have caused the other) as the hot water caused the ice to melt. We have plain causal changes here in the same causal order. In the case of God, we have something "outside the world," supposedly linked up in some mysterious way with something in the world, say Adam, but how that could be is a miracle and a mystery indeed. A causal theory of reference here works no better than to try to teach "God" through ostensive definition or by definite descriptions. What it could possibly come to to speak of causal relationships here is entirely unclear. If there is a causal relationship here, it is certainly quite unlike any other kind of causal relationship that we can reliably impute and clearly understand.

7. Willard rightly alludes to the existential import of our discussions. Belief in God, at least for people socialized as most of us have been and standing where we stand, is a major issue in dealing with our lives. It just does not come as a matter of course to us as it has to other peoples at other times. Perhaps this will not always be so. Indeed, I hope that it will not always be so, but it is so now for most of us and will be so for the foreseeable future. Here are raised questions about how

to make sense out of our tangled lives, questions about whether it is true, as Søren Kierkegaard believed, that to overcome despair or to achieve our fullest flourishing or to achieve our deepest good, we need (scandal to the intellect or not) to believe in God. This should have been, but unfortunately was not, at the center of our discussions. I regret very much that the religious side was represented by such religious rationalists bent on discussing scientific cosmology, "Big Bang mysticism," and the like, rather than what I take to be the really vital questions dividing belief and unbelief and of concern to both. I regret very much that I did not have Kierkegaardians or Wittgensteinians or Niebuhrians to debate so that we could really have discussed questions of religious and human import. Even when Moreland discussed morality and religion, he brought in a lot of noncentral metaethical questions, like a good metaphysician, about non-natural properties, contra-causal freedom, and cosmological considerations.[42]

Do we need a belief in God and (in some sense) immortality to make the moral life possible or at least in the fullest sense possible and to meet our deepest expectations of life—our secret hopes and wishes (if we have any)—in a life that can seem like just one damn thing after another? I argued in my lecture on ethics and religion in Chapter 8 and in considerable detail in my *Ethics Without God* that even in a world without God, we can have a firm knowledge of right and wrong, as firm a knowledge of right and wrong as in a world with God. Those of you who are parents consider this simple feature about the moral life. You love your children, care for their well-being, and do not want harm to come to them. Suppose you are a Jewish or Christian believer and you lose your faith. Would that make the slightest difference to the feelings I described above that you have for your children? Or *should* it? I think those questions answer themselves. What more solid foundation would a belief in God give you here? Suppose you have an infant utterly dependent on you. Would God's commanding you to love and care for that infant give you any more reason than you already have for not harming or neglecting her? It would not. Would—to replay the Abraham/Isaac story—God's commanding you to harm her or neglect her justify your doing so? It would not. (Kierkegaard strikingly dramatized things here, but Kant's attitude, believer that he was too, was far saner.)

There are not a few religious believers—including Kant—who would agree with me here. Only a few would bite the bullet and so crucify their moral sense that they would be prepared to do *whatever* God commands no matter *what* it is. In a crucial way ethics is autonomous. Crucially, God or belief in Him plays no role in the *justifying* of our moral beliefs. But Kant, who would agree with this, thought that in *another way* God entered into morality. Let me explain. As things stand, people of moral integrity—principled people who do what is right because it is right or who genuinely and unselfishly care for others—often come out badly, sometimes even go to the wall, as the world goes. There are even some who think they are suckers for so acting. That is their fate, while the intelligently unprincipled, discretely uncaring, and prudently freeloading typically do very well indeed. That strikes us—or at least most of us—as very unfair. But that is just how it is.[43] The virtuous typically do not get rewarded in this world. But if we postulate immortality and a heaven and hell under God's guidance, where the wicked get punished and the virtuous rewarded, justice reigns in the world and we gain a proper moral balance of things. *We do not need God to tell us that freeloading is wrong, but we need God to punish the free-loader and reward the person of moral integrity.* So we postulate God, whether it offends our intellect or not, as (as Kant put it) a pure *practical* necessity to make sure that moral integrity is rewarded. It, of course, doesn't guarantee that it will be rewarded, for *we cannot call into being cosmological realities out of moral need*, but it does show us what would have to be the case for moral integrity to be rewarded, given the world as it is.

I would respond by saying that moral integrity and related virtues need no reward. Rewarded or unrewarded, they are intrinsically worthwhile. If (to use Foucault's way of putting things) you care for self (and that is not the same as being selfish), this is just the sort of person you want to be and you will continue to want to be, even if the unprincipled flourish and you don't. You don't, of course, want a world in which people get suckered and the unprincipled flourish; you will, of course, try to protect yourself and others from that eventuality. But even if you fail, you will prize your moral integrity and that of others as something, rewarded or unrewarded, worth having for its own sake. Something *you* want for its own sake. Something which is a central part of *your* image of yourself. Is being decent something to be done *only* if you get rewarded for it?

However, it might be responded in turn, "Aren't you a spoil-sport? Wouldn't it be nice if virtue were rewarded?" Well, yes, of course. But this niceness here is not worth crucifying your intellect for and believing in something that would have no credibility otherwise: which you haul in as a *pure practical necessity* with no theoretical necessity or plausibility at all. Of course, if belief in God has some theoretical plausibility, you can then add pure practical necessity as a nice ancillary reason. It is frosting on the cake. But standing by itself, it is too much like a wish fulfillment that in reality will give us no guarantees at all. In such a context, it is better to set aside such hopes and to concentrate on the very difficult task of living with moral integrity *and* with a good Hobbesian sense of prudence in our nasty world. But we should, as well, and in accordance with these two things, take our morally nondestructive happiness where we can find it.

It is frequently said in these contexts that I am missing the most important reason for believing in God. In my atheist world, it is certain that we will die and (if we don't get cremated first) rot. I must face the fact—the unsettling fact as Leo Tolstoy would have it—that this will happen to me and to those I love, as it will inescapably happen to everyone, if my bleak atheist conception of the world is really so. To escape this, we are told, we must postulate God and immortality. Perhaps I am superficial, but I have never understood this Tolstoyian *angst*. If my physical and mental powers are intact, I would rather not die. And I certainly do not want to lose the people I love. But I must die, and they must die, and we can face this and, realizing that is all we have (and it is not a little), live that life to the full. Love is not worthless because the death of both lovers will bring it to an end. Fastening on what we know we have (among them thick relations between people) and what, if we are not too neurotic, we, by ourselves or with others, can make something of, without distracting ourselves with things (God and immortality), which at best are just barely intelligible, we can in a godless world have both a full moral life and really demanding and reciprocally fulfilling human relations. (Moralists and moral philosophers are too prone to think morality is everything and to neglect all the rest which gives life a point and that, where such things can be sustained, makes living such a wonderful thing. Moreover, that these things very, very often cannot be sustained does not mean that they never can be. And it certainly does not require a *deus ex machina* for their sustainment.) A central thing is, as Albert Camus dramatized, to relentlessly fight the plague, and to (as Michel Foucault argued toward the end of his life) cultivate the care of the self, and to (as Bertrand Russell might have put it) find—though without indifference to others—your happiness and human flourishing where you can. This is all fully available to you even if you are, as I am, utterly without religious faith.

NOTES

1. Jean Hampton, "Should Political Philosophy be Done Without Metaphysics?" *Ethics* 99: 4 (July 1989), 791–814. I should add here that, except where otherwise specified, discussions of and quotations from authors writing in this volume are from their contributions to this volume.
2. That impartiality and neutrality should be distinguished and how they are to be distinguished are clearly argued by Robert Paul Wolff in *The Ideal of the University* (Boston: Beacon Press, 1969), 69–76, and by Charles Taylor in "Neutrality in the University" in *Neutrality and Impartiality: The University and Political Commitment*, A. Montifiore, ed. (Cambridge, England: Cambridge University Press, 1975), 128–148.
3. This is the kind of consideration that Terence Penelhum tries to worry out in his *Problems of Religious Knowledge* (London, England: Macmillan Press, 1971).
4. J. L. Mackie, *The Miracle of Theism* (Oxford, England: Clarendon Press, 1982) is the best single statement of this view. But see as well Wallace Matson, *The Existence of God* (Ithaca, N.Y.: Cornell University Press, 1965) and Michael Scriven, *Primary Philosophy* (New York: McGraw-Hill, 1966), 87–167. Even the Christian philosopher Terence Penelhum comes to rather similar conclusions. See his *Religion and Rationality* (New York: Random House, 1971).
5. Keith Parsons, *God and the Burden of Proof* (Buffalo, N.Y.: Prometheus Books, 1989). In the first part of the book, he gives an acute critique of Alvin Plantinga. In the second part he gives similar attention to Richard Swinburne. See also his *Science, Confirmation and the Theistic Hypothesis* (New York: Peter Lang, 1990).
6. This distinction and its import is clearly articulated by Jean Hampton, *Ethics*, 810–14.
7. I discussed in some considerable detail the traditional proofs for the existence of God, the appeal to religious experience, and various fideistic strategies in my *Reason and Practice* (New York: Harper & Row, 1971), 135–194.
8. Stephen Toulmin, "Contemporary Scientific Mythology" in his *Metaphysical Beliefs* (London: SCM Press, 1957), 13–81.
9. Jürgen Habermas, *Toward a Rational Society*, translated by Jeremy Shapiro (Boston: Beacon Press, 1970), 81–127.
10. Kai Nielsen, *Reason and Practice*, 168–183. Paul Edwards in a widely read anthology has made those points very simply. It is a pity Willard makes no effort to meet such rather standard objections. Paul Edwards and Arthur Pap, eds., *A Modern Introduction to Philosophy*, 3rd ed. (London: Collier-Macmillan, 1973), 376–85.
11. Alasdair MacIntyre clearly articulates the view that they are even unde-

sirable. Alasdair MacIntyre, "The Logical Status of Religious Belief" in *Metaphysical Beliefs*, S. Toulmin et al, eds. (London: SCM Press, 1957), 169–211; *Difficulties in Christian Belief* (London: SCM Press, 1956). John Hick and Terence Penelhum make the more standard point that none of the arguments for God's existence work, but that provides no impediment to the reasonability of faith.

12. Kai Nielsen, "Can Faith Validate God-talk?" in *New Theology*, Martin E. Marty and Dean G. Peerman, eds. (New York: Macmillan, 1964), 131–49.

13. E. P. Evans-Pritchard, *Witchcraft, Oracles and Magic Among the Azande* (Oxford, England: Oxford University Press, 1937).

14. Rudolf Otto, *The Idea of the Holy*, trans. J.W. Harvey (Oxford, England: Oxford University Press, 1923). See also in this context the splendid anthology of nineteenth-century religious thought edited by Bernard M. G. Reardon, *Religious Thought in the Nineteenth Century* (Cambridge, England: Cambridge University Press, 1966).

15. John Wisdom, "Gods" in his *Philosophy and Psycho-Analysis* (Oxford, England: Basil Blackwell, 1953), and his "The Modes of Thought and the Logic of God" in *The Existence of God*, John Hick, ed. (New York: Macmillan, 1964), 275-98.

16. Antony Flew, *God and Philosophy* (London: Hutchinson, 1966), and his *The Presumption of Atheism* (New York: Barnes and Noble, 1976).

17. See Paul Ziff, "About God" in *Religious Experience and Truth*, Sidney Hook, ed. (New York: New York University Press, 1961), 195–202; Kai Nielsen, *An Introduction to the Philosophy of Religion* (London: Macmillan, 1982), 17–42.

18. See C. B. Martin, *Religious Belief* (Ithaca, N.Y.: Cornell University Press, 1959), and Ronald W. Hepburn, *Christianity and Paradox* (London: Watts, 1958). For a brief discussion of the essential points here, see Kai Nielsen, *Reason and Practice*, 195–203. An excellent discussion of this whole issue is contained in Louis Pojman's anthology *Philosophy of Religion* (Belmont, Calif.: Wadsworth, 1987), 91–149.

19. Norman Malcolm, "Anselm's Ontological Argument" in *The Existence of God*, John Hick, ed. (London: Collier-Macmillan, 1965), 48–70.

20. Kai Nielsen: *Scepticism* (New York: St. Martin's Press, 1973); *An Introduction to the Philosophy of Religion*, 140–70; *Philosophy and Atheism* (Buffalo, N.Y.: Prometheus Press, 1985), 77–106.

21. Kai Nielsen, *Philosophy and Atheism*, 9–28.

22. Susan Stebbing, "Critical Notice of *Language, Truth and Logic*," *Mind* 45 (1936).

23. Kai Nielsen, *An Introduction to the Philosophy of Religion*, 17-42, 140–70; *Philosophy and Atheism*, 77–106.

24. See my discussions of Wittgenstein and Wittgensteinian fideism in my *Introduction to the Philosophy of Religion*, 43–139, in my *Scepticism*, and in

my *God, Scepticism and Modernity* (Ottawa, Ontario: University of Ottawa Press, 1989), 94–159.

25. Where my central arguments about reference avoid verificationist appeals can be seen in my *Philosophy and Atheism*, 77–106, and my *God, Scepticism and Modernity*, 15–26.
26. Ludwig Wittgenstein, *Philosophical Investigations*, trans. G.E.M. Anscombe (Oxford: Basil Blackwell, 1953); *On Certainty*, trans. Denis Paul and G.E.M. Anscombe (Oxford: Basil Blackwell, 1969); Michael Dummett, *Truth and Other Enigmas* (Cambridge, Mass.: Harvard University Press, 1978), 437–58.
27. The article on atheism in the *Encyclopedia Britannica* was written by me. The article in the *Encyclopedia of Philosophy* was written by Paul Edwards. See also the article on agnosticism by Ronald Hepburn in the *Encyclopedia of Philosophy*, and my article "Agnosticism" in *Dictionary of the History of Ideas*, vol. I, Philip P. Wiener, ed. (New York: Charles Scribner & Sons, 1968), 17–27.
28. Antony Flew, *God and Philosophy; The Presumption of Atheism*. Paul Edwards, "Difficulties in the Idea of God" in *The Idea of God*, Edward H. Madden, ed. (Springfield, Ill.: Charles C. Thomas, 1968), 43–97. Kai Nielsen: *Contemporary Critiques of Religion* (New York: Herder and Herder, 1971); *Scepticism; An Introduction to the Philosophy of Religion; Philosophy and Atheism; God, Scepticism and Modernity*.
29. Antony Flew, *God and Philosophy; The Presumption of Atheism*.
30. The moving away from anthropomorphic thinking was particularly evident in nineteenth-century thought. See Bernard M. G. Reardon's anthology *Religious Thought in the Nineteenth Century*, and particularly the writings of Schliermacher, Ritschl, Kierkegaard, Maurice, Newman, and Mansel. For a brilliant worrying out of this issue, see the extended exchange between John Skorupski and Robin Horton. Robin Horton, "A Definition of Religion and Its Uses," *The Journal of the Royal Anthropological Institute of Great Britain and Ireland* 90: 201–26; Robin Horton, "African Traditional Thought and Western Science," *Africa* 17 (1967), 131–71; John Skorupski, "Science and Traditional Religious Thought I and II," *Philosophy of the Social Sciences* 3 (1973), 209–30; Robin Horton, "Paradox and Explanation: A Reply to Mr. Skorupski I," *Philosophy and the Social Sciences* 3 (1973), 289–314; Robin Horton, "Levy-Bruhl, Durkheim and the Scientific Revolution" in *Modes of Thought*, R. Horton and R. Finnegan, eds. (London: Faber and Faber, 1973), 249–305; John Skorupski, "Comment on Professor Horton's 'Paradox and Explanation'," *Philosophy of the Social Sciences* 5:1 (1975) 63–70; John Skorupski, *Symbol and Theory* (London: Cambridge University Press, 1976).
31. Rudolph Carnap, "The Elimination of Metaphysics through Logical Analysis of Language" in *Logical Positivism*, A. J. Ayer, ed. (Glencoe, Ill.: The

Free Press, 1959), 66–67. It should be noted that this article was first published in 1931.

32. See *Religious Thought in the Nineteenth Century,* Bernard M. G. Reardon, ed.

33. Rudolph Otto, *The Idea of the Holy.*

34. Kai Nielsen, *God, Scepticism and Modernity,* 220–21.

35. Nielsen, *God, Scepticism and Modernity,* 239–40.

36. Keith Parsons, *God and the Burden of Proof.*

37. Axel Hägerström, *Philosophy and Religion,* trans. Robert T. Sandin (London: Allen and Unwin, 1964), 175–305.

38. The Ayer/Copleston debate is published in the first edition of Paul Edwards and Arthur Pap, eds., *A Modern Introduction to Philosophy* (Glencoe, Ill.: The Free Press, 1957), 586–618 and the Russell/Copleston debate in the third edition of the same anthology, 473–490.

39. Fredrich Waismann, *How I see Philosophy* (New York: St. Martin's Press, 1968), 65.

40. Ludwig Wittgenstein, *Culture and Value,* trans. Peter Winch (Chicago: University of Chicago Press, 1980). See also Toulmin, "Contemporary Scientific Mythology," and MacIntyre, "The Logical Status of Religious Belief."

41. W. H. Newton-Smith, *The Rationality of Science* (London: Routledge and Kegan Paul, 1981).

42. John Rawls, Richard Rorty, and Bernard Williams have shown how irrelevant that is to pressing problems about the moral life. See John Rawls, "Justice as Fairness: Political Not Metaphysical," *Philosophy and Public Affairs* 14:3 (Summer 1985), 223–51; Richard Rorty, "The Priority of Democracy to Philosophy" in *The Virginia Statute for Religious Freedom,* Merrill D. Peterson and Robert Vaughan, eds. (Cambridge, England: Cambridge University Press, 1988), 257–82; Bernard Williams, *Ethics and the Limits of Philosophy* (Cambridge, Mass.: Harvard University Press, 1985). John Dewey in various writings stressed this long ago. The Christian philosopher-theologians writing in this volume are oblivious to these considerations. They write as if George Eliot, Ludwig Feurbach, Søren Kierkegaard, and William James had never lived. They seem dead to the complexities of the moral life and, I am inclined to say, of the religious life as well.

43. Kai Nielsen, *Why Be Moral?* (Buffalo, N.Y.: Prometheus Books, 1989).

PART V

HOW CAN I DECIDE FOR MYSELF?

The Debate Made Personal

The Choice of a Lifetime

We have heard the debate, and four responses to it. How shall *we* respond? And how can we decide rationally for ourselves whether to believe God exists or not? Can a rational debate help us decide, help convince us? Can minds be changed by argument?

I think it is unlikely that many strong theists will have been convinced by this debate (perhaps by any debate) to convert to atheism, and unlikely that many strong atheists will have been convinced by this debate to convert to theism—even if one side of this debate did in fact win decisively. But I think some uncertain and doubting readers, whether atheists or theists or agnostics, may have moved some significant way toward a different position than they started from, but they are probably still uncertain, not wholly convinced either way. It is to these people—the not-wholly-convinced-either-way—that I address the rest of this chapter, in hope of helping them to decide for themselves, intelligently and rationally and fairly, how to think about this issue of God.

I think there are three preconditions we can all agree on, three things everyone can and must do if they really want to know the truth.

First, *we must be totally honest and try to have motives as pure and as passionate as possible:* to deeply desire to know the truth for its own sake, regardless of the consequences, however uncertain and fearful, however personally inconvenient these may be. Honesty requires something from both the intellect and the will, but it begins in the will, in a resolve. Honesty with oneself is difficult—often much more difficult than honesty with others. Modern psychology has taught us how clever the unconscious mechanisms of self-deception can be. But unless both sides begin here, with an unqualified "I *will*" to honesty and truth, *whatever* it may turn out to be, there is no hope of really settling this issue, or any other, and debate becomes a mere entertainment, a sham.

Second, *we must all look at all the evidence on both sides, and not focus on only one side or only one part of the evidence.* In addition to confronting all the unresolved questions in this debate, which are summarized in the Appendix, some kind of overall logical scorecard must be drawn up for the sides of atheism and theism. If the preponderance of evidence lies on one side, then that fact should at least move the honest mind significantly closer to closure, at least increase the probability of the preponderant side being true. To find out where the preponderance of good evidence lies, other arguments than the few covered in this debate should be considered—especially the atheist's traditionally strongest argument, the problem of evil, and the theistic arguments such as the argument from the natural desire for God (see C. S. Lewis) and the argument from miracles. (If I were an atheist, I would examine doctors' reports of alleged miraculous cures, and carefully interview people who claim to have seen miracles or been miraculously healed, and see whether I could expose them all as either deceivers or deceived.)

Third, *we are not reduced to passive reading and learning; we can also perform active experiments,* as in science, as Solomon did in 1 Kings 3:16-28 and as Jesus did in John 8:2-11, especially verse 7. Here are four such experiments:

(1) Test not just ideas but lives. Find out what difference atheism or theism makes to people's lives, especially converts to both positions. A scientist wants to know not just what a theory means and how logical it is but also what difference it makes, what its consequences are, and how useful it is. G. K. Chesterton once said that the strongest argument against Christianity is Christians. He meant hypocritical, gloomy, or stupid Christians. Perhaps the strongest argument *for* Christianity is also Christians: saintly, joyful, and wise Christians. Find both kinds, and both kinds of atheists, and look at the difference. Gather data. Be scientific.

(2) Try on the two sets of clothing, so to speak, for a day's workout in each. Be an atheist for a day; see how it feels. Be a Christian for a day; see how that feels. Try consciously to live in a universe with no God; contemplate the fact of no-God often and deeply during the day. How do you live in this light? Then try consciously to live with God for a day; pray, love God and His immortal image in your neighbor, see the world as divine art and your life as divine providence. See what kind of difference it might make.

The second half of this experiment is suggested by the wise old guru Father Zossima in Dostoyevski's *The Brothers Karamazov* to "a woman of little faith" who confesses to him that she has lost her Naïve, childlike faith by learning that everything can apparently be explained by science without God. "What if when I come to die there are only the burdocks on my grave?" Zossima does not try to prove God or immortality to her, nor to return her to the unquestioning innocence of her lost childhood. Instead, he suggests to her an experiment. "Love your neighbor, actively and indefatigably," as if he or she were indeed an immortal soul made in the image of God and infinitely valuable. "Insofar as you advance in love, you will grow surer of the reality of God and of the immortality of your soul. This has been tried. This is certain."

The experiment is not a trick, a self-deception, a pair of blinders. It is a pair of glasses. It is a fair experiment to test a hypothesis. The believer's hypothesis is that there is not only a God in heaven but also an image of God on earth—namely, the human soul. And that hypothesis further stipulates that active, unselfish, self-forgetful love is not merely a subjective feeling but a seeing of an objective truth; that this kind of love is not blind (how could love be blind if "God is love"—is God blind?) but has an eye in it; and that this eye, when opened by the exercise of loving your concrete neighbor (not safe, abstract ideal "Humanity!"), will eventually perceive the image of God in the soul of the loved neighbor.

But the love must be genuine: other-centered, not self-centered. It must be the love of the other qua other, qua himself or herself. This is not sentimental love or desire, whether erotic or otherwise. It is not even merely friendship or bonhomie. It is treating your neighbor as if he or she really were God's son or daughter. For according to the theistic hypothesis, which we are supposed to be testing, that is exactly what he or she is.

It is a strictly no-risk, no-lose experiment. Who would attack love, whether there is or is not a God? What harm could it do to love?

Two results are possible. Either Zossima is right and the lover will begin to see an objective truth he or she did not see before, or Zossima is wrong. If wrong, then you have additional evidence for atheism, or at least for agnosticism; and also you have done something good in the meantime, something good for you as well as good for your neighbor.

(3) "Pascal's Wager" is another experiment, rather than an argument. It is based on the premise that though you may not know whether or not there is a God and a life after death, you do know that you will certainly die. What will happen then, according to theism and according to atheism? If there is no God and no immortality, you will no longer be alive to discover that fact, or anything else. So if there is no God, there is no "payoff" at the end on the "wager" for God or on the "wager" against God. You can neither gain nor lose anything if you do not exist. But if there is a God, the "wager" to believe in Him and make peace with Him during your lifetime will pay an infinite "payoff": eternal life in joy with God. The opposite "wager," to choose to think and live without God, at least *risks* losing this infinite gain. So if the evidence for God and the evidence against God are anywhere near equal

or uncertain, this practical consideration seems to decide which way it is reasonable to choose.

In other words, there are logically only four possibilities:

1. God does not exist, and you do not believe;
2. God does not exist, and you do believe;
3. God exists, and you do not believe;
4. God exists, and you do believe.

There is no chance of winning or losing the infinite prize of eternal life in either (1) or (2) because there is no such prize. The only chance of winning it is (4), and the only chance of losing it is (3). Faith is a "no-lose" bet and atheism a "no-win" bet.

If I had two sweepstakes tickets in my hat and one of them was worth a million dollars, would it be worth your while to pay a dollar for the privilege of drawing just one ticket, even though there was a 50 percent chance that it would be worth nothing? Of course. But, one may reply, what you must give up to buy the "ticket" by believing in God may be much more than a dollar. You are no longer your own god, your own lawgiver. The reply to that is first that the psychological loss in this life, the loss of ultimate autonomy over your own life, may not be a loss at all, and it may be more than compensated for by the sense of purpose and meaning that is added by adding God. Second, even if the price of the million dollar ticket is more than a dollar, the ticket is also worth much more than a million. It still comes out a good bet.

Of course, mere prudential "betting" on God is not yet love, or even faith, as distinct from belief. But it is hope. And according to the theistic hypothesis, God will honor that and bring something deeper out of it, like blowing a spark into a flame.

But what about agnosticism? Is that not a third possibility in addition to atheism and theism? Why not refuse to wager either way until the evidence is clearer? That would seem to be the more scientific attitude. The answer is, in Pascal's words, "You *must* wager. You are embarked." The ship of self is moving along the waters of time past the port of God. If it is not our true port, we should turn away; if it is our true home, we should turn to it. But why not stay anchored out at sea until the fog clears, and we can see better whether this is our true port or not? Because the fog will only clear when it is too late, after death. The ship has a finite amount of fuel. There is a point of no return. If Romeo proposed to Juliet daily, and her answer every day was neither 'Yes' nor 'No' but 'Wait,' then when she died her 'Wait' would turn into 'No.' To every question there are three possible answers: 'Yes,' 'No,' and 'Wait.' Death eliminates the third answer.

An agnostic came to the great philosopher-rabbi Martin Buber and demanded that Buber prove the existence of God to him. "You are the only believer in the world that I respect. If you do not prove to me that God exists, no one can do it, and I shall be an atheist till I die." Buber simply said that he could not prove the existence of God to him. As he turned to go, disappointed and angry, Buber shot this parting remark at him: "But can you be *sure* there is no God?" That writer wrote, many years later, autobiographically, "I still do not believe in God. But Buber's last word has haunted me every day of my life."

(4) The last and simplest experiment of all could be called "The Prayer of the Skeptic." The simplest way to test the religious hypothesis is to *pray*. Go out into the country some night, or into your back yard, where no one can hear you, and say something like this:

"God, I don't know if You exist or not. I suspect I'm only talking to a myth or to my own fantasies. But I'm not sure. So if You do exist, You must hear me now and know me and know my heart. So You know that I'm honestly seeking the truth, whatever it is. You supposedly promised that all who seek You, will find You. If You *are* the truth, I'm seeking You now, because I am seeking the truth. So please let me know that You're real, somehow, in Your own way and Your own time. Presumably, You know best how that's to be done. I'm open and ready if You are."

Who could quarrel with that experiment? It's like fairly testing the hypothesis that someone is in the closet, tied up, by knocking on the door. If the hypothesis is true, you may hear a reply. Why hesitate to knock?

The analogy is not perfect because in the case of the closet you can open the door and look with your eyes, while in the case of an invisible God you cannot. But you can still speak and listen with your mind and heart, and this constitutes a fair test, because the hypothesis maintains not only that God exists but also that this God wants to reveal Himself to you, to set up a relationship of love and faith for a lifetime and beyond.

The hypothesis claims that "all who seek, find." So test it. Seek.

I can think of only two reasons for hesitating: the fear that you will find nothing, and the fear that you will find something.

Honesty, like love, casts out fear.

APPENDIX

FACING THE
SPECIFIC
QUESTIONS

APPENDIX

Peter Kreeft

Facing the Specific Questions

In order to help the reader evaluate the debate more thoroughly, I shall enumerate the main specific questions that need to be answered, questions about which the debaters remain in disagreement, specific questions which would settle the general question of the debate—whether God exists—if they were answered one way or the other. For the sake of easy reference back to the speeches of the two debaters, I shall list the questions in the order they emerge from each speech, rather than re-ordering the questions myself in a more logical order. Dr. Craig in his essay has already done such a logical outline of the debaters' arguments anyway that I will not repeat it here. You should find his outline of the issues very helpful in sorting out the different questions and subquestions.

Moreland's First Speech (Chapter 1)

1. What exactly is the thesis Moreland is defending? He says, "The thesis I wish to defend is that it is rational to believe that God exists. I do not mean that God's existence can be proved with mathematical certainty. . . ." Where does Moreland stand on the following spectrum of opinions?

a. God's existence can be proved with mathematical certainty.
b. God's existence can be proved with non-mathematical certainty.
c. God's existence can be proved to be probable, but not certain.
d. God's existence can be proved to be possible, or not rationally impossible.
e. No proof is possible at all, but even in the absence of all proof, it is still rational to believe in God; believers are within their "epistemic rights."

Moreland seems to begin by claiming only (e), but it soon becomes evident that he is claiming either (b), (c), or (d).

It may be helpful to distinguish six questions which are easily confused with each other—six questions about anything, any x, whether God, quasars, self, snarks, or Oreo cookies:

(1) Is the sentence "x exists" logically and linguistically meaningful?
(2) If so, does x exist?
(3) If so, can we know that x exists?
(4) If so, can that knowledge be certain?
(5) If so, is there a proof of that certainty?
(6) If so, is it a mathematical or scientific proof?

(1) If x is not linguistically or logically meaningful, neither are all five subsequent questions about x. This seems to be Nielsen's basic contention regarding God.

(2) X could be meaningful without really existing—e.g., x could be Salem witches, Martians, or unicorns.

(3) X could exist without us knowing it—e.g., a certain crater on the dark side of the moon.

(4) We could know x without being certain of it—e.g., that Caesar was assassinated, or that the North Pole is still cold right now.

(5) We could be certain of x without being able to prove it—e.g., the existence of other minds, or perhaps even of our own.

(6) We could prove x without having a mathematical or scientific proof, as philosophers down through the centuries have tried to prove things—unless philosophy is folly.

Now, where does Moreland stand on this spectrum? I think he maintains that he can prove with certainty that a being exists that possesses at least some of the distinctive, unique attributes ascribed by orthodox Jews, Christians, and Muslims to God. But perhaps I am mistaken, and his claim really is as modest as it seems to be from the quotation at the beginning of this question. You decide.

2. Who has the burden of proof? Alvin Plantinga and his followers maintain that the believer has no burden of proof, for belief in God is "properly basic," and believers are within their "epistemic rights" not to give any proofs for this belief, just as those who believe there are other human minds besides their own (i.e., everyone but solipsists) need not give proofs for this "properly basic" belief. Plantinga disagrees with "Clifford's Rule," which states that everyone ought to apportion his or her beliefs to the evidence; that if there is compelling evidence, that fact justifies a sure belief, and if there is probable evidence, that fact justifies a probable belief, and if there is no evidence,

that does not justify any belief. Both Moreland and Nielsen would maintain, I think, that the believer in God, like the believer in Bigfoot or the Big Bang, has the burden of proof, for they would both (I think) agree with Clifford's Rule.

(I think Moreland would want to add the following important qualification to Clifford's Rule, however: It is right for *initially* deciding whether to believe in anything, but not always for *continuing* to believe, when there is a personal factor involved. There are personal relationships where every one admits we ought to continue to believe—for instance, that a friend or spouse is trustworthy even when strong but not conclusive evidence to the contrary seems to turn up. (See C. S. Lewis's essay "On Obstinacy in Belief" in his *Christian Reflections*.)

If either Nielsen or Moreland believed that believers were not rationally obliged to give reasons for their faith, I do not see how they would still have been able and willing to debate as they did.

The Bible itself seems to address this issue in 1 Peter 3:15, in which believers are commanded to give reasons, at least to unbelievers. (And if believers do not first give reasons to themselves, how can they give them to others?)

3. Moreland made many points; Nielsen essentially only one. Craig argues, at the beginning of his response paper (Chapter 11), that Moreland clearly won the debate because he answered all of Nielsen's arguments while Nielsen answered few of Moreland's. Does Craig mean to say merely that Moreland put forward *more* unanswered arguments than Nielsen did? If so, does he mean to imply that all you need to do to win a debate is to come up with more arguments, quantitatively, than your opponent? If not this, then what?

Nielsen's strategy was to put all his eggs in one basket and charge Moreland with linguistic sins, or at least "irregularities." Thus, he did not directly answer many of Moreland's arguments. To complete the score card, the reader should ask: (1) Which of Moreland's arguments *did* Nielsen address successfully? (2) Which did he address unsuccessfully? (3) Which did he not address at all? Also, of the arguments in (2) and (3), which of them, if any, did Flew and/or Parsons answer successfully in their response papers (Chapters 12 and 13)?

4. Did Moreland's strategic decision to mention, however briefly, archeological evidence for the trustworthiness of the Bible and also his own religious experience add to the evidence for his case, or did it distract from it? Why?

5. Moreland also argued for Christ's divinity and resurrection. Was this relevant evidence for his thesis that God exists, or not? Should one say yes, because if Christ really resurrected, this miracle proves his divinity, and if Christ is God, then God exists? Or should one say it is not logically pertinent, because history is not an exact science and no historical event can be quite certain?

Why did neither Nielsen nor Parsons address this question of Christ's resurrection? Flew did, briefly—only briefly because he argued the issue at great length against Gary Habermas at Liberty University in debate on another occasion. The reader is referred to this debate, published by Harper & Row under the title *Did Jesus Rise from the Dead?*

6. Moreland concentrated on two cosmological arguments: the argument from design and the *kalam* (time) argument. Is Flew right in contending (in Chapter 12) that choosing the *kalam* argument was bad strategy because it tried to prove too much, more than could be proved? Thomas Aquinas thought so. He thought one could prove that the universe required God as a First Cause, but not that this "first" could be proved by reason alone to be temporally first—that God created the world in time, that God had created a universe with a finite time span—because God *could* have created a universe with an infinite time span. Which is the stronger strategy, Moreland's or Aquinas's? Did the *kalam* argument prove its conclusion? Did Nielsen refute it?

Nielsen's First Speech (Chapter 2)

1. Both debaters accept "the grand tradition of natural theology." Nielsen says that this tradition is rare and dying today; that few Christians today, especially Christian philosophers, still believe you can give rational arguments, even probable ones, for the existence of God. Is this true? If anyone does not know the answer to this question and wants to know, it can be found by a brief research foray into *Books In Print*, "Subject" volume, under "Apologetics."

2. Nielsen argues that Moreland must mean by "God" either (1) something meaningful and identifiable but obviously false, like Zeus, or (2) something not obviously false but also not meaningful or identifiable—an eternal, infinite, transcendent being. Everyone in this debate, in fact everyone in the world today, seems to accept, without ever questioning it, the assumption that "anthropomorphic" gods like

Zeus do not exist and never did. How do we know this? Can this be proved?

3. *Why* did Nielsen use his "all eggs in one basket" strategy? Was it because his one argument was adequate and unanswerable? Or was it because he had no other answers to Moreland's arguments? Does the text of the debate answer this question, or must we play amateur psychologist and guess?

4. Nielsen contended that Moreland could give no ostensive definition (referent) to "God," and Moreland contended that religious experience provided such a referent. In other words, Nielsen said "God" was in principle not a being you could *meet* and Moreland replied that he had really met Him. How can this difference be resolved?

5. How can one "identify" God? Why does not Nielsen accept the common-sensical answer that "God" is a very distinctive concept and could not be confused with anything else because *only* God is infinitely powerful, good, wise, etc.? What would Nielsen say to Thomas Aquinas's answer (*Summa* I, 14) that though "God" cannot be defined, He can be meaningfully "identified" as (1) the efficient *cause* of the universe, (2) *not* possessing any of the limitations or imperfections in the universe (such as ignorance, sin, death, or movement from or to less perfect states), (3) *analogous* to perfections in the universe, somewhat as "good man" is analogous to "good doggy," and (4) as *more* perfect than anything in the universe?

6. Is Nielsen's claim that God and God's attributes are logically *meaningless* or just that they are (as he says) "linguistic irregularities"? Is he prescribing linguistic Ex-Lax? The claim that God-talk is *meaningless* seems too strong, as Flew admits in his response paper; for this was the claim of A. J. Ayer's *Language, Truth and Logic* and of early Logical Positivism, which had to be modified because its strictures on meaning were so strict as to be self-excluding and self-contradictory. Its "Verification Principle," which stipulated that all propositions which were not either empirically verifiable or tautologies were meaningless, was neither empirically verifiable nor a tautology, therefore it was meaningless by its own criterion. But the weaker claim, that "God-talk" is merely "linguistically irregular," does not seem very damaging; many meaningful expressions are linguistically irregular (e.g., exclamatory sentences). Presumably Nielsen wants to stand somewhere between these two extremes, one too strong and one too weak, perhaps

with Flew's more serious challenge (as it seems to me) that the existence of God is not a legitimate notion because it is not *in principle falsifiable*. That is, the believer will not accept any possible state of affairs as disproving God. (See John Wisdom's famous paper, "Gods.") Did Moreland say anything which would indicate how he would respond to this challenge of Flew's?

7. Is it an intellectual cop-out to say that we should not *expect* "God-talk" to be clear or reasonable because God is a "mystery"? Would Moreland agree with Nielsen's statement that "some minimal understanding is necessary for faith to be possible"? Could anyone disagree with that? Why or why not?

8. Is God observable or detectable in any way? Nielsen argues that He is not, and therefore He is not identifiable. "Identifiable" seems to be a slightly weakened form of "meaningful." Nielsen seems to be saying God-talk is not really meaningful because God is not in principle knowable as an object. Moreland replies, in effect, that this conclusion follows from the premise *only if* we assume the second premise that whatever is in principle not knowable in this way is meaningless. He goes on to argue that this premise is false because there are some things, like the chemical processes in my brain, that are meaningful but not in principle knowable in the way Nielsen means, namely observable, detectable. This criterion of *observability* seems to be a slightly weakened form of "empirically verifiable," just as "not identifiable" seems to be a slightly weakened form of "meaningless," so that Nielsen seems to be arguing essentially in the same way as the Logical Positivists.

Well, *are* the chemical processes in my brain unobservable in principle (by anyone, ever) or only contingently (by me, now)? Is God unobservable in principle (by anyone, ever) or only contingently (by us, now)? Would Moreland say we can see God after death? (See Aquinas, *Summa Theologica* I, 12, esp. 3, ad 2, where he says we can "see" God after death as we "see" life now, as an indirect object.)

Nielsen contends that "you can't encounter a transcendent being." Does Nielsen restrict "encounter" to "empirically encounter"? Are there any other things besides God that people claim to "encounter" nonempirically? e.g., other human minds?

9. Would Moreland agree with Nielsen's statement that "we have no understanding of what it is for an individual . . . to be eternal, such that it could not *not* exist in any possible world"? Is this concept of a

"necessary being" a "category confusion" as the Logical Positivists claimed? Their argument was that only *propositions* can properly be said to be necessary or contingent (a necessary proposition is a tautology, or at least one true in all possible worlds, one whose contradictory is intrinsically impossible or self-contradictory), but real beings cannot be said to be necessary or contingent (nonnecessary). Is this contention (1) self-evidently true, (2) an arbitrary and unjustifiable restriction, or (3) arguable? If (3), how?

10. Nielsen says, "Suppose I ask you to believe in poy, an utterly nonsensical term . . . But I can't tell you what poy is. You can't in that circumstance, no matter how much you want to, believe in poy or have faith in poy." The implication is that since no one can tell you what God is, you can't really (meaningfully) believe in God. Would Moreland accept Nielsen's quotation as a premise and conclude instead that since people do meaningfully believe in God, therefore they must be able to tell you what God is? If so, why can't Moreland tell Nielsen what God is to Nielsen's satisfaction? Moreland argues that "it seems . . . preposterous and prima facie odd to say that 99.9 percent of the entire human race has literally not known what they were talking about when they used the word 'God.'" Must Nielsen believe that? Is it preposterous?

Moreland's Second Speech (Chapter 3)

1. How closely does Moreland connect his position to Platonism?

2. Do we see the Platonic Form or timeless type of redness itself, or only a material thing with the quality red? How does this question logically relate to the argument about whether "God" is meaningful?

3. Does Nielsen commit what Moreland calls the "centipede fallacy"? Can we know what love, or time, or God is without being able to give a satisfactory reflective account or definition of it? Can knowledge be meaningful without being clear, true without being adequate, rational without being defined? Can we know what a thing is without being able to give an account of it? If so, why does Nielsen think we can't? If not, why does Moreland think we can?

4. How do you evaluate Moreland's argument from the fact that the human brain works to give us true knowledge of the universe, to the existence of something such as God (a version of the argument from design)? His argument claims that we must posit an intelligent and

trustable Designer to account for the fact that reason knows truth. (See C. S. Lewis, *Miracles*, Chap. 3, for a longer version of this argument.) If we look at the brain as analogous to a computer, the argument asks why we should trust it if its programmer was only blind, unintelligent chance, rather than an intelligent superhuman mind guiding whatever cosmic forces brought it into being by evolutionary stages. Why would we trust a computer programmed by a random fall of hailstones on its keyboard?

The atheist or agnostic usually replies that "natural selection" has worked for the "survival of the fittest" without requiring any intelligence behind the process. And the theist argues back that (1) "survival of the fittest" is self-referential, circular, or tautological since the "fittest" are identified as such only by their survival, and that (2) truth is not necessary for survival, only consistency. (See endnote 13 of Chap. 3, Moreland's second speech.) How would the argument continue from that point?

Nielsen's Second Speech (Chapter 4)

1. How can Nielsen be "not terribly interested in" whether Jesus rose from the dead or not? If the resurrection is a myth or a lie, is it not at least a very interesting one, especially if many people believe it literally and base their lives on it? Moreland points out that most people find *Nielsen*'s issue boring—the issue about whether "God-talk" is linguistically and logically meaningful and proper or not. For that issue, unlike the issue of the resurrection of Jesus, is a technical and "second-order" question about language, rather than a concrete and "first-order" question about real events. If you feel as Nielsen does about which question is more interesting, why do you think most people feel the opposite? If you feel as Moreland does, why do you think Nielsen feels as he does?

In Samuel Beckett's nihilistic, agnostic classic "Waiting for Godot," two tramps who spend a meaningless life doing nothing but waiting for a God who never comes argue about the two thieves who were crucified with Christ. One is very interested in the fact that one of the two, the "good thief," repented before he died and was saved, because if the story is true, it suggests they have one in two chances of being saved. The other, however, can find no more meaning in the story, and in the whole Bible, than the pretty colors he remembers from the Bible maps. Do Moreland and Nielsen correspond to these two attitudes? Are they irreconcilable? Are they arguable? Pascal, for one, tries to argue about it. See the challenging section in the *Pensees* "Against Indifference."

2. Nielsen says he does not claim that all God-talk is simply meaningless, but he does say that "we literally don't know what we are talking about" when we talk about God. Is there a difference between these two claims? If so, what is it?

3. How does Nielsen distinguish between "identifying," "defining" and "pointing to" something? Is "identifying" the generic term here? If so, is there a third subdivision of "identifying" in addition to ordinary "defining" (which, since a definition must be logically convertible, is presumably tautological), and "pointing," or "ostensive definition" (which presumably, is empirical)? If there is not any third possibility, is this not simply the old Verification Principle again? If there is a third possibility, a third kind of "identifying," what is it and could it include God?

Or might the identification of God be by a definition but not by a definition by genus, since God has no genus, but only by difference in the form of negation: infinite (not finite), eternal (not temporal), etc.? Or perhaps a nonempirical ostensive (pointing) identification? Is that what Moreland answers?

4. Why does Nielsen think that even if it were possible to "identify" God, this would not link us up with Jesus and the claim that He rose from death? Would Nielsen accept the seemingly-obvious linkage that if Jesus, who claimed to be God, really rose from the dead, that that is evidence for the truth of the claim, and if the claim is true, then there is indeed a God? See the Flew-Habermas debate *(Did Jesus Rise from the Dead?)* on this. Consult also my *Between Heaven and Hell* (InterVarsity Press) on the logic of the argument about Jesus' claim to divinity.

Nielsen's Third Speech (Chapter 5)

1. *Why* does Nielsen think that "there couldn't be a nonsensory awareness of an infinite eternal God transcendent to the universe"? What does Moreland reply?

2. Does Nielsen presuppose empiricism when he says (in Chap. 7) that "the only models we have for self-authenticating experi-

ences are things like headaches or sensations" (and *not* consciousness)?

3. In the audience participation section of the debate, Nielsen says he has the same difficulty understanding the coherence or meaningfulness of immortality—a disembodied soul—as he has understanding the meaningfulness of God. Is *this* empiricism? How would he explain the apparent ability of nearly everyone to at least conceive and understand this thought, whether they believe it true or not, and even to write stories about it?

Moreland's Third Speech (Chapter 6)

1. What does Moreland claim is distinctive about Christianity? Does this answer Nielsen's "Comparative Religions" challenge adequately (see Chaps. 4 and 5)?

2. Is Moreland arguing for Christianity specifically or for a generic theism common to orthodox Judaism, Christianity, and Islam? How would a Jew or a Moslem explain Moreland's personal experience of Christ? Of God? How would Nielsen?

Nielsen's Speech on Ethics (Chapter 8)

1. The "divine command theory" of morality, which both debaters reject, was stated by Euthyphro in Plato's dialogue by that name. For Euthyphro, an act was right or wrong only because the gods commanded or forbade it. Socrates easily refutes this theory by pointing out that the gods contradict themselves, thus the same act is simultaneously right and wrong by the standard of different gods. But if we substitute only one God who never contradicts Himself for the many Greek gods who do, why is the divine command theory still untenable? Moreland implicitly accepts Nielsen's argument against it. However, many, especially Calvinists, would accept that theory and try to answer Nielsen's argument against it.

(a) What is Nielsen's argument against the divine command theory? (b) Why does Moreland accept this argument and believe a natural law theory instead? (c) How would a Calvinist answer Nielsen's argument? (d) How adequate is that answer?

2. Moreland's answer to Socrates' dilemma "Is something good because God wills it, or does God will it because it is good?" is: nei-

ther. Goodness is based on God's *nature*. (See the example of Chicago in Chap. 10.) Nielsen contends that this is still circular, just as the divine command theory is, for it (a) bases morality on religion—goodness reflects the nature of God—and (b) bases religion on morality—God is to be trusted and obeyed *because* He is good. How would Moreland escape this charge of circularity?

3. Dostoyevski wrote, "If God does not exist, everything is permissible." Would Moreland agree with this?

Is Moreland's contention merely that "Christian theism is a background theory (cosmology or metaphysics) that makes the existence and knowability of morality more likely than does the background theory of atheism," or is it something more, namely the moral argument for God's existence? One form of the moral argument begins with Dostoyevski's premise ("If God does not exist, everything is permissible"), adds that *not* everything is permissible, and concludes that God must exist. Ivan Karamazov, Dostoyevski's atheistic character in *The Brothers Karamazov,* concludes instead that since God does not in fact exist, everything *is* permissible. Both Nietzsche and Sartre follow Ivan's reasoning. Why doesn't Nielsen?

4. Nielsen contends not only that God is not logically necessary for morality, but that God is psychologically harmful to morality, for faith and hope in God keep humanity from maturity, self-reliance, and independence. This is a very common claim among modern atheists. How can it be fairly evaluated? What would one look at to decide?

5. Nielsen claims there can be purpose *in* life without any overall purpose *to* life—there can be short-range purposes without any overall, long-range purpose. The same applies to immortality and to God: the theist claims that both God and immortality are necessary to give purpose to human life, because if the end is nothingness, then all the means to that end become meaningless, merely steps to the abyss. (In the words of *Waiting for Godot,* "they give birth astride a grave.") Theists like Moreland and existentialist atheists like Beckett both say they do not or would not find life's short-range ends meaningful without a long-range final end; while humanistic atheists like Nielsen say they still find meaning *in* life without any purpose *to* life. Is there any way to argue about this issue logically and objectively rather than psychologically and subjectively?

6. If there is no God and no immortality, is there *less* love between people, as Moreland would claim, or *more,* as Nielsen would claim?

Stephen Crane's short story "The Open Boat" takes Nielsen's position, and Dostoyevski's *The Brothers Karamazov* takes Moreland's position. Camus's *The Plague* seems undecided about the possibility of morality and love without God. Its hero, Camus's mouthpiece the agnostic Dr. Rieux, knows he must fight "the plague" (evil) with or without God, and he does, heroically. But he agonizes over the question "How can one be a saint without God?" Nielsen refers to this book when he says we can still "fight the plague" without God. But Sartre, in "Existentialism and Humanism," says that "the existentialist, on the contrary [as vs. the humanist], finds it very distressing that God does not exist, for all possibility of finding meaning in some heaven of Ideas disappears along with God. There can no longer be any *a priori* Good because there is no infinite and perfect consciousness to think it."

Thus we seem to have four possible positions:

(a) The divine command theory: there is a God, there is a moral law, and God is the only possible basis for the moral law.

(b) Moreland's traditional Natural Law Theory: there is a God, there is a moral law, and God is in fact the basis for morality, but (1) not through His unknowable will but through His knowable nature, and (2) we can *know* the effect (the moral law) without *knowing* the cause (God), just as we can know God's effects in physical nature by science without knowing their divine creative cause. But knowledge of God makes morality much more explainable and is the only adequate answer to the question of morality's ultimate basis.

(c) Existential atheism (Ivan Karamazov, Sartre): since there is no God, there is no real moral law, only arbitrary man-made rules of the man-made moral game.

(d) Humanism, whether atheistic (Nielsen) or theistic (Kant): morality is self-justifying, for human persons are ends in themselves, intrinsically valuable.

Would Moreland argue against position (d) that God is the *only possible* rationally adequate explanation of *why* all people are intrinsically valuable—namely that they are made in God's image? Or would he claim only that God is only the *best* "background explanation" for this morality?

Might someone argue that belief in God, far from *grounding* morality, actually *contradicts* the morality of each person as intrinsically valuable and as an end in him/herself? For if God is the only absolute, can each individual also be absolute in value? How would Moreland reply to this question?

Moreland's Speech on Ethics (Chapter 9)

1. Moreland argues that if there is no God, then "the same process that coughed up human beings coughed up amoebas." In other words, if we are not made in the image of King God, we are made in the image of King Kong. So what? What follows from this? What difference must it make to morality?

2. One answer Moreland gives to question 1 is that "if we are mere creatures of matter . . . it is hard to see how we could ever have the requisite freedom to be morally responsible." Must a metaphysical materialist be a psychological determinist? And must an atheist be a materialist? Must therefore an atheist be a determinist? Moreland argues that atheism logically entails materialism, materialism determinism, and determinism the loss of moral responsibility. How would Nielsen reply to this *reductio ad absurdum* argument?

3. Moreland argues that one must have some objective cosmological or metaphysical basis for morality; that what we are morally obligated to *do* depends on what we *are*, where we come from, what our end and purpose is, and what our real, objective value is. Nielsen would argue that this is the fallacy of trying to derive an "ought" from an "is," thus smuggling more into your conclusion than you had in your premises. Both arguments seem to make an obvious point, but at least one must be wrong. Which, and where?

4. Are moral propositions like "Mercy as such is good" synthetic a priori propositions? If so, how do we know them? (See Chap. 9, endnote 6.) Moreland's answer is that we know them by intellectual intuition, or intuitive understanding—something Kant denied existed, and something which does not fit into either of the two categories of meaningful propositions (the empirically verifiable and the tautological) according to Positivism. Is this why Nielsen rejects such knowledge? Is Nielsen presupposing the Verification Principle in practice, if not in theory?

5. Would Platonism be a viable alternative to both theism and atheism in accounting for moral absolutes (as Platonic Forms—divine Ideas without a divine mind)? Could an atheist be a Platonist? Could a theist be a Platonist? Could the two agree about morality on a Platonic level without agreeing about God? If so, does that mean God is dispensable, not indispensable, to morality?

6. If the universe is merely the sum of all facts, and facts do not include values, then where do we get values from? If we make them up, why are they really binding, and how can our opinions about them be either true or false? For example, why is someone who believes that cruelty is better than kindness *wrong*? If we don't make up values but discover them as objective truths, where are they, or where do they come from, or where do we get them from? Five possible answers to this last question are:

(a) God alone, by His will, creates values (the divine command theory);
(b) God's nature is the standard of values, and the human soul, made in the image of God, is the natural basis for a "natural law" morality;
(c) values are Platonic Forms;
(d) values are certain facts: "The thing that is intrinsically valuable . . . is an ideal form of DNA molecules (i.e., human beings);"
(e) values are subjectively invented by human beings, either individually (as in Sartre) or culturally (as in John Dewey).

What are the strengths and weaknesses of each of these explanations of our awareness of values?

7. Moreland criticizes Nielsen's "optimistic humanism" as arbitrary, as giving no answer to the crucial question: *Why* should I be altruistic rather than egotistic? Does Nielsen have any answer to this question? See Chapter 9, endnote 10, and Nielsen's response in the discussion in Chapter 10. Does Nielsen give a logical answer, or only a practical, pragmatic one? Does Nielsen say there is any ontological, metaphysical, objective basis for morality at all? If so, what is it? If not, does he give any reason for putting that question aside? If not, is this "putting aside" simply arbitrary?

8. In his *Republic*, Plato gives an answer to the question *Why* be moral? Why not use the "Ring of Gyges" (power) unjustly if you can get away with it? He did this without bringing in gods or life after death (until his argument was all over, in Book 10). His argument was essentially that justice is health and harmony of soul, and is thus always more profitable than injustice, as health is more profitable than disease. Would Nielsen agree with this essential argument of Plato's *Republic*?

Would Moreland? It is a natural law morality, so how could Nielsen agree with it? It is a morality without God, so how could Moreland?

9. Nielsen seems to take a lead from Kant rather than from Plato in referring to people as a "kingdom of ends" and in contending that that is an adequate basis for a morality of obligation to treat them well. Is the criterion of moral worth, then, the membership in the human *species,* or is it the possession of *intelligence?* Would an intelligent, non-human extraterrestrial have the same moral rights as we? Would a severely retarded human? If the criterion of moral worth is intelligence, does that mean the more intelligent have more moral worth? That the intrinsically valuable thing is I.Q.? If not, if it is not intelligence but membership in the human species that confers intrinsic moral value as an end on each person, then is this not mere species-egotism or species-prejudice? Wouldn't donkeys say the same about their species? (See Chap. 9, endnote 3.) How would Nielsen answer these questions? How would Moreland?

10. In Chapter 10, Nielsen maintains that "Hitler was a vile man" is not the same kind of sentence as "Snow is white" because "it isn't quite so clear what [the statement about Hitler] refers to." Is it clear to Moreland? If so, why isn't it clear to Nielsen? (Cf. question 4 above.)

Conclusions

In general, the two debaters' strategies ran the danger of avoiding direct contact with each other, for Moreland's arguments were usually factual (Big Bang, Anthropic Principle, historical evidence for Jesus' resurrection, encountering God in religious experience) while Nielsen's objections were linguistic (how can we "identify" God?). Were their strategies the best for this debate? Would Moreland have weakened or strengthened his case if he had concentrated on linguistic answers as much as Nielsen concentrated on linguistic questions? Would Nielsen have weakened or strengthened his case if he had concentrated on factual, onotological answers to Moreland's challenges?

The two concluding questions of judgment are not *necessarily* related: (1) Which debater won? (2) Which position won? You decide, but do so in the best spirit of this debate—with good reasons supporting your decision.

BIBLIOGRAPHY

Atheism

Atheism in General

Edwards, Paul. "Atheism," *Encyclopedia of Philosophy*.

Flew, Antony. *The Presumption of Atheism*. New York: Barnes and Noble, 1976.

Hepburn, Ronald W. "Agnosticism," *Encyclopedia of Philosophy*.

Martin, Michael. *Atheism: A Philosophical Justification*. Philadelphia: Temple University Press, 1990.

Nielsen, Kai. "Agnosticism," *Dictionary of the History of Ideas*, ed. P. P. Wiener. Scribner's, 17–27.

———. "Atheism," *Encyclopedia Britannica* (1983).

———. "In Defense of Atheism," *Perspectives in Education, Religion and the Arts*, ed. H. Kiefer and M. Munitz. New York, 1970.

———. "Philosophy and Atheism—Again," *Teaching Philosophy* 10:3 (September 1987).

———. *Philosophy and Atheism: In Defense of Atheism*. Buffalo, N.Y.: Prometheus Books, 1985.

Stein, Gordon, ed. *An Anthology of Atheism and Rationalism*. Buffalo, N.Y.: Prometheus Books, 1980.

Atheism and Morality

Nielsen, Kai. *Ethics Without God*, second edition, revised and expanded with new chapters. Buffalo, N.Y.: Prometheus Books, 1989.

———. *God and the Grounding of Morality*. Ottawa: University of Ottawa Press, 1991.

———. "On Sticking with Secular Morality," *Religion and Irreligion*, ed. Hugo Meynell. Calgary, Alb.: University of Calgary Press, 1985.

———. "On 'The Meaning of Life'," *Religion and Human Purpose*, ed. C. Hovosz. Martinus Nijhoff, 1984.

——. "Religion and the Grounds of Moral Belief," *New Zealand Rationalist and Humanist* XXXVIII, 8 (May 1977). Also in *Religious Humanism* 11:1 (Winter 1977).

——. "Some Remarks on the Independence of Morality from Religion," *Mind* 70 (April 1961). Reprinted in *Contemporary Philosophy and Christian Morality,* ed. I. T. Ramsay. London, 1966; in *Modern Critical Readings in the Philosophy of Religion,* ed. P. Angeles, Basic Books; and in *Readings in Ethics,* ed. W. Frankena and W. Granrose. New York: Prentice-Hall, 1974.

——. *Why Be Moral?* Buffalo, N.Y.: Prometheus Books, 1989.

General Critiques of Religion

Carnap, Rudolph. "The Elimination of Metaphysics Through Logical Analysis of Language," *Logical Positivism,* ed. A. J. Ayer. Glencoe, Ill.: The Free Press, 1959, 66–67.

Edwards, P. and Pap, A., eds. *A Modern Introduction to Philosophy,* first edition. Glencoe, Ill.: The Free Press, 1957; third edition, New York: Macmillan, 1973.

Flew, Antony. *God and Philosophy.* London: Hutchinson, 1966.

Hägerström, Axel. *Philosophy and Religion,* transl. Robert T. Sandin. London: Allen and Unwin, 1964.

Johnson, B. C. *The Atheist Debater's Handbook.* Buffalo, N.Y.: Prometheus Books, 1983.

MacIntyre, Alasdair. *Difficulties in Christian Belief.* London: SCM Press, 1956.

——. "The Logical Status of Religious Belief," *Metaphysical Beliefs,* ed. S. Toulmin, et al. London: SCM Press, 1957, 169–211.

Mackie, J. L. *The Miracle of Theism.* Oxford: Clarendon Press, 1982.

Martin, C.B. *Religious Belief.* Ithaca, N.Y.: Cornell University Press, 1959.

Nielsen, Kai. *Contemporary Critiques of Religion.* New York: Herder and Herder, 1971.

——. *God, Scepticism and Modernity.* Ottawa: University of Ottawa Press, 1989.

——. *An Introduction to the Philosophy of Religion.* New York: Macmillan, 1982.

——. "On Speaking of God," *Theoria* XXVIII (1962). Reprinted in *Analytical Philosophy of Religion in Canada,* ed. M. Faghfoury. Ottawa: University of Ottawa Press, 1992.

——. *Scepticism*. New York: St. Martin's Press, 1973.

——. "A Sceptic's Reply," *Faith and the Philosophers*, ed. J. Hick. New York: St. Martin's Press, 1964.

Penelhum, Terence. *Problems of Religious Knowledge*. London: Macmillan Press, 1971.

Reason and Belief

Hepburn, Ronald W. *Christianity and Paradox*. London: Watts, 1958.

Nielsen, Kai. "Faith and Authority," *Open Mind* (1979). With an ending exchange with S. Brown.

——. "God and The Self," *Journal of Religion* (October 1973).

——. "Religion and Groundless Believing," *The Autonomy of Religious Belief*, ed. F. Crosson. Notre Dame, Ind.: University of Notre Dame Press, 1981.

——. "Religion and Modern Predicament," *The Humanist* (1958).

——. "Religious Perplexity and Faith," *Crane Review* VIII: 1 (Fall 1965).

——. "Skepticism and Belief," *Dialogue* 22 (1983).

——. "Wittgensteinian Fideism," *Philosophy* 42 (July 1967).

Nielsen, Kai, and Hart, Hendrik. *Search for Community in a Withering Tradition: Conversations between a Marxian Atheist and a Calvinian Christian*. Toronto, Canada: Lanham University Press of America, 1990.

Pojman, Louis, ed. *Philosophy of Religion*. Belmont, Calif.: Wadsworth, 1987.

Reardon, Bernard M. G., ed. *Religious Thought in the Nineteenth Century*. Cambridge: Cambridge University Press, 1966.

Science and Belief

Newton-Smith, W. H. *The Rationality of Science*. London: Routledge and Kegan Paul, 1981.

Parsons, Keith. *Science, Confirmation and the Theistic Hypothesis*. New York: Peter Lang, 1990.

Toulmin, Stephen. "Contemporary Scientific Mythology," *Metaphysical Beliefs*, ed. S. Toulmin. London: SCM Press, 1957, 13–81.

The Concept of God

Edwards, Paul. "Difficulties in the Idea of God," *The Idea of God*, ed.

Edward H. Madden. Springfield, Ill.: Charles C. Thomas, 1968, 43–97.

Nielsen, Kai. "God and Postulated Entities," *Southern Journal of Philosophy* (Summer 1974).

——. "God as a Human Projection," *The Lockhaven Review* 9 (1967).

——. "The Intelligibility of God-Talk," *Religious Studies* 6 (1970).

——. "Is God So Powerful that He Doesn't Have to Exist?" *Religious Experience and Truth*, ed. S. Hook. New York: New York University Press, 1961.

——. "Reductionism and Religious Truth Claims," *Dialogos* (1976).

——. "Religion and Ideology," *Sophia* (1983).

Wisdom, John. "Gods," *Philosophy and Psycho-Analysis*, ed. J. Wisdom. Oxford: Blackwell, 1953.

——. "The Modes of Thought and the Logic of God," *The Existence of God*, ed. John Hick. New York: Macmillan, 1964, 275–298.

Ziff, Paul. "About God," *Religious Experience and Truth*, ed. S. Hook. New York: New York University Press, 1961, 195–202.

The Existence of God

Malcolm, Norman. "Anselm's Ontological Argument," *The Existence of God*, ed. John Hick. London: Collier-Macmillan, 1965, 48–70.

Matson, Wallace. *The Existence of God*. Ithaca, N.Y.: Cornell University Press, 1959.

Nielsen, Kai. "Eschatological Verification," *Canadian Journal of Theology* 11:14 (1962). Reprinted in *The Logic of God*, ed. M. Diamond and P. Litzenburg. Bobbs-Merrill, 1974; in *Philosophy of Religion*, ed. S. M. Cahn. New York: Harper & Row, 1970; and in *Philosophy of Religion: A Book of Readings*, second edition, ed. G. L. Abernathy and T. A. Langford. New York: Macmillan, 1968.

——. "A False Move in Reasoning About God," *Understanding* (1975).

——. "God and Verification Again," *Canadian Journal of Theology* 11:2 (1965). Reprinted in *The Logic of God*, ed. M. Diamond and P. Litzenburg. Bobbs-Merrill, 1974.

——. *Reason and Practice*. New York: Harper & Row, 1971.

Parsons, Keith. *God and the Burden of Proof*. Buffalo, N.Y.: Prometheus Books, 1989.

Penelhum, Terence. *Religion and Rationality*. New York: Random House, 1971.

Scriven, Michael. *Primary Philosophy*. New York: McGraw-Hill, 1966.

Religious Language

Nielsen, Kai. "Can Faith Validate God-talk?" *Theology Today* (July 1963). Reprinted in *New Theology*, ed. M. Marty and D. Peerman. Collier-Macmillan, 1964; and in *Philosophy and Religion: Some Contemporary Perspectives*, ed. J. Gill. Burgess Press, 1968.

———. "Religion and Rationality," *Analytical Philosophy of Religion in Canada*, ed. M. Faghfoury. Ottawa: University of Ottawa Press, 1982.

Religious Experience

Nielsen, Kai. "Christian Positivism and the Appeal to Religious Experience," *The Journal of Religion* 42 (October 1962).

Otto, Rudolf. *The Idea of the Holy*, transl. J. W. Harvey. Oxford: Oxford University Press, 1923.

Resurrection and Immortality

Brown, Raymond E. *The Virginal Conception and Bodily Resurrection of Jesus*. New York: Paulist Press, 1973.

Fuller, Reginald H. *The Formation of the Resurrection Narratives*. New York: Macmillan, 1971.

Marxsen, Willi. *The Resurrection of Jesus of Nazareth*. Philadelphia: Fortress Press.

Naland, John K. "The First Easter: The Evidence for the Resurrection Evaluated," *Free Inquiry* 3:2 (Spring 1988).

Nielsen, Kai. "The Faces of Immortality," *Death and Afterlife*, ed. John Hick. London: Macmillan, 1990.

———. "God, Disembodied Existence and Incoherence," *Sophia* 26:3 (October 1987).

———. "Inconceivability and Immortality," *Death and Afterlife*, ed. John Hick. London: Macmillan, 1990.

The Bible

Hayes, John H. *Introduction to the Bible*. Philadelphia: Westminster Press, 1971.

Helms, Randel. *Gospel Fictions*. Buffalo, N.Y.: Prometheus Books, 1989.

Hoffmann, R. Joseph. "The Origins of Christianity: A Guide to Answering Fundamentalists," *Free Inquiry* 5:2 (Spring 1985).

Christian Theism

General Works on the Existence of God

Audi, Robert, and Wainwright, William J., eds. *Rationality, Religious Belief, and Moral Commitment*. Ithaca, N.Y.: Cornell University Press, 1986.

Collins, James. *God in Modern Philosophy*. Chicago: Henry Regnery Company, 1959.

Ewing, A. C. *Value and Reality*. London: George Allen and Unwin, 1973.

Geisler, Norman L., and Corduan, Winfried. *Philosophy of Religion*. 2d ed. Grand Rapids, Mich.: Baker, 1989.

Grisez, Germain. *Beyond the New Theism: A Philosophy of Religion*. Notre Dame: University of Notre Dame Press, 1975.

Moreland, J. P. *Scaling the Secular City*. Grand Rapids, Mich.: Baker, 1987.

Nash, Ronald H. *Faith and Reason*. Grand Rapids, Mich.: Zondervan, 1988.

Swinburne, Richard. *The Existence of God*. Oxford: Clarendon Press, 1979.

Yandell, Keith E. *Christianity and Philosophy*. Grand Rapids, Mich.: Eerdmans, 1984.

The Cosmological Argument

Craig, William Lane. *The Kalam Cosmological Argument*. N.Y.: Macmillan, 1979.

Reichenbach, Bruce R. *The Cosmological Argument: A Reassessment*. Springfield, Ill.: Charles C. Thomas Publishers, 1972.

Rowe, William L. *The Cosmological Argument*. Princeton: Princeton University Press, 1975.

The Design Argument

Clark, Robert E. D. *The Universe: Plan or Accident?* Grand Rapids, Mich.: Zondervan, 1949.

Horigan, James E. *Chance or Design?* N.Y.: Philosophical Library, 1979.

Leslie, John. *Universes*. New York: Routledge, 1989.

McPherson, Thomas. *The Argument from Design*. London: Macmillan, 1972.

Tennant, F. R. *Philosophical Theology*. Vol. 2: *The World, the Soul, and God*. Cambridge: Cambridge University Press, 1956.

The Moral Argument

Adams, Robert M. *The Virtue of Faith*. N.Y.: Oxford University Press, 1987. Chapters 7–12.

Helm, Paul. ed. *Divine Commands and Morality*. N.Y.: Oxford University Press, 1981.

Lewis, C. S. *Mere Christianity*. N.Y.: Macmillan, 1943; rev. ed., 1952.

Mavrodes, George I. "Religion and the Queerness of Morality." In *Rationality, Religious Belief, and Moral Commitment*, 213–26. edited by Robert Audi and William J. Wainwright, Ithaca, N.Y.: Cornell University Press, 1986.

Mitchell, Basil. *Morality: Religious and Secular*. Oxford: Clarendon Press, 1980.

Owen, H. P. *The Moral Argument for Christian Theism*. London: Allen and Unwin, 1965.

Sorley, W. R. *Moral Values and the Idea of God*. Cambridge: Cambridge University Press, 1981.

Religious Experience

Evans, C. Stephen. *Subjectivity and Religious Belief*. Grand Rapids, Mich.: Eerdmans, 1978.

Gutting, Gary. *Religious Belief and Religious Skepticism*. Notre Dame: University of Notre Dame Press, 1982.

James, William. *The Varieties of Religious Experience*. N.Y.: Modern Library, 1902.

Long, Eugene Thomas, ed. *Experience Reason, and God*. Washington, D.C.: The Catholic University of America Press, 1980.

Sherry, Patrick. *Spirit, Saints,* and *Immortality*. Albany, N.Y.: State University of New York Press, 1984.

Underhill, Evelyn. *Mysticism*. N.Y.: New American Library, 1955.

Wainwright, William J. *Mysticism: A Study of its Nature, Cognitive Value and Moral Implications*. Madison: University of Wisconsin Press, 1981.

——. *Philosophy of Religion*. Belmont, Ca.: Wadsworth, 1988. Chapter 5.

Religious Belief and Evidence

Geehan, E. R. ed. *Jerusalem and Athens*. Grand Rapids, Mich.: Presbyterian and Reformed, 1974.

Kennedy, Leonard A. *Thomistic Papers IV*. Houston: Center for Thomistic Studies, 1988.

Plantinga, Alvin, and Wolterstorff, Nicholas, eds. *Faith and Rationality*. Notre Dame: University of Notre Dame Press, 1983.

Rescher, Nicholas. *Pascal's Wager*. Notre Dame, Ind.: University of Notre Dame Press, 1985.

The Concept and Attributes of God

Davis, Stephen T. *Logic and the Nature of God*. Grand Rapids, Mich.: Eerdmans, 1983.

Morris, Thomas V., ed. *The Concept of God*. Oxford: Oxford University Press, 1987.

———. *Divine and Human Action*. Ithaca, N.Y.: Cornell University Press, 1988.

Nash, Ronald H. *The Concept of God*. Grand Rapids, Mich.: Zondervan, 1983.

Swinburne, Richard. *The Coherence of Theism*. Oxford: Clarendon, 1977.

The Problem of Evil

Geisler, Norman L. *The Roots of Evil*. Grand Rapids, Mich.: Zondervan, 1978.

Hick, John. *Evil and the God of Love*. Rev. ed. San Francisco: Harper & Row, 1977.

Lewis, C. S. *The Problem of Pain*. N.Y.: Macmillan, 1962.

Plantinga, Alvin. *God, Freedom, and Evil*. N.Y.: Harper & Row, 1974.

Swinburne, Richard. *The Existence of God*. Oxford: Clarendon Press, 1979. Chapter 11.

Historicity of the New Testament Documents

Blomberg, Craig. *The Historical Reliability of the Gospels*. Downers Grove, Ill.: InterVarsity Press, 1987.

Bruce, F. F. *The New Testament Documents: Are They Reliable?* 5th rev. ed. Grand Rapids, Mich.: Eerdmans, 1960.

Dunn, James D. G. *The Evidence for Jesus*. Philadelphia: Westminster Press, 1985.

France, R. T. *The Evidence for Jesus*. Downers Grove, Ill.: InterVarsity Press, 1986.

Habermas, Gary. *The Verdict of History*. Nashville: Thomas Nelson, 1988.

Marshall, I. Howard. *I Believe in the Historical Jesus*. Grand Rapids, Mich.: Eerdmans, 1977.

Moule, C.F.D. *The Birth of the New Testament*. 3d. rev. ed. San Francisco: Harper & Row, 1981.

Robinson, John A. T. *Redating the New Testament*. Philadelphia: Westminster, 1976.

Stanton, G. N. *Jesus of Nazareth in New Testament Preaching*. Cambridge: Cambridge University Press, 1974.

Historicity of the Resurrection of Jesus

Bode, E. L. *The First Easter Morning*. Rome: Biblical Institute Press, 1970.

Craig, William Lane. *Knowing the Truth About the Resurrection*. Ann Arbor, Mich.: Servant, 1988.

Ladd, George E. *I Believe in the Resurrection of Jesus*. Grand Rapids, Mich.: Eerdmans, 1975.

Lapide, Pinchas. *The Resurrection of Jesus: A Jewish Perspective*. Translated by Wilhelm C. Linss. Minneapolis: Augsburg, 1983.

Miethe, Terry L., ed. *Did Jesus Rise From the Dead? The Resurrection Debate*. San Francisco: Harper & Row, 1987.

O'Collins, Gerald. *The Resurrection of Jesus Christ*. Valley Forge: Judson, 1973.

Wilkins, Ulrich. *Resurrection*. Translated by A. M. Stewart. Atlanta: John Knox, 1978.

Miracles and Philosophy

Brown, Colin. *Miracles and the Critical Mind*. Grand Rapids, Mich.: Eerdmans, 1984.

Geisler, Norman L. *Miracles and Modern Thought*. Grand Rapids, Mich.: Zondervan, 1982.

Lewis, C. S. *Miracles: A Preliminary Study*. N.Y.: Macmillan, 1947.

Swinburne, Richard. *The Concept of Miracle*. N.Y.: St. Martin's Press, 1970.

Christianity and Science

Davis, Percival, and Kenyon, Dean H. *Of Pandas and People*. Dallas, Tex.: Houghton, 1989.

Denton, Michael. *Evolution: A Theory in Crisis*. London: Burnett Books, 1985.

Geisler, Norman L., and Anderson, J. Kerby. *Origin Science: A Proposal for the Creation-Evolution Controversy*. Grand Rapids, Mich.: Baker, 1987.

Jaki, Stanley L. *The Origin of Science and the Science of Its Origin*. South Bend, Ind.: Regnery/Gateway, Inc., 1978.

Jastrow, Robert. *God and the Astronomers*. New York: W. W. Norton & Co., 1978.

Lester, Lane P., and Bohlin, Raymond G. *The Natural Limits to Biological Change*. Grand Rapids, Mich.: Zondervan, 1984.

Moreland, J. P. *Christianity and the Nature of Science*. Grand Rapids, Mich.: Baker, 1989.

Pitman, Michael. *Adam and Evolution*. London: Rider, 1984.

Schoen, Edward L. *Religious Explanations: A Model from the Sciences*. Durham, N.C.: Duke University Press, 1985.

Thaxton, Charles B.; Bradley, Walter L.; and Olsen, Roger L. *The Mystery of Life's Origin: Reassessing Current Theories*. New York: Philosophical Library, 1984.

About the Contributors

WILLIAM LANE CRAIG has taught philosophy of religion at Trinity Evangelical Divinity School (Deerfield, IL) and is associate professor of philosophy and religious studies at Westmont College (Santa Barbara, CA). He has two earned doctorates—one in philosophy under John Hick from the University of Birmingham (England) and one in theology under Wolfhart Pannenberg from the University of Munich (West Germany). He has written extensively on the existence and nature of God and on the resurrection of Jesus. Among his scholarly and popular writings are *The Kalam Cosmological Argument* (Macmillan), *The Only Wise God* (Baker), *Knowing the Truth about the Resurrection* (Servant), and *The Cosmological Argument from Plato to Leibniz* (Macmillan).

ANTONY FLEW, since 1949, has taught philosophy or moral philosophy in England at Christ Church, King's College, the University of Keele, and the University of Reading. He has also been visiting professor at several schools in the United States, including the University of Minnesota, New York University, the University of Pittsburgh, and the University of Southern California. Probably one of the most well-known atheistic philosophers today, his writings include *Hume's Philosophy of Belief* (Routledge and Kegan Paul), *God: A Critical Enquiry* (Open Court), *An Introduction to Western Philosophy* (Bobbs-Merrill), and *God, Freedom and Immortality* (Prometheus).

PETER KREEFT is professor of philosophy at Boston College (Boston, MA), where he has been since 1965. After receiving his Ph.D. from Fordham University, he taught philosophy at Villanova University for three years. He is a prolific and creative writer, with such books to his credit as *Love Is Stronger Than Death* (Ignatius), *Heaven, the Heart's Deepest Longing* (Ignatius), *Between Heaven and Hell* (InterVarsity), *Making Sense Out of Suffering* (Servant), *Socrates Meets Jesus* (Servant), and *Knowing the Truth of God's Love* (Servant).

J. P. MORELAND has a Th.M. in theology from Dallas Theological Seminary, an M.A. in philosophy from the University of California at Riverside, and a Ph.D. in philosophy from the University of Southern California, where he studied under Dallas Willard. He has taught philosophy at Liberty University (Lynchburg, VA) and is beginning a teaching position at Talbot School of Theology, Biola University (La Mirada, CA) as professor of philosophy of religion. His articles have appeared in various journals, including *Philosophy and Phenomenological Research, The Australasian Journal of Philosophy, Process Studies,* and *The American Philosophical Quarterly. Scaling the Secular City* (Baker), *Christianity and the Nature of Science* (Baker), *The Life and Death Debate* (Praeger Books), and *Universals, Qualities, and Quality Instances: A Defense of Realism* (University Press of America) are four of his recent books.

KAI NIELSEN, since earning his Ph.D. in philosophy from Duke University in 1955, has generated almost four hundred scholarly articles and twenty-five books, among which are *Reason and Practice* (Harper & Row), *Contemporary Critiques of Religion* (Macmillan), *Ethics Without God* (Prometheus), *God, Scepticism and Modernity* (University of Ottawa Press), and *Philosophy and Atheism: In Defense of Atheism* (Prometheus). He is an editor of the *Canadian Journal of Philosophy,* and the former president of the Greater New York chapter, "Society for Philosophy and Public Policy." Currently he is professor and head of the Department of Philosophy at the University of Calgary. Aside from Antony Flew, he is perhaps the most prominent atheist in contemporary philosophy.

LOUIS POJMAN, who moderated the debate between J. P. Moreland and Kai Nielsen, received a D. Phil. at Oxford University and a Ph.D. in theology from Union Theological Seminary. He has taught philosophy at Notre Dame University and the University of Texas at Dallas, and he is currently professor of philosophy at the University of Mississippi. Along with the publication of his numerous articles, he has written several books, including *The Logic of Subjectivity* (University of Alabama Press), *Religious Belief and the Will* (Routledge and Kegan Paul), and *Ethics: Discovering Right and Wrong* (Wadsworth).

KEITH PARSONS earned his Ph.D. in philosophy at Queen's University (Ontario, Canada). He teaches philosophy at Berry College (Rome, GA), and he is the founder and chairman of Georgia Skeptics—an educational organization committed to the critical investigation of pseudoscientific and paranormal claims. His most recent publications include *God and the Burden of Proof* (Prometheus) and *Science, Confirmation, and the Theistic Hypothesis* (Peter Lang).

DALLAS WILLARD is a professor in the School of Philosophy at the University of Southern California, where he was the Director of the School of Philosophy from 1982 to 1985. He has taught at UCLA, the University of Colorado, and the University of Wisconsin at Madison. His writing has been done primarily in the areas of epistemology, the philosophy of mind and of logic, and the philosophy of Edmund Husserl. However, his two popular books on the Christian faith—*In Search of Guidance* (Regal) and *The Spirit of the Disciplines* (Harper & Row)—have made him well-known to general readers.